S0-AHJ-909

CHURCH POLITY AND AMERICAN POLITICS

GARLAND REFERENCE LIBRARY
OF SOCIAL SCIENCE
(VOL. 455)

Church Polity and American Politics: Issues in Contemporary American Catholicism

edited by
Mary C. Segers

GARLAND PUBLISHING, INC. • NEW YORK & LONDON
1990

Library of Congress Cataloging-in-Publication Data

Church polity and American politics: issues in contemporary American Catholicism / [edited by] Mary C. Segers.
p. cm. — (Garland reference library of social science ; vol. 455)
Includes bibliographical references.
ISBN 0–8240–4440–1 (alk. paper)
1. Catholic Church—United States—Political activity. 2. Sociology, Christian (Catholic)—United States—History of doctrines—20th century. 3. United States—Politics and government—1945– . 4. Catholic Church—United States—History—1945– 5. United States—Church history—20th century. 6. Catholic Church—Doctrines—History—20th century. I. Segers, Mary C. II. Series: Garland reference library of social science; v. 455.
BX1407.P63C48 1990
261.7'08'822—dc20 89–29915
CIP

Printed on acid-free, 250-year-life paper
Manufactured in the United States of America

To Jerry, Suzanne, and Jean-Paul

CONTENTS

Church Polity and American Politics: Issues in Contemporary American Catholicism

INTRODUCTION

THE AMERICAN CATHOLIC CHURCH IN CONTEMPORARY AMERICAN POLITICS

Mary C. Segers

A conventionally held thesis is that U.S. Catholics have "arrived" in American society and have taken their rightful places in the worlds of business, education, politics, and culture. The election of the first Catholic president in 1960 has been considered a watershed, an indication that lay Catholics had by then achieved a maturity and competence in the ways of secular society. But the last thirty years have also seen the American church itself assume a new public role in American society and culture. Here the Second Vatican Council, which met in Rome from 1962–1965, is the watershed. Before Vatican II the American church's political activity was conducted behind closed chancery doors; moreover, its purpose was largely to protect church institutions—for example, to secure federal aid for parochial schools. Today the post-Vatican II American church has assumed a new, prophetic role in American society, issuing forceful, comprehensive statements on war and peace and economic justice, which are critical of the conventional, mainstream views of American domestic and foreign policymakers. American bishops have monitored U.S. policy in Central America, for example; they have also been highly critical of *Roe v. Wade*, the 1973 U.S. Supreme Court decision legalizing abortion, and have pressed and lobbied actively for the reinstatement of restrictive abortion laws. In assuming this new public role, Catholics have not been alone, of course; the conservative evangelical churches of the religious right have been even more active, perhaps, in attempting to shape public policy in the 1980s. Inevitably, the activities of these churches have raised questions about religious liberty, tolerance, and church-state separation in a pluralist constitutional democracy.

This book examines some of these issues, as well as the connections between the Catholic religion and American culture. During much of American history, Roman Catholicism was thought to be incompatible with American democratic ideals, laws, and practices. Throughout the colonial period, and especially during the great immigration of the nineteenth century, Catholics were viewed as poor, ignorant foreigners who owed primary allegiance to the Roman papacy and were therefore potentially, if not actually, subversive. For their part, Catholics bent over backward to prove their loyalty, patriotism, and good citizenship. In the first half of the twentieth century, Catholics' general support of American involvement in two world wars, the New Deal, McCarthyism, and the Korean War often caused the Catholic community to be blamed for an excess rather than a deficiency of patriotism.[1] Only within the last thirty years has the American Catholic Church achieved some balance between the function of legitimator and the role of critic in American culture. The election of President John F. Kennedy in 1960 seemed to signal an end to overt anti-Catholicism in American politics. The emergence of a Catholic left opposition to the Vietnam War in the 1960s and the Catholic bishops' search for a new role in the nation's public life during the 1980s confirmed the prophetic potential of Catholic Christianity in the United States.

Indeed, several Protestant thinkers have pronounced the present to be a distinctively "Catholic moment" in the nation's history. William Lee Miller urges, "In the late twentieth century, now is the moment for Catholicism to have its desirable effect upon the America within which at last it is coming to be at home."[2] Peter Berger, a sociologist of religion, told a Catholic audience in 1976 (during the bicentennial of the American Revolution) that its church stood as the foremost defender of a central idea of the Declaration of Independence: that men and women have rights independent of the state.[3] Finally, Lutheran pastor Richard Neuhaus has entitled a recent book *The Catholic Moment*, by which he means that

> This . . . is the moment in which the Roman Catholic Church in the world can and should be the lead church in proclaiming the Gospel. This can and should also be the moment in which the Roman Catholic Church in the United States assumes its rightful role in the culture-forming task of constructing a religiously-informed public philosophy for the American experiment in ordered liberty.[4]

While it may be gratifying to American Catholics to realize that they have finally "arrived" in American society, it is also sobering. Reaching political, social, and economic maturity has brought with it a new sense of responsibility and an awareness of risk and danger, as the church seeks to contribute to the improvement of American public life. In the 1970s and 1980s the church has sought to address the moral dimensions of public affairs and to act as a moral critic of public policy. This search for a new voice in American public life is the subject of this book.

In discussing the political involvement of the American church, it is important to be clear about various meanings of the term church. "Church" can refer to the general community of the faithful (all believing Catholics or "the People of God," to use Vatican II terminology) or to the institutional church (the hierarchially structured organization of clergy and laity in parishes and dioceses throughout the United States). In this introductory chapter, I will be discussing the church in this latter sense, focusing for the most part on the activities of the episcopal hierarchy in the United States (the bishops and prominent organizational leaders). The reader may legitimately ask: why the concentration on the hierarchy? There are several reasons. Historically, fear of the political power of the American Catholic bishops has been a principal driving force behind anti-Catholicism in the United States. Yet today the efforts of the bishops to influence public policy are, for the most part, warmly welcomed (with the exception of their interventions on issues of abortion and contraception). This change is significant for all Americans, Catholic and non-Catholic. Secondly, the political involvement of the bishops is easier to chronicle than the activities of American Catholics in the general electorate. By examining episcopal statements of the pre-Vatican II church of the 1940s and 1950s, and comparing them with the bishops' pronouncements of the 1970s and 1980s, we can gauge some measure of the distance the American church has traveled in the space of little more than a generation. In the 1950s, the average Catholic heard his bishop complain about secularism and materialism in the larger culture, about salacious movies banned by the Legion of Decency (the church's movie screening agency), and about atheistic Communism. In the 1980s, the average American Catholic heard his bishops address critically public policies on defense, economic justice, reproductive technologies, human rights, abortion, racism, healthcare, poverty, hunger, child welfare, and capital punishment. Something happened in the intervening years. The institutional church has gone from being a parochial, defensive church entering the political arena only to defend its organizational interests—to a forceful public presence regularly lobbying on Capitol Hill on a wide range of issues. In this search for a public voice in American life, the church has sought to address non-Catholic as well as Catholic Americans, and to speak about issues of concern to all, not narrowly "Catholic" interests (such as federal aid to parochial schools). This coming of age of American Catholicism represents, I submit, a political, social, economic, even theological maturity. This is no longer an immigrant church, defensive, and bound up in its own alternative culture within the larger society.

While the American bishops have contributed positively in articulating the moral dimensions of economic and nuclear policy over the last fifteen years, on the negative side they have failed to support public policies to enhance the status of women in society. The institutional church has also failed to resist repressive measures taken by the Vatican against Catholic theologians, religious sisters, priests and laywomen. It has been unable to stem declines in membership, church attendance, numbers of priests and women religious, parish and school closings. The church in the United States is changing. Yet these changes may not be altogether negative. Indeed, I would suggest that what is happening among many American Catholic women is one of the more promising and hopeful signs in the contemporary church.

In examining the American Catholic church today, we are confronted with a large, resourceful institution (53 million Catholics in 1989) which has found its voice in American public life at the same time that it is experiencing internal difficulties in church polity and governance. This introductory chapter examines these external and internal aspects of American Catholicism.

THE BISHOPS AND PUBLIC AFFAIRS

The increased political activism of the American Catholic church inevitably raises questions about why this activism is happening now and what it portends for the future relation of religion and politics in the United States.[5] Several factors may be said to account for the emergence of the U.S. Catholic church as a prominent political actor in the 1980s. Among these are changes in *ideology* and *organization* within the episcopal hierarchy of the American church.

Many contributors to this volume acknowledge the Second Vatican Council, the great assembly of the world's Catholic bishops, which met in Rome from 1962–1965, as providing the ideological framework within which greater Catholic political involvement could occur. The speeches and documents of Vatican II insisted that the hopes and fears of *all* people were the concern of the church. The Council stressed that both the institutional church and individual Catholics had a moral obligation to work to alleviate global problems such as poverty, famine, illiteracy, and political repression. The Council's renewal of theology and philosophy provided the ideas necessary to stimulate greater involvement in efforts to eradicate those political, social, and economic ills.

Organizational changes in the U.S. Catholic hierarchy have also made possible greater political involvement by the church. The bishops themselves have come to act as political leaders in American politics partly because, in the years immediately following Vatican II, they set up an institutional framework which facilitated political activity. Prior to Vatican II (from 1919 to 1966), the bishops had a small-scale national organization, the National Catholic Welfare Conference, which was weak, poorly financed, and understaffed. In 1966, pursuant to a Vatican Council Decree calling for national episcopal councils, the U.S. bishops set up a much stronger national organization, the National Conference of Catholic Bishops (NCCB). Twice annually, the NCCB brings together at its general meeting the more than 350 bishops of the United States. At these assemblies, the bishops debate positions on public policy as well as pastoral concerns, elect their own officers, and appoint fellow bishops to the twenty-six standing committees and nearly twenty ad hoc committees which carry on the NCCB's work between general meetings.

The NCCB is assisted by the United States Catholic Conference (USCC), an administrative and operational staff of professionally trained experts who help the bishops research problems, draft policy statements, and communicate their concerns to Congress, to executive branch officials, and to the general public. The USCC, located in Washington, D.C., is divided into three major departments: communications, education, and social development and world peace. It has a professional staff of almost fifty people and runs its own publishing and documentary services. In 1986, the combined budget for the NCCB/USCC was $26,582,848.[6]

As should be evident, the NCCB and USCC are essential to the political leadership role the bishops have been taking in the 1970s and 1980s. These agencies provide the bishops with an organizational network and a national forum from which to address public issues. At their 1983 meeting the bishops passed their pastoral letter on war on peace, and at their 1986 meeting they approved the letter on the U.S. economy. At other national meetings, they have condemned capital punishment, urged amnesty for Vietnam War resisters, and adopted a position of neutrality on the Equal Rights Amendment. The bishops and their staff representatives also testify before and regularly lobby Congressional committees and file *amicus curiae* briefs in selected court cases. From this strong organizational base the U.S. bishops have worked, in accordance with the Vatican Council's injunctions, to alleviate the social and economic ills of modern society.

While the last two decades have seen the emergence of the bishops as national political leaders, this has not resulted in the imposition of Catholic power in American public life. That is, the Catholic church's presence in American politics has not, by and large, resulted in coercive, sectarian policies for non-Catholic Americans. For one thing, a diversity of church-related and Catholic-identified pressure groups comprise what might be called the Catholic lobbying effort in Washington. These groups, as Thomas O'Hara shows in chapter 7, do not necessarily speak with one voice; and they may sometimes oppose the policy recommendations of the NCCB/USCC. Secondly, individual Catholic citizens do not always agree with the bishops on how to translate Gospel norms and Catholic social teaching into public policy. This is clear in the case of the bishops' pastoral letter on nuclear war, which elicited broad agreement but also sharp dissent.[7] It was also evident in the case of the bishops' pastoral letter on the U.S. economy. One week before the bishops issued this letter, a commission of lay Catholics, which included former Treasury Secretary William Simon and former Secretary of State Alexander Haig, issued their own counter-pastoral on the economy taking strong exception to the bishops' call for policies of distributive justice.[8]

Thirdly, it should be noted that divisions within the NCCB preclude any monolithic exercise of power by the Catholic church in the

United States. In 1984 the bishops disagreed openly about the priority given abortion as a campaign issue; in 1987 another episcopal disagreement about AIDS and sex education erupted on the front pages of *The New York Times*.[9] Fourthly, there is serious question whether the U.S. bishops can "deliver the Catholic vote" today to any one candidate during a major election. As Timothy Byrnes shows in chapter 6, Catholic voters do not necessarily follow the policy guidelines or suggestions of their pastoral shepherds. Catholic citizens take the bishops' recommendations under consideration, but, like other American voters, they are cross-pressured by competing loyalties and affiliations, and they have a typically American distrust of clerical partisanship. Nor, for that matter, do Catholic public officials and lawmakers necessarily follow the lead of their bishops in matters of public policy. This is abundantly clear on the abortion issue, for example, where, according to one report, 41 percent of Catholics in Congress do not follow the NCCB's recommended policy suggestions to reverse *Roe v. Wade* and outlaw abortion.[10] Especially noteworthy is the position of New York Governor Mario M. Cuomo, in which he argues that his personal moral opposition to abortion does not necessarily translate into public opposition to legalized abortion. This view has caused considerable controversy within both Catholic and non-Catholic circles, as evident in the discussions by Peter A. Lawler and this author in chapters 8 and 9.

Thus, although Catholics have arrived in American politics and Catholic bishops have assumed a leadership role in public affairs, the specter of a monolithic American Catholic church, beholden to a foreign power and somehow tyrannically imposing its religious beliefs on non-Catholic Americans, has not taken shape. Instead, the U.S. Catholic community has been politically assimilated and acculturated. One may claim, as Neuhaus does, that once the Protestant hegemony in American public life was broken (as now clearly has taken place), it was almost inevitable that the Catholic church, large and dynamic, would step in to articulate its moral concerns about public affairs. But the nativist fear of "Catholic power" has proven groundless. In fact, the opposite seems to have occurred. During the 1980s, the bishops' statements on economic justice and nuclear war have been welcomed and applauded by a secular society in need of moral reflection and guidance.

However, there is a down side to the church's increased political activism. It is one thing for the church to speak, and quite another thing for the church to be heard. Over the last fifteen years the institutional church has learned some hard lessons about its mode and style of political participation. The American bishops have learned that in addressing all citizens, Catholic and non-Catholic, they must attempt to persuade through reasoned argument rather than by appealing to authoritative papal pronouncements. Moreover, as R. Bruce Douglass shows in chapter 4, whether the church moves beyond a sectarian perspective to find a public voice depends in part on its manner of speaking, on whether it speaks in Biblical language or employs the discourse of natural law and right reason. In the public forum of a pluralistic society, rational argument is more often more appropriate than sectarian appeals to the sacred books of diverse traditions. The bishops have learned that they cannot engage in partisan politics or speak for or against political candidates without jeopardizing their tax-exempt status.[11] They have discovered the pitfalls and political liabilities of a single-issue focus in public policy. And they have learned that they must resist the tendency to become yet another special-interest group in American politics.

The catalyst for all this learning has been the abortion issue. The movement in the United States for reform of restrictive state abortion laws began in the 1930s and gathered momentum through the 1950s, and especially, 1960s. Nevertheless, American Catholics were, by all accounts, stunned by the U.S. Supreme Court's 1973 ruling in *Roe v. Wade* legalizing abortion.[12] The response of the institutional church was immediate denunciation of the decision and quick mobilization to restrict the scope of the court's ruling and work for its ultimate reversal.

Indeed, since 1973, American Catholic bishops have been engaged in an unprecedented, unparalleled effort to overturn the Court's ruling in *Roe v. Wade*. The NCCB's 1975 Pastoral Plan for Pro-Life Activities, reissued in 1985, contains the most detailed and explicit proposal for political action ever to emanate from the offices of the American Catholic hierarchy.[13] Convinced that they face, in the abortion decision, an ethical issue which is not a matter of sectarian belief but a question of moral reasoning about which all Americans can come to some common agreement, the bishops have pressed for changes in law and public policy reflective of their convictions.

Representatives of the NCCB/USCC have testified in numerous Congressional committee hearings in support of antiabortion legislative riders and constitutional amendments. The USCC general counsel has filed numerous *amicus curiae* briefs in court cases on abortion. The bishops' aggressive posture on abortion policy is reflected in their efforts to influence major presidential candidates in the 1976, 1980, and 1984 election campaigns. Churches have engaged in a variety of electioneering activities, thus threatening their tax-exempt status. On an issue of signal importance to women's rights advocates, the bishops failed to endorse the Equal Rights Amendment in the late 1970s and early 1980s, because they feared that ERA approval would constitutionally legitimize abortion. They refused to support other legislation of importance to women's rights groups—the Pregnancy Discrimination Act of 1978 and the Civil Rights Restoration Act of 1988—unless antiabortion riders were attached to these bills.

Although the NCCB was politically active on many issues before 1973, the intensity of their opposition to legalized abortion marked this issue as somehow different and rendered them liable to the charge that the Catholic church's political involvement had a single-issue focus. To counter this charge, in 1983 Cardinal Joseph Bernardin of Chicago began to articulate a "consistent life ethic," a political-ethical perspective which held that the church was committed to a broad range of policy issues concerning the dignity and sacredness of human life.[14] These included abortion, capital punishment, war and peace, euthanasia, and quality-of-life issues such as poverty, hunger, the environment, and immigration and naturalization issues. Although Bernardin's consistent life ethic, or "seamless garment" approach to political issues is heavily criticized by many Catholic pro-lifers,[15] it is regarded by many other Catholics as a more appropriate policy perspective than a single-issue focus. Employing this policy framework, Cardinal Bernardin and his allies within the NCCB have managed to move the institutional church away from a sole preoccupation with abortion to a concern for a broad, respect-for-life agenda. Some observers of the NCCB, therefore, regard abortion as the issue on which the church "cut its political teeth" and learned to take the heat in contemporary American politics,[16] and as the entering wedge that forced the bishops to address seriously other "life" issues such as war and peace, the nuclear arms race, and the U.S. economy.[17]

As a result of their political activism on the abortion issue, the bishops have learned the importance of not being partisan, the necessity of a multi-issue approach to American politics, and the necessity of presenting a rational and convincing case for their position rather than appealing to scriptural or papal authority for justification.[18] The NCCB's approach to other topics—in the peace pastoral and the letter on the U.S. economy, for example—gives evidence that the lessons have been learned well. However, one significant difference between the NCCB's development of public policy recommendations on nuclear war and the economy, on the one hand, and on abortion, on the other, is that the peace and economic pastorals were written only after consultation with specialists who in many cases opposed church views, whereas the development of policy recommendations on abortion has not involved formal consultation with demographers, family planners, feminists, and legal and medical experts who do not accept the church's moral teachings on abortion.

To summarize, in the wake of the Second Vatican Council and the political-economic assimilation of Catholics in the United States, the American Catholic church—led by able and talented bishops—has found a voice in American public life and has addressed issues at the national level. If this is "the Catholic moment" in American society and if the church is to continue to address the moral dimensions of policy issues, then the church must continue to use rational ethics rather than scriptural precepts to speak to a religiously diverse society. Moreover, as David Hollenbach argues in chapter 5, the church can and perhaps should draw upon the communitarian emphases in Catholic social teaching when addressing economic and social issues. These positive elements in the deeper Catholic approach to state and society can help to counteract the excessive individualism of American life. Finally, while the NCCB/USCC may at times lobby to protect its own particular views and interests in the policy process, the church would do well to remember that it is not just another interest group with headquarters in Washington. Churches, it seems to me, are more than interest groups. They have a special duty to attend to the common good and to articulate universal values of peace and justice. In its pastoral letters on war and peace and on economic justice during the 1980s, the American Catholic bishops have carried out this duty admirably and effectively.

CHURCH POLITY AND AMERICAN POLITICS

While the American church has functioned effectively during the last two decades in its external public role in our society, Catholicism itself has experienced considerable internal difficulties during this same time period. It is one of the ironies of contemporary American Catholic history that at the very moment when the hierarchy is making its mark in terms of public affairs, it is losing internal ground among Catholic adherents. There is disaffection among many Catholics, who are more educated and affluent than their immigrant forbears. Many of the 53 million Catholics in the United States harbor private reservations about the most recent directions of their church.

The statistics tell a good part of the story. Since the mid-1960s, Andrew Greeley and William McCready of the National Opinion Research Center in Chicago have been studying Catholic trends in the

United States and documenting continuing declines in Catholic life in the form of school closings, fewer worshipers in the pews, and the exodus of priests and nuns from the active ministry. There has also been a weakening of financial support among American Catholics, although in 1979 and again in 1986, American bishops came to the rescue of the Vatican and mobilized resources to offset estimated budgetary shortfalls in Rome's finances.[19] As U.S. Catholics have moved from urban to suburban areas, the shape of Catholic elementary and secondary education has changed. And in the 1980s, small inner city parishes have had to close up or merge with other neighboring urban parishes in order to survive.[20]

The number of American religious sisters declined from 180,000 in 1965 to 113,000 in 1986, a tremendous drop in the space of one generation.[21] The number of Catholic sisters teaching in Catholic schools declined by almost 75 percent during this period,[22] necessitating increasingly greater reliance on lay faculty to staff the parochial school systems. And since lay teachers, unlike the sisters in the past, must now be paid salaries close to their public-school counterparts, they have become a major item for strained church budgets. Catholic school enrollments have declined from more than six million in the mid–1960s to fewer than three million now.

Difficult as these declines may be, they pale in comparison with yet another problem: the U.S. church confronts a major shortage of priests. According to one estimate, eight percent of diocesan priests, and nine percent of religious-order priests, resigned from the ministry between 1966 and 1970. According to a second estimate, 12.5 to 13.5 percent of all diocesan priests active in 1970 resigned over the next ten years. Apart from the exodus of already ordained priests, there has also been a dramatic decrease in the number of seminarians—from 48,992 in 1965 to 10,440 in 1986 (a drop of 38,552).[23] Enrollment at Catholic seminaries continues to decline; in 1988, there were 8,921 student candidates for the priesthood in the United States.[24] The implications of this for Catholic life are dramatic and far-reaching. Whereas in 1965 a Catholic parish without a resident priest was virtually unheard of, in 1986, no fewer than 1,183 of the 19,313 Catholic parishes in the United States had no resident pastor. Married deacons (the office of permanent deacon was reinstituted at Vatican II) can pick up some of the slack, but they cannot replace ordained priests who, in the Catholic church, are the only persons who can celebrate mass. For Catholics, the mass is the essential form of worship, the very center of the sacramental life of the church. To the extent that a lack of priests means that the Eucharist must be celebrated less frequently, this is a major ministerial problem for U.S.

Catholics. Parenthetically, it should be noted, although no causal relation is implied, that there is a marked decline in Catholics' attendance at weekly Sunday mass. Whereas, in 1958, an estimated 74 percent of American Catholics attended weekly Sunday mass, by 1984, only 51 percent of U.S. Catholics were fulfilling this primary obligation of church law.[25]

However, statistics do not tell the whole story nor do they convey adequately the sense of dismay pervading the American Catholic community as it approaches the 1990s. A central concern is with Rome's interventions in the affairs of the U.S. church. Beginning in 1980, Pope John Paul II began to "get tough" with U.S. Catholics, ordering Jesuit Father Robert Drinan not to seek a sixth term as Congressman from Massachusetts' Fourth Congressional District. Although Vatican spokesmen claimed that, under a stricter interpretation of canon law, priests should not hold political office, it was clear that church authorities were dismayed at Drinan's positive votes for public funding of abortion. A similar issue was at stake in 1982, when a Sister of Mercy, Agnes Mary Mansour, was appointed director of Michigan's Department of Social Services. Archbishop Edmund Szoka of Detroit bowed to pressure from antiabortion groups, who wrote to the Vatican and to the Detroit archdiocese protesting Mansour's being permitted to accept the appointment. The antiabortion forces were disturbed over the department's administration of a publicly funded abortion program. When Szoka called on Mansour to resign her post, she refused, declaring that, although she was personally opposed to abortion, she could tolerate public funding of abortion out of consideration for American pluralism. Again, this rationale proved unacceptable to diocesan and Vatican authorities, and Mansour was forced to resign as a nun in order to continue service as Director of the Michigan Department of Social Services.

In 1984, when Democratic vice-presidential candidate Geraldine Ferraro was attacked by Cardinals John O'Connor of New York and Bernard Law of Boston for her political position on abortion policy, ninety-seven Catholics, including four men religious and twenty-four female religious, signed a paid advertisement in *The New York Times* declaring that Catholics held a "diversity of opinions" on abortion and calling for open discussion of the issue.[26] Almost immediately, the Vatican intervened in the person of Cardinal Jerome Hamer of the Congregation for Religious and Secular Institutes, who ordered these men and women religious to retract their statement or risk expulsion from their congregations. The male signatories—two priests and two brothers—immediately issued clarifications acceptable to the Vatican, but the nuns were not so quick to comply, and their cases took four years to resolve. The faithful dissent of these nuns is discussed by Maureen Fiedler in chapter 15 of this volume.

Through the 1980s, Rome's interventions in the affairs of the American Catholic community continued.[27] Two of the more celebrated cases of discipline and suppression concerned Father Charles Curran, a theologian at Catholic University in Washington, D.C., and Archbishop Raymond Hunthausen of Seattle. From 1979 to 1985, Father Curran was investigated by the Vatican Congregation for the Doctrine of the Faith, headed by Cardinal Joseph Ratzinger, concerning his writings in moral theology on human sexuality and abortion. In 1986 he was stripped of his license to teach Catholic theology and suspended as a theology professor at Catholic University. Although he is a dedicated and loyal priest, Father Curran, who is interviewed in chapter 14 by Anne Lally Milhaven, did not go quietly out to pasture but challenged the actions of Catholic University in court. His legal challenge was unsuccessful; in February, 1989, District of Columbia Judge Frederick H. Weisberg ruled that Catholic University did not violate Father Curran's tenure contract and was within its legal rights to bar him from teaching Roman Catholic theology at the University. The Curran case carries major implications for Catholic theologians, for ecumenists, and for those who support academic freedom in the more than two hundred American Catholic colleges and universities, many of whom are chartered and partially funded by state and federal governments.

Perhaps the most astonishing case of church discipline in American Catholic history, involves Seattle Archbishop Hunthausen, who was criticized by political conservatives for his opposition to nuclear weapons and for his decision in 1982 to begin withholding 50 percent of his income tax in protest against U.S. arms policies. Religious conservatives in Seattle complained to Rome about Hunthausen's allegedly lax policies in areas of sexual morality (principally with respect to contraceptive sterilization and homosexuality). Hunthausen first came under official Vatican investigation in 1983. In 1985, Rome sent an auxiliary bishop, Donald Wuerl, to act as a watchdog in Seattle; and by 1986, Hunthausen was stripped of decision–making power in major areas of responsibility traditionally belonging to the head of a diocese. This highly unusual treatment of an American bishop was deeply shocking, not least to the vast majority of Seattle's 300,000 Catholics, who had great respect for Hunthausen. The NCCB discussed the Hunthausen case in closed session at its 1986 annual meeting. Eventually, an oversight committee made up of American cardinals and archbishops mediated between Seattle and Rome and, in May 1987, the Vatican reversed itself on many of its positions.

These cases indicate that Pope John Paul II and his Vatican advisers are indeed worried about the state of American Catholicism. As John Deedy has written:

> It can no longer be doubted that Rome has now decided to come to grips with what it sees as the problem of the American church. The disciplining of so many American Catholics, from relatively anonymous nuns to prominent priests, including even an archbishop, allows no other conclusion. Confirming the impression further are actions such as the withdrawal of the imprimatur (the church's seal of approval on a published work) from several books and catechisms that enjoyed an earlier clearance, as well as the tightening of reigns generally over U.S. dioceses, seminaries, colleges, and universities. The pope . . . has got tough—and he remains tough, so tough, in fact, that it sometimes appears that his reach or the long arm of one of his lieutenants is now everywhere in American Catholicism.[28]

Needless to say, the American church is not the only regional Catholic community feeling the direct impact of John Paul II. Church communities in Brazil, Peru, the Netherlands, Germany, and Austria have all been confronted by this pontiff with questions about their direction and orthodoxy. Latin American liberation theologians such as Leonardo Boff and Gustavo Gutierrez have either been censured or are in danger of being silenced. A post–Vatican II church seems to be going through a period of reaction and retrenchment under a strong pope who wants to reassert central control over a worldwide Catholic communion of over 800 million adherents. This is the most well-traveled pontiff in Vatican history. Through his power of episcopal appointments, through his revival of *ad limina* visits—a practice in which the bishop heading a diocese must return to Rome every five years to give a personal accounting of his episcopacy—and through his worldwide travels, John Paul II has sought to emphasize the unity of faith and doctrine under the centralized control of a papacy made visible and palpable through his journeys.

Vatican reassertion of an authoritarian mode of leadership has prompted fresh protests, among them an essay by the Reverend Bernard Haring, a distinguished and respected moral theologian, which originally appeared in the January 15, 1989 issue of a biweekly Italian Catholic magazine, *Il Regno*.[29] Haring protested against the inflexible position the Vatican has taken on artificial birth control and against anonymous denunciations of theologians regarded as unreliable on the birth control question. At the same time, a protest statement, the "Cologne Declaration," was signed by 163 German-speaking theologians from Germany, Austria, the Netherlands, and Switzerland. This document describes, in strong language, three specific problem areas in the worldwide Roman Catholic church:

> 1. The Roman curia is aggressively pursuing a strategy of unilaterally filling vacant episcopal seats around the world, without regard for the recommendations of the local church and without respect for their established rights.
> 2. All over the world, many qualified theologians, men and women, are being denied ecclesiastical permission to teach. This represents a serious and dangerous interference in the free exercise of scholarly research and teaching, and in the pursuit of theological understanding through dialogue, principles which Vatican II repeatedly emphasized. The power to withhold official permission to teach is being abused; it has become an instrument to discipline theologians.
> 3. There have been theoretically questionable attempts to assert the pope's doctrinal and jurisdictional authority in an exaggerated form.[30]

The Cologne statement criticizes Rome's efforts at centralization; the theologians claim that collegiality between pope and bishops has been bypassed or ignored, local churches have been progressively undermined, theological debate has been suppressed, and the role of the laity in the church has been reduced. They are especially critical of recent papal teaching statements on birth control; in a November 12, 1988 address, the pope said that the church's teaching against contraception is not a man-made doctrine, but that it was "written by the creative hand of God in the nature of the human person" and confirmed by God's hand. It is these recent papal statements on artificial contraception which have so alarmed Father Haring and other signers of the Cologne Declaration. They claim that, "A pope who refers so often to the responsibility of Christian women and men in secular activities should not systematically disregard it in this area. Moreover, we regret the intense fixation of the papal teaching office on this single problem area." The Cologne theologians contend that the pope has erroneously connected a particular church teaching on birth control with the fundamental truths of the faith such as redemption through Jesus Christ and that, in so doing, he has exceeded the prerogatives and responsibilities of his teaching office. They conclude: "If the pope does what does not belong to his office, he cannot demand obedience in the name of Catholicism. Then he must expect contradiction."[31]

These recent events indicate that issues of internal church governance and ecclesiology remain contested areas twenty-five years after the last session of Vatican II. Both the Cologne Declaration and Father Haring's essay stress ecclesiological issues—collegiality among pope and bishops, the principle of subsidiarity whereby central authority is not to monopolize or usurp the power and authority of local institutions, and the conception of the church as not merely the Vatican bureaucracy but the worldwide communion of all believers. Though the Catholic church may not necessarily be a democracy, it is not an autocracy either. Historically, forms of church governance have changed many times through the centuries. Throughout its history, the church as a cultural institution has been influenced by models of government in civil society, and this is still true today. In a recent article, "Autocracy Isn't the Catholic Style," Philip Kaufman, a Benedectine historian, maintains that change in forms of church polity is inevitable and that the criteria for appropriate governance will be harmony with contemporary needs and fidelity to gospel values.[32] Autocratic rule seems particularly inappropriate to a contemporary world characterized by a growing concern for individual rights and human dignity. Perhaps the church would do well to think about more democratic forms of governance which would embody these values. Indeed, the church might apply the Vatican II Declaration on Religious Liberty (*Dignitatis Humanae*) to its own internal affairs as well as to its external relations with governments and societies.[33]

What does all of this mean for the American Catholic church? Not unexpectedly, the kinds of tensions and divisions existing within worldwide Catholicism have surfaced in American Catholicism as well. As the church has adjusted to the changes effected at Vatican II, it has had to contend with divisions among American Catholics between those who welcomed the Council's reforms and those who have opposed liturgical reform, theological development, and changing conceptions of the church. Among the latter are groups such as Catholics United for the Faith (CUF), Women for Faith and Family, Opus Dei (which has about 2,500 members in the United States), and followers of French Archbishop Marcel Lefebvre who favor a return to the Latin Tridentine Mass. These groups tend to emphasize an uncritical adherence to Vatican papal and curial statements as the litmus test for Catholic orthodoxy.

They complain that secular humanism and modernism have made major inroads in American Catholicism. They consider themselves to be vigilant watchdogs for any deviation from the true faith, and engage in extensive correspondence with Vatican agencies reporting on sermons, theologians, liturgical practices, and other details of church life. CUF, for example, was the group in the Seattle archdiocese that complained to Rome about Archbishop Hunthausen's leadership. So militantly vigilant are these groups that a theologian recently described their approach as a kind of Catholic fundamentalism, which treats the ecclesiastical magisterium in the same manner as Protestant fundamentalists treat the Bible. That is, Catholic fundamentalism "appeals to a literal, ahistorical, and nonhermeneutical reading of papal or curial pronouncements as a sure bulwark against the tides of relativism, the claims of science, and other inroads of modernity."[34] Unlike contemporary Protestant fundamentalists of the Religious Right for whom *sola scriptura* (the Bible alone, regarded as literally true) is the key to salvation, these Catholic fundamentalists have as their rallying cry *solum magisterium* or *solus papa*.

Liberal Catholics whom these fundamentalists criticize as deviant have formed groups such as Network (a social-justice lobby in Washington), the Association for the Rights of Catholics in the Church (ARCC), the National Association of Religious Women (NARW), Catholics Speak Out, the Center for Concern, the National Coalition of American Nuns (NCAN), and the Quixote Center, to name a few. There are also large numbers of American Catholics who maintain their parish affiliations and devotional lives somewhat immune to the charges and counter-charges swirling about them. However, even these Catholics, now more educated and affluent than their immigrant forbears, have changed, in the sense that a sizable percentage of them take the church on their own terms rather than on its terms. They are no longer content to "pray, pay, and obey." On issues of birth control, divorce and remarriage, homosexuality, the role of women in the church, even abortion, they prefer to think for themselves and to make their own accommodations to church teaching. A huge percentage of American Catholics have settled the birth control issue on the basis of their individual consciences, as opposed to the official teaching of their church. Perhaps it was to be expected that a church, which at Vatican II proclaimed the supremacy of conscience for people in the world at large, would have to cope with the logical extension of such primacy of conscience to its own believers.

Inevitably, these ecclesiological tensions within the American church have carried over to the church's external relations with the larger society and government. Nowhere is this more apparent than on questions of women's rights and status. Within Catholicism, women are still second-class citizens. They are excluded from ordination to the Roman Catholic priesthood on grounds that they do not physically "image" the male Christ who, moreover, ordained only men as priests. The sensitivities and sensibilities of many Catholic women are offended by the exclusive language of the church's liturgy and formal documents which often refer to God as "he" and to the faithful as "our brothers in Christ." The church's traditional teachings on sexuality, fertility control, and the family are intimately related to traditional conceptions of the role of woman as primarily wife-and-mother.

These traditional views are reflected in the primacy accorded by the church to the abortion issue in American politics. In the 1970s and 1980s, no other issue in American public life has occupied so large a pace in the NCCB's public agenda as has the antiabortion cause. Finances, resources, energy, attention and public rhetoric have all been focused in a sustained effort to delegalize abortion. Moreover, the American church has used the abortion issue to justify its refusal to support public policy initiatives—the Equal Rights Amendment, the Pregnancy Discrimination Act of 1978, the Civil Rights Restoration Act of 1988—designed to end discrimination against women and improve the quality of their lives.

Despite, or maybe because of, their second-class status in a patriarchal church, many Catholic women have worked to reform church structures and policies they regard as sexist. Perhaps it is no accident that three of the leading feminist theologians in contemporary American society come from the Roman Catholic tradition (Mary Daly of Boston College, Rosemary Radford Ruether of Garret Evangelical Seminary, and Elisabeth Schussler-Fiorenza at Harvard Divinity School). Led by such theologians, many Catholic women have formed organizations such as the Women's Ordination Conference, the National Coalition of American Nuns, Women's Alliance for Theology, Ethics and Ritual (WATER), Chicago Catholic Women, the National Association of Religious Women, and Boston Catholic Women—all groups organized by women to work for peace, social justice, and issues of women's rights and equity. Many religious sisters are among the most dedicated of Catholic feminists. In 1972, the Leadership Conference of Women Religious, an organization of major superiors of women's religious communities in the United States, made a conscientious decision to work insistently to accommodate the insights of contemporary feminism. The LCWR decision coincided with a general reexamination and renewal of religious life undertaken by congregations in accordance with the instructions of the Second Vatican Council. These communities of religious women rediscovered the intentions of their Founders, redefined their spirituality, and undertook new forms of ministry. In the process, many Catholic sisters became dedicated participants in the movement for equity and equality of the sexes in church and society.

Feminism among Catholic women is evident in the formation of Women-Church, which is not an alternative institution but the recognition that women as much as men *are* the church, the People of God. The first gathering of Women-Church was held in 1983; the second "Women-Church Convergence" drew more than 3,000 women to Cincinnati in October, 1987. In addition, groups of women have been in dialogue with various NCCB committees in the 1970s and 1980s on issues of concern to women. In April, 1988, the NCCB released the first draft of "Partners in the Mystery of Redemption," a controversial pastoral letter on women's concerns for church and society. While this pastoral statement is severely deficient in many respects (for example, it contains no systematic analysis of the causes of sexism in society),[35] it does at least decry sexism as sinful and represents a small step towards church reform in the treatment of women.

Nevertheless, one cannot be sanguine about what are essentially limited efforts to include women as full participants in church structures and institutions. The American hierarchy chooses a path of constant mediation between a recalcitrant Roman curia which fears "radical feminism" without knowing quite what feminism is—and many American Catholic women who argue increasingly for a greater say in church life. What is needed is a realization that change is not necessarily negative but can be positive, even empowering. The struggle for justice and equality of the sexes can be especially instructive to Catholics; after all, respect for one another as equals would seem to be a *sine qua non* of a church which bases itself upon the fundamental Christian ethic of love. In this sense, the emancipation of women can be a redemptive moment for the church.

In sum, the American Catholic community is still feeling the impact of that signal Catholic event of the last generation, the Second Vatican Council. Vatican II resulted in many innovations, including major changes in theology, liturgy, ecclesiology, ecumenism, monastic and religious life, episcopal organization, and church-society relations. These changes have had a lasting impact on a global church. This book tries to gauge some of the impact by chronicling the search for a public voice in American Catholicism and by examining some of the connections between contemporary Catholicism and American culture. The essays in Part I focus on the relation between the liberal political tradition that has been dominant in American public life and the rich tradition of Catholic thinking about politics and society. In addition to the essays by Douglass and Hollenbach, Jo Renee Formicola, Patrick Allitt, and James Muldoon discuss the development and historical antecedents of American Catholic political theology. The selections in Part II examine specific ways contemporary American Catholics have sought to express their religious beliefs in the political arena—from electoral activities of bishops to interest-group lobbying to the efforts of Catholic lawmakers to achieve consistency between moral conviction and public duty.

Public policy issues and questions of political acculturation, especially issues of Americanization and assimilation, have been important throughout American Catholic history and have taken on renewed significance in the contemporary church. As the Vatican's papal and curial pronouncements on family life, sexual ethics, reproductive technologies, and orthodox belief have become more stringent, the American traits of dissent, criticism, and democratic participation have become more evident. Many women, homosexuals, nuns, and theologians have found themselves dissenting; many remain deeply loyal Catholics. The essays in Part III focus on issues of sexuality and reproduction, one of the major areas of modern life in which Catholic teaching is openly counter-cultural. In these selections, Patrick Allitt, Jo Renee Formicola, Thomas Shannon, and this author describe the concerns of American Catholics about the morality and legality of contraception and abortion, the ethical implications of new forms of reproduction, and the tensions between church teachings on sexuality and institutional recognition of the civil rights of homosexual women and men.

The chapters in Part IV approach political-cultural questions of Americanization and assimilation from another angle—the influence of the democratic ethos of American life upon a hierarchially structured church. In addition to the chapters by Maureen Fiedler and Anne Lally Milhaven, Karen Sue Smith and Leonard Doohan discuss the role of the laity in church and society, the place and function of dissent, and the status of women in the church. The concern here is with ecclesiology and community and especially with matters of internal church governance.

Editing an anthology of original essays on contemporary American Catholicism requires enormous cooperation and coordination between editor and contributors in shaping the volume. I would like to thank the contributing authors for their thoughtful analyses written so well and so efficiently. Special thanks also to Marie Ellen Larcada for suggesting this project and to Meryl L. McDuffie for invaluable assistance in preparing the manuscript for publication. It is a pleasure to acknowledge Dean Donald G. Stein and the Graduate School at Rutgers University in Newark, New Jersey, for the partial support provided by a 1988–89 Graduate Research Award. Finally, this book was begun and completed while I served as Henry Luce Fellow in Theology at the Harvard Divinity School. I am grateful to the faculty and students of HDS for providing a collegial atmosphere and for many hours of stimulating conversation about theology, religion, politics, and society.

NOTES

1. See Dorothy Dohen, *Nationalism and American Catholicism* (New York: Sheed and Ward, 1967).

2. William Lee Miller, *The First Liberty: Religion and the American Republic* (New York: A. Knopf, 1986), 280, 291.

3. The Berger statement is reported in David O'Brien, "American Catholics and American Society," *Catholics and Nuclear War*, ed. Philip J. Murnion (New York: Crossroad, 1983), 16.

4. Richard John Neuhaus, *The Catholic Moment: The Paradox of the Church in the Modern World* (San Francisco: Harper & Row, 1987), 283.

5. The general relation between religion and politics has received increasing attention from political scientists in the last decade. See, for example, Robert Booth Fowler, *Religion and Politics in America* (Metuchen, N.J.: Scarecrow, 1984); A. James Reichley, *Religion in American Public Life* (Washington, D.C.: Brookings, 1985); Kenneth D. Wald, *Religion and Politics in the United States* (New York: St. Martin's Press, 1987); and Mary Hanna, *Catholics and American Politics* (Cambridge: Harvard University Press, 1979). See also Charles W. Dunn, ed., *Religion in American Politics* (Washington, D.C.: CQ Press, 1989).

6. NCCB/USCC, *Agenda Report: Documentation for General Meeting, Action Items 1–19* (Washington, D.C.: NCCB/USCC, 1986), 253, as

reported in Mary Hanna, "Bishops as Political Leaders," *Religion in American Politics*, ed. Charles W. Dunn (Washington, D.C.: CQ Press, 1989), 79.

7. See George Weigel, *Tranquillitas Ordinis: The Present Failure and Future Promise of American Catholic Thought on War and Peace* (New York: Oxford University Press, 1987).

8. Lay Catholic Commission on Catholic Social Teaching, *Toward the Future*, (New York, 1984).

9. *The New York Times*, December 27, 1987, p. A1 and December 29, 1987, p. A1.

10. David Shaneyfelt, "Pro-Abortion Catholics in Congress," *Crisis* 6:11 (December 1988), 14–17. This analysis is based on a study of the second session of the 100th Congress, in which Catholics numbered 28 percent of the U.S. House of Representatives (121 out of 432 voting members) and 19 percent of the U.S. Senate (19 of 100 Senators).

11. See the Memorandum by General Counsel Mark Chopko to the NCCB, reprinted in *Origins* 18:12 (September 1, 1988), 181–186. See also *United States Catholic Conference and National Conference of Catholic Bishops v. Abortion Rights Mobilization, Inc., et al.* (1987), Supreme Court Docket Number 87–416.

12. 410 *U.S.* 113.

13. NCCB, "Pastoral Plan for Pro-Life Activities," in *Pastoral Letters of the United States Catholic Bishops*, ed. Hugh J. Nolan, 4 vols. (Washington, D.C.: NCCB/USCC, 1984), 4:84.

14. See the following by Cardinal Joseph Bernardin: "Toward a Consistent Ethic of Life," Origins 13 (29 December 1983): 491–494; "Religion and Politics: The Future Agenda," *Origins* 14 (8 November 1984): 325; "The Consistent Ethic: What Sort of Framework?" *Origins* 16 (30 October 1986): 345, 347–350. See also Thomas G. Fuechtmann, ed., *Consistent Ethic of Life* (Kansas City, MO: Sheed and Ward, 1988).

15. See Michael Pakaluk, "A Cardinal Error: Does the 'Seamless Garment' Make Sense?" *Crisis* 6:10 (November 1988), 10–14.

16. Remarks of the Rev. J. Bryan Hehir, Panel on "The Catholic Bishops on War and Peace," Joint Meeting of the American Historical Association and the American Catholic Historical Association, Washington, D.C., December 29, 1987.

17. Remarks of the Rev. Francis X. Winters, S.J., Panel on "The Catholic Bishops' Pastoral Letter on War and Peace," Annual Meeting of the American Political Science Association, Washington, D.C., September 1984.

18. Bishop James K. Malone, Address of the President to Annual Meeting of the NCCB, November 12, 1984; reprinted in *Origins* 14 (29 November 1984): 384–390.

19. See John Deedy, *American Catholicism—And Now Where?* (New York: Plenum Press, 1987), chapter 1.

20. The parish reorganization in Detroit ordered by Archbishop Edmund Szoka in 1988–1989 is a case in point.

21. These statistics are from the *Official Catholic Directory*, published annually by P.J. Kennedy & Sons in New York.

22. John Deedy, *American Catholicism—And Now Where?*, p. 9.

23. *Ibid.*, 12–14.

24. *National Catholic Reporter*, November 25, 1988, p. 3.

25. John Deedy, *American Catholicism—And Now Where?*, p. 24.

26. *The New York Times*, October 7, 1984, p. 7.

27. Other Americans who have been disciplined directly or indirectly by the Vatican in the 1980s include: three Jesuit priests, John J. Mc Neill, Michael Buckley, Terrance A. Sweeney, and the Dominican priest, Matthew Fox.

28. John Deedy, *American Catholicism—And Now Where?*, pp. xi–xii.

29. Bernard Haring, "Does God Condemn Contraception? A Question for the Whole Church," *Commonweal*, February 10, 1989, pp. 69–71.

30. "The Cologne Declaration," *Commonweal*, February 24, 1989, pp. 102–104.

31. *Ibid.*, p. 104.

32. Philip S. Kaufman, O.S.B., "Autocracy Isn't the Catholic Style: Toward a Divine-Right Democracy," *Commonweal*, February 24, 1989, pp. 110–114.

33. One of the most important of the sixteen conciliar documents of Vatican II was the *Declaration on Religious Liberty (Dignitatis Humanae)* which was approved in 1965. This conciliar declaration is sometimes said to be the American contribution to the Second Vatican Council, since one of its principal architects was the Jesuit theologian, John Courtney Murray. Murray argued that the American conception of religious freedom and nonestablishment had positive advantages for the worldwide church as it sought to coexist with different governments in the late twentieth century. He and other theologians persuaded the Council to declare strong support for freedom of religion and for correlative duties of tolerance and respect. *The Declaration on Religious Liberty* put to rest the notion of "the Catholic state" and transformed the church-state question into a new theological consideration of the church's role in the world. Perhaps inevitably, it has also extended questions of freedom of religious belief and conscience to intramural or internal Catholic church affairs as well. The *Declaration* may be read in Walter M. Abbott, S.J., general editor, *The Documents of Vatican II* (New York: Guild Press, America Press, Association Press, 1966). See also John Courtney Murray, "Church and State at Vatican II," *Theological Studies* 27 (1966), 581–585.

34. John A. Coleman, "Who Are the Catholic Fundamentalists?" *Commonweal*, January 27, 1989, pp. 42–47.

35. See the Symposium, "Sexism, Sin and Grace: Responses to the Pastoral on Women," *Commonweal*, June 17, 1988, pp. 361–366. See also "Comments on the First Draft of the NCCB Pastoral Letter, prepared by the Center of Concern (Washington, D.C., June 13, 1988).

PART I

CATHOLIC SOCIAL TEACHING AND AMERICAN POLITICAL THOUGHT

This section focuses on the relation between the liberal political tradition that has been dominant in American public life and the rich tradition of Catholic thinking about politics and society. The essay by Jo Renee Formicola, which opens this section, traces the development of modern Catholic social teaching over the last century, culminating in the declarations of the Second Vatican Council and the emergence of an American Catholic political theology within the last thirty years. This new political theology accepts the constitutional principles of religious liberty and church-state separation as part of its core of religious beliefs, thereby reconciling the religious and political beliefs of American Catholics and dispelling the notion that a true Catholic could not be a loyal American. In showing how this new theology justifies political activism by the institutional church as well as by individual Catholic citizens, Formicola sets in context the recent pastoral statements of the Catholic bishops on war and peace, on economic justice, and on racism and sexism.

The American theologian chiefly responsible for demonstrating the compatibility of Catholicism and American political thought was the Jesuit scholar John Courtney Murray. Patrick Allitt examines the significance of Murray's achievement and shows how Murray's historical method enabled him to cull from pre-Reformation sources an antiabsolutist political tradition in Catholicism.

The bishops' use of the "just war" tradition in their 1983 peace pastoral is the subject of James Muldoon's essay, which questions why the pastoral's authors relied only upon medieval sources and ignored the work of sixteenth-century Spanish theologians and lawyers who attempted to address the fundamental issues raised by the discovery of the New World. Muldoon points to Francisco de Victoria, Bartolomeo de las Casas, and Francisco Suarez as creative thinkers who confronted the moral pluralism of the non-European world. By comparison, he argues, the American bishops do not yet fully realize that, in a pluralistic society such as the United States, the common good as expressed in public policy is the product of negotiation and compromise. He wonders why the bishops, who seek to join other non-Catholic opponents of nuclear war, articulate an absolutist view of abortion, which undermines the practical possibility of such antinuclear coalitions. Although Muldoon does not mention the bishops' consistent life ethic, his conclusion clearly questions its political applicability.

Finally, the essays by R. Bruce Douglass and David Hollenbach address directly the compatibility of liberalism and Catholic social thought through analysis of the presuppositions of the bishops' 1986 pastoral letter on the U.S. economy. Douglass argues, like Muldoon, that our political and religious culture is now more self-consciously pluralistic than ever before. Given such diversity, he wonders why the bishops in their economics pastoral have abandoned the language of rational ethics so prominent in previous Catholic social teaching, and couched their arguments in Biblical and theological terms. He also questions the emphasis on individual rights in the pastoral, which has supplanted the old natural law mode of reasoning, and he warns against confusing Catholic teaching with liberalism, even in its more benign forms.

David Hollenbach also examines the basic ethical framework of the bishops' letter as a case study of the relationship between Catholic social teaching and liberalism as a political and economic ideology. However, he argues that the bishops' letter embodies a reasonably coherent moral theory, one which incorporates both a liberal emphasis on personal dignity and rights, and a communitarian stress on the common good. Drawing upon the work of theologians Reinhold Niebuhr and John Courtney Murray and political theorists Michael Walzer and John Rawls, Hollenbach defends the pastoral letter's synthesis of liberal and communitarian perspectives. He also suggests that the pastoral letter, in proposing a conception of justice as participation in society, makes a significant contribution to contemporary theoretical discussions of liberalism in American politics and society.

CHAPTER I

AMERICAN CATHOLIC POLITICAL THEOLOGY

Jo Renee Formicola

During the last twenty-five years, a Catholic political theology has emerged in the United States, one designed to reorient the relationship between church and state in America. Indeed, the Bishops' pastoral on nuclear arms and their more recent letter on the economy attest to this fact. The new Catholic political theology reflects a shift from the traditional, apologetic teachings of the past, which merely defended the narrow dogmatic interests of the Catholic Church, to an assertive theology that now justifies political activism on behalf of "social justice" issues. Such a major shift within Catholic church-state teachings during the last quarter century requires identification and analysis of the stages in the development of a Catholic political theology. These periods can be defined and described as: the reactionary papal stance of the nineteenth century; the American conservative posture of the 1920s; the era of progressive reevaluation of the 1950s; the reforms of Vatican II during the 1960s; and the current liberal, activist nature of American political theology.

PAPAL REACTIONISM

The conscious development of an American Catholic political theology did not begin until the mid-1950s. Prior to that time, traditional papal encyclicals and teachings, particularly those of Leo XIII (1878–1903), were regarded as the final word on church-state theory. The Catholic clergy and faithful understood those documents to be religious, definitive, and nonpolitical. On the one hand, while the encyclicals and writings, which often covered political issues, were binding on the consciences of Catholics, they attached no sin to noncompliance and were not to be interpreted in a partisan manner. On the other hand, these writings were perceived by many non-Catholics, particularly those in the United States, as political, not religious, tenets. Thus, such promulgations helped to reenforce the notion that a true Catholic could not be a loyal American, an idea that fueled the Catholic-Protestant rivalry in the United States until the middle of the twentieth century.

When Leo XIII assumed the papacy, the Catholic Church had lost considerable religious and temporal power in Europe, especially as a result of the unification of Italy in 1870. In order to reassert its eroding power at the time, the Holy See issued a series of encyclicals and letters to stem what it perceived as the degenerating secularization of government in the world. The most significant of these documents were: *Inscrutibili* (1878), *Diuturnum* (1881), *Immortale Dei* (1885), *Libertas Praestantissimum* (1888), *Testem Benevolentiae* (1888), *Sapientiae Christianae* (1890), and *Longinque Oceani* (1895).

Basically, four principles of church and state characterized the writings of Leo XIII. First, they were predicated on the belief that the spiritual is superior to the temporal order. Second, they called for the public profession of religion by governments. Third, they supported the notion that the Catholic Church should be protected by the state. And fourth, they encouraged the harmonious relationship between the Church and the state. Such ideas were construed as reactionary by American non-Catholics, most of whom perceived Catholic church-state beliefs to be a threat to the constitutional principle of the separation of church and state.

Pope Leo defended his primary premise, the belief in the superiority of spiritual over temporal power, by writing in *Immortale Dei* that the authority of the Church is "the most exalted of all authority."[1] Even in jurisdictional disputes between the Church and the state, he argued that the authority of the Church should prevail. "But if the laws of the State are manifestly at variance with the divine law containing enactments hurtful to the Church, or conveying injunctions adverse to the duties imposed by religion, or if they violate the person of the Supreme Pontiff or the authority of Jesus Christ, then truly to resist is a positive duty, to obey, a crime."[2]

In his second principle, Leo called for the public profession of religion, as well as the recognition of Catholicism as the one, true religion. Justification for such a stance rested on his belief in the divine origin of all power and the need of the state to recognize and submit to God as the author of all authority. "All public power must proceed from God. For God alone is the true and supreme Lord of the World. Everything without exception must be subject to Him and must serve Him. . . . As a consequence, the State constituted as it is, is clearly bound to act up to the manifold duties linking it to God, by the public profession of religion."[3]

Once the state agreed to make a public profession of faith, Leo expected that the religion to be affirmed and protected would be that of Roman Catholicism. For, he wrote, "It is not lawful for the State, anymore than for the individual, either to disregard all religious duties or to hold in equal favor different kinds of religion.[4] He stated further, "Men who really believe in the existence of God must . . . understand that differing modes of divine worship . . . cannot be all equally . . . good and equally acceptable to God."[5]

In *Longinque Oceani*, Leo even went so far as to criticize the concepts of separation of church and state and religious liberty as they existed in the United States. "It would be very erroneous to draw the conclusion that in America is to be sought the type of the most desirable status of the Church, or that it would be universally lawful or expedient for State and Church to be, as in America, dissevered and divorced."[6] He also held that the Catholic Church in America would flourish more if "in addition to liberty, she enjoyed the favor of the laws and the patronage of the public authority."[7]

Leo's ideas on the supremacy of the spiritual over the temporal order and the public profession of Catholicism were augmented by his third principle of church and state: the belief that the Church should be protected by the state. By this he meant that the Catholic Church should not be limited in any way by the state. To him, the Church should not be "looked upon as inferior to the civil power, or in any manner dependent upon it."[8] Rather, he believed that the Church should administer "freely and without hindrance, in accordance with her own judgement all matters that fall within its competence."[9] Such "matters" included marriage, education, and church property, sources of continuous conflict between civil and church leaders during much of the nineteenth and twentieth centuries.

Finally, Leo completed his church-state theory with his fourth principle, that a harmonious relationship between both institutions should be sought. Viewing such unity as both possible and necessary, the pontiff wrote that the church and the state were to work for the ultimate good of man and function in a complementary, orderly way.

> The nature and scope of that connection can be determined only, as We have laid down, by having regard to the nature of each power, and by taking account of the relative excellence and nobleness of their purpose. One of the two has for its proximate and chief object the well-being of this mortal life; the other the everlasting joys of heaven. Whatever, therefore, in things human is of a sacred character, whatever belongs either of its own nature or by reason of the end to which it is referred, to the salvation of souls or to the worship of God, is subject to the power and judgement of the Church. Whatever is to be ranged under the civil and political order is rightly subject to the civil authority.[10]

Thus, reflection on the four tenets of Pope Leo's church-state theory—the supremacy of the spiritual over the temporal order, the public profession of Catholicism, the complete freedom of the church in its sphere of authority, and the harmonious working of both institutions—reveals ideas that were clearly antagonistic to the American constitutional principles of church and state. And, even more significantly, no attempts were made by succeeding pontiffs to alter these principles until Vatican II, almost a hundred years later. Rather, all adhered to the papal admonition of Leo: "There are some among you who conceive of and desire a Church in America different from that which is in the rest of the world. One in unity of doctrine as in the unity of government, such is the Catholic Church, and since God has established its center and foundation in the Chair of St. Peter, one which is rightly called Roman, for where Peter is, there is the Church."[11]

CLERICAL CONSERVATISM

In the 1920s, American Catholic church-state theory took on a distinctly conservative cast, as Father John A. Ryan sought to interpret and apply the Leonine theories in light of the American democratic experience. Holding a doctorate from Catholic University, Ryan authored the "Bishops' Plan for Reconstruction" after World War I, became a leading member for the newly formed National Catholic Welfare Council (NCWC), and eventually was appointed the dean of theology at Catholic University of America. In 1920, he wrote his most significant political work, *The State and the Church* with F. X. Millar, S.J., to explain the view of the Catholic Church on American politics.

Ryan was a strict conservative on matters of moral theology. Since he viewed Pope Leo's theories on church and state as religious teachings, he explained, defended, and applied them to the United States from a purely dogmatic perspective. Technically, he supported the notion of the primacy of the spiritual over the temporal order. Even though he was willing to admit that the authority of the state is supreme in civil affairs, he ultimately concluded that the state is not in every respect "unlimited."[12] He wrote: "It is true that the actions of the State when in the field of legislation or administration have moral aspects, inasmuch as they are human actions. Therefore, they are in some manner subject to the Church as the interpreter of the moral law."[13]

Ryan also insisted, abstractly, on the public profession of faith and Catholicism, but understood that some qualifications were necessary to adapt to the system of religious plurality in America. Again, shifting from Pope Leo's view somewhat, he called on the government to evidence a "positive friendliness toward religion."[14] His opposition to strict government neutrality toward religion was based on his contention that such behavior always resulted in a state policy of moral hostility.

As for the recognition of Catholicism as the one, true religion, Ryan held the pontiff's stand to be "thoroughly logical."[15] Basing his defense on the medieval theological premise that "error has no rights," he condescended to allow a limited religious liberty based on expediency, a fact of life so long as Catholics remained in the minority of America. He wrote: "It is true, indeed, that some zealots and bigots will continue to attack the Church because they fear that some 5,000 years hence the U.S. may become overwhelmingly Catholic and may then restrict the freedom of non-Catholic denominations. Nevertheless, we cannot yield up the principles of eternal and unchangeable truth in order to avoid the enmity of such unreasonable persons."[16]

Ryan accepted Leo's other two principles, freedom of the Church in deciding its sphere of work and the harmonious collaboration of the Church and the state, as axiomatic truths. He spent little time on these matters, dismissing the first as an historical problem of the papal states to be solved by adequate international recognition and guarantees. As for the second principle, however, Ryan believed that if both the Church and the state maintained independence in their own spheres, no conflict would arise. In the two possible areas of jurisdictional dispute, education and marriage, the state should simply adhere to Catholic moral principles in Catholic states, and in the case of disagreements in non-Catholic countries, governments should simply leave the Church alone! "It is possible to arrive at an adjustment, which though not in full accord with Catholic claims, will forestall misunderstanding and actual friction. All that is necessary for this purpose is that civil authorities should seek merely to promote the public welfare and not make any difficulties for the Church."[17] It should come as no surprise that such condescending, inflexible statements and conservative interpretations of all the Leonine principles of church and state reenforced perceptions among non-Catholics of the Church as an alien, autocratic, religious institution bent on the political fusion of the Holy See and the United States government. These fears were exacerbated by Ryan's extensive literary influence and considerable involvement in both church and government administration. *The State and the Church* remained in print from 1922 until 1940, when it was revised and given the new title, *Catholic Principles of Politics*. Having been through eleven printings by 1958, it was viewed as the definitive text on the subject of Catholic church-state principles in the United States. Ryan himself went on to found *Social Action*, a magazine supported by the NCWC, to publish numerous books on distributive justice, to serve as religious adviser to Al Smith, to work for Franklin D. Roosevelt on unemployment insurance, and to lead the fight against the progressive theologians of the 1950s.

PROGRESSIVE REEVALUATION

By the 1950s, John Courtney Murray, S.J., challenged, and ultimately shattered, the prevailing religious notions of church and state in America. A theologian himself, Murray was the perfect foil for Ryan and his followers. Having served as a professor of theology at Woodstock, the Jesuit seminary, Murray was chosen as the religion editor of the order's magazine, *America*, and, simultaneously, as the editor-in-chief of *Theological Studies*. The latter journal served as a vehicle for investigation on a wide range of social, as well as political, questions from a theological perspective. From this vantage point, Murray could attack not only Ryan and his conservative fellow clerics, but the ideas of Leo XIII as well.

Working within the confines of Catholic dogma, Murray began with one basic premise, that is, that church-state theory is evolutionary, subject to historical, political variables. This assumption led him inevitably to the conclusion that the Church would have to adapt its principles of ecclesiastical rights and duties to the political contingencies of time and place in America. A simple methodology characterized his approach to church-state theory. Using the three perspectives of ethics, theology, and politics, he set out to separate dogma from rhetoric and then to reformulate the existent papal and conservative ideas of church and state. Murray's first major article[18] was written from an ethical perspective and was designed to explore the obligations of the individual as man and citizen, as well as the responsibilities of the state to its citizens and to God. Murray believed that man qua man was to search for the truth about God and worship him, to work for his own self-perfection, and to assist his neighbor to come to a knowledge of God. Man qua citizen had the ethical duty to practice social charity and justice and to obey the positive law.

The ethical responsibilities of the state were similar to those of man in the abstract, but quite different in the concrete. In the *abstract*, Murray believed that the state should acknowledge God as its author and worship him, promote religion and morality through civil law based on natural law, and prohibit those internal forces which could destroy morality or the belief in God. In the *concrete*, however, Murray held that such state actions were to be regulated by the "norms of political prudence."[19] Thus, for the first time, the Catholic approach to politics was tempered by the addition of a discerning, yet pragmatic, dimension. It encouraged the flexibility needed to reach an accommodation between Catholicism and democracy in the United States and, as a result, led to the rejection of the Leonine notion of the public profession of religion by many of the other progressive theologians in America, most notably Gustav Weigel, S.J., John Tracey Ellis, and John A. O'Brien.

Murray's second major article, written from a political perspective, narrowed the conservative religious concept of church freedom in order to reach an accommodation between Catholicism and the political system of the United States.[20] To Murray, the ordering of freedoms and the maintenance of institutions that protected freedom, were the political ends of the state. Thus, building on earlier ideas, he asserted that the only responsibility of the state to the Church was the secular obligation to maintain its freedom. The state, in Murray's view, had no moral responsibility to profess religion. Differing with Leo XIII and Ryan, Murray claimed that the state was to aid the Church in maintaining its freedom by guaranteeing its right to pursue its traditional ends: to teach, rule, and sanctify its members. The clear obligation to preserve such authority depended, according to Murray, not solely on government protection, as previously held, but instead, on a personal act of faith of church members acting as citizens. The relationship of church and society was to become the subject of Murray's third significant paper. Standing apart from fifteen hundred years of Catholic practice, Murray contended that contemporary Catholicism had to forge a new relationship with society. He proposed one based on the growing power of citizenry rather than on maintaining the traditional marriage of the institutional Catholic Church and government. "The problem is no longer *sacredotium* and *regnum*, but *sacredotium* and *civis*. . . . It is with this new *libertas civila* that the old *libertas ecclesiastica* has to establish proper relations."[21]

Emphasis on the individual within society eventually emerged as the crucial underpinning of Murray's future break with the conservative stance on the church and state. Trying to reconcile the traditional theological understanding of man as an individual with the modern political view of man as a citizen, Murray argued that the citizenry, not the Catholic Church, should perform the two most important functions in the society. These included the reconciliation of institutions within the temporal and spiritual orders and the correction of problems within the temporal order through the institutions of the state, rather than the Church. Thus, he shifted such major responsibilities from the jurisdiction of the institutional Catholic Church to the conscience of the citizen acting as church member. "In the native structure of the American system, the citizen of religious conscience is placed in the mediating position between Church and State. The Church is free to form the consciences of her members; and they as citizens are free to conform in the life of the City to the demands of their consciences. Both freedoms are part of an organic system of freedom. And the system . . . rests on the collective judgement of the people that this whole system is for the common good."[22]

Murray's emphasis on the individual changed the interpretation of the place of the institutional church within the totality of society. Although he still viewed the Catholic Church as the prime force within the temporal order, in contrast to the conservatives, Murray could no longer justify it as an institution above the temporal order. By the 1950s, then, Murray's task was quite clear: to find a way to support religious toleration and separation of church and state within the American democratic infrastructure without compromising the Catholic view of its own religious perfection. To do this, Murray proposed a massive study of the Leonine writings in order to separate the polemic from the theological arguments, and then to reformulate the Catholic notion of church and state.

Murray began, but never finished, his critiques of Pope Leo's writings in 1953. Claiming that Leo's writings had a "powerful polemic bias," and that they were "dated,"[23] Murray attacked the pontiff for viewing church-state theory too simplistically. Murray argued that the nineteenth-century European state, about which Leo wrote, was an example of a social and juridical monism, to be sure, but that the twentieth-century American democratic, pluralistic system was vastly different. The uniqueness of the American situation rested on the existence of a limited government and, according to Murray, that fact precluded the need for an established state religion to maintain a legal, social, or moral duality.

On the whole, then, Murray differed with the ideas of Leo XIII and John A. Ryan in four ways. First, he did not accept the theory of the primacy of the spiritual over the temporal order. Instead, he believed in the existence of the spiritual within the temporal order, as defined and exercised through the citizens of the state, rather than by juridical decision of the institutional Church. Second, he held that the public profession of religion in the concrete was neither a function nor responsibility of the state. He viewed the state, pragmatically, as a natural, secular institution having no supernatural right or obligation to acknowledge God. Third, he held that the preservation of the freedom of the church was essential to maintain a social and juridical dualism. He believed, however, that the autonomy of the church was to be preserved by the faith of the citizens, not by the power of the government. Finally, while Murray believed in the necessity and harmony of all law, he felt that the Catholic Church had to adapt itself to contemporary democratic principles such as freedom of religion and separation of church and state in order to maintain its own autonomy and authority.

These ideas met with fierce opposition from John A. Ryan and other conservative clerics such as Joseph Clifford Fenton and George Connell. The Vatican, too, looked askance at the beginnings of Murray's reformulation of Leonine church-state theory. Quickly censuring him in 1955, the Holy See forbade him to write on church-state in the future.

Indeed, it was not until Vatican II, almost a decade later, that Murray was again allowed to be heard on these issues and was vindicated.

Vatican II was convened by Pope John XXIII in 1962 for the purpose of *aggiornamento*, that is, for internal reform, church renewal, and a reassessment of the external relationship of the Catholic Church with the world, particularly government. Such purposes rankled the defenders of the status quo and inspired the progressives, yet it would be too simplistic to characterize the Council as a struggle for dominance between conservatives and liberals. Rather, many of the problems, theological, social, and political, which had arisen since the previous synod a century earlier, were the result of two different, complex mind sets. One group, composed largely of Italian cardinals, tended to see problems in nonhistorical, abstract principles. They supported an unchanging orthodoxy suspended in time. A second group, made up of theologians *(periti)*, supported the evolution of church doctrine in response to modern problems. They stressed the formulation of a theology alive to, and formed by, history and circumstance. Eventually, the mentality of the latter group prevailed, with the hierarchy supporting a mandate to look at the times and interpret them in the light of the gospel of Christ.

The Council lasted for three years, and during that time issued sixteen decrees on diverse matters of theology, ethics, social justice, and church organization. For the purpose of this essay, four documents are most significant: *Lumen Gentium*, also known as *De Ecclesia (The Dogmatic Constitution of the Church), Gaudium et Spes (The Pastoral Constitution on the Church in the Modern World), Unitatis Reintegratio (The Decree on Ecumenism),* and *Dignitatis Humanae (The Declaration on Religious Freedom).*

With the formulation of *Lumen Gentium* and *Gaudium et Spes*, the Council set about to redefine the role and relationship of the Catholic Church to man and the world. The thrust of these two documents was to stress the Church's role as servant of mankind: "to foster brotherhood," "to give witness to the truth, to rescue and not sit in judgement, to serve and not be served."[24] While supporting the quest for freedom and human rights, it took a cautious stand on attempts to secure those rights. "Christ, to be sure, gave his Church no proper mission in the political, economic or social order. The purpose He set before us is a religious one."[25]

Further, with regard to politics, the Council stressed the autonomy of the Catholic Church, *not* its superiority over the political order.

> The role and competence of the Church being what it is, she must in no way be confused with the political community, nor be bound to any political system. For, she is at once, a sign and a significant of the transcendence of the human person.
>
> In their proper spheres, the political community and the Church are mutually independent and self-governing. Yet, but with a different title, each serves the personal and social vocation of the same human beings. This service can be more effectively rendered for the good of all, if each works better for wholesome mutual cooperation, depending on the circumstances of time and place. . . . The Church does not lodge her hope in privileges conferred by civil authority. Indeed, she stands ready to renounce the exercise of certain legitimately acquired rights if it becomes clear that their use raises doubt about the sincerity of her witness or that new conditions of life demand some other arrangement.[26]

Thus, Vatican II reflected a fundamental change in the attitude of the Catholic Church toward the state: the council agreed that the contingencies of time, place, and circumstance had to play a role in determining how the Church should interact with the state for the benefit of mankind. The Church was even willing to give up rights, as well as privileges, if such positions compromised its proper functioning in a changing world. As a result of Vatican II, then, the four immutable principles of church and state which had been expounded by Leo XIII and reenforced by his successors, were understood to be no longer sacrosanct. Instead, the Council admitted that the Church had to adapt those doctrines to the political realities of the present. Ironically, the ideas of John Courtney Murray had now come full circle and were recognized as the proper guide for church-state interaction.

The Council also dealt with ecumenism and religious freedom in the documents *Unitatis Reintegratio* and *Dignitatis Humanae*. Framed by the Americans Gustav Weigel, S.J., and John Courtney Murray,[27] one of these documents reflected a complete shift in the former Vatican policy, from religious separation and aloofness to one of cooperation and tolerance. *Unitatis Reintegratio* accepted the fact that all Christian churches play an important role in salvation, supported the notion of dialogue with non-Catholics, and suggested that Catholics take the first steps to help bring about religious unity by changing their own personal attitudes.

Dignitatis Humanae further augmented ecumenism by stressing religious freedom. Using Murray's methodology, it discussed religious liberty on three planes: ethical, political, and theological. On an ethical level, religious freedom was conceived as an inalienable human right. On a political plane, it was understood as a right worthy of preservation and protection by the government. On a theological level, it was considered the right that justified the juridical freedom of Church. The bishops, through Murray's document, agreed that:

> This Vatican Synod declares that the human person has a right to religious freedom. This freedom means that all men are to be immune from coercion on the part of individuals or of social groups and of any human power, in such wise that in matters religious no one is to be forced to act in a manner contrary to his own beliefs. Nor is anyone to be restrained from acting in accordance with his own beliefs, whether privately or publicly, whether alone or in association with others, within limits. . . . This right of the human person to religious freedom is to be recognized in the constitutional law whereby society is governed. Thus it is to become a civil right.[28]

Vatican II, therefore, shifted the Church's attitude toward religious tolerance, replacing expediency with genuine respect for the moral convictions of others. Again, the Council confirmed and validated the American ideal of religious freedom.

What, then, did Vatican II accomplish with regard to church-state theory? In general, it promulgated principles which, for the United States, had the effect of reconciling Catholic religious beliefs with American political principles. It supported and affirmed the constitutional ideals of democracy: belief in the worth and dignity of man, separation of church and state, adherence to freedom of conscience, and respect for religious diversity.

The significance of such a turn of events cannot be overestimated, especially in the United States. Since Catholic teaching on church and state finally mirrored American constitutional principles, Catholics could at last be considered loyal Americans *and* good Catholics! And, perhaps even more importantly, the seeds were being sown for the beginnings of significant Catholic political activism on behalf of social justice issues in the United States.

AMERICAN CATHOLIC POLITICAL THEORY

Post–Vatican II writings have again changed Catholic church-state theory significantly, taking the Church a step further toward the left as it now attempts to put its social and theological teachings into practice in a more positive, often political, way. On the papal level, two encyclicals, *Populorum Progressio* and *Octagesima Adveniens*, written by Pope Paul VI, followed up on Vatican II's mandate to look at the times and reinterpret them in light of the gospel of Christ. These writings show the shift in church emphasis from talk about economic and political reform, to action on behalf of social justice concerns. *Populorum Progressio* urged the integral development of the whole person, while *Octagesima Adveniens* called for political action to make such advancement a reality.

Other incentives, particularly those of the Latin American hierarchy, further attempted to fulfill the Vatican II mandate. During the 1960s, statements by the hierarchy at Mar Del Plata (1966) and Medellin (1968) helped to crystallize the political attitudes and behavior of the Catholic Church. The bishops pledged to bring about a transformation in the social order by working to restructure the society of Latin America, not on the principles of either the left or the right, but on the social *magisterium* of the Church.

This notion was quickly radicalized by Gustavo Gutierrez and others in the 1970s, and soon became the starting point for a new religio-political phenomenon: liberation theology. Stressing the class struggle and the need for the Church to play a role in eradicating it, the Latin American clergy responded swiftly and enthusiastically by increased political activism to effect the transformation of society in the southern hemisphere.

Many of these ideas were summarized and validated by the Catholic hierarchy meeting in Rome in 1971. Issuing a statement entitled *Justice in the World*, they declared that the new role of the Church was to be the voice of the voiceless. Writing that the mission of the Church is "the redemption of the human race and its liberation from every oppressive situation,"[29] they equated spiritual evangelization with social action to make the gospel more intelligible in the world, work, and life of forgotten people.

By 1974, at their general assembly, the bishops extended the notion of the Church's mission by contending that there is a mutual relationship between evangelization and liberation, indeed, "an intimate connection."[30] Clearly, the hierarchy had begun officially to view theological obligation as more than mere social action, but stopped just short of viewing religious responsibility as a political mandate, as the liberation theologians would have liked. At Puebla in 1979, the notion was carried even farther, as the bishops claimed that the Church exists to evangelize, to eliminate poverty, to create a just world, to support workers, and to defend human rights. The philosophy of the hierarchy and some of the radicalism of the Latin American bishops has spilled over into the United States. As a result, the American Catholic religious community is moving toward a more liberal posture, supporting increased political activity in the United States for what it considers to be social justice concerns.

Trends and writings, however, clearly indicate that American Catholic church-state theory still lies within the framework established by John Courtney Murray and the hierarchy at Vatican II. Many of those guidelines, however, have been augmented by more radical American Catholic thinkers anxious to take the challenge of Vatican II further and scrutinize the signs of the times in order to interpret them in the light of the gospel. As a result, they have changed American Catholic church-state theory into a new political theology. That is, Catholic theologians have justified, by a current secular reinterpretation of theology, the active involvement of the Catholic Church within the American political process today. That is particularly true with regard to the current understanding of the agenda, the role, and the means that the Catholic Church should use to attain its goals within the American pluralistic infrastructure.

Since Vatican II, the Catholic Church has increasingly broadened its agenda, moving from narrow, dogmatic, domestic interests such as abortion and education, to wider social justice and "moral" matters such as international human rights, disarmament, and the economy. For the first time, the Church has become involved politically, not only injecting what it views as transcendent values into the foreign policy decision-making process, but making program and legislative recommendations as well. A good case in point is human rights.

As early as 1973, the Church gave significant, reliable, testimony to the Fraser Committee in the United States House of Representatives, the first congressional body constituted to investigate human rights abuses abroad.[31] It did not stop there, however. Drawing on their own resources and information, the bishops, through their policy agency, the United States Catholic Conference (USCC), lobbied for the enactment of a series of bills that would tie economic and military assistance to respect for human rights.[32] The USCC publicized examples of repression and created a constituency within government and the public sector committed to adoption of public policies which supported open criticism of governments that violated human rights. Currently, the bishops have challenged President Ronald Reagan's use of "quiet diplomacy" to gloss over repression in many parts of the world, and they have taken the lead, politically, to oppose current United States policy in El Salvador and Nicaragua.

By the end of the 1970s, theologians such as David Hollenbach, S.J., were already reinterpreting theology to justify church activity on behalf of human rights. In his work, *Claims in Conflict*, Hollenbach argued, first, that the moral perspective of human rights is what links together an understanding of the economic, social, and political rights of man. Then, by using and reinterpreting the theological concept of *imago Dei*, the belief that man is made in the image and likeness of God, Hollenbach justified a Catholic commitment to support action on behalf of human rights in the present socio-political circumstances. He also claimed that the Catholic Church must take up its social mandate and support the needs of the poor over the wants of the rich, encourage the freedom of the dominated over the liberty of the powerful, and support the participation of the marginalized over the preservation of the order which excludes them.[33] Thus, Hollenbach had theologically validated the claims of the oppressed against the status quo while arguing for an activist and theologically vigorous approach to the problem of human rights by the Church.

The understanding of the role of the Catholic Church within the American infrastructure has also changed. For a long time, politics in America was regarded as a partisan pastime, one that the Church should avoid.[34] Now, however, politics has come to be recognized as one of the most important means by which the Church should make its views known in a pluralist society. J. Bryan Hehir, director of the Office of International Justice and Peace and an architect of the bishops' pastoral on nuclear arms and the economy, believes that it is the responsibility of the Church to enrich the public debate, to act as a moral critic on public policy, and to teach Catholic views on dogmatic and social justice issues.[35] He also believes that the Catholic Church should act like any other interest group within the American infrastructure, presenting its views in the political arena by using the political process to influence the course of United States domestic and foreign policy.[36]

Such ideas are reflected by Bishop James Malone, President of National Council of Catholic Bishops. During the 1984 presidential campaign, he attempted to clarify the role of religion and politics in America. Justifying the traditional right of the Catholic Church to teach, inform, judge, and bring attention to issues involving significant moral dimensions, he urged all Catholics to "involve themselves in the political process," and to "convince others of the rightness of the Catholic position."[37] Thus, it is possible to see within the Catholic Church a trend to support a more vocal, aggressive, and political Catholic membership and hierarchy in the future.

Finally, political activism has emerged as an acceptable, viable means to carry out the broadened agenda and new role of the Church in the 1980s and beyond. Supported by theologians and members of the hierarchy and clergy, increased, intense political activity is being used by the Catholic Church in America to effect social justice changes in society. Theologians such as John Coleman have stressed the need to follow a practical, activist theology. In his major work, *An American Strategic Theology*, Coleman argues that the Church has the right to intervene *institutionally* in political/economic matters because of its mission to sustain man and effect escatalogical transformation of the community. Action for social justice, he believes, is simply another element of the Church's evangelization duty. Love of God and love of neighbor demand that the Church give attention to economic and political justice. Therefore, according to Coleman, the Church must intervene in the political process *qua* the Church and hierarchy. Acting as a forum for moral discussion, the Church should nourish and support the good in society by mobilizing it for social action. More importantly, he believes that the Catholic Church should form "voluntary associations . . . who form lobby groups to effect social policy."[38] Thus, Coleman also uses theology as a justification for social change and envisions the Catholic Church as the means to effect the course of such a transformation by political action.

The international Catholic theological organization, Concilium, also agrees. With many prominent American Catholic theologians numbered among its members, Concilium recently defended the Catholic Church's political involvement throughout the world. Justifying such activism as a way of entering the world of the poor, sharing their destiny, and promoting their liberation, these theologians have protested current Vatican efforts by Pope John Paul to limit religious involvement in politics. They stated: "As these movements are a sign of hope for the whole Church, any premature intervention from higher authorities risks stifling the Spirit, which animates and guides local Churches. We express our strong solidarity with these movements of liberation and their theology. . . . We firmly believe that the future of the Church, the coming of the kingdom and the judgment of the world are tied up with these movements."[39] Again, a theological justification for political action is being used. In this case, political activism is defended on the basis of the exposition of the Holy Spirit in the world, and the coming of God's kingdom in the future.

Yet these cases are not unique. A trend is developing, one in which the American hierarchy and theologians are increasingly reinterpreting theology to validate action, both social and political, on behalf of religious issues. Space and time dictate only a cursory look at the two major works of the bishops in the 1980s, the pastoral on nuclear arms and the pastoral on the economy. Both "scrutinize the times" and view these concepts in light of the gospel. Both also make policy recommendations, with the pastoral on disarmament already serving as the basis for demonstrations, lobbying, and testimony against the MX missile and increased defense expenditures.

How, then, can we summarize the new political theology of the American Catholic Church? First, it is a political theology that accepts the constitutional principles of separation of church and state as well as the notion of religious liberty as part of its core of *religious* belief. Thus, the religious and political beliefs of American Catholics have finally been reconciled. Second, it is a political theology that justifies political activism, not only by citizens, but by the Catholic Church as well, for the advancement of moral principles in American domestic and foreign policy. Viewing itself as a special interest group within the American infrastructure, the Church intends to continue political action to advance human rights, to bring about disarmament, and to reform the economy. Third, it is a political theology that is evolutionary, changing as the Church continually views the times through the prism of the gospel of Christ. Thus, its concerns may vary, and the choice of methods to support them may change as well.

NOTES

This article originally appeared in *Journal of Church and State* 29 (Autumn 1987), pp. 457–474.

1. John J. Wayne, *The Great Encyclical Letters of Pope Leo XIII* (New York: Benzinger Brothers, 1903), p. 113. *Immortale Dei.*

2. Ibid., p. 185. *Sapientiae Christianae.*

3. Ibid., pp. 109–110. *Immortale Dei.*

4. Ibid., p. 26. *Immortale Dei.*

5. Ibid., p. 123. *Immortale Dei.*

6. Ibid., p. 323. *Longinque Oceani.*

7. Ibid., p. 324. *Longinque Oceani.*

8. Ibid., p. 113. *Immortale Dei.*

9. Ibid., p. 124

10. Ibid., p. 115.

11. Ibid., p. 452. *Testem Benevolentiae.*

12. John A. Ryan and Moorehouse F. X. Millar, *The State and the Church* (New York: Macmillan, 1922), p. 43.

13. Ibid., p. 42.

14. Ibid., p. 31.

15. Ibid., p. 32.

16. Ibid., p. 39.

17. Ibid., p. 52.

18. John Courtney Murray, "Freedom of Religion I: The Ethical Problem," *Theological Studies* 6 (June 1945): pp. 229–286.

19. Ibid., p. 267.

20. John Courtney Murray, "Contemporary Orientations of Catholic Thought on Church and State," *Theological Studies* 10 (June 1949): pp. 177–234.

21. Ibid., p. 193.

22. Ibid., p. 225.

23. John Courtney Murray, "Leo XIII on Church and State: General Structure of the Controversy," *Theological Studies* 14 (March 1953): pp. 1–30.

24. Walter Abbott, *The Documents of Vatican II* (New York: Herder and Herder, 1966), p. 201. *Gaudium et Spes*, Sec. 3.

25. Ibid., p. 241. *Lumen Gentium*, Sec. 42.

26. Ibid., pp. 287–288. *Lumen Gentium*, Sec. 76.

27. Murray was not invited to the first session of the general council. However, he was taken as a *periti*, that is, a theological expert, by Francis Cardinal Spellman to the second session. As a result of such action, Murray's "intellectual exile" ended, and he was invited to author the document on religious freedom.

28. Abbott, *The Documents*, pp. 678–679. *Dignitatis Humanae*, Sec. 2.

29. Joseph Gremillion, *The Gospel of Peace and Justice* (Maryknoll, New York: Orbis), 514. *Justice in the World*, Sec. 6.

30. Ibid., p. 597. *Evangelization of the Modern World*, Sec. 12.

31. Correspondence of Congressman Donald Fraser to the author, 16 March 1980, and interview, Dr. John Salzberg on 18 February 1980.

32. Twenty-nine recommendations for incorporating human rights into U.S. foreign policy emerged from those hearings, as well as seven significant pieces of legislation. These include: Resolution 556, 20 September 1973 (Better use of the International Court of Justice at The Hague); House Resolution 557, 20 September 1973 (To ratify the U.N. Covenants on Human Rights); House Concurrent Resolution 307, 20 September 1973 (To strengthen the U.N. Human Rights Commission); House Concurrent Resolution 321, 20 September 1973 (To establish rules for the treatment of prisoners); House Concurrent Resolution 313, 20 September 1973 (To support U.N. efforts to establish a program for the decade to combat racism and radical discrimination); and House Resolution 10455, 20 September 1973 (To establish an office within the State Department on Humanitarian Affairs).

33. David Hollenbach, *Claims in Conflict* (Ramsey, New Jersey: Paulist Press, 1979), p. 204.

34. Interview, Bishop Peter Gerety, 8 February 1980.

35. Interview, Father J. Bryan Hehir, 4 January 1980.

36. Interview, Father J. Bryan Hehir, 16 July 1984.

37. Bishop James Malone, "Text of Statement from Leader of National Conference of Catholic Bishops," *The New York Times*, 10 July 1984, p. B4.

38. John Coleman, *An American Strategic Theology* (Ramsey, New Jersey: Paulist Press, 1979), p. 270.

39. Concilium, "Text of Statement Issued by Catholic Theologians," *The New York Times*, 25 June 1984, p. A8.

CHAPTER II

THE SIGNIFICANCE OF JOHN COURTNEY MURRAY

Patrick Allitt

Since the Second Vatican Council, Catholic intellectuals, conservative and liberal alike, have acknowledged a large debt to John Courtney Murray, S.J., for his work on religious freedom and church-state relations. The essays in this collection are a case in point: tributes to Murray's fertile mind and conceptual brilliance appear every few pages. This essay shows *how* Murray argued, in the last "triumphalist" decade before the Council, and how he offered American Catholics a new avenue of self-understanding. It also demonstrates that Murray sometimes creatively misinterpreted the historical record to fortify his theological claims. In every way "jesuitical," Murray defeated his clerical antagonists on their own ground, through an imaginative re-reading of orthodox classics.[1]

Murray was born in 1904 and spent his adult life as a Jesuit priest, largely at the Jesuit seminary in Woodstock, Maryland. Highly regarded within the order for his intellectual powers and his scholastic virtuosity, he was made editor of the Jesuit journals *America* and *Theological Studies* in the mid 1940s. He became a controversial figure in the Church in the early 1950s for publishing a bold reinterpretation of Catholic political theology. The Vatican was dismayed by his argument that the American constitutional system was more congenial to Catholic tradition than any integralist alternative and that the Church should embrace religious pluralism. Rome censured him in the mid–1950s and restrained him from publishing a sequence of articles on the church-state question. The censure fell short of disgrace or suspension from his teaching duties, however, and Murray was rehabilitated soon after Pope John XXIII announced the policy of *aggiornamento*. In 1960, he published an influential series of essays on Catholicism and the American political tradition, *We Hold These Truths*. In 1963 he went to the second session of Vatican II as an advisor to New York's Cardinal Francis Spellman, and drafted the Conciliar document on religious liberty, *Dignitatis Humanae*. His vindication was a source of satisfaction to American delegates at the Council.[2]

Murray lived to enjoy this vindication only until 1967. Since then, he has been commended widely as a prophet of the postconciliar Church. Despite his intellectual daring, however, Murray maintained the demeanor of a pious and orthodox priest. His arguments on the nature of the State and the Church were based not upon new or "liberal" premises, he said, but upon a more thorough reading of Church tradition. His advocacy of theological novelties was couched in the language, and supported by the example of, venerable figures in Church history: Pope Gelasius I, St. Thomas Aquinas, St. Peter Damian. It was not from contemporary liberalism but from pre-Reformation sources that he claimed to have discovered an antiabsolutist political tradition in Catholicism.[3]

Murray's historical method placed him at odds with his contemporaries. He approached papal statements as elements of an evolving, ever-changing tradition, not as truths cast in bronze. He emphasized that the Church has lived in history, not above it, and that its pontiffs and scholars wrote and disputed in response to particular historical circumstances. Champions of papal absolutism appealed to declarations of Popes Pius IX and Leo XIII solely as proof texts (a method which a fellow reformer, Michael Novak, termed "non-historical orthodoxy"). Murray, by contrast, *situated* these texts in history, distinguishing within them the doctrine from the historical, contingent, and polemical aspects. The Church had never explicitly prohibited this method, but Catholic theologians had neglected a critical historical method for almost a hundred years following the First Vatican Council.

The practical consequences of Murray's technique were considerable. He resolved American Catholics' ambivalence about contact with their non-Catholic fellow citizens, and he enabled them to relinquish the old imperative of building a monolithic Catholic America.[4]

Until 1908, the Vatican had treated the United States as mission territory. In 1884 the American hierarchy at the Third Plenary Council of Baltimore decided to insulate itself against the prevailing Protestant culture by establishing a comprehensive Catholic educational system. Catholics throughout America pursued this immense and costly task for the next seventy years. At the end of the 1890s, "Americanizing" bishops suffered a papal rebuke for taking cautious ecumenical steps. Late nineteenth- and early twentieth-century popes warned repeatedly that "indifferentism" was a grave sin; as a result, Catholic education through the first half of the twentieth century was energetically anti-Protestant. Murray addressed an audience educated in Catholic institutions, many of whom viewed their Protestant compatriots through jaundiced eyes. His message, however, contradicted the inherited Catholic wisdom by speaking enthusiastically of American life. In his view, the American republic was agreeable to Catholics because its people, though Protestant, were guided by adherence to the natural law, a faith made explicit in Jefferson's Declaration of Independence. "Catholic participation in the American consensus," said Murray,

> has been full, free, unreserved and unembarrassed, because the contents of this consensus—the ethical and political principles drawn from the tradition of the natural law—approve themselves to the Catholic intelligence and the Catholic conscience. Where this kind of language is talked, the Catholic joins the conversation with complete ease. It is his language. . . . The ideas are expressed in a way native to his own universe of discourse. Even the accent, being American, suits his tongue.

Claims like this were more than a little surprising to Catholic readers of the 1950s. It was true that a large number of them prospered as never before in postwar America, but Murray was being disingenuous when he said they participated in the American consensus "unembarrassed" or that they joined political dialogue with "complete ease." He and his fellow reformers *wished* it were so, but the claim was premature—designed more as a goad to reform than as a report of actual conditions.[5]

Murray was alert to the persistence of American anti-Catholicism in the 1950s; one of his tasks was to show that Catholics were not latently disloyal to the republic. Well into the 1950s, Paul Blanshard and others attacked the Church as a foreign, authoritarian power, no less mendacious than communism itself. Murray wanted to silence the fears of anti-Catholics. He argued that adherence to both Catholicism and the American political system were compatible, not merely in practice, as Cardinal Spellman, Bishop Fulton Sheen, and other patriotic priests had long made evident, but also *in theory.* Throughout most of its history, he said, the Church had not claimed temporal authority. A Catholic's spiritual adherence to his faith did not vitiate his patriotic adherence to the nation. Murray went on to show that, according to early Catholic teaching, the state was a purely secular organization, concerned with the welfare of people on earth as it found them, saints and sinners alike, but not concerned with their spiritual destiny. This was a role, said Murray, which the American Constitutional system had facilitated, perhaps better than the polity of any other nation, making it entirely consonant with Catholic political theory. He went so far as to claim that the American system of limited government retained more vestiges of the medieval political ideal than any of the "Catholic" nations of Europe. The Catholic Church in Europe, said Murray, struggling first against the Reformation and then against the French Revolution, distorted its own political heritage and lost sight of its best exemplar.

> The Roman advisors of Leo XIII knew their Rousseau; they had probably never heard of the Federalist Papers. It is indeed a curious paradox that, at a time when the Roman Curia was intensely preoccupied with problems of political realizations and the philosophy behind them, they had apparently no interest in the most striking and successful political realization of modern times, despite the fact that the philosophy behind it was of linear descent from the central political tradition of the West, which the Church herself had helped fashion out of Greek, Roman and Germanic elements.

In other words, said Murray, the Vatican had forgotten its own teaching on the relationship of Church and state. He explained why. [6]

The political storms of the nineteenth century had produced a crisis of religious authority. The great popes of that era, under duress, confused general Catholic doctrines with momentary contingencies. When they condemned liberalism, said Murray, the popes had in mind the secularist liberalism of the Enlightenment, whose political manifestation was the Jacobins. The philosophical and political monism of the Enlightenment, subordinating all of society to the state and permitting the Church no more than a private role on political sufferance was, he agreed, indefensible: he opposed it as ardently as the Vatican did. But, he went on, there was another tradition of church-state separation which Catholics could embrace gladly, the separation spelled out in the First Amendment to the American Constitution. Murray showed that the First Amendment was a declaration of the state's inability to judge affairs of the spirit, a statement of the government's confinement to temporal affairs, and *not* an assertion of indifferentism. He quoted an exchange of letters between the Holy Office and Benjamin Franklin, written in the first days of the Constitutional republic, when the Church wanted to establish a bishopric in America. Franklin informed the Holy Office that the affair, being purely ecclesiastical, was beyond the competence of the American government, which was not empowered to make any objections. "The good nuncio must have been mightily surprised," says Murray about Rome's reception of these good tidings. "Not for centuries had the Holy See been free to erect a bishopric without the prior consent of government" and without negotiation of complex political obstacles.[7]

Murray argued that Catholic accord with the principles of the American Constitution had been obscured because of the long history of papal-monarchical collaboration in Europe. Originally, he said, Catholic political theory assumed the existence of two distinct human "societies," the Church and the State, each with its proper guardians. However, the pretensions of popes and princes in early modern Europe broke down this dualism and substituted a theory of two powers within the broad embrace of a single society; the Erastianism of the absolutist era obscured it almost completely. Recovery of the tradition obliged both Church and State to recognize that each had its peculiar sphere of operation, and that the two were united only to the degree that persons belong, by nature, to both. There are, said Murray, areas where the natural spirituality of man permits the Church to intrude into the temporal sphere (in facilitating of public worship, for example), but there is no area where the state can override its exclusively temporal character and intervene in affairs spiritual.

> The essential duty of government is not directly towards religion in society, even though religion be integral to the common good. It is directly a duty to the autonomous natively free society—in this case the Church—to which alone the religious salvation both of individuals and of society itself has been committed.

Such nations as Franco's Spain, in which the Church believed itself "fortified" by the state, actually violated the principle of the two societies by permitting undue state encroachments in the realm of the Church. America was more scrupulous! Murray's hispanophobia was unusual for a Catholic of the 1950s; he treated Spanish history as a protracted object lesson in how *not* to conduct Church-State relations. In one abnormally outspoken passage, he noted that the Spanish Inquisition, the most notorious effort at coercion of consciences in Catholic history, had left a legacy of anticlericalism in Spain and an international hatred of Spanish Catholicism that were not fully dissipated even four centuries later. Catholic intolerance in Spain gave rise to "that peculiarly militant form of unbelief which, on the evidence of history, tends to ensue upon government efforts to suppress unbelief. The price in the rest of the world has been a shadow, still unerased, upon the Catholic name." Here was the most vivid warning of what the Church should avoid in America.[8]

Murray's arguments on church-state relations hinged upon careful distinctions between "society," "state," and "government," distinctions he believed the Enlightenment tradition had neglected. He took pains to emphasize, first, that the "state" should be confined as narrowly as possible, subordinate to "society," and second, that "government" should be no more than one element of the state. Murray limned this hierarchy in contrast to the Enlightenment political monism which, he said, treated society as an emanation of the state. In the monistic system, human rights were granted by the state whereas, according to the natural law, human rights and the pre-existing society took ontological priority over the state. European "totalitarian democracy," said Murray, jeopardized the Church, which, by natural law, was not dependent on the state for its existence and welfare, but drew its legitimacy from God Himself.[9]

Murray's America, then, was a latently Catholic polity. He treated American politicians less as heirs of the Puritans than as participants in a Christian tradition dating far back before the Reformation. Murray was rhetorically deft and knew how to make his case by invocation of old American heroes. Roger Williams, for example, was no protoliberal in Murray's eyes but rather a perpetuator of the Old Catholic tradition of separation. As Murray told it, Williams feared that unification of Church and state in the Massachusetts Bay Colony impaired the dignity of the Church. It was not from reasons of indifferentism that Williams demanded separation, but for the *dignity* of his faith (albeit an erroneous one), a principle which Catholics could applaud in this old American hero. Murray juxtaposed Williams's views with recent allocutions of Pope Pius XII to show how closely the two accorded on this point.[10]

Scattered through Murray's articles of the 1950s are other unexpected juxtapositions of this sort. He described St. Thomas Aquinas as "the first Whig" and claimed that Thomas would have rejoiced in the American concept of "a free people under a limited government." He argued that "the American Bill of Rights is not a piece of eighteenth-century rationalist theory; it is far more the product of Christian history." Elsewhere, in a discussion of limited government, Murray threw in another of these patriotic *obiter dicta*, arguing that Andrew Jackson anticipated Leo XIII's social encyclical *Rerum Novarum* by six decades when he assumed a role for government in regulating the economy. Leo's principle, said Murray, had a Jacksonian resonance: "As much freedom as possible, as much government as necessary. . . . The phrase has a good American ring whatever one's judgment may be on the manner and success with which America has applied it." More than a little rhetorical legerdemain was needed to transform Jefferson, Madison, and Jackson into heroes manqué of the Catholic political tradition. Murray was equal to the task, and his dramatic historical "revisionism" had lasting consequences.[11]

Murray's use of history implicitly denigrated papal authority by relativizing papal statements; no longer could the word of a pope be incontrovertible. He provoked energetic opposition. Murray's principal opponents, John Ryan, Joseph Fenton (in America), and Cardinal Alfred Ottaviani (in Rome), examined papal documents for granitic truths and assembled statements from papal encyclicals and allocutions without regard to their historical sequence or the circumstances in which they had been published. They placed great emphasis on the statements of Pius IX (1846–1878) and Leo XIII (1878–1902). These two Popes had turned the Church decisively away from reconciliation with the political, economic, and intellectual trends of modernity and were the two most often quoted in defense of "non-historical orthodoxy." It was Leo who unequivocally condemned Catholic "Americanization" in the 1890s. In the encyclical letter *Longinque Oceani* (1895) Leo XIII declared: "It would be very erroneous to draw the conclusion that in America is to be sought the type of the most desirable status of the Church, or that it would be universally lawful or expedient for State and Church to be, as in America, dissevered and divorced. "

Murray seems to have recognized that if he were to succeed he must make his case where his adversaries felt strongest, by reinterpreting the words of Pius IX and Leo XIII, especially the latter. The composition of his path-breaking articles of the 1950s bears witness to this imperative. Often extraordinarily long, they led off with a declaration of the main point and then subjected papal statements to microscopic scrutiny in a quest for remarks suitable to Murray's needs. In the eyes of his rivals, papal statements possessed far greater authority than Murray's own words. Therefore, he had to tease out of papal declarations a meaning congruent with his own views; he must overcome his antagonists on their own ground by showing that their champion was actually on Murray's side all along.[12]

Leo XIII turned away from industrialization, democracy, and evolutionary thought. America led the world in all three. Undeterred, Murray argued that Leo, if properly reinterpreted, had enunciated principles which all Americans, Catholic and non-Catholic alike, could applaud. He spent several years levering open what chinks he could find in the old Pope's armor, doggedly isolating statements of *principle* and separating them from Leo's application of principles to events. He showed, for example, that Leo XIII, in his struggle against secularist French governments, erred on a point of historical truth when he traced the engrossing appetites of the state to the French Revolution. Absolutist kings long before the Revolution had aggrandized themselves by domesticating the French Church. The papal infallibility enjoyed by Leo XIII did not extend to questions of historical fact. As Murray said, the principles are timeless but their historical application is not. Without spelling it out, Murray left readers to wonder whether the principles, which were themselves based on the interpretation of historical experience, could really play so magisterial a role in his theology as they did in the work of nonhistorical interpreters.[13]

Murray was, however, too shrewd a politician to find fault with any pontiff, past or present. Moreover, he went to considerable pains to point out cases where Leo had acted in ways of which Americans of the 1950s would approve. For instance, he noted Leo's belief that governments should be able to adopt emergency police powers in their struggle against political "sects" which advocated "totalitarian democracy." Proletarian illiteracy in the late nineteenth century had left the masses defenseless against the polemical depredations of atheist and statist "sects." In this emergency, said Murray, Leo XIII had recognized that strong counter-measures were essential, and so he supported counter-revolutionary politicians. Murray claimed that these papally approved counter-measures suspended, but did not invalidate, Papal commitment to the idea that the legitimacy of government springs from the consent of the governed. In the same way, said Murray, Americans in the 1950s believed that combatting communism could justify suspending or overriding civil rights. He took it for granted, first, that communism represented a clear and present danger, and second, that a nation cannot make observance of due process a higher value than national self-preservation. To compare the political outlook of Leo XIII and Presidents Truman and Eisenhower, however, was to obscure far more than he clarified. This farfetched analogy was of little historical value, but it suited Murray's *theological* purposes admirably. Once again he was able to claim that the papacy and the United States had common interests, never more clearly than in the face of "Godless Communism."[14]

Murray's stern anticommunism placed him comfortably inside the American consensus of the 1950s; unanimity against communism was one of the leitmotifs of *We Hold These Truths*, and it is possible to read some sections of the book as examples of "the thinking man's McCarthyism." Murray's fear that the centrifugal forces of American culture were breaking down the American consensus broods over these pages. He argued in favor of religious freedom but premised it upon moral consensus within society. Like other advocates of the public philosophy, he feared that American social libertarianism and ethical "situationism" augured the development of an unstable moral pluralism. Murray thought of human rights as commensurate with duties, rather than as claims over against others. Likewise, he saw freedom as a function of man in society; freedom meant congruence with the order embedded in nature and did not mean the absence of external restraint. If the latter view, based on Enlightenment individualism, flourished, the fabric of the American consensus would tear—we would no longer "hold these truths."[15]

Murray, juxtaposing these definitions of freedom, rarely quoted his Enlightenment antagonists. Instead, he summarized their case with broad strokes, drawing the worst possible consequences out of Rousseau, for example, rather than following Rousseau's own lines of argument. It is as though Murray, in his determination to challenge one point of Catholic orthodoxy (the religious-liberty teaching of the preconciliar Church), leaned with extra weight upon another (Catholic hatred of the French Enlightenment). As a result, he exaggerated the cleavage between the American version of church-state separation and the French version, and the notions of freedom that accompanied each. American historians know that the Founding Fathers were far from immune to French philosophy, and that many of them adapted its insights in addressing their own political exigencies. By "freedom" they sometimes meant the absence of restraint rather than Murray's "positive" freedom. Murray belittled this influence in his attempt to convince Rome of the positive qualities of the "American idea." (Later, in articles written when the battle for religious freedom was won, he did acknowledge possible tensions between freedom and authority that he had not previously admitted.)[16]

Murray's work on the "two societies" laid unprecedented emphasis upon the purely secular character of the state. The natural consensus by which "we hold these truths" is a moral, not a religious, consensus. Similarly, religious liberty is a civil question, not a religious one. Nevertheless, Murray believed it was no paradox to say that the health of civil society depended upon the religious faith of its citizens; he believed that to be a Christian of any sort was superior to atheism or secularism. The people of a nation, he argued repeatedly, must "hold these truths," must hold in common a set of propositions about the character of human life and social forms. Jefferson's Declaration of Independence expressly set out from an acknowledgement of "held truths," which he and his American contemporaries took to be self-evident, so fully accepted in themselves as to need no debate: truths upon which the political project of American independence was premised. Murray believed that the nation could not survive if this political consensus foundered on the rock of irreconcilable metaphysical systems, of which communism was certainly one. From the experience of American history, Murray believed that the coexistence of Protestants, Catholics, and Jews had permitted a tolerable proximity of metaphysical systems and had facilitated the health and growth of the nation. His essay "E Pluribus Unum" ended with a dystopian vision of a future when philosophical novelties have led irreligious citizens away from the natural law:

> If that evil day should come, the results would introduce one more paradox into history. The Catholic community would still be speaking in the ethical and political idiom familiar to them as it was familiar to their fathers, both the Fathers of the Church and the Fathers of the American Republic. The guardianship of the original American consensus, based on the Western heritage, was elaborated long before America was.

Whether the "evil day" has arrived remains open to question, though there can be no doubt that the American religious landscape is transformed in ways Murray could not have anticipated thirty years ago.[17]

Ironically, elements of Murray's own Church now doubt the value of the public philosophy and natural law traditions. Much of the religious energy of Catholicism in the 1960s gloried in the "prophetic" mode of conduct and denigrated the "priestly," of which Murray was a supreme embodiment. Several contributors to a 1979 symposium on "Murray's Unfinished Agenda" argued, in the pages of his old journal *Theological Studies*, that his dogged rationalism was excessive and that Catholics should emphasize the Biblical resources of their tradition, something he almost never did. When the American Catholic bishops wrote their pastoral letter on nuclear weapons in the early 1980s, they considered both Biblical sources and the rationalistic just-war theory. Their use of just–war theory would have been cold comfort to Murray, however, since they concluded that the structure of deterrence was incongruent with the theory. Where Murray concentrated on the character of the communist foe and found in favor of the weapons, the bishops of the 1980s concentrated on the character of the weapons and found against them, whatever the character of the foe.[18]

Murray's lasting contributions to American Catholicism are his advocacy of religious freedom and his historically engaged theological method. The Vatican of the 1950s did not want to hear that it did not know its own history. Under Pius XII it valued the image of Catholicism as an outpost of eternity in a world of flux. Murray's historical method undermined this self-image and encouraged the Church to acknowledge that it too had changed over time, doctrinally, ecclesiologically, and politically. Vatican II was a symbolic acknowledgement of Murray's superiority. And yet, ironically, this historically minded theologian was a poor historian, tendentious and misleading. His objectives were theological; history was simply the medium through which, sometimes opportunisitically, he pursued them. His attempted transformation of Leo XIII into a proto-American was probably his most audacious coup, though it has to face the competition of his "Catholicization" of several prominent Americans. American Catholics can welcome the outcome of his labors for their renewed Church without taking him as a reliable guide to Catholic and American history.

NOTES

1. I wish to thank David Hollenbach, S.J., for introducing me to the work of John Courtney Murray, and Mary Segers, for many profitable discussions of Murray and his work. For references to Murray in this collection see below.

2. For biographical details, see Donald E. Pelotte, *John Courtney Murray: Theologian in Conflict* (New York: Paulist Press, 1975). Murray's principal articles, on which the following analysis is based, were as follows:

"Governmental Repression of Heresy," *Proceedings of the Catholic Theological Society of America*, III, 1948, pp. 26–98;

"The Problem of the Religion of the State," *American Ecclesiastical Review*, 124 (1951), pp. 327–352;

"Contemporary Orientations of Catholic Thought on Church and State in the Light of History," *Theological Studies* (hereafter *TS*), 10 (1949), pp. 177-234;

"The Church and Totalitarian Democracy," *TS* (1952), pp. 525–563;

"Leo XIII on Church and State: The General Structure of the Controversy," *TS* 14 (1953), pp. 1–30;

"Leo XIII: Separation of Church and State," *TS* 14 (1953), pp. 145–214;

"Leo XIII: Two Concepts of Government," *TS* 14 (1953), pp. 551–567;

"Leo XIII: Two Concepts of Government, II: Government and the Order of Culture," *TS*, 15 (1954), pp. 1–33. A fifth article in the Leo XIII series was already written and drawn up in galleys when the Vatican notified Murray's superiors that it should not be published.

J. C. Murray, *We Hold These Truths: Catholic Reflections on the American Proposition* (New York: Sheed and Ward, 1960).

On the American role at the Second Vatican Council, see Vincent Yzermans, *American Participation in the Second Vatican Council* (New York: Sheed and War, 1967).

3. On Gelasius I, see *We Hold These Truths*, p. 202; on Aquinas, ibid., p. 32, on Damian, "The Problem of the Religion of the State," p. 328, note 3.

4. Michael Novak, *The Open Church* (London: Darton, Longman and Todd, 1964).

5. On the historical background to these issues, see Jay P. Dolan, *The American Catholic Experience* (Garden City, New York: Doubleday, 1985). On Catholic education in the early twentieth century see William Halsey, *The Survival of American Innocence: American Catholics in an Age of Disillusionment* (Notre Dame, Indiana: Notre Dame University Press, 1980). On the "Americanism" controversy see Robert Cross, *The Emergence of Liberal Catholicism in America* (Cambridge, MA: Harvard University Press, 1958). Quotation: *We Hold These Truths*, p. 41.

6. On anti-Catholicism, see Paul Blanshard, *American Freedom and Catholic Power* (Boston: Beacon Press, 1949). On Catholic cultivation of American patriotism, see Edward Kantowicz, "Cardinal Mundelein of Chicago and the Shaping of Twentieth Century American Catholicism," *Journal of American History* Vol. 68, No. 1, June 1981, pp. 52–68; and John Cooney, *The American Pope: The Life and Times of Francis Cardinal Spellman* (New York: New York Times Books, 1984). Quotation: "The Church and Totalitarian Democracy," p. 554.

7. Murray against secularist liberalism: "In addition to being the embodiment of an absolutist political theory, the state became the active vehicle of a secularist ideology that assumed the character of a religious faith, a faith as exclusive, as universal in pretension, and as exigent of total devotion, as any religious faith." "The Church and Totalitarian Democracy," p. 527. On Franklin and the nuncio, *We Hold These Truths*, p. 71. Murray adds, "The American state does not presume to define the Church or in any way to supervise her exercise of authority in pursuit of her own distinct ends. The Church is entirely free to define herself and to exercise to the full her spiritual jurisdiction. It is legally recognized that there is an area which lies outside the competence of government." Ibid., p. 70.

8. On the ancient theory: J. C. Murray, "St. Robert Bellarmine on the Indirect Power," *TS*, 9 (1948), pp. 291–334. On the secular character of government and the Spanish example, "Leo XIII: Two Concepts of Government, II," p. 14.

9. On distinguishing state, society, and government, see "The Problem of the Religion of the State," pp. 330–331. On the ontological priority of society see "The Church and Totalitarian Democracy" and *We Hold These Truths*,

chapter 9, "Are there Two or One?" (pp. 197–217), which describes the traditional Catholic doctrine of the freedom of the Church. The doctrine had been thrown into jeopardy by modernism and its unified theory of freedom and rationality. Properly understood, it recognized the Church and the State as coeval "perfect societies." The freedom of the Church comprised its exercise of spiritual authority, the freedom of the Christian people to worship and learn, and the restraints against government which ensued from their observation (pp. 202–205). Murray emphasized that the consequences of Church alliance with government under absolutist monarchies were almost as baleful as those of state absorption of all other freedoms and sovereignties in the Revolution, and that American resistance to this absorption made it the genuine carrier of the ancient order.

10. *We Hold These Truths*, pp. 55–61.

11. On Aquinas, ibid., p. 32. On the Bill of Rights, ibid., p. 39. On Jackson, "Two Concepts of Government," pp. 556–557, 559.

12. Against Murray, see for example Joseph Fenton, "The Theology of Church and State" *Proceedings of the Catholic Theological Society of America*, II (1947), pp. 15–46; Alfred Cardinal Ottaviani, " 'Church and State': Some Present problems in the Light of the Teaching of Pope Pius XII," *American Ecclesiastical Review* (May 1953), pp. 321–334. Leo XIII quotation, cited in Jo Formicola, "American Catholic Political Theology," *Journal of Church and State*, Vol. 29, No. 3, Autumn, 1987, p. 460.

13. On Leo XIII's erring history: Murray stressed that encyclicals are not to be regarded as authoritative scholarship but as exhortations to the faithful. The encyclical *Immortale Dei* (1885), he said, is "a tract for the times, confined in its outlook, concerned with an historical situation," "The Church and Totalitarian Democracy," pp. 551–552. On principles separable from examples, see "Leo XIII on Church and State: The General Structure," p. 15.

14. "Leo XIII: Two Concepts of Government II," p. 31. For Murray on anticommunism, see *We Hold These Truths*, pp. 221–273.

15. On the jeopardized consensus, see *We Hold These Truths*, pp. 79-123. Murray's book bears comparison with Walter Lippmann, *Essays in the Public Philosophy* (Boston: Little Brown, 1955), an analogous lament for the dissolution of the shared American consensus. On the positive and social character of freedom, see "Leo XIII: Two Concepts of Government: II," pp. 4–5.

16. J. C. Murray, "Freedom, Authority, Community," *America*, December 3, 1966, pp.734–741; and "The Declaration of Religious Freedom: Its Deeper Significance," *America*, April 23, 1966, pp. 592–593.

17. On the superiority of errant Christianity: Murray stressed that Leo XIII had been more preoccupied with political sects than with Protestants and had intimated the need for the "separated brethren" and "all men of good will" (i.e., all Christians) to unite in the fight against secularism. "Leo XIII on Church and State, the general structure . . .," pp. 2–3. On the "held truths" of the Declaration of Independence, *We Hold These Truths*, intro. "The Civilization of the Pluralist Society." On the "evil day," ibid., pp. 42–43. Note the graceful blending here of the two sets of "fathers" for American Catholics.

18. Symposium: "Theology and Philosophy in Public: A Symposium on John Courtney Murray's Unfinished Agenda," *TS* 40 (1979), pp. 700–715. John Coleman, S.J., and Robert Lovin argue for a more Biblical approach: Bryan Hehir favors the preservation of Murray's "public philosophy" rhetoric. The bishops' letter: National Conference of Catholic Bishops, *The Challenge of Peace: God's Promise and Our Response* (Washington D.C.: USCC, 1983). For Murray on nuclear weapons, see *We Hold These Truths*, pp. 249–273.

CHAPTER III

THE BISHOPS' PASTORAL ON PEACE: THE MEDIEVAL JUST WAR IN THE MODERN WORLD

James Muldoon

The Challenge of Peace is one of the most important official statements on any matter of public policy in the history of the Catholic Church in America. Its publication marked a significant step in the creation of a critical Catholic stance on matters of public policy. The American Catholic hierarchy had traditionally supported a strong policy of anticommunism and a strong defense posture. With the pastoral on nuclear war, however, the bishops were taking a stand that varied in tone and in substance with positions taken by their predecessors since 1945.

The pastoral letter generated a great deal of discussion, especially within conservative Catholic circles. Conservative Catholics saw it as a rejection of traditional Catholic positions on war and peace.[1] It might have seemed possible for the bishops to argue that the contemporary international situation, resting as it does on the threat of nuclear holocaust, is radically different from anything in the past and so the traditional arguments about the just war would no longer apply. The bishops did not, however, take that approach, and indeed they could not have done so. The bishops are not after all free to speak prophetically as the Spirit moves them. They function within an intellectual tradition that has been evolving over two thousand years. Just as papal encyclicals invariably refer to previous statements on the topic under discussion in order to place the present statement within the context of Catholic thought, so too the bishops must place their statement on nuclear war within the context of Catholic thought on this issue. As a result, early on in the pastoral, the bishops noted: "The Catholic tradition on war and peace is a long and complex one, reaching from the Sermon on the Mount to the statements of Pope John Paul II. Its development cannot be sketched in a straight line and it seldom gives a simple answer to complex questions."[2]

A bit later on, the letter narrowed the issues further and indicated more specifically the intellectual sources of the tradition within which the bishops were operating. "The just war argument has taken several forms in the history of Catholic theology. . . . In the 20th century, papal teaching has used the logic of Augustine and Aquinas to articulate a right of self-defense for states in a decentralized international order and to state the criteria for exercising that right."[3]

The first statement, the one that emphasizes the antiquity of Catholic thought on war and peace, indicates broadly the development of this tradition over almost 2,000 years of continuous growth and development. The second statement, however, indicates some narrower limits on the chronological span of this tradition. A common teaching device illustrates this point. Imagine, if you will, a time-line 20 feet long, drawn along a blackboard in a large classroom. Each foot of the line represents one century. The line would begin at one end with the New Testament. At the four-foot mark stands St. Augustine, who died in 431. Between 12 feet and 13 feet stands Thomas Aquinas, who died in 1274. Finally, after making a leap of several feet [or centuries] we find, standing in a neat line at the 20-foot mark, the twentieth-century popes. This is not indicative of an organically evolving and coherent intellectual tradition. It suggests rather the search for applicable precedents in an ahistorical fashion. This is not to say that the bishops did this with malice or with intent to deceive. This approach to materials from the past is characteristic of several disciplines, most notably, theology and law. Decisions of the United States Supreme Court are often subjected to the same criticism. In each case, official statements must be framed in such a way as to demonstrate the place of the statement, whether it be a pastoral letter or a court decision, within an historical tradition. Bishops can no more issue pastoral statements that explicitly reject the teaching tradition of the Church than the justices of the Supreme can reject the doctrine of *stare decisis*.

If we turn to the actual historical development of Catholic teaching on war and peace, we find a tradition that is substantially less than 2,000 years old. This thought is very much the product of developments that began around the year 1000 with the Peace of God and Truce of God movements in France. It reached its fullest development during the thirteenth century in the work of theologians, philosophers, and canon lawyers. Even the place of St. Augustine in the just-war tradition was very much the result of the excerpts from his writings that Gratian incorporated into his *Decretum* during the mid-twelfth century. In fact, the development of a Catholic tradition on war and peace is the product of about three hundred years of medieval experience, not two thousand years of ancient, medieval, and modern experience.

When modern popes began to indicate an interest in serious, positive responses to the problems that the modern world faced, they turned to the intellectual tradition of the Middle Ages for guidance, because they had nowhere else to turn in the Catholic tradition. From the Avignon popes of the fourteenth century to the papal prisoners of the Vatican in the early twentieth century, the papacy found itself at odds with the world for almost six centuries, first having to deal with enemies from within and then those from without. As recently as 1864, Pius IX summed up several hundred years of papal opposition to the modern world in the *Syllabus of Errors*. When Leo XIII sought to initiate a more positive dialogue with the modern world, he had to reach all the way back to Thomas Aquinas in order to provide an intellectual basis for this dialogue. Fifteen years after the publication of the *Syllabus* came Leo XIII's *Aeterni Patris,* which asserted the central role of Thomistic thought in Catholic teaching, Thus, when Leo XIII turned to dealing with the social, economic, and political problems of the modern world, as he did, for example, in *Rerum Novarum* (1891), he did so on an essentially medieval foundation. Placing discussion of modern problems on a purely medieval base is, however, rather like taking an ancient giant redwood tree, cutting it off about ten feet above the ground, then cutting off the last ten feet of the fallen trunk, grafting it back onto the stump, and then announcing that there is an ancient redwood tree that is only about twenty feet tall. In effect, papal social and political thought has developed as if the modern world had never come into existence. Perhaps it is fairer to say that papal thought has come into existence in opposition to the modern world and often demands a return to a romanticized medieval social order.

The bishops' letter on war and peace reflects some awareness of the difficulty of approaching the issue of modern war in medieval terms. As the bishops say at the very beginning of the letter: "Nuclear weaponry has drastically changed the nature of warfare, and the arms race poses a threat to human life and human civilization which is without precedent."[4]

If nuclear weapons have in fact so changed warfare, then it would seem that restrictions on the use of weapons developed in an age of swords, lances, and longbows would not be of much help in dealing with modern technological tools of war. Grafting the modern situation onto the medieval stump is necessary, however, because of the obligation of the official teachers of Catholic doctrine to remain within the medieval tradition that is equated with the entire history of Catholic intellectual development. If, however, the bishops examine the development of thought on war, peace, and international relations by Catholic writers who worked after Aquinas, they might find a more effective way to express their views on these issues. Furthermore, they might be able to express their views in an idiom that is closer to the modern way of discussing these issues than is the medieval tradition.

The key to approaching the issue of war and peace from a new perspective is to recognize that the bishops are not quite accurate when they describe the current world situation as being "without precedent." The discovery of the New World had an impact on mankind that was not simply a threat of something dire that might happen in the future. Dire things did happen on a large scale. William H. McNeill has argued that by "1568, less than fifty years from the time Cortez inaugurated epidemiological as well as other exchanges between Amerindian and European populations, the population of central Mexico had shrunk to about three million, i.e., to about one tenth of what had been there when Cortez landed."[5]

The epidemiological effects of the discovery and conquest of the New World were only part of the story. The effects of these discoveries on the economic and agricultural structures of the entire world were equally great. The effect on the world political structure was even greater. Furthermore, the capacity of mankind to rebound from traumatic events is much greater in the modern world than in the past. Not even the massive, non-nuclear bloodletting in the twentieth century has hindered the rapid growth of the world's population. The dropping of two atomic bombs on Japan in 1945 not only killed fewer people than did the conquest of Mexico by a handful of Spaniards, the long-term effects of those bombs on the growth of the Japanese population has been negligible. According to McNeill, the population of sixteenth-century

Mexico continued to decline until it reached "a low point of about 1.6 million by 1620. Recovery did not definitely set in for another thirty years or so and remained very slow until the eighteenth century."[6]

Obviously there are significant differences between the current situation and that of the sixteenth century, but the sixteenth century is not only closer to us chronologically than the thirteenth century, its problems are more akin to ours.

The Spanish experience in the sixteenth century should interest the twentieth-century American bishops in their search for an intellectual basis consistent with traditional Catholic thought on which to construct a critique of public policy in the twentieth century. Spanish philosophers, theologians, and lawyers attempted to deal with the fundamental issues that the discovery of the New World raised. The Dominican Francisco de Victoria (d. 1546) and the Jesuit Francisco Suarez (d. 1617), along with their numerous students, struggled to comprehend the conquest of the Americas within the theory of the just war and also in terms of the Church's responsibility to preach Christ's message to all men. The just-war theory was difficult to apply in these circumstances, because it assumed defensive war as the norm of the just war. The inhabitants of the New World were not, however, a military threat to the Spanish. They were not about to invade Europe and attack Christians. Furthermore, they did not occupy lands that had once been Christian, a situation that could traditionally authorize a just war of recuperation.

Victoria's solution to the problem of applying the theory of the just war to the Americas was to deny to European Christians any general right to conquer the Americas. The fact that the inhabitants were idolators or that they committed acts that were against the natural law did not justify conquest. Reaching back to the thirteenth century, Victoria stressed Pope Innocent IV's arguments about the natural right of all men to govern themselves according to their own lights.[7] He rejected all religiously based arguments that could justify the conquest. Instead, Victoria emphasized an essentially secular reason for sending Spanish troops into the Americas, an action that might lead to a permanent conquest. According to the Spanish Dominican, there exists "natural society and fellowship" among all mankind.[8] The result, according to Victoria, was that the "Spanish have a right to travel into the lands in question [the Americas] and to sojourn there, provided they do no harm to the natives, and the natives may not prevent them" from so traveling. This right of free and peaceful travel throughout the world belongs to all men. In effect, Victoria was postulating the existence of a sort of international society, a universal fellowship of all mankind. He derived his from the "law of nations [ius gentium], which is either natural law or is derived from natural law."

After presenting the general premises of the argument, Victoria went on to give concrete examples of the kinds of travel he meant. The first example, interesting enough, concerned merchants, not missionaries.

> The Spaniards may lawfully carry on trade among the native Indians, so long as they do no harm to their country, as, for instance, by importing thither wares which the natives lack and by exporting thence either gold or silver or other wares of which the natives have abundance. Neither may the native princes hinder their subjects from carrying on trade with the Spanish; nor on the other hand, may the princes of Spain prevent commerce with the natives.[9]

Should the Indians seek to prevent the Spanish from enjoying their rights to free and unimpeded travel and trade, the "Spaniards ought in the first place to use reason and persuasion" in order to convince the natives of their peaceful intentions. If peaceful argument does not work and if Spanish travelers and merchants are attacked by the natives, they "can defend themselves and do all that consists with their own safety, it being lawful to repel force by force." If a show of defensive force is not sufficient to ward off attacks, then the Spanish "may build fortresses and defensive works, and, if they have sustained a wrong, they may follow it up with war on the authorization of their sovereign and may avail themselves of the other rights of war."[10] Victoria did not encourage recourse to war. War is to be begun only after every possible step has been taken to avoid it.

Only after discussing the right to travel and to trade freely throughout the world did Victoria move to discussing the rights of Christian missionaries. Christians have an obligation to preach the Gospel to all men because Christ specifically enjoined them to do so. Furthermore, "if the Spaniards have a right to travel and trade among the Indians, they can teach the truth to those willing to hear them, especially as regards matters pertaining to salvation and happiness, much more than as regards matters pertaining to any human subject of instruction."[11] If the Indians or their rulers attempt to prevent the preaching of the Gospel in the Americas, the Spanish should first, as in the case of the merchants, seek to convince the people of their peaceful intentions. If reason fails to convince the people to admit the missionaries, the Spanish may legitimately wage war against them "until they succeed in obtaining facilities and safety for preaching the Gospel."[12]

Victoria went on further to discuss other possible justifications for the Spanish conquest of the Americas, but they are not relevant here. The significant point is that he tried to develop a basis for peaceful relations between Spanish Catholics and the pagan inhabitants of the Americas on essentially secular or natural law grounds, that is, on the right to travel freely throughout the world. A generation later, Francisco Suarez sought to develop the theory of natural law and the law of nations even more fully to provide a basis for an international order. In addition, the students that Victoria and Suarez trained wrote numerous treatises on the just war and related matters, providing an extensive theoretical basis for the situation that the discovery of the New World provided. Finally, as the work of Lewis Hanke demonstrated long ago, the Spanish imperial government, especially during the reign of Charles V in the first half of the sixteenth century, was very interested in the moral problems that the discoveries posed.[13]

By the early seventeenth century, however, even as Suarez was still teaching and writing, the intellectual lead in dealing with the problems of international relations and the new political and economic order that was emerging was passing from Catholic writers to Protestant writers such as Hugo Grotius (1583–1645). Grotius's great work, *The Law of War and Peace*, could not have been written without the earlier work of men like Victoria and Suarez. Grotius admitted his debt to the Spanish tradition while pointing out what he saw as the fundamental weakness of this school's approach to the question of international law and relations.

> I have seen also special books on the law of war, some by theologians, such as Franciscus de Victoria, Henry of Gorkum, William Matthaei; others by doctors of law... All of these, however, have said nothing upon a most fertile subject; some of them have done their work without system, and in such a way as to intermingle and utterly confuse what belongs to the law of nature, to divine law, to the law of nations, to civil law, and to the body of law which is found in the canons.[14]

As Professor James T. Johnson has pointed out in his study of the just war tradition, "the commitment of Victoria remains strongest to the Middle Ages, and that of Grotius is directed forward in time."[15] The work of the Spanish thinkers was capable of being expanded and developed in the process of developing a theory of international law and relations, including the issues of war and peace, if anyone was interested in doing so. Because Catholic thinkers stopped engaging in such work by the seventeenth century, however, non-Catholic scholars provided all the subsequent work on these issues. The failure of Catholic thinkers, at least of official Catholic thinkers and teachers, to engage the later developments of the modern world meant that a Catholic intellectual response to that emerging world was simply lacking, except for the sort of response that Pius IX expressed in the *Syllabus of Errors*. Thus, when the American Catholic bishops came to the study of the problem of nuclear war, they came equipped with intellectually primitive tools. They sought to examine a complex twentieth-century problem in a thirteenth-century context and then attempt to propose a solution to that problem as if modern, pluralistic societies did not exist.

Having condemned the bishops for failing to deal with the world as it exists in the late twentieth century, I am obliged to suggest what I think they ought to do. As one might expect, my suggestion is that before issuing any more pronouncements on contemporary problems, the bishops give serious consideration to the intellectual and historical basis upon which they wish to construct their critique of contemporary society. As the work of Victoria, Suarez, and their contemporaries makes clear, there were orthodox Catholic thinkers who have provided some of the basis for a reasoned Catholic approach to the problems of the modern world. A critic might say at this point that there is nothing wrong with employing thirteenth-century standards for judging twentieth-century society, because truth is truth regardless of time and place. That is so, of course, and neither Victoria nor Suarez would disagree. It is also true, however, that social and political thought is not simply a matter of metaphysical truth. It involves the application of general principles to concrete, historical situations. The modern world contains a number of situations not envisioned by Thomas Aquinas. For example, Aquinas gave no serious consideration to the problem of applying the moral principles of the just war in a society where sovereignty rests in the hands of a population that votes for its leaders on a regular basis. In his world, the achievement of moral goals in the political order was very much the task of the prince, guided by his nobles and clerics. Such a ruler did not have to take into account the views of a large and diverse population. In the modern world, the making of public policy is a much more complex process than it was in the thirteenth century.

Furthermore, the pluralistic nature of modern society is something that no ancient or medieval philosopher ever considered. Not only does the contemporary American public official have to consider what the people want, he must consider what the various peoples or political communities that comprise his constituency want. Near the end of their pastoral letter, the bishops allude to the pluralistic nature of American society and how they intend to deal with it. They declare that:

> we look forward in a special way to cooperating with all other Christians with whom we share common traditions. We also treasure cooperative efforts with Jewish and Islamic communities, which possess a long and abiding concern for peace as a religious and human value. Finally, we reaffirm our desire to participate in a common effort with all men and women of good will who seek to reverse the arms race and secure the peace of the world.[16]

This is a fine-sounding platitude. In modern American society, however, applying this principle would mean the creation of a political coalition designed to unite people who agree with the bishops on the nuclear threat and who agree to work with them to end that threat. The implication here is that it will be easy for those who agree on the nuclear issue to join forces in order to affect public policy. A few pages earlier, however, the pastoral contained a statement that would virtually negate the possibility of creating the broad coalition the bishops wish to create: "Abortion in particular blunts a sense of the sacredness of human life. In a society where the innocent unborn are killed wantonly, how can we expect people to feel righteous revulsion at the act or threat of killing non-combatants in war?"[17]

It is one of the better known ironies of the contemporary political scene that many of those who support the bishops' position on nuclear war also support legalized abortion, while many of those who oppose abortion are in favor of nuclear arms and so oppose the bishops on that issue. What the pastoral fails to appreciate is that a pluralistic society is not simply one in which people attend different churches but believe the same fundamental truths. A pluralistic society is one in which people of quite different moral beliefs live together in harmony. The common good of the society as a whole is not, therefore, the common good as defined by the moral principles of any one group. In a pluralistic society, the common good, as expressed in public policy, is the product of negotiation and compromise. If the bishops wish the support of the groups they named in their pastoral in order to achieve the goal they propose in nuclear matters, will they be willing to surrender their opposition to legalized abortion as the price they must pay? I do not mean to trivialize the seriousness of this dilemma. If anything, the bishops have trivialized it by making the common American assumption that men of good will can always get along. This is not so. In a pluralistic society, men of good will can differ fundamentally because they proceed from different, incompatible premises. Even though groups can agree to join forces on a particular issue because they agree on the end involved, this does not mean that they will agree on all issues. One solution to this problem is, of course, to deny good will to one's opponents. It is characteristic of American politics to define one's opponents' position as being immoral and so avoid having to deal with them on a rational basis. While this may lead to a warm and cosy sense of righteousness in those who act this way, it does not do much for the formation of public policy.

In conclusion, then, it seems to me that the American Catholic bishops do not really rest their pastoral on nuclear war on two thousand years of Catholic social and political thought but rather, on about three hundred years of Catholic thought. As a result, they leave contemporary American Catholics in a terrible dilemma. What is the responsible Catholic citizen of a pluralistic society to do when faced with a public policy that his pastors define as evil? Is he to oppose it, even to the extent of overturning the government, or is he to turn his back on public life? What is that citizen to do when his bishops hold positions that are in conflict in the practical order? This, I would suggest, is not some scholastic *reductio ad absurdam*, it is a dilemma that millions of American Catholic voters increasingly will face in congressional, senatorial and presidential elections during the final decade of the twentieth century. What is the voter to do when entering the polling booth to choose between a candidate who opposes abortion and supports the use of nuclear weapons and a candidate who has taken the opposite position on each of these issues? This is the real and immediate test of the bishops' role as moral teachers.

The writings of Thomas Aquinas will be of little help to the perplexed voter in forthcoming elections on many issues that are central to twentieth-century public life. His writings will not provide much guidance for the bishops either. Aquinas did not begin to consider the nature of pluralistic societies and the moral dilemmas they present. There was no reason for him to do so because such a society would have been very alien to his world. Victoria, Suarez and their contemporaries, however, provide at least a beginning in the process of fitting a pluralistic world into the Catholic political tradition. Whereas Aquinas operated within a society with a single official moral order, a society that for the most part saw itself at war with a competing moral order—the Islamic world—the sixteenth-century Spaniards in contrast, were beginning to appreciate the existence of a pluralistic international order. Neither Victoria nor Suarez argued for the destruction of non-Christian societies and the creation of a universal Christian order by force. They asserted the natural right of other peoples to govern themselves, even when engaged in behavior that violated natural law. They began to grapple with the problems of a morally pluralistic international society and so began to deal with one of the fundamental moral problems of modern society.

Just as the sixteenth-century Spanish theologians had to learn how to apply the moral principles created within a morally unified medieval European intellectual world to a morally pluralistic world beyond Europe, so the American Catholic bishops now have to learn how to apply those principles within a morally pluralistic nation-state. Just as Victoria and Suarez had to come to terms with societies that were based on different moral principles than those on which European society was based in order to create a peaceful international order, so too the American bishops must now take into account the fact that American society is morally pluralistic and that the achievement of some of the moral goals that the bishops desire may entail acceptance of goals desired by other groups but which the bishops find immoral. In short, if the bishops want political support for the abolition of nuclear weapons, then they may have to accept abortion as the price. At the very least, if the bishops wish to influence public policy, they will have to come to terms with the pluralistic nature of American society and make their choices accordingly.

NOTES

An earlier version of this paper was presented at the annual meeting of the American Catholic Historical Association, Washington, D.C., December 27–30, 1987.

1. Conservative responses to the pastoral include: Michael Novak, "Moral Clarity in the Nuclear Age," *National Review*, April 1, 1983, pp. 354–392; and "The Bishops Speak Out," ibid., June 10, 1983, pp. 674–681; George

Weigel, *Tranquillitas Ordinis: The Present Failure and Future Promise of American Catholic Thought on War and Peace* (New York: Oxford University Press, 1987). See also: William A. Au, *The Cross, the Flag, and the Bomb: American Catholics Debate War and Peace* (Westport, Conn.: Greenwood Press, 1985); and *Peace in a Nuclear Age: The Bishops' Pastoral Letter in Perspective*, ed. Charles J. Reid, Jr. (Washington, D.C.: Catholic University Press, 1986).

2. *The Challenge of Peace: God's Promise and Our Response*, Pastoral Statement of the U.S. Conference of Catholic Bishops (Boston: St. Paul Editions, 1983), p. 10.

3. Ibid., p. 28.

4. Ibid., p. 3.

5. William H. McNeill, *Plagues and People* (Garden City: Doubleday, 1976), p. 204.

6. Ibid.

7. For Innocent IV's views and the development of the medieval theory of the rights of infidels, see James Muldoon, *Popes, Lawyers, and Infidels* (Philadelphia: University of Pennsylvania Press, 1979), pp. 5-15.

8. Franciscus de Victoria, *De Indis et de Ivre Belli Relectiones*, ed. Ernest Nys, The Classics of International Law , reprint ed. (New York: Oceana Publications, 1964), p. 151.

9. Ibid., p. 152.

10. Ibid., p. 154.

11. Ibid., p. 156.

12. Ibid., p. 157.

13. Lewis Hanke, *The Spanish struggle for Justice in the Conquest of America*, reprint ed. (Boston: Little, Brown, 1965).

14. Hugo Grotius, *The Law of War and Peace*, trans. Francis W. Kelsey, The Classics of International Law, reprint ed.(Indianapolis: Bobbs-Merrill, n.d.), 22.

15. James T. Johnson, *Ideology, Reason and the Limitation of War* (Princeton: Princeton University Press, 1975), p. 210.

16. *The Challenge of Peace*, p. 79.

17. Ibid., p. 71.

CHAPTER IV

THE SEARCH FOR A NEW PUBLIC VOICE IN AMERICAN CATHOLICISM: REASON AND REVELATION IN THE PASTORAL LETTER ON THE ECONOMY

R. Bruce Douglass

The reader will be forgiven for wondering whether there is anything to be gained from yet another analysis of the American Catholic bishops' pastoral letter on the economy.[1] Presented with much fanfare initially in 1984 and subsequently the subject of extended discussion in a very public process of revision that extended well into the fall of 1986, the letter has elicited commentary in countless articles and even several books, and one might think that by now, all that was worth saying about the subject had already been said. To some extent, I think this is undeniable. Especially with respect to the merits of the substantive claims made in the letter about the character of the American economy, it is difficult to imagine what else profitably remains to be considered. In the church itself, of course, there will surely be ongoing follow-up, and there may well be complementary initiatives undertaken by the bishops in the years ahead. But critical commentary is something else, and in the absence of such new initiatives, it is reasonable to expect even the readers of a volume of this sort to turn their attention elsewhere.

Considerations of method, however, are a somewhat different matter. Despite the fact that the letter represents a major—and in some respects dramatic—departure from the form of past Catholic social teaching on more than one count, it has received only minimal attention in this regard. The innovation has been noted in passing, to be sure, by numerous observers. But rarely has there been anything like a sustained effort to explore its meaning and significance. In particular, there has been hardly any attempt to make sense of *why* the authors chose to cast their argument in the form that they did. Nor has there been much discussion at all of the wisdom of casting the Church's message in such terms. Aside from the occasional blanket affirmation or condemnation, there has been scarcely an informed word spoken about the subject.

This is a silence which, I think, deserves to be broken. Especially now that the dust has settled in the controversy over other issues raised by the letter, it is appropriate to focus attention on such methodological considerations. For whatever the fate of the particular argument about economics in the letter turns out to be, the challenge of relating the Church's teaching to the affairs of the wider society will endure, presumably, and it can be expected, if anything, to become increasingly important in the years ahead. In a time, moreover, when the Church is clearly positioning itself to become a more influential force in American life than it has been before, this is obviously of more than just passing interest. How it is met is almost certain to be an important factor in determining the effectiveness with which the American Church responds to the opportunity that is now opening up to it in this country, and it can be expected to have an effect on the larger relationship between religion and politics in American society as well.

Analysis of what the letter represents in this respect is particularly in order, furthermore, because there is more than one reason to think that the innovations in question are not in the least accidental. There is evidence to suggest that they reflect not only recent trends in the intellectual life of the American church but also, more specifically, a considered judgment about how to communicate the message the hierarchy is seeking to articulate as it goes about trying to establish itself as a force in American public life. Those responsible for the drafting ended up structuring the theoretical part of their argument in particular as they did at least in part because of a conviction that a new voice was needed if they were effectively to make themselves heard.

Such, at least, is what I propose to argue. And if what I have to say in this regard is at all persuasive, the obvious question to which it leads is, what merit is there in the strategic judgment involved? Is the calculus it entails sound? What implications does it have for the character of the message that is conveyed? And can it be expected to produce anything like the desired effect? This, too, I shall also explore in the latter part of my remarks, arguing for somewhat skeptical conclusions while at the same time acknowledging in principle the point of what I think lies behind the innovations in question. There is definite merit, I think, in the desire to give indigenous expression to the church's teaching which is reflected in the letter. Especially at this particular time in history does it make sense for the American hierarchy to be undertaking such a project. But the particular manner in which it is pursued in this most recent pastoral is not, I think, to be judged a success. For more than one reason it needs to be considered more a suggestive probe than an example to be followed.

I.

In principle, of course, there is nothing in the least novel about what this particular letter represents. Nothing could be more in keeping, in fact, with the Church's historic understanding of its role in society than such an attempt to influence the underlying assumptions on which the economic life of the nation is conducted. There is, to be sure, a certain element of novelty in the *American* bishops casting themselves in the role that the letter suggests. But once the Protestant hegemony in American public life was broken (as now clearly is taking place), it was almost inevitable that the Church would step forward to assert itself in this way, and it is altogether in keeping with the size, resources, and dynamism that now characterize the American Catholic church that this should happen.

What *is* novel, however, is the ground on which the letter attempts to pursue this project. For, in marked contrast to its own prior history, the American Catholic hierarchy has chosen in this letter at least to adopt a mode of expressing itself which is not at all that of the by-now-familiar tradition of the social encyclicals. The break is by no means complete, of course. Appropriate references to such concepts as the common good and subsidiarity are scattered through the text , and it may well be, as this author has sought to argue elsewhere, that much of the content of the Church's traditional teaching is retained in one way or another in the substance of what the letter proposes.[2] But the fact remains that both the idiom in which the authors have chosen to cast their argument and the structure of what they have to say are very different from what informed students of Catholic teaching on these matters are accustomed to encountering, and the difference does not appear to be merely cosmetic.

In saying this, I have in mind two principal considerations. The most obvious is the role that theology and the Bible play in the letter. This above all has to stand out in any reading of this document that is at all informed by a sense of the prior history of Catholic teaching. For in the past, theological assertions simply did not figure significantly in the claims that were made or the arguments advanced on their behalf. Nor did the Bible. For quite specific reasons Catholic thought in this area tended, in fact, as a matter of principle to be characterized by an avoidance of theological discourse. There were, of course, references made where appropriate to the underlying religious rationale for the Church's teaching, and there was never any doubt left about its ultimate importance in the minds of the authors. But at the same time they were not central to the argument.

The whole point, indeed, was to speak in terms that did not require any sort of reliance on religious belief (or practice). Catholics themselves were expected, of course, to read and appropriate what was said through the eyes of faith, and respond accordingly. But the Church's *social* teaching, as a body of thought intended to apply to matters of general, public concern, was to be cast in a form that would be accessible just as much to those outside of the community of faith as to those within. As a form of public discourse, addressed to all people of good will, irrespective of their particular religious loyalties, it was intended to rest solely on premises that could be derived from reason alone, and none of the particularity of the specifically religious part of Catholicism was to enter into the argument. Scripture especially was not to play a role, but more broadly, even the larger theological teaching that the Church embraced as well.

Nothing could be farther, however, from the style of reasoning adopted by the authors of the pastoral letter on the economy. For not only do they base much of what they have to say on explicitly Christian theological premises, but they go out of their way to emphasize the importance of this part of their argument. From beginning to end it is stressed, and it figures so prominently in the way the argument unfolds that it has to be considered central to it. It is, moreover, not just this invocation of theological themes that is noteworthy; it is also the particular kind of theology on which the authors rely. There is scarcely a hint, in fact, of the kind of elaborate philosophical reflection that has come to be the hallmark of Catholic theology, and in its place is substituted an exposition that is almost entirely exegetical. It is in no sense abstract theological argument to which appeal is made, but rather the Biblical story itself, with very little effort at mediation.

This emphasis on Scripture does not extend, admittedly, to making it the sole source of the argument. For all of the attention they devote to the Bible, the authors of the letter are still sufficiently attuned to the complementarity of reason and revelation to want to avoid exclusive reliance on revelation. Biblical themes may constitute the foundation of the point of view that they seek to propound, but for both practical and substantive reasons they clearly see the need to speak in another voice as well. This is the case especially in dealing with distributive justice, which of course is at the core of what they have to say, and the more one explores the logic of this part their argument, the more obvious it becomes how important this other line of reasoning is to the cogency of their case as well.

The thing that is noteworthy about this other source, in turn, is what it is—and is not. For once again novelty prevails. There is scarcely a hint of the old natural law mode of reasoning, and in its place is substituted a heavy emphasis on rights. The character of the rights in question is such, moreover, that it soon becomes evident that another way of thinking is being introduced that in its own way is, in this country at least, every bit as familiar. The rights in question are in principle equal; public institutions are construed primarily as means to secure their fulfillment; and justice is said to be done when there is in fact equal protection. It is, predictably, life and liberty which in the first instance are meant to be served, but ultimately what is sought is something much more expansive that is characterized as self-realization.

All of this is developed, of course, in a way that is highly revisionist. It is hardly the sort of "rugged" individualism that has come to be associated with the purer forms of "life, liberty and the pursuit of happiness" with which we are familiar. As a matter of fact, there is nothing in the least "rugged" about it whatsoever. There is plenty of talk about community and social responsibility, so that the anti-social tendency in liberalism is largely muted, and the thrust of the argument is clearly directed against sanctioning any sort of self-absorption. But the fact remains that the philosophical part of the letter is based on a set of essentially liberal premises, and the logic of liberalism clearly has more than a small role to play in defining the vision of social and economic order that is being advanced.

II.

None of this can be altogether surprising to anyone who is at all familiar with recent developments in American Catholicism. Change has been so much a part of the life of the Church in this country of late that one would be surprised, in fact, if the letter did *not* entail some departure from the pattern of past Catholic teaching. But at the same time the actual form which the innovation does in fact take is not at all to be taken for granted, and the more one reflects on the issues it raises, the more in need of explanation it becomes. Especially is this so, I might add, if attention is focused on the role the letter is intended to play as part of the Catholic hierarchy's recent attempt to establish its place in American public life. The elaborate process of deliberation that went into the letter means, presumably, that its design is anything but accidental, and the obvious question, in turn, is why, in view of this purpose, the authors chose to cast the argument in the way that they did.

There can be no simple answer to such a question, I am sure, that does justice to all of the relevant considerations. Too many different forces are at work in any large, complex process of this sort for it to be reduced to any single factor. It is only a slight exaggeration to say that the whole recent history of the Church comes into play whenever its leaders dedicate themselves to a project of this sort. But at the same time some factors are almost always more influential than others, and in this case I think it makes sense to focus attention on certain factors that have figured prominently in the thinking of those most directly responsible for the actual drafting.

Of these none is more important, I think, than a concern that is appropriately linked to the legacy of John Courtney Murray.[3] That legacy extends, of course, in a number of different directions, and I certainly do not mean to invoke all of it. The pastoral letter on the economy is hardly a "Murrayesque" document in every sense, and in some respects it is in fact so much out of keeping with the spirit of his work as to be considered alien to his intent. But in at least one critical respect it is so much informed by the precedent he set as to be virtually an extension of his work. Particularly with respect to the attitude it represents toward American institutions and, more broadly, the American way of life, the letter follows squarely in the path he pioneered, and it is probably inexplicable without reference to the successful initiative he took in this regard.

For it was Murray who, more effectively than any other single figure, challenged the notion that things American were alien to the life and teaching of the Catholic church. Indeed, he went further, suggesting not just that it was appropriate for American Catholics to affirm the American "proposition" (and much of the rest of what went with it) on their own, but even (by implication) that the wider church had something to learn from the American experiment. Moreover, not just with respect to the sensitive issue of church and state, but more broadly, with the larger issues of social and political order as well, he deftly made the case that, despite its appearance of heterodox origins, the way of life that had developed on these shores was worthy to the point of being exemplary. It was badly understood, he suggested, if it was viewed as the fruit of ideas that were alien to the principles on which the Church based its teaching, and while there were obviously elements in the American experience that were inimical to Catholicism, there was nothing about it alien in principle to Catholic values and aspirations whatsoever. Indeed, the impression he sought to convey was that, for all of its warts, the experiment that had taken place in this country deserved even to be counted as providential.

Murray was thus a pioneer of a style of reflection that has subsequently come to be very popular among Catholic intellectuals. For, ever since Vatican II, the quest for the indigenization of the Church's teaching has flourished, often with dramatic results. Much of the impetus for liberation theology, for example, has come from the new warrant to relate the Gospel specifically to the circumstances in which particular parts of the Church find themselves. To be sure, nothing quite so dramatic has appeared on this continent. To date, at least, there is no specifically American theology that presents itself as such to the wider world. But there is, clearly, a distinctive American way of viewing the world and in particular of construing problems of social and political order, and the pastoral letter on the economy is the most important piece of evidence to date of how deeply that mentality is coming to affect the Church's life and teaching in this country.

For virtually the whole design of the letter is to be attributed—I think it is manifest—to a deliberate attempt to speak in terms that are appropriate to the specific context presented by this society. From the invocation of Biblical motifs to the appeal to rights, it is one extended effort to appropriate the characteristic themes of the religious and political culture of this country for the purpose of situating the Church's teaching squarely within the mainstream of American life. Much like Murray, the authors of the letter seek to employ ideas and symbols that are already well known and respected among the American people (including Catholics) to draw them in the direction of behavior that is consonant with the Church's concept of what this society can and should be.

Building on the premise that there is an essential affinity between things American and the purposes that the Church seeks to uphold, they then use ideas that appear, at least, to be almost entirely indigenous in order to convey the points they wish to make.

In speaking thus, I do not mean for a moment to suggest, of course, that it is tactical considerations alone that dictate the form the letter takes. Just as Murray was surely convinced of the truth of every affirmative word that he had to say about the American experiment, so, too, one can rest assured that the authors of the pastoral letter on the economy themselves affirm the whole of the argument they have elaborated. It is because they themselves embrace both the theological and the philosophical premises on which the letter is based that they find it possible to speak in the manner that they do. Especially is this true, I am confident, of the emphasis on Scripture: a document of this sort simply would not have been possible had not the Catholic church undergone the rediscovery of the Bible it has experienced in recent years. It is because the life of the church in this country is increasingly infused by Scripture that its leaders find themselves capable of speaking in this manner.

But for all this, it is still above all, I would submit, the fact that the authors believe the themes they have chosen to emphasize are capable of speaking to the American people at large that their argument is cast in the way that it is. They are not just out to expound their own view of the subject, but to persuade as well. They want, in fact, to establish a mode of discourse for the Church that will enable it to function as an effective force in the affairs of this society. And they are drawn to speak in the way that they do, in turn, because of a conviction that it is in this form that Catholic teaching is most likely to be accessible and appealing to the wider society.

III.

Obviously this presupposes a certain conception of what the American public mind is—and is likely to be in the foreseeable future as well. Specifically, it assumes that whatever else it may have become, the American nation is still composed largely of people who are more likely to be responsive to the imagery and logic of Biblical religion, on the one hand, and liberal politics and economics, on the other, than any of the available alternatives. It is still this historic combination that has been at the foundation of the American political culture since well before the founding of the republic that constitutes, the authors believe, the moral and spiritual center of our public life, and if it is going to be possible to reform American institutions in the way they have in mind, this is the ground that will have to be occupied. They are betting, moreover, that both elements will endure. There may be changes in the way they are interpreted, and in the comparative respect they are accorded. But neither will fade. They will show continuing vitality. So for all of the change that now swirls about us, there will still continue to be an underlying continuity with the past with respect to the most basic assumptions Americans bring to bear in attempting to make moral and religious sense of their life together.

It goes without saying, of course, that this is a highly controversial reading, which flies in the face of some of the more popular assumptions commonly made today about what is happening in this society and where it is headed. In the bishops' defense, it must be said that there is much more evidence to confirm it than might initially be supposed. The continuing vitality of liberalism among the American people is manifest, I assume, and requires no extended discussion. But it is only slightly less obvious, if one is willing to acknowledge the relevant facts, that Americans continue to be a people whose life and thought is characterized by an unusually high degree of religiosity. For all of the talk about secularization, there is in fact today, by some informed estimates, more evidence of identifiable religious practice in this country than ever before in its history. Millions of Americans—the vast majority in fact—continue to identify themselves as practitioners of one or another religious creed, and at this moment in our history in particular it is being demonstrated once again how strong is the tendency for religious belief to intrude itself into public affairs. Whatever doctrines the Supreme Court may choose to enunciate in handling the discord that arises from such incursions, the fact remains that this is still very much a "nation with the soul of a church,"[4] and it can be expected to continue to be such for the foreseeable future.

Moreover, biblical religion in particular continues to figure very prominently in the religious practice going on in this nation. For all the evidence of increased religious pluralism, the vast majority of religious observance in this country is still based, in one way or another, on the Book. In fact, with the increased attention to Scripture today on the part of Catholics (who now comprise approximately one–fourth of the population), on the one hand, and the enormous growth Protestant evangelicals have experienced, on the other, the religious culture of the American people today could well be as Biblical as it has ever been. It is not, it needs to be remembered, the more rationalistic forms of religion that have flourished in recent years. They, if anything, have waned, and even among the more educated segments of the population, it is the religions of revelation that are in the ascendancy.

Still, for all of this, the fact remains that this is a highly pluralistic society with respect to religious beliefs and practices, and it appears to be getting more so every day. It is indisputably, I would submit, more pluralistic now than at any previous time in its history, and is surely destined to become even more so in the years ahead. Not only is the traditional mix of Protestants, Catholics, and Jews much more evenly distributed now than before, but it is now complemented by what appears to be a steadily expanding proliferation of new religious identities as well. It is not, however, just the mere fact of this heterogeneity that distinguishes the present moment; it is also the effect that it is having on the ethos of American life. For, as a result of it, the nation is much more *self-consciously* pluralistic than ever before as well. The days of Protestant hegemony are fast fading, and in its place is emerging a way of life that defies homogenization. Respect for the sensibilities of religious minorities is increasingly the norm, and even the rights of nonbelievers are an increasingly important part of the equation of factors that have to be taken into account in determining the role that religion will play in our public life.

Carried to its logical conclusion, of course, the tendency this represents could well be expected to produce such a fundamental change in the identity of the nation that most of the tradition to which the pastoral letter seeks to appeal would be rendered obsolete. Biblical themes in particular simply would no longer be able to function as a basis for any sort of credible construction of the purposes actually operating in public life. For even if they continued to have meaning for large numbers of citizens, they would in principle be reduced to the status of one alternative view among others, and whatever understandings developed out of their interaction with the various other views with which they would come into contact would almost certainly entail major compromises. Especially could this be expected the more they were forced to come to terms with the challenge of specifically secular and antireligious influences. One could well imagine, in fact, a situation developing in which the Christian influence in American public life was so diminished that the invocation of any sort of Biblical themes to interpret public events would be positively incongruous.

It is easy to understand, in turn, why the church would want to do all it could to prevent the advance of religious pluralism in this country from ending up yielding this result, and up to a point, such resistance makes perfectly good sense. But at the same time, there would appear to be definite limits as to how far it legitimately can go. Even the degree of pluralism achieved to date imposes constraints on the invocation of religious themes in public contexts that simply have to be respected if the rights of minorities are to be taken seriously, and the obvious question that is posed by any sort of explicit reference to theological concepts drawn from the Bible is whether this can be done in a way that will not amount to a new form of triumphalism. It is all well and good to want to insure that the religious part of the American tradition is preserved and maintains its vitality, but it remains to be seen how this is to be reconciled with the sort of complex pluralism now taking shape in this extraordinarily heterogeneous society.

Whatever else may be said for the pastoral letter, in turn, it does not provide much illumination on this score. Perhaps it may be possible to speak theologically about public things in a way that does not exclude a substantial part of the electorate. Perhaps it may even be possible to speak Biblically to such effect. But the example of the letter is not encouraging. Precisely because it is so explicitly Biblical and unequivocally exegetical, the letter reads all too much like a confessional statement. It is spoken from faith to faith, in language that can hardly help but be incomprehensible to those who do not look upon the Bible with the same sort of respect. Indeed, my hunch is that to the extent that it is taken at all seriously, such language is likely to inspire mistrust among those that it excludes, and no amount of explaining will remove the fear that what it signals is a Catholic endorsement of the historic Protestant effort to make Christianity the unofficial religion of the republic.

IV.

It is to meet this problem, of course, that the line of argument having to do with rights is introduced. Having spoken at length specifically in the language of faith, the authors turn quite deliberately to adopt the very different language of liberal deontology as they go about addressing the wider society. Citing the familiar Catholic notion of the complementarity of reason and revelation, they then indicate that all of the conclusions reached by the community of faith about distributive justice and other matters pertaining to the public good can be expected to be corroborated by reason acting independently, and the clear implication is that all that they have had to say theologically that is of relevance to such issues can be contained adequately in the version of rights theory that they embrace. So with respect to the ordering of economic life at least, Biblical theology and revisionist liberalism are two paths to reach essentially the same conclusions, and there is no reason, therefore, for anyone to feel excluded or threatened by the appeal to specifically Christian ideas.

None of this is explained, however, much less defended. It is just stipulated. And the obvious question is why it is to be believed. Broadly, of course, it is easy enough to comprehend—and appreciate—the logic of the connection the authors mean to suggest between what the Bible suggests about distributive justice and the priority they believe should be attached today to the fate of the poor. One might even concede, more generally, the symmetry between the sort of notion of community that is held out as normative in Scripture and the vision of social inclusiveness that those responsible for the design of the letter believe is to be found in the best of liberal thinking today. But it is one thing to make connections of this sort and quite another to establish the larger identity they appear to have in mind. For as nonbelievers surely must sense intuitively and believers know with certainty, both Scripture and contemporary liberalism are whole, complex intellectual worlds unto themselves, involving assumptions that, on their face at least, are every bit as much in tension as in harmony, and the only way that such differences can be eliminated is by doing violence to one or the other. It hardly takes a learned student of the Bible, for example, to sense that what is involved in taking it seriously as a basis for the conduct of economic life is much more than just a certain attitude toward the poor, and some of what this entails is almost certainly in direct contradiction to what liberal ideas would incline one to favor. Nor, by the same token, does one need to have mastered all of the complicated nuances of contemporary rights theory to sense that the logic of rights as it is customarily employed today involves a way of thinking about human life and its purposes that is not at all easily reconciled with the understanding represented by the Bible.

Especially do such differences matter, moreover, with respect to the larger issues of meaning and purpose the letter seeks to address. For even if it could be established that the teaching of Scripture and the version of contemporary liberalism that the authors of the letter have chosen to embrace converge in what they entail for the ordering of certain basic features of human relations, it does not then follow that agreement is likely with respect to the more fundamental issues of purpose raised by the quest for moral vision in which the bishops claim to be engaged. Far from it. One could well imagine, in fact, the two leading in diametrically opposed directions the more attention is focused on the ends to be pursued. Especially with respect to economic life, I might add, is this likely to be the case, and no amount of laudatory talk about the promise of the "American experiment" will overcome it.[5]

V.

In speaking thus, I do not mean to build a case for the *status quo ante*. The judgment that the method of reasoning traditionally employed by the Church in the elaboration of its social teaching was deficient because of its neglect of Scripture is, in my opinion, very much to the point and deserves to be upheld. At the least, it deserves a very serious hearing. So too, does the inference that overtly religious symbols and ideas are almost inescapably destined to play a role in public life, and that therefore it is appropriate and indeed necessary that they should form a part of the Church's public witness. The neat separation between reason and revelation that characterized the traditional teaching is overly simple on a number of counts, and simply does not do justice to the complexities of the realities involved.[6] The authors of the letter are perfectly justified, therefore, in seeking to make a fresh start in this regard.

Nor is there anything problematic at all in principle about showing respect for the value of the rights and liberties that have come to be associated with liberalism, or in giving support to their further development in the sense that is being proposed in some of the more recent versions of liberal theory. There is, as Murray showed so effectively, something of fundamental and lasting value in the protections and opportunities that individuals have come to take for granted in societies like the United States, where free institutions have prevailed. And it is altogether fitting, in turn, that this should find direct reflection in the Church's teaching. In this day and age, one would have to wonder, in fact, about the adequacy of any formulation that did not acknowledge, in one way or another, the historic accomplishment that this represents.

But it is one thing to affirm in principle the appropriateness of such steps and quite another to endorse the specific form they take in the letter. The invocation of theological and even Biblical themes has long been associated with that part of the political culture of this nation that we have come to characterize as civil religion, and there is no reason to think, unless one is dedicated to the complete secularization of our public life, that this can or should be abandoned. But the use of such themes in this manner has almost always been significantly different from their sectarian usage. Even if, as has been the case with most of the major components of our civic religion, the symbols and concepts in question have obviously been derived from one or another particular sectarian tradition, they have been invested with new meaning that has turned them into vehicles of wider, more inclusive purposes. In the process of transposition into public symbols, they have been made into something rather different from what they originally were, and it is precisely this protean quality, in turn, that has enabled them to function plausibly as embodiments of meanings meant to be shared by the whole nation.[7]

The problem, in turn, with the way theological themes are employed in the letter is that they do not have this character. Some of those invoked almost certainly have the potential, I am confident, to function as the instruments of more than just sectarian belief. But that is not the way they are presented. For the most part, they are presented in an unequivocally confessional manner that leaves little or no room for their appropriation by persons of other faiths. All too much like that type of Protestant who today arouses such mistrust because of an insistence on a straightforward, unmediated application of the Scripture to public life, the authors of the letter simply assert what they believe the Bible teaches and leave it at that, with little or no attempt to adapt the relevant concepts to the conditions created by a pluralistic society.

Nor, by the same token, need acknowledgment of the virtues of the American experience entail an embrace of liberalism. As inheritors of the Catholic tradition in particular should appreciate, there are ways of affirming what is valuable in the way of life that has been established in this society without ever adopting directly the logic of liberalism. For tactical reasons, of course, it may be decided that some concessions to the language of that brand of liberalism that has come to be associated with the American institutions are required in order to communicate more effectively one or another aspect of what needs to be said. But there should be no confusion left about the essential differences that separate Catholic teaching from even the more benign forms of liberalism on matters of fundamental importance. For the sake of both the integrity and the plausibility of the Church's teaching, it is essential that this distinction be maintained. Especially, one might add, is it important for the American Catholic Church's *own membership* that there be no confusion on this score.

VI.

In a period when informed observers increasingly are given, with good reason, to characterizing the present moment as a time of special opportunity for Catholicism in this nation, it goes without saying that what is at stake in this matter is of more than just academic interest. The size and growing influence of the American Catholic community alone give the church's social teaching a significance it has not previously had, and when this is combined with the intention the hierarchy obviously now has to assert itself as a force in the nation's affairs, it is clear that the stage is being set for what is almost certain to be a major change in the role Catholicism plays in American life. This is not for a moment to suggest, of course, that we are about to enter a period of Catholic hegemony. But it is to suggest that Catholic ideas and interests can be expected to influence the course of events as never before in American history.

Exactly how much of a difference this will make will depend very much, however, on the way in which the Church chooses to conduct itself. To some extent, of course, it is bound to make a difference. An articulate and assertive Catholic community of the size and power this nation now has cannot help but have an impact on the course of events, almost regardless of what it seeks and how it presents itself. But there is, at the same time, an enormous difference between the assertion of sectarian interests and permeation of the wider society. One can easily be successful at the one without ever having much success at the other, and it is the latter, as the bishops must surely recognize, that presents the real challenge. Catholics are almost certain to have more "muscle" in the years ahead in this society and to be able to defend their interests, therefore, with greater effectiveness. But it remains to be seen whether the wider purposes that their leaders would have prevail in the nation as a whole can be anything more than one more sectarian point of view.

What takes place in this regard will almost certainly be influenced, in turn, by the manner in which the issue that has been under discussion here is handled. It is one thing to speak and quite another to be heard, and the Catholic voice in American public life is bound to remain a sectarian one until the Church finds a way to speak in terms that can be appreciated (and appropriated) by the non-Catholic majority. Now that it has broken out of the ghetto and into the mainstream of American life, the challenge confronting the Catholic community in this country is to discover a way of expressing itself that can enable Catholic substance to become a force in the lives of non-Catholics.

There is no assurance, of course, of success in such an undertaking. It is a tall order, and ultimately may prove to be beyond the resources available to the American church. If the critique of the pastoral letter on the economy that has been developed in these pages is at all valid, it still has a long way to go. Indeed, it has only begun, and the journey it faces is filled with pitfalls. It appears especially daunting when one takes into account the strength of the prejudice against things Catholic that surely still exists in this country, on the one hand, and the continuing pull of the ghetto mentality within the Catholic community, on the other. But this is hardly the first time the Church has faced such a challenge, and the historic experience it can bring to bear in confronting it is also enormous. Of no small importance, moreover, is that those responsible for giving leadership in this regard are recognizing the task that confronts them for what it is. This, too, is part of what the letter reveals, and when all is said and done, it could well turn out to be the most important part of all.

NOTES

1. The letter went through a series of drafts, all of which have been available in published form through the National Conference of Catholic Bishops in Washington, D.C. The final text is now available under the title *Economic Justice for All* (Washington, D.C.: NCCB, 1986).

2. Cf. "First Things First: The Letter and the Common Good Tradition" in R. Bruce Douglass, ed., *The Deeper Meaning of Economic Life* (Washington, D.C.: Georgetown University Press, 1986), pp. 21–36.

3. Cf. "Theology and Philosophy in Public: A Symposium on John Courtney Murray's Unfinished Agenda," *Theological Studies*, XL, 4 (December 1979), pp. 700–715. This series of essays is very important, I believe, for understanding the design of the pastoral letter on the economy, because several of those directly responsible for the drafting are given the opportunity to speak directly to the strategic issues the letter raises. There are a variety of views presented, but the weight of the argument falls, I think it fair to say, on the side

of departing from the specific strategy Murray employed in the direction of a more explicitly theological mode of discourse. The symposium reveals clearly, however, the enormous significance of the precedent Murray set for those responsible for articulating the American Catholic Church's social teaching today even as they stand in judgment on some of what he said and did.

4. Cf. Sydney Mead, *The Nation With the Soul of a Church* (New York: Harper, 1975).

5. A lot more needs to be said on this topic, which takes into account the more recent developments in both Catholic and liberal teaching. There is, of course, a long history of quarrel and controversy between Catholicism and liberalism, but of late the topic has not received the scholarly attention it deserves. Two essays that I believe deserve to be read in this connection are: Gerald Mara, "Poverty and Justice: The Bishops and Contemporary Liberalism" and Diane Yeager, "The Bishops and the Kingdom," both of which appear in the aforementioned *The Deeper Meaning of Economic Life*.

6. I have developed the argument which is presupposed here at length in "Civil Religion and Western Christianity," *Thought*, IV, June 1980, pp. 169–183.

7. Robert Bellah's now classic essay on civil religion in this country explains this process in some detail. Cf. "Civil Religion in America" in *Beyond Belief: Essays on Religion in a Post-Traditional World* (New York: Harper, 1970), pp. 168–189.

CHAPTER V

LIBERALISM, COMMUNITARIANISM, AND THE BISHOPS' PASTORAL LETTER ON THE ECONOMY

David Hollenbach, S. J.

In November 1986, the Roman Catholic Bishops of the United States approved the final text of their pastoral letter on the U.S. economy. The document has already been the subject of considerable analysis and debate. Most of this discussion has focused on the concrete policy recommendations contained in the letter. Though these practical questions remain important, this essay will address the more basic question of the document's fundamental ethical framework. I propose to approach the pastoral letter from a somewhat more theoretical and analytical standpoint than the letter itself adopts. The genre of a pastoral letter is, of course, quite different from that of critical moral theory. Therefore, it would be an exaggeration to claim that the bishops deal with all of the important questions of moral theory relevant to the subjects treated by the letter. At the same time, the letter is based on the long tradition of Catholic social thought, a tradition that is strongly committed to reasoned and systematic analysis of social morality. I think the letter does embody a reasonably coherent moral theory, but this theory needs to be made more explicit.

CLARIFYING THE MORAL THEORY OF THE LETTER

In particular, I want to address an issue raised in a recent essay by Bruce Douglass and William Gould, namely, "the relationship between Catholic teaching and liberalism as a political and economic ideology." Douglass and Gould argue that, in an effort to relate the letter to the mainstream of American public life, the bishops "embrace what to all appearances is an essentially liberal theory of rights and then employ that theory as the primary philosophical instrument available to them in developing their evaluation of the American economy."[1] Though it is a "revisionist liberalism" that they find present in the letter, Douglass and Gould argue that any accommodation between Catholicism and liberalism is risky business. It threatens to undermine the communitarian motifs that are central in biblical faith and in the Catholic tradition, motifs that the bishops themselves want to emphasize. They ask pointedly: "Does it really make sense to reinforce the individualist and even egoist orientation which tends to accompany talk about rights in this society, when the professed goal is the creation of a political and economic order characterized by a sense of mutual care and accountability?"[2]

By "liberalism" Douglass and Gould are not referring to the political program of the left wing of the Democratic party. Others have criticized the bishops' policy recommendations for uncritically blessing neo–New Deal and neo–Great Society programs. In my view, most of these criticisms are themselves uncritical and more than a little ideological. Douglass and Gould have a deeper concern that lies on the level of the cultural and philosophical underpinnings of political life. The liberalism they think the letter may be too quick to embrace is that mode of moral philosophy and political theory developed in the eighteenth and nineteenth centuries by such thinkers as John Locke, Adam Smith, Immanuel Kant, and John Stuart Mill. In our own time this approach has been powerfully reformulated and given new life, preeminently by John Rawls, but also by thinkers such as Ronald Dworkin, Amy Gutmann, William Galston, Bruce Ackerman, and a number of others. There are important differences among these contemporary interpretations of liberalism. They do, however, exhibit a number of common assumptions about the appropriate normative standpoint toward social and political activity and institutions:

1. They take as the fundamental norm of social morality the right of every person to equal concern and respect.[3]

2. They are committed to organizing the basic political, and social structure of society in a way that will insure that society is a fair system of cooperation between free and equal persons.[4]

3. They are especially sensitive to the pluralism of modern moral and political life. Because free and equal persons hold different and sometimes conflicting philosophical, moral, and religious convictions about the full human good, an effort to implement a comprehensive vision of the good society through law or state power is excluded. Such an effort would violate some persons' right to equal concern and respect.[5] This perspective is summarized by affirming that the right is prior to the good.

4. Because persons cannot be said to deserve the circumstances of their birth, such as special talents or economic advantages, the tendency of these circumstances to lead to disproportionate outcomes must be counteracted by appropriate societal intervention.[6] (Note that this does not exclude all inequality of economic resources or political power.)

These four assumptions do not indicate the rich content of the discussion of liberalism that has been taking place in recent years, nor do they do justice to the differences among the participants in the debate. They do provide a starting point for assessing the claim of Douglass and Gould that the bishops' letter embodies a classical liberal view of social morality. An examination of these assumptions will also provide an opportunity to discuss some of the important recent refinements in liberal theory.

Douglass and Gould's concerns reflect a vigorous debate underway today among moral philosophers and political theorists about the merits of the liberal tradition. Critics of liberalism such as Alasdair MacIntyre and Michael Sandel believe that liberalism is incapable of addressing the urgent problems of modern society because it rests on an erroneous individualistic and ahistorical conception of the self. They argue that the liberal effort to develop basic moral norms independent of a vision of the full human good is doomed to failure. Therefore, they reject an ethic and politics built on the notion of rights in favor of an ethic and politics of the common good. In the communitarian view, the liberal philosophical framework embedded in our culture is the source of the problems in present-day social, political, and economic life, not the basis for their solution.

As in the case of contemporary liberal thinkers, there are important differences among the communitarian critics. They, too, however, share several assumptions:

1. The human person is essentially a social being. A person's communal roles, commitments, and social bonds are constitutive of selfhood.[7]

2. The determination of how persons ought to live, therefore, depends on a prior determination of what kinds of social relationship and communal participation are to be valued as good in themselves. Therefore, the good is prior to the right.[8] In fact, the very notion of "rights," as it functions in liberalism, denies the constitutive role of community in forming the self.

3. Human beings do not know the good spontaneously, and they cannot learn it either by deeper and deeper introspection or by philosophical analysis of selfhood apart from the ends the self ought to pursue. Therefore, if we are to know how persons should live and how communities should be organized, we must be schooled in virtue. That is, we must serve as apprentices in a community with a tradition that has taught it virtue.[9]

4. How society as a whole ought to be organized will depend on a vision of the integral good of the whole community, that is, the common good. But because of the deep pluralism of modern social life, we lack a civic community with the traditions and virtues that are needed to teach us what the common good is. Therefore, for the time being, we must concentrate on learning these virtues in communities that are smaller than humanity as a whole or than the nation, that is, in local and intentional groups that do share a vision of the human good.[10]

These four communitarian convictions will also serve as reference points for determining what kind of moral theory the pastoral letter embodies. The extent to which they are found in the letter will indicate the extent of its rejection or revision of classical liberal theory.

CATHOLICISM AND LIBERALISM AS ADVERSARIES

It is a historical fact that, from the time of the Enlightenment to the Second Vatican Council, Catholicism and liberalism stood in a vigorously adversarial relation to each other. Michael Novak anticipated the publication of the pastoral letter with a book entitled *Freedom with Justice: Catholic Social Thought and Liberal Institutions.*[11] Novak quite rightly notes the persistent antipathy of the popes and of most Catholic authors generally toward the liberalism of Locke, Smith, and Mill. He identifies three sources of this antipathy. As a *moral* doctrine, this liberalism valued tradition and authority too lightly and gave insufficient weight to the communal context for the formation of a right conscience. As a *political* doctrine, the liberal stress on freedom of religion and democracy was seen as a direct challenge to the truth claims of Christianity and, less admirably, to the church's stake in the *ancien régime.* And as an *economic* doctrine, liberal stress on the individual offended Catholicism's strong sense of the importance of community and its frequent nostalgia for agrarian, local, organic forms of social life.[12]

I fully agree with Novak's argument that most Catholic responses to liberalism up to Vatican II were insufficiently attentive to the ways that the institutions of liberal democracy significantly advanced the protection of human dignity under new social conditions. He is also right—up to a point—when he states that "Catholic Social thought has slowly but steadily come to embrace the institutions of liberal society."[13] It is clear, however, that Novak believes that the bishops have not gone far enough in their reconciliation with liberalism. Thus, while Douglass and Gould worry that there is too much liberalism in the letter, Novak thinks there is not enough, especially not enough of those aspects of liberalism that are most supportive of free markets and the institutions of democratic capitalism.

I would summarize Novak's critique this way: the pastoral letter contains an overly optimistic, too broadly extended conception of human beings' capacity for social union, and it is naive about the unintended negative consequences of pursuing too much communitarian solidarity. In a recent essay, he begins by praising the bishops for their strong emphasis on the classical notion of the common good. But he turns swiftly to a vigorous description of how this concept is freighted with dangers of paternalism, authoritarianism, and even tyranny.[14] He argues that the common good is not in fact *a* good, but rather many goods that are not necessarily in harmony with each other. For example, in the economic sphere, the common good of society will include such things as low inflation, low unemployment, steady growth, low interest rates, gains in productivity, protection of the environment, and the alleviation of poverty.[15] These goods may often be in direct conflict. Further, in a pluralistic society, different persons will rank these various goods differently in relation to each other, and in relation to non-economic goods. Therefore any attempt directly and intentionally to pursue one unified vision of the common good of society as a whole will stifle pluralism and choke freedom.

For Novak, however, the genius of liberalism is that it has discovered a set of political and economic institutions that enable human communities to maximize all these social values without relying on some intentional, overarching plan of how to do so. In his words:

> A society respectful of the freedom and dignity of persons would have to forebear any direct and conscious effort to produce the common good. Under conditions of pluralism, that citadel could no longer be taken by frontal assault. On the other hand, it could with high probability be taken by an indirect, less paternalistic route.[16]

It will come as no surprise that this indirect route is through the establishment of the institutions of democratic capitalism, with their emphases on free markets, private property, entrepreneurship, economic activism, individual initiative, and their deep suspicion of government.

THE LETTER'S TWO LANGUAGES

Who is right? Douglass and Gould, or Novak? Is the philosophical framework of the letter basically liberal with certain revisions to save what can be saved of the Catholic communitarian tradition? Or does the letter advocate a communitarian ethic and a politics of the common good, with certain elements of liberalism grudgingly accepted? In order to answer these questions, we need to turn to the text of the document itself.

It is clear on almost every page of the letter that its normative framework includes a commitment *both* to the dignity of all persons (every person's right to equal concern and respect) *and* to a strongly communitarian understanding of what it is to be a person. The letter employs the language of rights and freedoms associated with liberalism; it also speaks the language of the virtues and the common good associated with communitarianism. Let me give a few examples of the way the letter blends these two vocabularies:

> The dignity of the human person, realized in community with others, is the criterion against which all aspects of economic life must be measured. All human beings, therefore, are ends to be served by the institutions that make up the economy, not means to be exploited for more narrowly defined goals. . . . Similarly, all economic institutions must support the bonds of community and solidarity that are essential to the dignity of persons.[17]

> Being free and being a co-responsible community are God's intentions for us (no. 36).

> In Catholic social thought, therefore, respect for human rights and a strong sense of both personal and community responsibility are linked, not opposed (no. 79).

> The common good demands justice for all, the protection of the human rights of all (no. 85).

These quotations from the letter incorporate both a liberal emphasis on personal dignity and rights, and the communitarian stress on the common good. It links these polarities by insisting, with Aristotle and Thomas Aquinas, and more recently with Sandel and MacIntyre, that community is constitutive of selfhood.[18] As the bishops put it: "Human life is life in community" (no. 63). Thus we must ask: do the bishops simply want the best of both worlds without seeing that there are tensions if not contradictions between these two views? Or is a coherent and stable synthesis possible?

Without doubt the letter proposes a capacious vision of the good society, not simply what Rawls called a "thin theory of the good" in *A Theory of Justice.*[19] Like MacIntyre and Sandel, the bishops are distressed by the lack of shared vision of a good society that marks our culture. The pluralism and differentiation of modern societies have brought many benefits, but they also exact high costs: social fragmentation, anomie, and increased emphasis on personal goals disconnected from a sense of larger social purpose. These problems, the letter states, are "vividly clear in discussions of economic justice. Here it is often difficult to find a common ground among people with differing backgrounds and concerns. One of our chief purposes in writing this letter is to encourage and contribute to the development of this common ground" (no. 22).

The development of such common ground, the bishops imply, calls for a renewed vision of the common good among both Roman Catholics and all members of society. In words quoted by the letter, the Second Vatican Council described the common good as "the sum of those conditions of social life which allow social groups and their members relatively thorough and ready access to their own fulfillment."[20] So described, the common good is the comprehensive human good of all who make up society. It includes all aspects of human living that make for human flourishing and happiness. It has both material and spiritual dimensions.

Thus the full scope of the common good will be achieved when all members of society attain wisdom, knowledge, true belief, and holiness: "knowledge and love of the living God in communion with others" (no. 30). In more philosophical language, the very notion of the common good rests on the recognition that the human person is a "social animal" (no. 65). Further, realizing the common good depends on the development of moral virtue among all members of the society in their interpersonal relationships, in their working lives, and in their lives as citizens. Thus the letter emphasizes the virtues of citizenship, which "grow out of a lively sense of one's dependence on the commonweal and obligations to it" (no. 66). The common good includes strong family life, strong educational institutions, rich artistic and cultural activity. Material goods sufficient to meet the needs of all members of society and active participation by all who are able in the economic and political life of society are also crucial elements in this understanding of the common good.

In line with the importance of tradition in shaping a rich conception of the good and of the virtuous life so much stressed by contemporary communitarian critics of liberalism, the letter as a whole is deeply rooted in the biblical and Roman Catholic traditions. The pastoral letter is itself part of what Alasdair MacIntyre has called a living tradition: "an historically extended, socially embodied argument, and an argument precisely in part about the goods which constitute that tradition."[21]

The four central affirmations of communitarianism are, therefore, richly woven through the fabric of the pastoral letter: community as constitutive of the self; the foundation of moral norms in the values of different kinds of human relatedness; the indispensable role of education in the virtues; and the importance of living tradition in shaping virtuous lives. If the letter reflects a liberal social theory, then it is surely liberalism of a strongly revisionist kind.

WHY NOT PURE COMMUNITARIANISM?

There are at least two important sets of reasons, however, why the pastoral letter introduces certain liberal constraints on the pursuit of a purely communitarian vision of the good society. The first of these is theological, and the second concerns the nature of the state and is therefore both moral and political.

The strictly theological reason has two aspects, one positive, the other negative. Positively, Christians believe that persons are created in the image of God and therefore possess a sacredness that can never be simply subordinate to the good of society as a whole. Further, in the biblical perspective, the creation of the covenanted community is the outcome of the liberation of slaves from bondage. Therefore any vision of a good society that would legitimate the dominance of some persons over others is biblically and theologically excluded. In his fine study of the political significance of the exodus and the Sinai covenant, Michael Walzer has cogently argued that though the covenant was initiated by God, its completion demanded the consent of the people. "So Moses came and called the elders of the people, and set before them these words which the Lord had commanded him. *And all the people answered together* and said 'All that the Lord has spoken we will do'" (Ex. 19:7–8). It is perhaps tendentious to draw too close a parallel between the covenant theology of Exodus and liberal contract theory. Nevertheless, Walzer is quite correct in stressing that there can be no covenant without consent. Thus he concludes that "The human agents of the covenant are, in contemporary philosophical language, *moral agents*. . . . It follows from a covenant of this sort that the individuals who commit themselves [to the covenant] are moral equals."[22] Members of such a community, therefore, have the duty to treat each other as free and equal, as well as the right to be so treated. The covenant community will be genuine and lasting only when these conditions are met, as the prophets had to remind Israel repeatedly. This theological perspective, therefore, leads to the more philosophical principle that the duty to promote the common good includes the obligation to protect the freedom and equality of all.

Negatively, theological argumentation calls for certain liberal constraints on pure communitarianism, because it insists that, though persons are created in the image of God, they are not themselves gods. They are creatures subject to the conditions of finitude, with limited knowledge of the full human good and imperfect understanding of how to achieve the good that they do know. In addition, human beings are sinners, not fully virtuous, and prone to advance their own interests as identical with the common good. The pastoral letter, in words that could have been written by Reinhold Niebuhr, puts it this way:

> The Christian tradition recognizes, of course, that the fullness of love and community will be achieved only when God's work in Christ comes to completion in the kingdom of God. This kingdom has been inaugurated among us, but God's redeeming and transforming work is not yet complete. Within history, knowledge of how to achieve the goal of social unity is limited. Human sin continues to wound the lives of both individuals and larger social bodies and places obstacles in the path toward greater social solidarity. If efforts to protect human dignity are to be effective, they must take these limits on knowledge and love into account (no. 67).

The document as a whole, of course, is considerably more positive about the possibilities of achieving a solid measure of community and social unity than Niebuhr usually was. But this note of "Christian realism" puts the letter on guard against the chief temptation of purely communitarian social theories: mistaking the good of a part of the community for the good of the whole. This is one of the chief objectives of liberalism as well.

The second set of reasons why the pastoral letter introduces certain liberal principles into its communitarian perspective is rooted in its understanding of the proper role of government in securing the full human good. The bishops argue that the government has a limited but indispensable role to play in securing the common good: "*Government has a moral function: protecting human rights and securing basic justice for all members of the commonwealth.* Society as a whole and in all its diversity is responsible for building up the common good. But it is government's role to guarantee the minimum conditions that make this rich social activity possible, namely, human rights and justice" (no. 122, emphasis in the original).

The letter's citations indicate that the bishops have been influenced here by the thought of John Courtney Murray. Murray's writings represent the most creative synthesis of Catholic communitarianism and modern liberalism yet achieved.[23] The letter's location within the liberal/communitarian debate can be further clarified by highlighting several of the arguments by which he brought this synthesis about.

Both Murray and the pastoral letter draw a clear distinction between society and the state. Society is a more inclusive reality than the state. It includes many forms of community and association that are not political in form: families, neighborhoods, voluntary associations of innumerable kinds, labor unions, small businesses, giant corporations, and religious communities. The political community is part of this rich communal existence, and though it is an extremely important part, it is not to be identified with the whole (nos. 121–125).

The distinction between society and the state leads to a moral/juridical distinction between the common good and what Murray called public order. Public order is that minimal level of social cohesion needed if a society in all its diversity is to be able to pursue the full common good. It is important to note that public order, as Murray and the Second Vatican Council used the term, is itself a moral notion. It includes those moral goods that are essential for "the coexistence of citizens within conditions of elemental social order."[24] It is that set of conditions that are prerequisite for any communal life that is based on mutual respect. There are four such prerequisites: justice (which secures for all people what is due them, namely their fundamental human rights), public peace (which will only be genuine peace when it is built on justice), public morality (the minimum standards of public behavior on which consensus exists in society), and public prosperity (which makes possible the material welfare of the people).[25]

What Murray called public order, therefore, bears a remarkable resemblance to what Rawls would call a just basic structure of social, political, and economic institutions. This resemblance is particularly clear in Rawls' most recent writings. Since the publication of *A Theory of Justice*, Rawls has acknowledged that that work failed to stress sufficiently that his notion of justice as fairness was intended as a political conception of justice. It is a moral framework to be applied to a particular subject, namely to political, social, and economic institutions.[26] Rawls' liberal theory of justice, therefore, is a theory of political morality and of political community. It is not a comprehensive conception of the full human good, and therefore it is not the whole of morality. But neither is it simply a *modus vivendi* worked among persons or groups in order to maximize their self-interests. It has a moral content, namely a conception of the political good as a fair system of cooperation among free and equal citizens. This conception of the just basic structure also presupposes a normative conception of the human person. In Rawls' words:

> Since Greek times, both in philosophy and law, the concept of the person has been understood as the concept of someone who can take part in, or who can play a role in, social life, and hence exercise and respect its various rights and duties. Thus, we say that a person is someone who can be a citizen, that is, a fully cooperating member of society over a complete life. We add the phrase, "over a complete life" because a society is viewed as a more or less complete and self-sufficient scheme of cooperation, making room within itself for all the necessities and activities of life, from birth to death. A society is not an association for more limited purposes; citizens do not join society voluntarily but are born into it, where, for our aims here, we assume they are to lead their lives.[27]

Rawls' citizen, therefore, is no egoist. It also stretches language to speak of a person who is a "fully cooperating member of society over a complete life" as an individualist or an "unencumbered self." This citizen is, however, a liberal. He or she insists on being treated, within the basic structure of society, as a free and equal citizen and is prepared to treat others similarly.

For Rawls, this political conception of the person does not exhaustively describe what it is to be a human being, and the conception of political community to which it is tied is only a part of human sociality. The good of political justice is not the full human good, but it does constitute a *very great* good.[28] Similarly, Murray observed that the political association is a distinctive kind of community. It lacks the family's warm ties of affection and loyalty. Its unity is different from the bonds of charity that make for the solidarity of the church. The source of social unity in the political community is neither paternal nor ecclesial; it is civil. This civility is a moral virtue that seeks the public weal through reasoned argument about what it means to be a community of free and equal citizens. As Murray put it, "there should be only one passion in the City—the passion for justice . . . [for] what is due to the equal citizen from the City and to the citizenry according to the mode of their equality."[29]

For Murray, then, liberalism does not rest on the supposition that the right is prior to the good, or that political justice can be defined from the standpoint of the autonomous individual. Rather, the right is part of the good, and the achievement of justice is part of the quest for the common good. On this view, then, even if all persons in a society came to share the same metaphysics, the same religion, and the same ultimate end, society would still need to be institutionally differentiated to some degree. Government is not the church, the corporation is not the family. Though it is surely true that these different kinds of relationships are differentiated to greater or lesser degrees in different societies, their complete collapse into each other is inevitably a form of tyranny.[30] I am not certain how Rawls would react to the suggestion that he is moving toward a similar way of understanding a liberal political order. One thing is clear though. Neither Murray nor the recent Rawls see liberalism and community as totally opposed. The same can be said, I believe, about the bishops' pastoral letter.

A REVISED CONCEPTION OF JUSTICE

From this it should be evident that the pastoral letter's synthesis of liberal and communitarian perspectives depends on its normative endorsement of institutional pluralism and social differentiation. The bishops' letter does not simply split the difference between the two alternative social theories. Rather, it argues that each of them is relevant to a different domain of social existence—the liberal theory of justice and rights to the political order, and the communitarian vision of the common good to the rest of social activity. However, the letter makes what is perhaps its most challenging contribution to the current theoretical debate by proposing a significant revision of the liberal conception of justice and rights.

The pastoral letter argues for a significantly more communitarian understanding of justice than do liberals like Rawls and Dworkin, even though it follows them in separating justice and rights, as elements of the political good, from the more inclusive notion of the common good. For Rawls, political justice as fairness seeks to create the conditions under which all citizens can be fully cooperating members of society over a complete life. The bishops, by way of contrast, state that "*Basic justice demands the establishment of minimum levels of participation in the life of the human community for all persons*" (no. 77). The notion of participation has a "thicker" communitarian meaning than does Rawls' notion of cooperation. Negatively, the letter states the norm of basic justice this way: "The ultimate injustice is for a person or group to be actively treated or passively abandoned as if they were non-members of the human race" (no. 77). This means that a conception of the human race as a moral community undergirds the notion of political justice. Communitarian bonds are present at the very foundation of the moral and political theory of the letter. Participation in community is presented as essential to the realization of human dignity from beginning to end in the letter's moral argument. *Full* participation by all, to the extent of their talents and nurtured capabilities, in the diverse forms of communal existence, is identical with the attainment of the *common good.* But the securing of *basic* levels of participation in social life for all is a demand of *justice.* Thus the pastoral letter advocates a conception of justice that can be called justice-as-participation. To be a person is to be a *member* of society, active within it in many ways through numerous sets of relationships. The key contribution that the bishops' letter makes to the liberal/communitarian debate lies in conceptualizing justice in terms of this link between personhood and the basic prerequisites of social participation.

The antithesis of this basic participation the letter calls marginalization—exclusion from active membership in the human community. Unjust exclusion can take many forms, as justice can take many forms (nos. 77–78). There is political marginalization: the denial of the vote, restriction of free speech, the tyrannical concentration of power in the hands of a ruling elite, or straightforward totalitarianism. It can also be economic in nature. Where persons are unable to find work even after searching for many months, or where they are thrown out of work by decisions they are powerless to influence, they are effectively marginalized. They are implicitly told by the community: "We don't need your talent, we don't need your initiative, we don't need *you*" (no. 141). If society acquiesces in this situation when remedial steps could be taken, injustice is being done. One can hardly think of a more effective way to deny people any active participation in the economic life of society than to cause or allow them to remain unemployed. Similarly, persons who face hunger, homelessness, and the extremes of poverty, when society possesses the resources to meet their needs, are treated as non-members. As Michael Walzer puts it: "Men and women who appropriate vast sums of money for themselves, while needs are unmet, act like tyrants, dominating and distorting the distribution of security and welfare. . . . The indifference of Britain's rulers during the Irish potato famine of the 1840s is a sure sign that Ireland was a colony, a conquered land, no real part of Great Britain."[31] In the same way, the hungry and homeless people in this nation today are no part of anything worthy of being called a commonwealth. The extent of their suffering shows how far we are from being a community of persons (no. 88).

In this understanding of the demands of justice, the letter expands the scope of the rights-language associated with the liberal tradition. It argues that all persons have rights not only to the conditions necessary for political cooperation or participation, but also to basic conditions necessary to be participants in the economic and social spheres as well. The bishops' letter defines rights as "the minimum conditions for life in community" (no. 79, section title). It maintains that among these rights are those to basic nutrition, housing, and employment for all who are able to work.

A problem that the letter has not addressed in a fully adequate way is that of specifying what constitutes the minimally acceptable levels of participation. Rawls seemingly avoids this problem, because his "difference principle" does not call for any specific level of basic goods; it only requires that they be maximized for the least advantaged. The concrete application of the difference principle in public policy, however, inevitably calls for substantive judgments about conflicting values. There is, I think, no way of avoiding a realist moral epistemology at some level of this argument. The bishops' letter adopts it sooner than Rawls, Dworkin, and Walzer do, but in the end all are forced to make claims about real values in the lives of real human beings.

An additional objection has been raised to this modification of the theory of justice and rights by critics such as Novak. In their view it will lead to an anti-liberal, paternalistic concept of the state. Were this charge true, the pastoral letter would contain a profound internal contradiction, for the letter is strongly committed to a liberal concept of limited government. In fact it contains no such contradiction. As noted above, government does have a moral function, that of securing basic justice and protecting human rights for all citizens. This does not mean that government has the sole responsibility for justice and human rights. All the diverse communities and associations that make up the whole society have such responsibilities as well, in ways appropriate to their roles and capacities. When, however, these nongovernmental agents lack the capacity or willingness to act in ways that secure the economic rights of some citizens, government ought to intervene. This is the substance of what the Catholic tradition calls the "principle of subsidiarity" (see nos. 98–100, 124, 308, 314). It was restated by Murray in typically American idiom: "As much freedom as possible, as much government as necessary."[32] If people are homeless, unemployed, hungry, and illiterate despite the vigorous growth of a democratic capitalist economy, government intervention is both necessary and justified.

The letter, therefore, embodies a moral theory that is fully compatible with the liberal commitment to pluralism in the institutional life of society. But it presses beyond classical liberalism and agrees with the communitarian critics that classical liberalism is an inadequate response to the anomie and disillusionment with public life that is very much around us. It urges the cultivation of the virtues needed to move society toward the realization of its full conception of the common good. In contrast to liberalism, the letter also assumes that there is a fundamental coherence among the diverse dimensions of modern social life. Its moral argument presupposes that the religious, political, economic, familial, technological, and other kinds of relationships that bind us together or drive us apart in advanced industrial societies can be brought into an imperfect but tolerable harmony with each other.

There is perhaps no more fundamental or important question facing Christian ethicists today than this issue of the conflict or coherence between the religious and socioeconomic spheres of human existence. The content of one's religious faith and theology impinges quite directly on the way this question is addressed. The bishops adopt the typically Roman Catholic view that the doctrines of creation and redemption together imply that the many fragments of our lives have a deeper unity in God. This prevents us from despair as we seek the connections between our many kinds of relationships and our many partial communities. In the bishops' words: "To worship and pray to the God of the universe is to acknowledge that the healing love of God extends to all persons and to every part of existence, including work, leisure, money, economic and political power and their use, and to all those practical policies that either lead to justice or impede it" [no. 329]. The crosscurrents among our various communal relationships, the different virtues we must cultivate, and the diverse kinds of obligations we must acknowledge in our chopped-up world are not a trap set for us by God in order finally to tear us apart. They are opportunities for the realization of capacities for mutual concern and respect that can be realized in no other way. They are, in short, opportunities and invitations to love all our neighbors as ourselves. Different persons are no doubt to be loved in different ways, but none in a way that says implicitly or explicitly: you don't count as my neighbor; you don't count as a human being.

Amy Gutmann has suggested that the contemporary communitarian critics of liberalism have failed to make their full contribution to contemporary political theory because they have not tapped the full constructive potential of their values. They have not sought to show the implications of a communitarian vision of personhood for the *political* life of a modern, pluralistic society. Instead, they show signs of despair over the very possibility of political life itself, and have backed off into a defense of local, small-scale enclaves of virtue, both secular and religious. My hope is that this essay has at least opened up a way of moving toward a synthesis of the values of both liberalism and communitarianism, a synthesis that can help address some of the urgent moral problems of our society. The bishops' letter does not provide a fully developed synthesis of this sort. But I hope I have shown that it, and the living tradition it represents and seeks to advance, makes a contribution to the endeavor to create a society that is more free, more equal, more just—in short, a society where every person's dignity can be realized through at least a minimum degree of social participation.

NOTES

1. R. Bruce Douglass and William J. Gould, "After the Pastoral: The Beginning of a Discussion," *Commonweal* 113 (December 5, 1986), p. 653.

2. Ibid.

3. See Ronald Dworkin, *Taking Rights Seriously* (Cambridge, Mass.: Harvard University Press, 1977), chapter 6, esp. pp. 178–83.

4. See John Rawls, "Justice as Fairness: Political Not Metaphysical," *Philosophy and Public Affairs,* 14 (1985), pp. 231–234.

5. See John Rawls, *A Theory of Justice* (Cambridge, Mass.: Harvard University Press, 1971), sections 33 and 50.

6. See Ronald Dworkin, "Why Liberals Should Care about Equality," *A Matter of Principle* (Cambridge, Mass.: Harvard University Press, 1985), pp. 205–213.

7. Michael Sandel, *Liberalism and the Limits of Justice* (New York: Cambridge University Press, 1982), pp. 147–154, 173–174.

8. Alasdair MacIntyre, *After Virtue* (Notre Dame, Ind.: University of Notre Dame, 1981), p. 240.

9. Ibid., chapter 15.

10. MacIntyre, *After Virtue*, pp. 244–245; Michael Sandel, "The Procedural Republic and the Unencumbered Self," *Political Theory,* 12 (1984), pp. 81–95, esp. pp. 91–95.

11. Michael Novak, *Freedom with Justice: Catholic Social Thought and Liberal Institutions* (San Francisco: Harper & Row, 1984).

12. Ibid., pp. 23–24.

13. Ibid., p. 38.

14. Michael Novak, "Free Persons and the Common Good," *Crisis* (October 1986), pp. 11–12.

15. Ibid., p. 14.

16. Ibid., p. 16.

17. National Conference of Catholic Bishops, *Economic Justice for All: Pastoral Letter on Catholic Social Teaching and the U.S. Economy* (Washington, D.C.: National Conference of Catholic Bishops/United States Catholic Conference, 1986), no. 28. Further references to the pastoral letter will be given parenthetically in the text, according to paragraph number.

18. See Sandel, *Liberalism and the Limits of Justice*, pp. 147–154; MacIntyre, *After Virtue*, chapter 15.

19. Rawls, *A Theory of Justice*, section 60.

20. Vatican Council II, *Pastoral Constitution on the Church in the Modern World*, no. 26; cited in *Economic Justice for All*, no. 79.

21. MacIntyre, *After Virtue*, p. 207.

22. Michael Walzer, *Exodus and Revolution* (New York: Basic Books, 1985), pp. 83–84.

23. Murray's writings on this subject are extensive. Here I will be relying primarily on the following: "Leo XIII: Two Concepts of Government," *Theological Studies*, 14 (1953), pp. 551–567; "Leo XIII: Two Concepts of Government II: Government and the Order of Culture," *Theological Studies*, 15 (1954), pp. 1–33; *We Hold These Truths: Catholic Reflections on the American Proposition* (New York: Sheed & Ward, 1960); *The Problem of Religious Freedom* (Westminster, Md.: Newman Press, 1965). See also Murray's notes and commentary on the Declaration on Religious Freedom of the Second Vatican Council, in W. Abbott and J. Gallagher, eds., *The Documents of Vatican II* (New York: America Press, 1966), pp. 672–696.

24. Murray, "The Declaration on Religious Liberty: A Moment in Its Legislative History," in Murray, ed., *Religious Liberty: An End and a Beginning* (New York: Macmillan, 1966), p. 35.

25. Murray, *The Problem of Religious Freedom*, p. 30.

26. Rawls, "*Justice as Fairness*," p. 224.

27. Ibid., p. 233.

28. John Rawls, "The Idea of an Overlapping Consensus," The Hart Lecture for 1986, forthcoming in the *Oxford Journal of Legal Studies*.

29. Murray, *We Hold These Truths*, p. 8.

30. Michael Walzer, in *Spheres of Justice: A Defense of Pluralism and Equality* (New York: Basic Books, 1983), has developed this line of reasoning in a very instructive way. Twelve years ago, Bishop James S. Rausch pointed out that an earlier and incipient formulation of Walzer's views had a marked similarity to Murray's perspective and to the traditional Roman Catholic principle of subsidiarity. See Rausch, "Dignitatis Humanae: The Unfinished Agenda," in Walter J. Burghardt, ed., *Religious Freedom: 1965 and 1975* (New

York: Paulist Press, 1977), pp. 45–47. This similarity is even more pronounced in *Spheres of Justice.*

31. Walzer, Spheres of Justice, pp. 76, 79.

32. Murray, "Leo XIII: Two Concepts of Government," p. 559.

33. Amy Gutmann, "Communitarian Critics of Liberalism," Journal of Philosophy and Public Affairs, *14 (1985), pp. 321–322.*

PART II

POLITICS, PUBLIC POLICY, AND AMERICAN CATHOLICISM

What role, if any, should religious interests in general, and U.S. Catholic interests in particular, play in American politics? The last thirty years have witnessed increased Catholic activism in the public forum, as Catholics have become fully participating members of American society. This section examines specific ways Catholics have expressed their religious beliefs in the political arena--from electoral activities of bishops to interest group lobbying to the efforts of Catholic lawmakers to achieve consistency between moral conviction and public duty. Timothy A. Byrnes offers a case study of the activities of the U.S. bishops in the 1976 presidential campaign to illustrate one form of politico–religious activity. Thomas J. O'Hara examines the many groups that comprise the Catholic lobbying effort in Washington. As he demonstrates, these groups lobby on many different issues, sometimes in opposition to the institutional church lobby (the NCCB and the USCC). O'Hara concludes that, like many American institutions, the Catholic lobby in Washington is not monolithic but is characterized by pluralism and diversity.

The last two essays in this section address conflicts between the bishops and lay Catholic political leaders over particular public policies, such as abortion. The problem of episcopal participation in partisan politics was dramatized by the claim of New York Cardinal John O'Connor and other bishops, during the 1984 elections, that Catholic politicians such as Democratic Vice-Presidential candidate Geraldine Ferraro and New York Governor Mario Cuomo were obligated to translate personal moral opposition to abortion into public policy outlawing abortion. Mary C. Segers examines how two Catholic public officials, Governor Cuomo and Joseph Califano, have resolved conflicts between religious belief, moral conviction, and their political duty to execute sound public policy in a pluralistic society. Peter Augustine Lawler argues that Cuomo should give more weight to the Catholic moral critique of abortion (as articulated by the bishops) and should oppose abortion politically.

CHAPTER VI

THE BISHOPS AND ELECTORAL POLITICS: A CASE STUDY

Timothy A. Byrnes

The role of the American Catholic hierarchy in modern presidential politics has been shaped by a dynamic relationship between its own publicly articulated policy agenda and the platforms and electoral strategies of the two major political parties. In recent decades, the bishops have played rather secondary roles during campaigns in which their agenda has cut across the policy and strategic differences between the parties. On the other hand, during campaigns in which their priorities have appeared to mirror the approach of one of the parties, then the bishops have found themselves at the very center of the partisan debate. In fact, in these latter cases, the bishops have inevitably been accused of endorsing one candidate over the other.

The 1976 presidential election was the key episode in the development of this relationship. Other events, such as the pastoral letters on war and the economy, and John O'Connor's criticism of Geraldine Ferraro's abortion views in 1984, have received more attention. However, none of these can rival the seminal and lasting influence that the 1976 campaign has had on the bishops' involvement in presidential politics. In fact, all of the bishops' political activities since 1976 can be characterized, to some extent, as responses to, or consequences of, the controversial events of that year.

Many bishops saw 1976, the first presidential election year after *Roe v. Wade*, as a propitious time to advocate strongly an antiabortion constitutional amendment. To that end, the National Conference of Catholic Bishops (NCCB) released the *Pastoral Plan for Pro-Life Activities* in late 1975 calling for "well-planned and coordinated [antiabortion] political action" and for the "development in each congressional district of an identifiable, tightly knit, and well organized pro-life unit."[1] In effect, the pastoral Plan was a blueprint for mobilization of American Catholics and other voters in a campaign to heighten the significance of abortion as a political and electoral issue in 1976.

However, not everyone within the bishops' conference was pleased with the tone and implications of this effort. Some members and officials of the bishops' conference were concerned that the Pastoral Plan's strong and expressly political language would limit the hierarchy's political role in 1976 to single-issue, antiabortion politics. They wanted to move beyond such an approach so as to avoid creating an impression that the NCCB would judge candidates and parties solely on the basis of abortion.

With that goal in mind, Bishop James Rausch, Secretary of the NCCB and General Secretary of the bishops' national secretariat—the United States Catholic Conference (USCC)—developed *Political Responsibility: Reflections on an Election Year*. This document placed abortion within the context of a broad range of issues to which the bishops had addressed themselves in the early 1970s. The statement, passed by the NCCB in the spring of 1976, conveyed the bishops' intention "to call attention to the moral and religious dimensions of secular issues, to keep alive the values of the Gospel as a norm for social and political life, and to point out the demands of Christian faith for a just transformation of society."[2] However, the statement also emphasized that the bishops "specifically do not seek the formation of a religious voting bloc," and that they would not "instruct persons on how they should vote by endorsing candidates."[3]

Moreover, the Political Responsibility Statement argued that "the church's concern for human rights and social justice should be comprehensive and consistent," and it listed "a broad range of topics on which the bishops of the United States have already expressed themselves." This list, presented in alphabetical order, included, in addition to abortion, the economy, education, food policy, housing, human rights, U.S. foreign policy, military expenditures, and the role of the mass media in the political process.[4]

In 1984, a great deal of attention was paid to an apparent split within the bishops' conference between supporters of Archbishop Bernard Law's designation of abortion as the "critical" issue of the day and supporters of Cardinal Joseph Bernardin's emphasis on a broader "consistent ethic of human life." It is clear from the above, however, that both of these positions had already been spelled out clearly and made public in official NCCB documents relating to the 1976 presidential campaign. It is clear, in other words, that by 1976 a debate had begun within the American hierarchy over the priority the bishops' conference should place on various public policy issues.

This setting of priorities is politically significant because it determines the way in which the bishops' agenda intersects with the platforms and strategies of the political parties. In 1976 the bishops' policy priorities were particularly significant because each of the presidential candidates tried to associate himself with the bishops and with limited segments of the NCCB agenda.

Both Jimmy Carter and Gerald Ford considered the support of Roman Catholic voters crucial to their electoral chances in 1976. Four years earlier a majority of Catholics had broken traditional ties to the Democratic party and had rejected George McGovern in favor of Richard Nixon.[5] This Catholic shift, along with a similar defection on the part of Southern whites, had dismantled the Democratic coalition that had dominated presidential politics since Franklin Roosevelt. Carter's primary task in 1976 was to rebuild the so-called New Deal coalition; Ford's was to hasten its decline and to solidify what some saw as an "emerging Republican majority."[6] As a former governor of Georgia, Carter was sure to return the white South to the Democratic column, but Catholics appeared to be up for grabs. In fact, Catholics were seen as vitally important swing voters, and they were actively sought by both campaigns. Moreover, since Carter and Ford both believed that the Catholic hierarchy could substantially influence the Catholic vote, both campaigns also paid particular attention to the hierarchy's policy agenda.

For his part, Jimmy Carter was concerned that the inevitable cultural gap between a "born-again" Southern Baptist candidate and Northern ethnic voters would create a "Catholic problem" for his campaign. In the hope of ameliorating this problem, Carter went out of his way to assure Catholics at every opportunity that he was personally sensitive to their particular concerns. It is not surprising, therefore, that

Carter worked diligently throughout the campaign to maintain friendly relations with the Catholic hierarchy. Cordiality between candidate and bishops, it was thought, would both symbolically downplay Carter's cultural distance from Catholics, and at the same time defuse active opposition to his candidacy by the bishops themselves.[7]

On the other side of the partisan fence, Gerald Ford had even more compelling reasons for associating himself with the Catholic hierarchy. Resigned to losing the South, Ford's only chance for victory in 1976 was to carry the heavily Catholic states of the Northeast and upper Midwest. As a result, Ford devised what his aides and some members of the press dubbed a Catholic strategy, involving direct appeals to Catholic voters and indirect efforts to "exploit the cultural combativeness between Baptists and Catholics."[8] Like their Democratic counterparts, the Republicans believed that a positive relationship between their candidate and the hierarchy would facilitate successful implementation of their campaign strategy. Friendly bishops could provide President Ford with valuable opportunities to speak directly to Catholic audiences, and public agreement between Ford and the bishops could highlight and exacerbate Carter's "Catholic problem."[9]

As it turned out, of course, both candidates overestimated the political influence, direct and indirect, that the hierarchy could exert on Catholic voters.[10] Nevertheless, in terms of the nature of the bishops' involvement in the 1976 campaign, the true extent of their influence on Catholic votes did not really matter that much. The fact that Jimmy Carter and Gerald Ford both *believed* that the bishops influenced the Catholic vote meant that the candidates were sensitive to the bishops' policy views and attentive to the bishops' statements and actions. As a result of this belief, the Catholic bishops were drawn into the very center of an intense, closely fought national election.

As we have seen, however, the official public policy agenda of the NCCB, as articulated in 1975 and early 1976, contained an apparent contradiction. On the one hand, the Pastoral Plan called for a single issue political mobilization designed to elect candidates who supported an antiabortion constitutional amendment. On the other, the Political Responsibility Statement declared that "the church's concern for human rights and social justice should be comprehensive and consistent." Now in abstract principle, these two positions may not be completely incompatible. However, in 1976 the Republican party agreed with the bishops *only* on abortion, while the Democratic party agreed with them on virtually everything *but* abortion. Given this political reality, it is difficult to see how the bishops' conference could encourage the election of antiabortion candidates and at the same time maintain a consistent

concern for other social-justice issues. In practical political terms, in terms of publicly articulated political priorities, the bishops would have to choose in 1976 between the *Pastoral Plan for Pro-Life Activities* and *Political Responsibility: Reflections on an Election Year*.

In effect, this is just what they did in the summer of 1976, when NCCB President Joseph Bernardin strongly denounced the abortion plank of the Democratic Party platform. Setting aside the fact that the platform agreed with NCCB policy on virtually every issue that followed abortion in the Political Responsibility list, Archbishop Bernardin called the Democratic platform "irresponsible" for "opposing protection of the life of the unborn and endorsing permissive abortion."[11]

This, of course, was an unwelcome development for a Democratic candidate trying to rebuild the New Deal coalition and concerned about a "Catholic problem." But even more ominously for Carter, Bernardin later added that he was "deeply concerned that this action by the Democratic platform committee may have the effect of increasing feelings of frustration and alienation from the political process felt by many Americans."[12] Though rather cryptic, these words seemed to suggest that the Democratic abortion plank had the potential of creating the type of wedge between Jimmy Carter and Catholic voters that could prove disastrous to the Democratic campaign.

In response to Bernardin's criticism, Carter quickly moved to "clarify" his own position on abortion. In an exclusive interview with Jim Castelli of the National Catholic News Service, Carter emphasized that he was strongly opposed to abortion on moral grounds, and argued that it was only the current proposals for a constitutional amendment that he could not support. Carter also tried to distance himself from some of the more uncompromising pro-choice implications of his Democratic platform. "The wording," Carter told Castelli, "of the Democratic plank was not in accordance with my own desires. . . . The insinuation of the plank's opposition to citizen effort to amend the Constitution as inappropriate is what I object to."[13] This platform wording, interestingly enough, had by all accounts been written by members of Carter's own campaign staff.

Nevertheless, if Carter thought that the bishops' conference would be mollified by this "clarification" of his position then he was immediately disappointed. Archbishop Bernardin, again speaking as President of the NCCB, promptly dismissed Carter's maneuvering:

> Despite [Governor Carter's] personal opposition to abortion, we regret that he continues to be unsupportive of a constitutional amendment to protect the life of the unborn. His reiteration of this stance reveals an inconsistency that is deeply disturbing to those who hold the right to life to be sacred and inalienable. . . . The pro-abortion plank of the Democratic platform remains seriously objectionable.[14]

A shift from "irresponsible" to "deeply disturbing" and "seriously objectionable" could not have been the change in rhetoric for which Carter had hoped when he arranged the interview with Castelli. Carter, it seemed, was not going to be able readily to sidestep the public criticism of the Catholic hierarchy. Indeed, the split between the Democratic candidate and the bishops' conference only widened when Archbishop Bernardin publicly praised a Republican platform that diverged from NCCB policy on virtually every issue except abortion. Deferring discussion of "other important issues" to "the days ahead," Bernardin lauded the Republican platform for its "timely and important" support of an antiabortion amendment.[15]

Not surprisingly, the bishops and conference staff aides who had originally devised and advocated the Political Responsibility Statement were unhappy with Bernardin's abortion-centered responses to the two party platforms. They were distressed at what they saw as the rapid degeneration of their broad, crosscutting policy agenda into a single-issue crusade, and they turned to personal contacts within the Democratic party in an effort to get Carter to take the initiative in broadening his public dialogue with Archbishop Bernardin. Their distress quickly gave birth to action. Several staff members at the bishops' national secretariat, the United States Catholic Conference (USCC), used personal contacts in the Democratic campaign to urge Carter to broaden his approach to the bishops and Catholic voters. They sent Carter copies of NCCB statements on policy issues other than abortion and they encouraged him to draw attention to this broader agenda in his public dialogue with Archbishop Bernardin. The key figure in these backchannel communications between the Catholic Conference and the Carter campaign was Bishop James Rausch.

As General Secretary, Rausch was, in effect, chief of staff of the entire NCCB/USCC bureaucracy. Unlike Archbishop Bernardin and most members and officers of the NCCB, Rausch lived and worked in Washington, D.C., where he directed the day-to-day operations of the conference and coordinated the hierarchy's various collective activities. He was also, according to everyone with whom I spoke about him, "fascinated with politics."[16] He was deeply committed to a broad range of social justice issues, and he felt that it was his job as General Secretary to lead the bishops' conference to more active, more broadly based participation in the national political process.

One of Bishop Rausch's many contacts in the Democratic party was a Washington lawyer named Thomas Farmer. Farmer, who by his own admission was looking for a way to "insinuate" himself into the Carter campaign, saw an opportunity for himself in Carter's public row with Bernardin over the Democratic platform.[17] Farmer presented himself to the Carter campaign as someone who understood the bishops, who had valuable contacts in the bishops' conference, and who could help Carter solve his deepening rift with the bishops' national leadership.

As a first step, Farmer arranged a face-to-face meeting between Bishop Rausch and Andrew Young of Governor Carter's campaign staff. Rausch and Young met, discussed Carter's relationship with the bishops, and readily agreed that more attention needed to be focused on the many policy issues on which the Democratic candidate and the National Conference of Catholic Bishops held virtually identical positions.

According to Farmer, Rausch's initial meeting with Young was followed by a phone call from Carter himself in which the candidate expressed his personal desire to resolve his difficulties with the hierarchy. Rausch assured Carter that he agreed with his objective, but added that as a bishop and an NCCB officer, he would not be able to play an active, public role in achieving it. However, Rausch encouraged Carter to continue to work through Farmer as an intermediary in establishing strategies and approaches for moving the public dialogue with the bishops beyond abortion.

Discussions concerning Carter's relationship with the bishops proceeded on several different levels over the next few weeks. Farmer, for example, traveled to Atlanta for a meeting with Carter's top advisers; Rausch sent one of his own aides from the USCC to a strategy session in Plains; and Rausch personally met with Walter Mondale (another old friend) to discuss their mutual interest in defusing public criticism of Carter's views.[18] In the end, Bishop Rausch, Mr. Farmer, and their interlocutors in the Carter campaign decided that the best way to lower the decibel level of the abortion dispute was to hold a personal meeting between Carter and the leaders of the bishops' conference. At such a meeting, they decided, a whole range of issues could be discussed, and the disagreement on abortion could be placed within a wider context of agreement.

Jimmy Carter, who had just captured the Democratic nomination for president through his ability to convince people of his sincerity and trustworthiness, thought a personal meeting with the bishops was an excellent idea. He reportedly believed that he could resolve his disagreements with the bishops by establishing "an intimate personal relationship" with their leaders.[19] Archbishop Bernardin was formally approached by the Carter campaign, and after some initial hesitation, let it be known that the NCCB Executive Committee would be willing to meet separately with both of the presidential candidates.

Jimmy Carter opened his meeting with the NCCB Executive Committee in late August 1976 by stressing his agreement with the bishops' positions on a wide range of issues and by pointedly assuring them of his strong support for parochial education.[20] However, turning very quickly to abortion, Carter reminded Archbishop Bernardin and the other bishops present that he shared their conviction that abortion was fundamentally immoral. His only difference with them on that issue, he argued, had to do with political strategy rather than ethical principle, and he expressed his hope that the bishops would not allow such a limited disagreement to continue to cast such a pervasive cloud over their relationship.

Carter's opening comments at the meeting revealed that he still thought it was possible for him to reach an accommodation with the bishops on abortion. Despite rather clear evidence that the disagreement was intractable, Carter clung to the notion that, in the words of an aide, "his position [on abortion] could be made minimally acceptable [to the bishops]."[21] Carter, in other words, went into the meeting wanting not merely to expand the scope of his discussions with the bishops (as he had been urged to do by Rausch and others), but also somehow to resolve the dispute that had dominated the discussion to that point.

The problem with this approach was that Archbishop Bernardin had no intention of resolving the dispute on any grounds other than Carter's agreement that an antiabortion constitutional amendment was necessary and desirable. Bernardin was quite willing to discuss other issues with Carter, but he was emphatically not open to compromise or accommodation on the central matter of a constitutional amendment banning abortion.

In a 16 August public statement, Bernardin had already made it clear how he, as NCCB President, felt abortion should be viewed in relation to other issues. "Human life is threatened in many ways in our society," he conceded. "Abortion, however, is a direct assault on the lives of those who are least able to defend themselves. If the church seems particularly concerned with abortion at the moment, it is for this reason: if we become insensitive to the violation of the basic human right to life, our sensitivity to the entire spectrum of human rights will ultimately be eroded."[22]

At the meeting with Carter, Bernardin read a prepared statement that repeated these comments verbatim and that directly challenged Carter to reassess his position on a constitutional amendment: "We . . . repeat today," Bernardin read, "with all the moral force we can muster, the need for a constitutional amendment to protect the life of the unborn. Indeed, without such a remedy, the effort to promote other human life causes for individual and social betterment, about which we are all so concerned, is seriously weakened."[23]

This statement made it quite clear that Carter was not going to be able to make his position on abortion palatable to the bishops. However, the hopes that Rausch and others had that the bishops' abortion dispute would be placed in a wider context of agreement and comity were also dashed. Following the meeting with Carter, Archbishop Bernardin held a press conference in which he indicated that abortion continued to be the focus of the bishops' approach to the candidates in 1976. Before taking any questions from reporters, Bernardin read a prepared statement reporting that abortion had been discussed "extensively" during the meeting, and that the bishops continued to be "disappointed" with Carter's position on that issue.[24]

This press conference and Bernardin's opening remarks in particular, dominated the media's coverage of Carter's meeting with the bishops. The meeting was depicted by the press as a cool rebuff of the Democratic candidate for president by the leaders of the American Catholic hierarchy. *Newsweek*, for example, reported that Carter had been "interrogated" by the Executive Committee.[25] *Time* spoke of "an hour's grilling" for Carter at the hands of the bishops.[26] Regardless of various characterizations, however, all of the major news stories emphasized one particularly descriptive word—"disappointed."

The Carter campaign was angered at the outcome of the meeting. What they had seen as an opportunity to draw attention *away* from abortion and the dispute with the bishops had had precisely the opposite effect. Moreover, members of Carter's staff apparently felt that they had been misled by Rausch and other conference officials who had strongly advocated the meeting. "We were sandbagged," complained a Carter aide. "We had assurances beforehand that the meeting would not degenerate into an abortion debate."[27]

Gerald Ford and his campaign staff, on the other hand, were, according to *The New York Times*, "nearly ecstatic" over Carter's deepening problems with the Catholic bishops.[28] Ford's strategy, you will recall, was to draw as much attention as possible to Carter's differences with the bishops in an effort to emphasize his own areas of agreement with them. Carter's public debate with Bernardin on abortion played right into those plans.

Ford, to be sure, was no right-to-lifer. In fact, his own moderation on abortion had brought him a great deal of criticism and pressure from Ronald Reagan during the Republican primary campaign. However, once Ford had acquiesced in an abortion platform plank written by the right wing of his party, he was able to distinguish himself sharply from his Democratic opponent on an issue that he took to be an important symbolic one for Catholic voters.

More to the point for our purposes, however, Ford's newfound pro-life vigor also allowed him to reach out and associate himself with the abortion-centered agenda that had been firmly identified with Joseph Bernardin and the NCCB. To that end, Ford invited Bernardin and the Executive Committee to meet with him at the White House. Having already announced that he was willing to meet with both candidates, Bernardin immediately accepted.

At a White House session with President Ford, Archbishop Bernardin once again opened with a prepared statement. "On August 18th," he read, "I issued a statement in which I called the Republican platform plank on abortion 'timely and important.' We would welcome a statement of your position on the plank as well as clarification concerning the kind of amendment you support and are prepared to work for."[29]

President Ford, like Carter, assured the bishops that he shared their moral opposition to abortion. However, unlike Carter, Ford also expressed support for the so-called "local option amendment" that would, in effect, reverse *Roe v. Wade* and return responsibility for abortion to the individual state legislatures. This was not the restrictive amendment that the bishops wanted, nor did it go even as far as Ford's own Republican platform had gone. Nevertheless, it was concrete support for a constitutional amendment of some kind and, as such, it clearly distinguished Ford's position from Carter's.

After the meeting, Bernardin once again proceeded immediately to a press conference, where he made remarks that completely dominated subsequent press coverage of the meeting. "Relative to the abortion issue," Bernardin read from a prepared statement, "we are encouraged that the President agrees on the need for a constitutional amendment. We urged him to support an amendment that will give the maximum protection possible to the unborn."[30]

Reporters, of course, pounced on "encouraged" as they had on "disappointed" ten days earlier, and Bernardin's comments made headlines throughout the country. In fact, this time the press explicitly concluded that the bishops had, in effect, endorsed the Republican ticket. *Time*, for example, reported that "the bishops' statement was a clear signal of support for Ford";[31] *The Washington Post* claimed that President Ford had won the "tacit support of the nation's Roman Catholic bishops."[32]

The bishops' participation in the 1976 presidential campaign, their meetings with the candidates and the public reaction to them, is a clear example of the way in which the bishops' political role in a given election is shaped by the particular intersection of the bishops' policy priorities with the platforms and strategies of the major party candidates. In truth, the bishops did not explicitly endorse Gerald Ford for President. However, Joseph Bernardin's responses to the party platforms, his statements to the candidates, and his remarks at two separate press conferences had clearly established an antiabortion amendment to the United States Constitution as the Catholic hierarchy's top political priority in 1976.

At the same time, Gerald Ford favored an antiabortion constitutional amendment and Jimmy Carter did not; Jimmy Carter's electoral strategy involved downplaying his policy differences with the bishops, Gerald Ford's involved highlighting them. It was a very short step from this relationship between the bishops' agenda and the policy positions and campaign strategies of the presidential candidates to a widely circulated conclusion that the bishops favored the Republican ticket. Given the political circumstances of 1976, in other words, Political Responsibility: Reflections on an Election Year had been routed by the Pastoral Plan for Pro-Life Activities.

Joseph Bernardin and other NCCB officials object to this formulation of their participation in the 1976 presidential campaign. They argued then, and they continue to argue today, that their actions that summer and fall were misunderstood and misrepresented. They maintain that the NCCB spokesmen limited themselves to addressing issues in 1976, and that it is inappropriate to infer opinions about candidates from positions on issues. They also claim that it is simply not true that abortion was their top priority in 1976. They argue that the media distorted their agenda by concentrating exclusively on abortion and completely ignoring NCCB positions on other issues. These same arguments, by the way, are used by NCCB officials in the context of other years and other elections as well.

First, let us look at the charge that the media misrepresented the bishops' actions and agenda in 1976. Following the Executive Committee's White House meeting with Gerald Ford, Russell Shaw, director of the bishops' Office of Public Affairs, wrote to *The Washington Post* to complain about the media's coverage of the session. Pointing out that no reporter had asked Archbishop Bernardin a question about anything but abortion, and that the subsequent news stories focused exclusively on that issue, Shaw asked, "Is it the bishops who have an exclusive preoccupation with abortion or is it—at least in their coverage of the bishops—the media?"[33]

The record of the Executive Committee's meetings with the candidates and of the press conferences that followed, however, indicates that Archbishop Bernardin himself did emphasize abortion over other issues. The fifty-five-line prepared statement that Bernardin read to Jimmy Carter during their meeting devoted eleven lines to general introductory remarks, ten to various other policy issues, and fully thirty-five lines to abortion specifically.[34] More to the point, Bernardin's opening statement at the press conference that followed the meeting was devoted exclusively to abortion. The statement deserves to be reproduced in full:

> The meeting was courteous; there was a good exchange of information. The abortion issue was discussed extensively. The Governor repeated his personal opposition to abortion and his opposition to government funding for abortion. He also indicated he would not oppose an effort to obtain a constitutional amendment. However, on the crucial point of whether he would support an amendment, he did not change his position. At this time he will not commit himself to supporting an amendment. We, therefore, continue to be disappointed with the Governor's position. And we repeat our call for a constitutional amendment.[35]

It hardly seems appropriate to blame the media for concentrating on abortion during the question-and-answer session that followed this opening statement. It was Bernardin's own characterization of the meeting, and not a media preoccupation, that caused abortion to dominate press coverage of the bishops' session with Carter. What of the coverage of the meeting with President Ford, the immediate cause of Mr. Shaw's complaint?

It is true that the prepared statement that Bernardin read to Gerald Ford was more even-handed in terms of its attention to the issues than his earlier statements had been. Abortion, on its own, occupied only fifteen lines in a seventy-three-line statement.[36] However, Bernardin's opening comments at his press conference, the subject of all of the news stories about which Shaw complained, once again directed reporters' attention to abortion and the candidates' views on it:

> The meeting was courteous; there was a good exchange of information on many issues. Relative to the abortion issue, we are encouraged that the President agrees on the need for a constitutional amendment. We urged him to support an amendment that will give the maximum protection possible to the unborn. We also discussed at some length the issues of employment, food, illegal aliens and the defense and protection of human rights as a key element in determining U.S. foreign policy. On these issues we explained our position which generally calls for sensitivity to human needs and an acknowledgement of the legitimate role of government in a free society. One final issue brought up by the President was aid to non-public schools.[37]

In contrast to the statement at his previous press conference, Bernardin did at least mention some other issues that were discussed with Ford. He was clearly making an attempt, based on the reaction to the Carter meeting, to indicate that abortion was not the *only* issue that interested the Catholic hierarchy. However, the statement nevertheless reinforced the existing impression that the bishops believed abortion was the most significant political issue of the 1976 campaign.

First of all, abortion is the first issue mentioned in the statement. Moreover, abortion is also the only issue on which Archbishop Bernardin acknowledged and evaluated President Ford's position. The statement said that the bishops were "encouraged" by Ford's support of a constitutional amendment, but it did not even mention what Ford's views were on the other issues that were discussed. In fact, concerning the many issues on which the bishops and the President clearly disagreed, Bernardin's statement was limited to a general call for "sensitivity" and an innocuous endorsement of the "legitimate role of government." Finally, when Archbishop Bernardin was later pointedly asked whether he was "disappointed" in any of President Ford's positions on these other issues, Bernardin allowed that "there was not total agreement on the approaches that should be taken to some issues."[38] It is impossible to square this record with Mr. Shaw's claim that the media was responsible for the emphasis on abortion.

Nevertheless, Joseph Bernardin, now the Cardinal-Archbishop of Chicago, continues to press Shaw's argument twelve years after the fact. In an interview with me, Cardinal Bernardin depicted himself as a victim of the media's fascination with abortion in 1976. He recalled that at his press conference "they asked me what I felt about Carter's position on abortion and what I felt about Ford's. Now it so happened that Ford's position was more in accord with our position than Carter's. In candor and truth I had to indicate that, and that was what was picked up as being the signal that we were favoring Ford over Carter."[39]

In fact, however, Bernardin's expression of encouragement at Ford's position, a clear distinction from his disappointment at Carter's, did not come in response to reporters' questions concerning the two candidates' views. Instead, it was offered in a prepared opening statement that he and his colleagues had independently crafted. Moreover, the expression of encouragement came ten days after the public uproar over the bishops' disappointment in Jimmy Carter's position. The NCCB Executive Committee, following that initial experience, must have known that their characterization of Ford's abortion position would be picked up and emphasized by the press. In fact, Cardinal Bernardin told me that he fully realized in 1976 that "the media were interested only in the abortion issue. It was very clear from the beginning that they were focusing only on the abortion issue and in particular they wanted to highlight the difference between Ford and Carter on that particular issue."[40] Why, then, if he realized this at the time, did Bernardin repeatedly emphasize abortion in his public comments on the candidates and the campaign?

The answer, it seems to me, is that Archbishop Bernardin and his colleagues believed that the 1976 presidential campaign represented a real opportunity for them to gather support for their proposal of an antiabortion constitutional amendment. For their own political reasons, which I mentioned earlier, the candidates, and especially Jimmy Carter, were sensitive to the views, statements, and actions of the Catholic hierarchy. Bernardin, speaking for that hierarchy, repeatedly emphasized abortion because he hoped that Carter would, in fact, change his position on that issue if he was put under sufficient pressure to do so.

It seems unlikely that the bishops were genuinely upset at the media's emphasis on abortion and the candidates' differences on that issue. Drawing attention to these matters, after all, was the whole point of the Pastoral Plan for Pro-Life Activities, the public responses to the party platforms, and the statements read to the candidates during the meetings with the Executive Committee. What seems more likely is that Archbishop Bernardin and his colleagues were upset that the media interpreted this emphasis on abortion as an endorsement of Gerald Ford's candidacy. In this regard, NCCB officials have consistently argued that the bishops' spokesmen addressed themselves to issues and not to candidates in 1976.

While more credible than the claims of media bias, this argument is also misleading, because it implies that the bishops played no role in creating the impression that they preferred Ford over Carter. The problem with this argument is that it neglects the political context in which the bishops' activities took place. Archbishop Bernardin's many comments on abortion and the candidates' abortion views were made in the middle of a heated presidential race in which one candidate pointedly supported the bishops' views on abortion and one did not. Moreover, Bernardin's comments were made at the same time that both candidates were actively maneuvering to maintain positive relations with the Catholic hierarchy in order to buttress their appeals to Catholic voters. Through their statements to the candidates and the press, the bishops articulated policy priorities that clearly reinforced the electoral strategy of the Republican candidate.

The press concluded that this reinforcement amounted to an endorsement of Gerald Ford by the Catholic hierarchy. Perhaps a more benign explanation would be that Bernardin and his colleagues sincerely but mistakenly believed that they had meaningfully and effectively distinguished between issues and candidates in 1976. Such a distinction can be made, of course, if one has spoken out on a range of issues that cut across the platforms and policy positions of the competing candidates. Then one can be perceived as putting forward an issues-based agenda that does not necessarily favor one candidate over another. This distinction between issues and candidates was lost in 1976, however, because the bishops' spokesmen repeatedly emphasized a single issue on which the candidates sharply disagreed. In that case, the press and the professional politicians did not recognize or accept a distinction between encouragement and endorsement.

As a matter of fact, this seems to be exactly the lesson that Joseph Bernardin and many of his NCCB colleagues have drawn from their experiences in 1976. Over the last twelve years the leadership of the bishops' conference has clearly been trying to identify the Catholic hierarchy with a broad-based policy agenda that can not be interpreted as favoring one party over the other.

Even before election day had passed in 1976, conference leaders were working to alter the public's perception of the hierarchy's agenda. Following the outcry over Bernardin's statements to the press, the NCCB Administrative Board (a larger governing body than the Executive Committee) released a statement which in both tone and content retreated to the broad, multi-issue approach of the Political Responsibility Statement. "There are elements of agreement and disagreement between our positions and those of the major parties, their platforms, and their candidates," the statement read.[41] *This* was what Jimmy Carter had hoped to hear from Archbishop Bernardin after his meeting with the Executive Committee.

In fact, this is pretty much what presidential candidates have heard from NCCB spokesmen since. In 1980, for example, the conference released an updated version of the Political Responsibility Statement and testified on those grounds before the platform committees of both parties. There were no public comparisons of the platforms, no meetings with the candidates, and no expressions of encouragement or disappointment. The bishops had apparently drawn the lesson from 1976 that if they wanted to be realistically perceived as nonpartisan and issue-oriented, then they had to adhere to their full agenda, which clearly cut across the policy differences of the major party candidates.

By 1983, of course, Bernardin himself was the leading proponent of such a crosscutting agenda. He called it the "seamless garment" or the "consistent ethic of life," and he argued that the bishops should focus on a large number of "pro-life" issues.[42] If they did not do so, Bernardin argued, if the bishops allowed themselves to be identified with one single issue, then they would continue to be perceived as partisan political operatives. "Without a [broad] framework or vision," Bernardin cautioned, "the bishops of this country would be severely pressured by those who [want] to push a particular issue with little or no concern for the rest."[43]

This is not to say, of course, that all of the American bishops agree with Joseph Bernardin on this point. They do not. The debate within the bishops' conference over the scope of the hierarchy's policy agenda, and over control of the way in which this agenda will intersect with partisan politics is still very much alive. Bernardin, for example, advocated the seamless garment in 1984, but Archbishop Law of Boston held that abortion was the "critical issue" of the election. The NCCB released another update of the Political Responsibility Statement that year, but Archbishop O'Connor of New York publicly challenged Geraldine Ferraro on abortion alone. In one sense, of course, Law's and O'Connor's activities in 1984 only reinforced the central lesson of 1976.

Their claims to be interested in issues rather than candidates were taken even less seriously by the press than Bernardin's had been in 1976. The events of 1984, however, also indicated that individual bishops, given access to the national media, could play as large a role as conference spokesmen and collective documents in determining the general perception of the hierarchy's agenda and priorities.

As I stated at the very beginning of this paper, the relationship between the Catholic hierarchy's publicly articulated policy agenda and American presidential politics is a very dynamic one. The relationship shifts and changes every four years according to the ongoing policy debate within the bishops' conference and the policies and strategies adopted by the political parties. Nevertheless, it is always some form of this fundamental relationship that shapes the bishops' role in a given presidential campaign. For that reason, students of the bishops' political activities would do well in the future to pay as much attention to *politics* as they do to the bishops themselves.

NOTES

1. "Pastoral Plan for Pro-Life Activities," in Hugh Nolan (ed.), *Pastoral Letters of the United States Catholic Bishop, Vol. IV* (Washington, D.C.: National Conference of Catholic Bishops, 1984), p. 87.

2. "Political Responsibility: Reflections on an Election Year," in Nolan, *Pastoral Letters*, p. 131.

3. Ibid., p. 133.

4. Ibid., pp. 134–136.

5. Catholics preferred Nixon to McGovern by 52% to 48%. For a recent discussion of Catholic voting behavior see George Gallup, Jr., and Jim Castelli, *The American Catholic People: Their Beliefs, Practices and Values* (Garden City, NY: Doubleday & Company, Inc., 1987), pp. 126–138.

6. This emerging majority was first predicted on the basis of the 1968 results. See Kevin B. Phillips, *The Emerging Republican Majority* (Garden City, NY: Anchor Books, 1969).

7. One of Carter's aides told me that Carter "needed desperately to win the Northern blue collar vote" and that the bishops were considered crucial to this effort, because they "could affect that vote at the margin." Stuart Eizenstat, telephone interview with author, 12 March 1987.

8. The quote is from an unidentified Ford aide in David M. Alpern, "Courting the Catholics," *Newsweek*, 20 September 1976, p. 16.

9. For a discussion of the Ford campaign's approach to the Catholic bishops, see James W. Naughton, "Ford Hopes Linked to Catholic Vote," *The New York Times*, 5 September 1976, p. 1.

10. In fact, Carter received 56% of the Catholic vote, indicating that his "Catholic problem" had been overblown by the press during the campaign. See Jim Castelli, "How Catholics Voted," *Commonweal*, 3 December 1976, pp. 780–781.

11. Bernardin's statement was part of a *United States Catholic Conference (USCC) News Release*, 22 June 1976. These releases were provided to me by the USCC Office of Public Affairs. The platform read: "We fully recognize the religious and ethical nature of the concerns which many Americans have on the subject of abortion. We feel, however, it is undesirable to attempt to amend the Constitution to overturn the Supreme Court decision in this area." See "*Democratic Platform 1976*," in Donald Bruce Johnson (ed.), *National Party Platforms: Volume II 1960–1976*, (Urbana: University of Illinois Press, 1978), p. 926.

12. *USCC News Release*, 23 June 1976.

13. The Castelli interview was reproduced in *Origins*, 2 September 1976, pp. 170–172. *Origins* is a documentary service of the United States Catholic Conference.

14. For Bernardin's statement, see ibid., p. 172.

15. Ibid., p. 173. The Republican platform endorsed the "efforts of those who seek enactment of a constitutional amendment to restore protection of the right-to-life for unborn children." See "Republican Platform 1976," in Johnson, *National Part Platforms*, p. 976.

16. The quote is from John Carr, a former Rausch aide and now a leading USCC official, interview with author, 10 March 1976. Bishop Rausch is deceased. I discussed his activities in 1976 and his general view of the bishops' conference's political role with several of his former colleagues.

17. Thomas Farmer, interview with author, 24 April 1987. Many of the details concerning Bishop Rausch's contacts with the Carter campaign were related to me by Mr. Farmer in this interview.

18. Walter Mondale recalled that he had "worked very closely" with Bishop Rausch in 1976. Personal correspondence with author, 3 September 1987.

19. See Martin Shram, *Running for President 1976: The Carter Campaign*, (New York, Stein and Day, 1977), p. 224. Several of Carter's campaign aides told me that it would be impossible to overstate Carter's self-confidence at the end of the summer of 1976.

20. I discussed the meeting with Cardinal Joseph Bernardin on 23 March 1988 and with Carter aide Greg Schneiders on 17 March 1987. Bernardin was the presiding bishop at the meeting, and Schneiders was the only aide to accompany Carter to it.

21. Greg Schneiders, telephone interview with author, 17 March 1987.

22. *Origins*, 2 September 1976, p. 170.

23. *Origins*, 16 September 1976, p. 207.

24. See Charles Mohr, "Abortion Stand by Carter Vexes Catholic Bishops," *The New York Times*, 1 September 1976, p. A1.

25. Alpern, "Courting the Catholics," *Newsweek*, 20 September 1976, p. 16.

26. "Flare-up Over Abortion," *Time*, 13 September 1976, p. 21.

27. Unidentified Carter aide, quoted in Alpern, "Courting the Catholics," *Newsweek*, 20 September 1976, p. 16.

28. See Naughton, "Ford Hopes Linked to Catholic Vote," *The New York Times*, 5 September 1976, p. 1.

29. *Origins*, 23 September 1976, p. 216.

30. Ibid., p. 218.

31. "On Abortion, the Bishops v. the Deacon," *Time*, 20 September 1976, p. 11.

32. Edward Walsh, "Bishops Like Ford's Stand on Abortion," *The Washington Post*, 11 September 1976, p. A1.

33. Shaw's letter was printed in a USCC News Release, 13 September 1976.

34. Based on the statement included in the *USCC News Release*, 1 September 1976.

35. *USCC News Release*, 1 September 1976.

36. Based on the statement included in the *USCC News Release*, 13 September 1976.

37. See *Origins*, 23 September 1976, p. 218.

38. Quoted in Rick Casey, "Bishops 'Encouraged' by Ford's Abortion Stand," *The National Catholic Reporter*, 17 September 1976, p. 1.

39. Cardinal Joseph Bernardin, interview with author, 23 March 1976.

40. Ibid.

41. *Origins*, 30 September 1976, p. 236.

42. The full text of Bernardin's 1983 speech on the "consistent ethic of life" was reproduced in *Origins*, 29 December 1983, pp. 491–493.

43. Bernardin made these remarks in a 1986 speech at the University of Portland in Portland, Oregon. I received a videotape of this speech from the office of Senator Mark Hatfield, (R-Ore).

CHAPTER VII

THE CATHOLIC LOBBY IN WASHINGTON: PLURALISM AND DIVERSITY AMONG U.S. CATHOLICS

Thomas J. O'Hara

The Roman Catholic Church clearly has become a significant actor in the public dialogue that leads to the formulation of United States public policy. In recent years the role of the church has been obvious in selected policy issues. For example, with regard to U.S. Central American policy, Michael Barnes, then chair of the House Inter-American Affairs Subcommittee, noted, "The Catholic Church has unquestionably had the most influence of any group on El Salvador policy."[1] Similarly, George Kennan, a respected foreign policy advisor, said of the Catholic bishops' 1983 statement on nuclear war, "This paper may fairly be described as the most profound and searching inquiry yet produced by any collective body into the relationship of nuclear weaponry and indeed of modern war in general, to moral philosophy, to politics, and to the conscience of the rational state."[2] The practical manifestations of increased church presence in the political arena are well documented. Within the past two decades the church has spoken on foreign policy issues ranging from the Vietnam War to aid to the Contras in Nicaragua, and on domestic issues from welfare to abortion. In many ways, the church has tried to take the initiative on several policy issues and set the framework for the public debate. The Catholic Church in this country has evolved from a relatively silent observer of policy debates to an increasingly active participant. From a religious-historical perspective, respected theologian Richard Neuhaus states, "This is the historical moment at which Roman Catholicism has a singular opportunity and obligation to take the lead in reconstructing a moral philosophy for the American experience in republican democracy. Now is the moment for Catholicism to have its desirable effect upon the America within which at least it is coming to be at home."[3]

It is undeniable that there is an increased awareness among politicians and scholars alike that the Catholic Church in America has become a serious political force. The object of this chapter is to examine that political force as it manifests itself within the complex world of lobbying the federal government in Washington, D.C. Studies of religious lobby groups have been somewhat slow in development; most studies of the political strength of religious groups have centered on the Religious Right.[4] For the most part, when scholarly attention has been paid to the lobbying effort of the Catholic Church, there have been some fundamental misconceptions that distort the analysis.

Analyses of the Catholic lobby up to this point often have been too simplistic in equating the institutional lobby of the bishops with the total Catholic interest in the policy progress. Political scientists have for the most part continued to examine the church only as an institution. There is a pronounced tendency to look at the bishops, who speak for the institution, and to ignore the broader membership of the church. To use the institution as the only definition or model of the church is not only inaccurate, it biases the research away from other, non institutional Catholic groups that also lobby in Washington. What is assessed in such a case is not the totality of the church, but only the clerical and hierarchical structures of the church—and in terms of lobbying, what is often described as a monolithic Catholic lobby. The central point of this chapter is that the Catholic lobby is actually much more diverse and pluralistic than has been popularly noted.

This chapter makes a serious attempt to document the political ramifications of diversity within the church. One of the clearest political manifestations of that diversity is to observe how particular groups within the church organize into their own lobby groups. While it is indeed true that the bishops' lobby, the United States Catholic

Conference, is a powerful religious voice, it is an organization that represents, in reality, the bishops of the Catholic Church in this country; and it is not the only Catholic advocacy group. The USCC is the preeminent institutional representation of the Catholic Church in policy circles. Yet numerous other Catholic-based groups have been functioning in Washington as well. These groups sometimes have organized to intensify a policy concern that perhaps the bishops' lobby did not give sufficient attention to; or sometimes these groups have organized to dispute the policy positions of the USCC.

This diversity has not been noted because for the most part social scientists have failed to appreciate the far-reaching effects the Second Vatican Council has had on the Catholic Church. Social scientists miss the political significance of an essential theme of Vatican II. That is, the church needs to be seen not just as a hierarchial and institutional entity; the church is comprised of all people, clerical and lay, united as "The People of God." The church clearly defines its nature in both hierarchial and communitarian terms. *The Dogmatic Constitution for the Church,* issued by the Second Vatican Council and the first systematic presentation of the Church's self-understanding in its history, speaks of the church in both forms. The second chapter of that document is entitled "The People of God," while the third chapter is entitled "The Church is Hierarchial."[5] Thus, according to the church, "The Church" is seen as both communitarian and hierarchial. However, most of the literature that assesses the political role of the Church only refers to the hierarchial church. Andrew Greeley, noted sociologist, makes this point as he states, "Most of the research done on American Catholicism is institutional, concerned with the Church as an organization and not as a population collectively."[6] It is clear that within the discipline of political science this has been the case. Using such an incomplete theological model of the church will necessarily produce incomplete political analyses when attempting to assess the role of the Catholic Church in public policy. A total analysis of the Catholic lobby thus would necessarily need to include all Catholic-based groups, institutional and hierarchial as well as those groups who define their Catholic status as part of "The People of God."

METHODOLOGY

A systematic study of all Catholic-based groups lobbying in Washington was conducted in order to document the totality of the Catholic lobby. For this study, all Catholic groups that advocated positions on public policy and maintained a Washington office were included. Catholic groups that dealt only with internal church matters or did not maintain a Washington office were excluded. Also, groups had to have a clear Catholic base; a few of the groups have expanded to include non-Catholics, but the essential Catholic character has been maintained.

The group itself is the unit of analysis; the information that describes each group was obtained by individual interviews with one or more members of that group. The data were collected through semi-focused interviews. Both open-ended and close-ended responses were coded and tabulated using dBase III Plus. Most interviews were conducted with the chief administration officer of the Washington office of each group. For some of the groups, the public liaison officers acted as spokespersons since the interview covered a variety of topics; for some groups, several interviews with persons of different expertise were necessary. All of those interviewed understood this was a study of Catholic-based lobby groups and agreed to include their group within the study.

LISTING OF GROUPS IN THE STUDY

Africa Faith and Justice Network
This group was founded in 1983. It is a network of religious communities that have people serving in Africa. It concerns itself with policy issues dealing with Africa, including human rights, development, refugees, and U.S. foreign aid programs.

Bureau of Catholic Indian Missions
This organization was founded in 1879. It is a church-sponsored agency that deals with issues pertinent to native Americans, including land settlement claims, education, and health issues.

Catholic Center
This group was founded in 1982. It was started as a project of the Free Congress Foundation and is lay organized. The group attempts to articulate the policy views of traditional Catholics who have conservative political views. The issues of the group are defense spending, abortion, Latin America, and free enterprise.

Catholic Charities U.S.A.
This organization was founded in 1910 to coordinate Catholic social work and social services throughout the United States. It serves as a federation of over seven hundred local autonomous branches of Catholic social service agencies. On policy issues, the organization concentrates on income maintenance issues, national housing policy, and child care programs.

Catholic Foreign Mission Society Justice and Peace Office
This office is part of the Maryknoll Mission Society. It was established in 1974. The group concerns itself with the impact of American foreign policy in the countries in which it serves, especially in Central America. It concentrates on development issues and questions of international debt.

Catholics for Free Choice
This group was founded in 1973 and is lay organized. The group was founded in direct opposition to the bishops' stand on abortion. The group concentrates on women's issues, most especially with regard to abortion.

Catholic Health Association
This group was founded in 1912 and is an association of Catholic health care facilities. Principally, this group concerns itself with health-related issues, including health costs, Medicaid, and health care subsidies, as well as protection of tax-exemption status.

Catholic League for Religious and Civil Rights
This group was founded in 1974 to monitor anti-Catholic bias and defamation in American society. Its main issues are tuition tax credit, abortion, and defamation issues of "traditional Catholics."

Catholic Relief Services
This group was founded in 1943 as War Relief Services, focusing on the needs of refugees from the Second World War. It is the largest private American agency that functions overseas. Principally, it attends to food assistance programs for stricken countries. It concerns itself with development issues as well as U.S. food assistance programs.

Catholic War Veterans of United States of America
This group was founded in 1953 to attend to the needs of Catholic war veterans. It is a lay-run organization and still provides service to Catholic veterans. Its policy issues include defense spending, SDI development, and veterans' benefits.

Center for New Creation
This group was founded in 1979. It is a lay-run organization whose membership can be described as peace activists. Their main issues have been disarmament, U.S. foreign policy, and defense spending. They have been organizers of numerous protests at the Pentagon.

Center of Concern
This group was founded in 1971. It was meant to be an ecumenical and cross-disciplinary think tank that concentrates on issues of development. The center is presently engaged in issues of international peace and development, especially the exploitation of women in development.

Christic Institute
This group was founded in 1980. Principally comprised of lawyers, its purpose is to use the legal system to advocate for social change. Its cases include the Silkwood case, the Greensboro case, the Eddie Carthen case, and presently, a suit contesting the legality of the Iran-Contra connection. Although founded by a priest and two Catholic laypersons, the group has a clear ecumenical approach.

Citizens for Education Freedom
This group was founded in 1959. The clear purpose of this group is to lobby for aid to parochial schools. This group has been willing to ally itself with the Religious Right in a manner in which the bishops have been unwilling to do. As a result, this group takes a somewhat critical view of the bishops' effort on parochial aid.

Columbian Fathers Justice and Peace Office U.S.A.
This office was founded in 1981. It concerns itself primarily with human rights issues in the countries in which its members work, especially South Korea, Chile, and Peru. This organization has also acted as a convener of ten of the groups in this study, all dealing with human rights issues, domestic or foreign.

Conference of Major Superiors of Men
This office was founded in 1957. It is an association of the leaders of all the male religious orders and congregations in the United States. On public policy issues, it concerns itself with South Africa, immigration and especially sanctuary, and Central America.

Dignity, Inc.
This group was founded in 1969, claiming that ministry to gay and lesbian Catholics was not fulfilled by the institutional church. It continues to argue for gay rights and for ministry to homosexuals, males and females. It also works on behalf of increased federal funding for AIDS research.

Franciscan Washington Desk
This office was founded in 1983, representing the concerns of the Franciscan community on policy issues. It is particularly active working against nuclear testing. This office also concerns itself with Central America.

Jesuit Social Ministries
This office was formed in 1968, representing the Jesuit religious order on social policy issues. It actively works on issues of disarmament and peace, issues of Central America, corporate responsibility with regard to South Africa, and issues of minorities in this country.

Leadership Conference of Women Religious
This conference was founded in 1959 as an association of the leadership of women's religious communities in this country. On policy issues, it is concerned with peace and disarmament issues, the foreign policy of the United States in the countries in which its members work, and some women's issues.

National Catholic Action Coalition
This group was founded in 1983. It is meant to represent "orthodox and conservative" Catholics. It works on tuition tax credits for religious schools, pornography issues, abortion, and opposes the bishops' economic pastoral as well as the peace pastoral.

National Catholic Conference for Interracial Justice
This national office was founded in 1960 (local chapters existed since 1935). It sole purpose is to promote interracial dialogue. This organization has been very much involved in the civil rights movement in this country.

National Catholic Eduction Association
This organization was founded in 1904 as an association of Catholic schools throughout the country. It works, in conjunction with the USCC, for continued governmental assistance to Catholic schools, and argues for the recognition of Catholic schools in this country.

National Council of Catholic Women
This organization was founded in 1920 as an association of Catholic women throughout the country. Its principal policy positions center on governmental economic assistance to women and children in poverty, including family medical leave and aid to dependent children.

National Committee of Catholic Laymen
This group was founded in 1977 because of "an absence of a voice for the traditional Catholic." On policy issues, this group focuses on abortion, tuition tax credits, and communist discrimination against Catholics in their native lands.

National Office of Black Catholics
This organization was formed in 1970 to meet the cultural and religious needs of black Catholics. On public policy issues, the group focuses on civil rights, South Africa, as well as hunger and housing issues.

Network, Catholic Social Justice Lobby
This group was founded in 1971. It originated with the experience of religious women working directly with the poor in this country. Present policy issues include disarmament, human rights, and economic redistribution questions in this country, as well as development and debt issues abroad.

New Ways Ministry
This group was founded in 1977 as a result of a perceived lack of ministry to the gay and lesbian community. It is an association of those who need the necessary education to work effectively within the homosexual community. As such, it argues for increased civil rights for the gay and lesbian community.

Quixote Center
This organization was founded in 1975. It focuses very strongly on Central American issues and peace issues. It is very actively involved in raising humanitarian aid for the people of Nicaragua. The center acts as an organizing force for training grass roots groups opposed to U.S. defense and foreign policy.

Society of African Missions Social Service Department
This group was formed in 1983 to express the policy positions of this religious community on foreign policy issues as they relate to countries in which members work. The group is also attempting to bring suit against

the Agency for International Development, based on violations of the Administrative Procedures Act.

United States Catholic Conference

The USCC was founded in 1922. It is the administrative agency of the American Catholic bishops. Its policy positions are on a wide-ranging set of issues. There are ten major areas of advocacy on public policy: agriculture, abortion, arms control, budget allocations, Central America, civil rights, immigration, communications, education, and welfare programs.

ANALYSIS

Closer examination of a few of the groups provides some insight into why the diversity of groups exists. Network was founded as religious sisters became involved in social ministry in the cities, community organizing, and civil rights following the Second Vatican Council. These sisters decided to come together in order to form a political action network of information and communication. From an original band of forty-five sisters, Network has expanded to a membership of over 8,000 women and men, religious and laity, in each state of the country. It has received high grades as an effective lobby organization that has pursued issues generally thought to be of a more progressive or liberal agenda. The social-activist bent of the original leadership still seems to be a primary motivating force behind the group today. Former Congressman, Fr. Robert Drinan, S.J., stated, "Network is the only Catholic lobbying group in America that expressly coordinates and implements the religious, the moral, and the political. It has been a strong and unique moral force in Washington and the nation in the past 15 years."[7]

On the other end of the ideological spectrum is an organization like the Catholic Center, formed as a project for the Free Congress Foundation. This group is supported by organizers who normally support conservative political causes. The Catholic Center essentially was formed to have a Catholic voice among the coalition of conservative groups that lobby for a strong defense and traditional moral values. It is a lay-organized group that conducts training workshops around the country in order to train "conservative or orthodox" Catholics how to be effective in the public policy arena. This group has consistently followed a conservative policy agenda, which often would place them at odds with some of the recent pastoral statements of the American bishops.

Two other groups bear special comment. The Quixote Center is a group that was originally formed to argue for the ordination of women within the church. Eventually the group became involved in the ERA movement as a public issue. In addition, members of the Quixote Center involved themselves in other "issues of justice." One of those issues was litigation on behalf of Karen Silkwood. A court suit sought damages for Silkwood's nuclear contamination and her death in 1974. Three staff members who successfully prosecuted the Silkwood case decided to form a separate group that would concern itself with "justice-oriented litigation." This new group became know as the Christic Institute. The Quixote Center continues to be an extremely active organization, its latest prospect being that of a major coordinator of the Quest for Peace, which was a campaign to lend 100 million dollars in humanitarian aid to the people of Nicaragua. In the meantime, the Christic Institute expanded a great deal. From the original Silkwood case, the group successfully prosecuted the Ku Klux Klan, the American Nazi Party, and the Greensboro Police Department after the murder of anti-Klan marchers in Greensboro, North Carolina. Since its inception, the Christic Institute has greatly enlarged its staff. It is now basically a public-interest law firm that litigates on behalf of issues of "personal freedom and social justice in the United States." Although the Christic Institute sprang forth from the Quixote Center, it has now become much more an interfaith group. It is the only group in the study that has become significantly more universal than a strict Catholic-based group. Yet it has remained in the analysis because it was born of the Quixote Center; the original leadership (former members of the Quixote Center) still guide the organization.

When we examine the data from the interviews of these groups, we observe interesting results. First of all, all 31 groups perceive that they represent definite parts of the Catholic community. While one group represents the bishops, other groups see themselves as representing black Catholics, or conservative Catholics, or progressive Catholics, or other types of Catholics. In essence, groups defined themselves as Catholic in several ways: as part of the institutional structure of the Church (i.e., firmly established by the bishops to be Catholic organizations), by juridical means (Catholic identity established by canon law), or by stressing the role of the laity within the Church. In all, 15 of the 31 groups defined themselves as Catholic groups based essentially on lay membership within the Church. These groups, enjoying neither institutional nor canonical status, clearly see themselves as Catholic groups. The absence of "official" or formal recognition does not deter these groups from defining themselves as Catholic, although Catholic identity for these groups is outside of institutional status. The point is that each group claims a Catholic constituency, but no one group represents the total constituency.

This is further documented by the perception of the groups themselves that there is no one Catholic lobby. Most of these groups rejected any notion of a monolithic lobby. Only 13 of the groups named the USCC as the principal lobby for the Catholic community. Fourteen groups thought the Catholic community was too diverse to be represented by one lobby group. Comments such as "too fragmented," "mosaic," "too diverse" indicated that for these 14 groups, no one group best spoke for the entire Catholic community. The assumption that the bishops' lobby speaks for the total Catholic community, a presumption made in much of the literature, is clearly disputed by the Catholic groups themselves.

In terms of the issues for which the groups lobbied, we again find evidence of diversity and pluralism within the Catholic lobby. Every single group claimed to lobby on an issue that was of particular concern to American Catholics. However, groups lobby on some of the same issues from opposing points of view. The following broad policy areas found groups on differing sides of the issue: welfare, defense spending, tuition tax credit, disarmament, abortion, the equal rights amendment, U.S. foreign policy in Central America, nuclear armaments, gay rights, and social security for urban America. Eleven of the 31 groups indicate particular policy disagreement with the positions of the institutional church. For example, various groups are opposed to the church's position on capital punishment, the economic pastoral, the peace pastoral, the document on Central America, on abortion, on homosexual rights, and on educational policies. Eight additional groups were not opposed to church policy positions but felt their issues needed to be stressed in a more focused way. Thus, rather than disagreement, there is a question of intensity of support for a particular issue. Individual groups have formed to highlight issues such as health care, international development, welfare concerns, women's issues, black and Catholic issues. Thus the data indicated that not only are there a number of groups in the Catholic lobby, these groups take various and often conflicting positions on public policy issues.

Of the 31 groups, 17 were formed after 1970. The groups that have a longer history are closely tied to the institutional church. Most of the newer groups were formed by lay persons or by religious orders of nuns, brothers, or priests. Part of the reason for the rise of those newer groups must be attributed to the proliferation of lobby groups in general within the last two decades. However, Vatican II is very likely an additional reason why there has been such an increase of Catholic-based lobbying groups. The theology of Vatican II, which stresses increased lay participation within the Church, gave added impetus to persons outside of the hierarchial structure of the church to organize as Catholics concerned about particular policy issues. Therefore, the formation of these newer groups may be due to external factors, i.e., the opening of the political process in the U.S., but to internal factors as well, i.e., the effect of Vatican II.

Thus the central finding of this chapter is that there is no monolithic Catholic lobby in the national policy process. For Catholic lobbyists involved in this study, that is no new insight. An overwhelming percentage of these persons reject the idea of a monolithic lobby. They know very well the pluralism within the church on policy matters. However, for political scientists who have a tendency to look only at the hierarchial model of the church, the documentation of a pluralistic lobby is slow in being noted. There is no longer one Catholic "actor" in the public policy world of lobbying; there are a multiplicity of "actors." Each actor claims to represent, in some manner, a Catholic constituency. To be sure, the institutional lobby, the bishops' lobby, still speaks powerfully. However, it no longer speaks solely.

NOTES

1. "Interest Groups Focus on El Salvador Policy," *Congressional Quarterly Weekly Report*, 24 April 1982, p. 896.

2. Kenneth Thompson, "Religion and Politics in the U.S.—An Overview," *Annals of American Academy of Political and Social Science*, 483 (January 1986), p. 24.

3. Richard John Neuhaus, "The Catholic Movement," *National Review*, 7 November 1986, p. 46.

4. Lake Ebersole, *Church Lobbying in the Nation's Capitol* (New York: Macmillan, 1951); James Adams, *The Growing Church Lobby in Washington* (Grand Rapids, Mich.: William Eerd, 1970); Alan Hertzke, *Representing God in Washington* (Knoxville: University of Tennessee Press, 1988).

5. Austin Flannery, ed. "The Dogmatic Constitution on the Church," *Vatican II: The Conciliar and Post Conciliar Documents* (Northport, N.Y.: Costello Publishing Co., 1975), pp. 359, 369.

6. Andrew Greeley, *The American Catholic* (New York: Basic Books, 1977), p. 32.

7. "Network Celebrates 1971–1986," *Network*, 1 April 1986, p. 16.

CHAPTER VIII

MORAL CONSISTENCY AND PUBLIC POLICY: CUOMO AND CALIFANO ON ABORTION

Mary C. Segers

What obligation does a Catholic lawmaker have to work toward the reinstatement of restrictive abortion laws? Does Church teaching *require*, as a matter of doctrine, Catholic officials to challenge the legal status of abortion? How can a public official personally believe that something is profoundly wrong morally, yet insist that he or she will not use political power to right the wrong?

These questions about moral consistency in public policy were raised by some prominent American Catholic bishops during the 1984 election campaign; they were directed rather pointedly at the position of vice-presidential candidate Geraldine Ferraro on abortion policy, and they may well be a recurring theme in American presidential campaigns, given the persistence of the abortion controversy and the possibility of future Catholic presidential nominees (Joseph Biden, Mario Cuomo, and Bruce Babbitt were, for example, possible contenders for the Democratic

Party's nomination in the 1988 elections). These questions are central in any discussion of the rights and duties of religiously committed lawmakers in a pluralistic democracy with constitutional bias toward religious and political liberty.

To address these questions, I propose to consider the cases of two Catholic male politicians who oppose abortion in conscience, yet have supported legalization and public funding of abortion: Joseph Califano, former Secretary of Health, Education and Welfare in President Jimmy Carter's Cabinet, and Mario Cuomo, the Governor of New York. In their political conduct and their written reflections on abortion policy, Califano and Cuomo illustrate how Catholic officials, faced with the vexing questions of public policy raised by the abortion issue, have sought to resolve conflicting obligations to conscience, constituents, the Constitution, and the common good. Examining the ways Cuomo and Califano have handled the abortion issue also provides an opportunity for reflection upon the role and function of law in a pluralistic democratic society, the constitutional bias toward freedom in American politics, and the nature of politics and political judgment in a liberal democracy such as ours. I suggest that the policy positions reached by Califano and Cuomo in carrying out their public duties are not only not inconsistent with their conscientious beliefs, but are perfectly consonant with traditional Catholic concepts of the limits of law and of state regulation.

CALIFANO AND ABORTION FUNDING

Joseph Califano served as the nation's chief health, education, and social service official during that period in the 1970s when public controversy and Congressional debate about abortion funding was at its peak. As Secretary of the Department of Health, Education, and Welfare, Califano had to oversee the administration of the Medicaid healthcare program for the indigent. In 1976, the House of Representatives, led by Congressman Henry Hyde (R.–Ill.) attached a restriction to the 1977 HEW appropriations bill prohibiting the use of HEW funds "to perform abortions except where the life of the mother would be endangered if the fetus were carried to term." This Hyde Amendment restricting federal funding of poor women's abortions became the subject of intense debate in Congress as well as a major federal court case (*Harris v. McRae*).[1] The Hyde Amendment also presented Cabinet Secretary Califano with a major dilemma: reconciling his private beliefs as a Roman Catholic with his public duties as HEW Secretary. In *Governing America*, Califano described it this way: "The issue was whether, and under what circumstances, HEW's Medicaid program to finance healthcare for poor people should pay for abortions. It would be debated and resolved in the language of the HEW appropriations law, and the regulations implementing the law. This made the Secretary of HEW an especially imposing and exposed figure on the abortion battlefield."[2] Califano, who opposed abortion, phrased his dilemma succinctly: "As Secretary of Health, Education, and Welfare, would I be able, in good conscience, to carry out the law of the land, even if that law provided for federal funding of all abortions?"

Califano's resolution of this dilemma is interesting and illustrative of how a Catholic public official can reconcile conflicting obligations to conscience and the Constitution. In public confirmation hearings before the House and Senate and in private informal conversations with feminist activists, Califano stated clearly his opposition to abortion and to public funding of abortions. Nevertheless, once Congress had authorized public funding of abortions in certain instances and Califano had to write specific regulations for administering the law, he correctly perceived his public duty to be paramount and to take precedence over his private religious convictions. As he wrote, "Neither President Carter's views nor mine were of any relevance to my legal duty to ascertain what Congress intended and write regulations that embodied that intent."

Three features of Califano's resolution of this dilemma are noteworthy. The first concerns the conformity of his views on abortion to Church teaching; the second concerns the intellectual style of his Catholicism and how that influenced his conception of the relation between private conscience and public duty; and the third concerns Califano's actual conduct as a government official.

First, although Califano describes his Catholic background and education in some detail and obviously considers himself Catholic, his discussion of abortion indicates that his view did not fully accord with Catholic teaching. In his book he wrote: "I consider abortion morally wrong unless the life of the mother would be at stake if the fetus were carried to term. Under such tragic and wrenching circumstances, no human being could be faulted for making either choice, between the life of the mother and the life of the unborn child. These are the only circumstances under which I considered federal financing of abortion appropriate."

While Califano clearly opposed abortion on demand, even his very strict, narrow grounds for permitting abortion did not reflect Catholic moral teaching. Church teaching holds that the direct killing of innocent unborn human life is never permissible. Califano's view, which prohibits abortion except to save the mother's life, is thus not in accord with church teaching. Yet bishops and other church leaders did not criticize Califano for this departure from church doctrine. (Note that although Califano's single qualification may seem minimal, it is actually very serious, because it undercuts the whole logic of the church's position.)

A second noteworthy aspect of Califano's approach to abortion was the manner in which he appropriated Catholic moral theology. From this comment it seems clear that, for Califano, his own judgment was the ultimate measure of Catholic orthodoxy. That is, Califano did not automatically submit will and judgment to Catholic moral teaching but reflected critically upon the church's teachings before accepting or rejecting them. This becomes clear when we compare his position on contraception with his position on abortion. Birth control and family planning policies were public issues that arose frequently in the 1960s when Califano was a White House adviser to President Lyndon B. Johnson. Johnson vigorously advocated birth control, especially in population policies for developing nations. Although the Catholic bishops publicly disagreed with Johnson's policies, Califano noted that birth control was a subject of intense debate and diverse opinion among theologians, and that he himself inclined toward the liberal view of contraception. In other words, contraception posed no ethical dilemma for him as a presidential policy adviser—because he essentially did not accept orthodox Catholic teaching on the immorality of artificial contraception. Because the intrinsic wrongness of contraception was neither obvious nor certain, Califano apparently did not think the Catholic view of birth control should influence, determine, or limit public policy options. He was able to reconcile private conscience with public policy on family planning because he was unconvinced of the correctness of the church's moral teachings on the immorality of contraception.

By contrast, Califano's own convictions were much closer to church teaching on abortion, and this made the task of reconciling private conscience with public policy that much more difficult. With abortion, Califano wrote, "I had to face direct conflict between personal religious conviction and public responsibility." Yet even in this case of rough consonance between Califano's own convictions and church teaching, he ultimately arrived at a public policy position that failed to reflect and, indeed, was at odds with, the church's position.

I wish to emphasize here the critical reflection and judgment Califano brought to these questions of reconciling his private conscience with public duties. Califano's adherence to Roman Catholicism seems clearly to be characterized by intellectual assent and dissent rather than simple rote conformity to church doctrine. For Califano, his own judgment was the ultimate arbiter of the extent to which he appropriated Catholic moral teaching. In the final analysis his own convictions about (a) the intrinsic rightness or wrongness of a practice, and (b) whether public policy should reflect/capture his moral convictions—were decisive. The intellectual style of Califano's Catholicism led him to be selective as to which church teachings elicited his assent. The same intellectual approach characterized his judgments about the relation between religious belief and public policy. Alluding to the work of John Courtney Murray, the Jesuit theologian prominent in the 1950s and 1960s, Califano stated, "His writings on the rights and duties of American Catholics in a pluralistic society and the need to accommodate private belief and public policy were guides for liberal Catholics of my generation."

A third noteworthy aspect of Califano's reconciliation of private conscience and public policy concerns his actual conduct as a public official. Califano's behavior was both *prophetic* and *prudent*. In public hearings and in private meetings, he stated his opposition to abortion and to the public funding of abortions in clear and unmistakable terms. At the level of public rhetoric and political discourse (moral suasion), Califano was willing to be prophetic—that is, critical of existing law in the name of moral convictions which put him against the cultural mainstream of American society. At the same time, he did not neglect the prudent regard for policy consequences, which Catholic jurisprudence has always insisted upon as the better part of political wisdom. Convinced that his obligation as a cabinet secretary was to carry out the law the nation enacts, and aware that appropriate public policy in a pluralistic democracy can differ significantly from one's own private religious or conscientious convictions, Califano went out of his way to discharge his public duties with scrupulous regard for fairness and objectivity in interpreting the Congressional statute on Medicaid. In a sense Califano bent over backward to prevent his Roman Catholic beliefs from influencing his conduct as a public official, on the grounds that this would be inappropriate in our constitutional democracy. Inevitably, of course, he was criticized by some Catholics and by diocesan newspapers for the regulations he issued on abortion funding. In dismay, Califano wrote, "The assumption of many bishops that I could impose my views on the law passed by the Congress reflected a misunderstanding of my constitutional role at that stage of the democratic process."

Califano's analysis of his experiences as HEW Secretary is illuminating for the light it sheds on later church criticism of other public officials' positions on the morality and legality of abortion. The dilemmas that confronted a Cuomo or a Ferraro in 1984 were anticipated by Califano:

> In personal terms, I was struck by how infinitely more complex it was to confront the abortion issue in the broader sphere of politics and public policy in our pluralistic society than it had been to face it only as a matter of private conscience. *I found no automatic answers in Christian theology and the teachings of my church to the vexing questions of public policy it raised*, even though I felt secure in my personal philosophical grounding.

If there were no easy answers or automatic policy inferences to be drawn from Catholic teaching, Califano found that there were also a variety of factors to be weighed and values to be balanced in American public life. Califano summarized the competing values and obligations every public servant must consider in exercising political judgment and executing constitutional responsibilities.

> Throughout the abortion debate, I did—as I believe I should have—espouse a position I deeply held. I tried to recognize that to have and be guided by convictions of conscience is not a license to impose them indiscriminately on others by one-dimensionally translating them into public policy. Public policy, if it is to serve the common good of a fundamentally just and free pluralistic society, must balance competing values, such as freedom, order, equity, and justice. If I failed to weigh those competing values—or to fulfill my public obligations to be firm without being provocative, or to recognize my public duty once the Congress had acted—I would have served neither my private conscience nor the public morality. I tried to do credit to both.

It should be noted that Califano was not publicly criticized by church leaders because his views on the morality of abortion did not conform fully to church teaching. Nor was he criticized for the manner in which he subjected church teaching to his own critical reflection. Church leaders did not publicly question the orthodoxy of his Catholicism. Some bishops *did* grumble about the Medicaid regulations he wrote, and they were critical of how he carried out his public duties. But Califano was never subjected to the kind of treatment accorded Geraldine Ferraro by several prominent bishops during the 1984 election campaign. The record suggests several factors that might account for this difference in treatment. First, Califano clearly and publicly stated his opposition to abortion. Second, Califano had served as an intermediary (a kind of "house Catholic") between the National Conference of Catholic Bishops and Presidents Johnson and Carter, both of whom used him to allay the bishops' criticism of their policies and positions. It seems unlikely that the bishops would have criticized the Catholic layman who served as their unofficial liaison with the President of the United States.

In a sense, Califano's task was easy, given his position as a high-level Cabinet official in the executive branch of the federal government. His constitutional duties were simply to execute and administer laws made by others and to carry out the policies of the President who appointed him. Presumably the task of reconciling private conscience and public duty on the abortion issue could be more difficult if one were a legislator or a chief executive. We turn now to Governor Mario Cuomo's experience as chief executive of the State of New York for further insight into questions of moral consistency in public policy.

CUOMO AND ABORTION POLICY

Governor Cuomo insists that he does not dissent from the church's teaching on abortion; therefore, a 1986 New York archdiocesan directive suggesting that dissenting Catholics not be invited to speak at parish functions does not apply to him.[3] In his celebrated 1984 address to the Theology Department of Notre Dame University, Cuomo stated:

> As a Catholic I accept the Church's teaching authority. While in the past some Catholic theologians may appear to have disagreed on the morality of some abortions . . ., and while some theologians still do, I accept the bishops' position that abortion is to be avoided.

> As Catholics, my wife and I were enjoined never to use abortion to destroy the life we created, and we never have. We thought church doctrine was clear on this, and—more than that—both of us felt in full agreement with what our hearts and consciences told us. For me life or fetal life in the womb should be protected, even if five of nine justices of the Supreme Court and my neighbor disagree with me. A fetus is different from an appendix or a set of tonsils. At the very least, even if the argument is made by some scientists or some theologians that in the early stages of fetal development we can't discern human life, the full potential of human life is indisputably there. That—to my less subtle mind—by itself should demand respect, caution, indeed . . . reverence. But not everyone in our society agrees with Matilda and me.[4]

It seems clear from Cuomo's statements on many different occasions that he accepts church teaching on abortion as authoritative for him and that he has critically reflected upon and appropriated the church's position. As a public official, however, Cuomo asks the following question: to what extent does one's full acceptance of Catholic teaching on birth control, abortion, divorce, and capital punishment obligate one as a matter of doctrine to translate church teaching into law?[5] As Cuomo himself stated, "Am I, as a Catholic governor who was elected to serve Protestants, Jews, Moslems, Sikhs, deists, animists, agnostics and atheists, obliged to seek to legislate my particular morality, in all of its exquisite detail? And if I fail, am I then required to surrender stewardship rather than risk hypocrisy?"[6]

Cuomo's negative answer to these questions emerges from a systematic analysis of the relation between religious belief and public policy.[7] This analysis may be crystallized in a series of propositions. *First*, Cuomo reaffirms the traditional relation in American history between religious values and public life: we are a religious people, yes, but "we are also a people of many religions, with no established church, who hold different beliefs on many matters." *Second*, as religious persons we have a right to articulate our personal views in the public forum and to seek to persuade others of the rightness of those views—even to the point of seeing them enacted into public policy. "The same amendment of the Constitution that forbids the establishment of a state church affirms my legal right to argue that my religious belief would serve well as an article of our universal public morality." *Third*, because this is a religiously diverse society, the values derived from religious belief will not—and should not—be accepted as part of the public morality *unless* they are shared by the pluralistic community at large, by consensus. "Our public morality—the moral standards we maintain for everyone, not just the ones we insist on in our private lives—depends on a consensus view of right and wrong." If, then, I seek to shape a public consensus in favor of outlawing abortion, I should appeal to common values and engage in reasoned debate with fellow citizens rather than appeal to religious authority. Persuasion, not coercion, is the proper method to employ. "That values happen to be religious values does not deny them acceptability as part of the consensus. But it does not require their acceptability, either. A decisive factor is public acceptability by a majority of Americans of the wisdom of a particular proposal."

Cuomo then asks what to do if there is no consensus on a given issue. Granted that I have a right to press my case, what if dissensus rather than consensus develops in the public forum? What if my efforts to influence public opinion to reinstate laws prohibiting abortion are polarizing, divisive, and threatening to our ability to function as a pluralistic community? "Should I continue to try to make my religious value your morality? My rule of conduct your limitation?"

As a Catholic public official, Cuomo, like Califano, finds no automatic answers in Christian theology and church teaching to the vexing public policy questions raised by the abortion issue. "There is neither an encyclical nor a catechism that spells out a political strategy for achieving legislative goals." Thus, whether a Catholic politician must use the power of his office to reinstate restrictive abortion laws is, for Cuomo, not a matter of doctrine but a matter of sound political judgment. "While we always owe our bishops' words respectful attention and careful consideration, the question whether to engage the political system in a struggle to have it adopt certain articles of our belief as part of public morality is not a matter of doctrine: it is a matter of prudential political judgment."

Cuomo suggests the elements that figure in a sound political judgment on whether to seek to enact religious beliefs into public morality and public policy. "The community," he wrote, "must decide if what is being proposed would be better left to private discretion than public policy; whether it restricts freedoms, and if so to what end, to whose benefit; whether it will produce a good or bad result; whether overall it will help the community or merely divide it." Citing "the American-Catholic tradition of political realism," Cuomo applies to abortion a distinction frequently made by the bishops themselves in their pastoral letters on peace and economic justice. This is the distinction between a moral principle and its political application. As the bishops stated in their pastoral letter, "The Challenge of Peace,"

> The Church's teaching authority does not carry the same force when it deals with technical solutions involving particular means as it does when it speaks of principles or ends. People may agree in abhorring an injustice, for instance, yet sincerely disagree as to what practical approach will achieve justice. Religious groups are entitled as others to their opinion in such cases, but they should not claim that their opinions are the only ones that people of good will may hold.[8]

According to Cuomo, the bishops themselves have honored this distinction on issues of divorce and birth control where they adhere to the traditional teaching of the church but abide by, and do not seek to change, the applicable civil laws as they now stand. Why is abortion treated differently? Why, on this issue, Cuomo asks, do the bishops hold Catholic politicians to account and insist that official Catholic teaching be translated into public policy?

If abortion policy is a matter of political judgment, and if church teaching does not automatically dictate any political strategy, then Catholic public officials must engage in a measured attempt to balance moral truths against political realities. And one of these realities is that while the Catholic Church insists that abortion, like racism, is an ethical rather than a religious issue, a number of other major religious organizations—the American Lutheran Church, the Central Conference of American Rabbis, the Presbyterian Church in the United States, B'nai Brith Women, the United Methodist Church, the United Church of Christ, the Unitarian-Universalist Association—all these groups oppose the Catholic position, reach different conclusions from Biblical norms, and conclude that abortion should be a legal option. As Cuomo argues, the existence of such a large diversity of views among religious and secular people is bound "to determine our ability—our realistic, political ability—to translate our Catholic morality into civil law, a law not for the believers who don't need it but for the disbelievers who reject it."

Cuomo's case rests largely but not solely on the contention that prudential political judgment must guide attempts to have one's values embodied as part of our public morality. As he notes, Catholic public officials take an oath to preserve the Constitution, which guarantees to Catholics and to all Americans religious and political freedom. Such freedom is not license; it imposes upon us duties of respect and tolerance for others and embodies an egalitarian *quid pro quo*. American Catholics know that "the price of seeking to force our beliefs on others is that they might someday force theirs on us."

Cuomo's position thus turns out to be the "I'm-personally opposed-in-conscience, but-I-publicly-support-legalized-abortion" view. He opposes a constitutional amendment outlawing abortion and supports Medicaid funding. It is important to note, however, that Governor Cuomo does not embrace either a religious or a political quietism on the subject. Instead, he suggests what has been called "a feminist social agenda" (although these are not his words)[9]—a wide range of public policies intended to enhance respect for all life and to reduce the incidence of abortion without coercing women. Advocating policies to provide food, clothing, housing, job training, education, and medical care for poor women, Cuomo states: "If we want to prove our regard for life in the womb, for the helpless infant—if we care about women having real choices in their lives and not being driven to abortions by a sense of helplessness and despair about the future of their child—then there is work enough for all of us. Lifetimes of it."

To summarize, Cuomo does not believe that church teaching requires him as a Catholic lawmaker to work toward the reinstatement of restrictive abortion laws. He does believe that abortion is profoundly wrong morally; moreover, he is willing to use political power to right the wrong by pressing for passage of laws and policies designed to enhance women's and children's lives and create genuine choice. He is not willing to use the coercive sanction of criminal law to right the wrong of abortion because, in his political judgment, such laws would not work and would have negative consequences. Moreover, in the absence of consensus, imposition of such laws risks violating constitutional freedoms. Cuomo concludes that "approval or rejection of legal restrictions on abortion should not be the exclusive litmus test of Catholic loyalty."

ANALYSIS

What conclusions can we draw from this account of the efforts of two Catholic politicians to achieve moral consistency in public policy on the abortion issue? The moral of these two tales is that, in a pluralistic democracy with a constitutional bias toward religious and political freedom, Catholic public officials can—with integrity—oppose abortion in conscience, yet consistently support the legality and public funding of abortion. We may summarize the reasons that religiously committed officials such as Cuomo and Califano are not required to seek to translate Catholic Church teaching on abortion into public policy.

First, these public officials have a moral duty to uphold the law; in fact they swear to God and on the Bible to support and preserve the Constitution. Upholding the Constitution means not merely supporting a system of governmental institutions but also maintaining and promoting the values, specifically the rights and freedoms, which the Constitution says are basic to the American polity. Chief among these is the "First Liberty," religious freedom, which the First Amendment anchored forever in fundamental law. Catholic public officials take an oath to preserve the Constitution that guarantees this freedom. As Cuomo states, "The Catholic public official lives the political truth most Catholics, throughout most of American history, have accepted and insisted on: the truth that to assure our freedom we must allow others the same freedom, even if occasionally it produces conduct by them that we would hold to be sinful."

Respect for First Amendment freedoms in a religiously diverse society imposes upon all citizens, Catholic and non-Catholic, duties of tolerance and restraint. Although Catholics regard abortion as not purely a religious proposition but as an ethical issue about which thinking people may come to some agreement, Catholics must confront the fact that major groups from another world religion, Judaism, reach different conclusions about the moral permissibility of abortion. Even within the Christian tradition, many churches interpret Gospel norms differently from Catholic Christians and reach opposite conclusions regarding the morality and legality of abortion within the framework of Christian moral thinking. Now all these people may have erroneous interpretations of Scripture, but in a pluralistic democracy who is to decide they are in error? Moreover, "error has rights" in the American and other democratic polities, and it is the genius of the American constitutional experiment to recognize this. The special *moral* duties of the public official qua public official are to preserve and uphold these constitutional freedoms and rights. In other words, the special character of the American polity affords a principled basis for resisting the temptation to impose, in the absence of consensus, one's religious beliefs or religiously derived ethical judgments upon non-believers.[10]

In addition, officials in the executive branch of federal and state government, such as Cuomo and Califano, have a special constitutional duty to enforce and administer laws enacted by legislatures and courts, not to change those rulings or to impose their own private interpretation of the meaning of those laws. It is unfair to criticize a Califano or a

Cuomo as somehow acquiescing in the *status quo* or failing to be prophetically critical of existing laws when in fact it is their sworn political duty to enforce the laws.

A second reason why religiously committed officials such as Cuomo and Califano are not required to seek to translate Catholic church teaching on abortion into civil law has to do with the nature of politics and the need to exercise sound political judgment in public life. Although in politics ends and goals may be set by the people through democratic elections or be derived, for example, in communist societies, from ideological commitments, it is the peculiar province of the lawmaker, the statesman, and the policymaker to determine the appropriate means to a given end. Prudence or practical wisdom in politics involves making judgments about the relation between means and ends. Since there are no automatic *policy* answers in the church's moral teaching on abortion, it is necessary for public officials to exercise sound political judgment in fashioning law and public policy on abortion. And prudent political judgment suggests a consequentialist approach to reinstating restrictive abortion laws. Policymakers must calculate the *efficacy* of restrictive laws (whether citizens will comply with them), the *enforceability* of such laws (whether police will enforce them selectively, uniformly, or not at all), and the *effects* of such laws—whether, on balance, the negative effects of reinstating restrictive laws will outweigh the positive benefits. Secular scholars and scholastics dating from Thomas Aquinas have insisted that good lawmaking requires the presence of clear sanctions attached to law, the possibility of compliance and enforceability, and acceptance as useful by the majority of the governed.[11] Traditional Catholic thought has always been realistic in acknowledging the possibilities and limits of lawmaking and state regulation.

Cuomo calls upon this tradition of "American Catholic realism" when he considers abortion law and policy. When he makes his judgment call, he says it would be better to enact policies that address the underlying causes of abortion than simply to outlaw abortion. Cuomo thinks we can best reduce the incidence of abortion and embody the crucial value of respect for life by using political power to pass laws and policies that get at the root causes of the high number of abortions in the United States: poverty, violence against women, the need for childcare assistance. Such generally pro-life policies also stand greater chances of being enacted than does a constitutional amendment banning abortion. In thus favoring policies which (a) seem better designed to achieve the goal of reducing abortions, and (b) have a better chance of being enacted, Cuomo fulfills his moral obligations as a public official to make and execute sound public policy.

It should be noted that although Cuomo cites dissensus about abortion in American society as a major factor influencing public policy prospects, consensus is not completely controlling for Cuomo. As Governor of New York, he has been willing to go against legislative and popular majorities favoring restoration of the death penalty and opposing mandatory seatbelts in automobiles. For reasons of sound public policy, Cuomo has opposed a majoritarian consensus on these issues. In the case of capital punishment, Cuomo does not believe the death penalty works as a deterrent or that it addresses adequately the roots of the crime problem. In the case of mandatory seatbelts, Cuomo accepts the evidence of empirical studies showing that the use of seat belts reduces automobile fatalities. In the case of abortion, Cuomo does not believe a human-life constitutional amendment will deter or reduce the incidence of abortion (it would be "Prohibition revisited," according to Cuomo). In each instance, after studying the available evidence as to the *consequences* of the proposed law or statute, Cuomo makes his own judgment regarding sound public policy. This is his job as governor having executive power and sharing legislative power. Thus, although consensus figures prominently in his thinking (as it should for any democratically elected public servant), the need to exercise sound political judgment in public life is ultimately decisive for Cuomo. In these instances he is not so much legislating personal moral beliefs as he is making prudential judgments about the probable results of proposed policies. This is the special province of the politician, and Cuomo is willing to contend for his right to that province.

Few Catholic moral theologians would contest the view that the task of the public official in modern government is to pursue laws and policies for the common good that are not divisive and that are feasible, practical, and efficacious. Yet throughout the controversy over public policy on abortion, the statements of bishops such as John Cardinal O'Connor of New York and of Catholic leaders in the Right to Life movement[12] suggest that they attach enormous importance to the idea of the educational function of law. Unlike legal positivists, who insist upon a certain disjunction between law and morality, these Catholics articulate a more traditional view of the law as both reflecting and shaping social mores. Socrates in the *Crito* spoke of the laws of Athens as his "parents," educating and instilling in him the mores and customs of Athenian society. Similarly, Cardinal O'Connor and others seem to fear that without statutes prohibiting abortion on the law books, ordinary citizens will come to think that abortion is morally acceptable and permissible.

However, Governor Cuomo asks whether the bishops, in calling for civil laws banning abortion, are asking government to do what they have failed to do. If the Catholic bishops, whose primary function is to teach the faithful, cannot persuade believing Catholics through explication of the church's moral theology that abortion is to be avoided, how can public officials persuade non-believers, through the imposition of restrictive laws, that abortion is wrong? Cuomo contends that Catholics should teach by their own example and by persuasion, not through the imposition of coercive laws.

To summarize, Catholic lawmakers are not morally required to challenge the legal status of abortion or to work toward the reinstatement of restrictive abortion laws. They do have a moral and political obligation to protect the constitutional freedom of religion and to exercise prudent political judgment in pursuing policies and laws for the common good that are feasible, practical, and efficacious. On abortion, public officials must judge which policies will enhance respect for all human life and work to reduce the incidence of abortion without coercing women.

The church insists that its moral teaching on abortion is universal, not sectarian or parochial. However, many Catholics ask why, if this is true, so many right-minded non-Catholics do not reach the same conclusions about the morality of abortion as does the church. As Richard McBrien has written, "The *clarity* of the church's official teaching on abortion is not in question. Its *persuasiveness* is."[13] The conclusion seems inescapable that, in a pluralistic society, religiously derived and religiously justified convictions must be subject to the tests of rational argument and persuasiveness if they are to be universalized and made into public policy for all. Moreover, prudent political judgments must be made in any attempt to have one's values embodied as part of our public morality. The thoughtful positions of Governor Cuomo and former Secretary Califano on abortion politics and policy illustrate well these "hard truths" about the relation between religion and politics in American society.

NOTES

1. *Harris v. McRae*, 448 U.S. *297* (1980).

2. Joseph A. Califano, Jr., *Governing America: An Insider's Report from the White House and the Cabinet* (New York: Simon & Schuster, 1981), p. 53. This and the following quotations are from Califano's account in chapter 2, "Abortion," pp. 49–87.

3. On August 18, 1986, New York's Archdiocesan Vicar General, Bishop Joseph T. O'Keefe, issued the following directive: "Great care and prudence must be exercised in extending invitations to individuals to speak at parish-sponsored events, e.g., Communion breakfasts, graduations, meetings of parish societies, etc. It is not only inappropriate, it is unacceptable and inconsistent with diocesan policy to invite those individuals to speak at such events whose public position is contrary to and in opposition to the clear, unambiguous teaching of the church. This policy applies, as well, to all Archdiocesan-owned or sponsored institutions and organizations." Since Governor Cuomo distinguishes between church teaching on the morality of abortion and clerical opinion on abortion policy, and since he insists that he accepts the church's moral teaching on the immorality of abortion, he immediately noted that the Archdiocesan directive did not apply to him. See Harry J. Byrne, "Thou Shalt Not Speak," *America* (December 6, 1986), pp. 356–362.

4. Mario M. Cuomo, "Religious Belief and Public Morality," *The Human Life Review*, Vol. XI, Nos. 1 and 2 (Winter/Spring 1985), pp. 31–32.

5. This is how Cuomo phrased the question in his address, "Those Who Love the World: Catholics and the Commonweal," at the Peter Turner Forum, St. James Cathedral, Brooklyn, New York, on October 2, 1986.

6. Mario M. Cuomo, *The Diaries of Mario M. Cuomo: The Campaign for Governor* (New York: Random House, 1984), p. 16.

7. Although Cuomo has addressed these questions on many different occasions in his public life, his most complete statement is his address to the Theology Department, University of Notre Dame, Notre Dame, Indiana, in September 1984 (see note 4 above for the citation of the same address in the *Human Life Review*). The following quotations are from that address.

8. National Conference of Catholic Bishops, "The Challenge of Peace: God's Promise and Our Response," (1983), sections 9 & 10 reprinted in Phillip J. Murnion, ed., *Catholics and Nuclear War* (New York: Crossroad, 1983), p. 258.

9. This phrase was used by Beverly Harrison and Barbara Ehrenreich at a conference on "Ethical Issues in Reproductive Health: Religious Perspectives," sponsored by Catholics for a Free Choice, Washington, D.C., December 5–6, 1986.

10. Of course, as John Courtney Murray pointed out in *We Hold These Truths: Catholic Reflections on the American Proposition* (New York: Sheed & Ward, 1960), acceptance of the First Amendment religion clauses does not commit one to an acceptance of religious indifferentism (e.g., the notion that one religion is as good as another or that all religions are equally valid). Rather, the establishment and free exercise clauses are not so much theological doctrines as they are articles of civil peace to which all can agree for the sake of social stability and harmony.

11. Thomas Aquinas, *Summa Theologiae*, ed. Blackfriars Dominicans (New York: McGraw–Hill, 1964), 1a2ae. 99,6; 1a2ae. 95,3; 1a2ae. 97,2. See also Timothy O'Connell, *Principles for a Catholic Morality* (New York: Seabury, 1978), pp. 185–187.

12. Cardinal John J. O'Connor, "Human Lives, Human Rights," *The Human Life Review*, Vol. XI, Nos. 1 & 2 (Winter/Spring 1985), pp. 41–65. See also John Noonan, *A Private Choice: Abortion in America in the 1970s* (New York: The Free Press, 1979).

13. Richard McBrien, "Religion and Politics in America," *America*, November 1, 1986, p. 255.

CHAPTER IX

THE BISHOPS VS. MARIO CUOMO

Peter Augustine Lawler

Mario Cuomo's rhetoric, unrivaled in its excellence among American political leaders today, means to arouse in Americans a respect for the moral dimension of politics, especially the political relevance of "our noblest aspirations."[1] He seeks to show that the Constitution is more than a selfish compact, that it creates a political life centered on the common good. The most morally charged American political issue today is abortion. "Not since slavery," observes Richard John Neuhaus, "have such elementary questions been raised about the legitimacy of the controlling ideas by which our society is ordered."[2] But Cuomo seems to exempt the abortion controversy from his generally moral approach to politics. He refuses to use his rhetorical talents to convince his fellow Americans that his moral opinion concerning the evil abortion is one that they should share.

Cuomo, politically speaking, is "pro-choice"; he seems to endorse uncritically the legal *status quo*. Some Catholic bishops, with varying degrees of insistency, have called attention to the "absurdity" of personally opposing abortion while doing nothing, politically, to oppose it. In 1986, Bishop James Malone, speaking for the National Conference of Catholic Bishops, said that the legitimate "diversity of views" among Catholics does not extend to the opinion that the question of abortion "falls outside of law and public policy."[3]

Cuomo calls his position not absurd but prudent. He claims to disagree with the bishops not on moral principle but on questions of practical, political judgement about which bishops have no special competence and hence ought to leave to the discretion of political actors. Cuomo suggests that the bishops' criticism, especially insofar as it implies that his position is morally deficient, is meddlesome, even aggressive "moral fundamentalism." Cuomo claims to oppose such criticism with reason, with "the American Catholic tradition of political realism."[4]

My conclusion will be that the bishops have a good case against Cuomo, but I will not present it with the intention of discrediting Cuomo as a political leader. My position is that Cuomo ought to listen to the bishops and oppose abortion politically. I will assume, not without reason, that he is open to reason, and that, as a result, he will eventually change his position. Cuomo is certainly worth criticizing, and I will begin by explaining why.

CUOMO'S DISTINCTIVENESS

Mario Cuomo, despite his presidential non-candidacy, remains the hope, even the soul, of the Democratic party. His visionary eloquence, his extraordinary intelligence, combining political astuteness with a taste and aptitude for theory and even theology, and his remarkable reputation for personal integrity point in many respects to his party's moral reinvigoration, to the possibility that it may soon be morning again for his party's political vision. They also, just as importantly, point to the party's success. The breath of Cuomo's appeal may eventually bring together once more the now seemingly irreparably fragmented elements of the New Deal coalition.

What distinguishes Cuomo from most of his fellow liberal Democrats, his biographer observes, is that "his progressive social philosophy" is rooted in "deep religious commitment."[5] In Cuomo's own words, "my politics is, as far as I can make it happen, an extension of . . . [my Catholic] faith and the understanding [my faith gives me]."[6] His "policies and goals" often "coincide" with those of other liberals, but Cuomo "reached them along a very different route." His "basic moral and religious values" are the products of his interpretation of the theory and spirit of Vatican II Catholicism. They owe little to the self-indulgent intellectual arrogance and moral destructiveness of the American sixties, which inspirited so many contemporary liberals. Cuomo's "social consciousness," as a result, is "more profound" that that of "secular" or pretentiously sophisticated or allegedly morally liberated liberals.[7]

Cuomo presents his theology as thoughtful, informed by contemporary insights, socially involved and hopeful, and yet in accord with authoritatively Catholic moral teaching. His task, as he presents it, is to show how such theological reflection can deepen the Democratic party's liberalism, to show how being a good Catholic can make one a better Democrat. This lesson is especially needed by those Democratic "activists" who have become contemptuous of the moral opinions of those middle class Americans who really work and really believe in God. On at least a moral and cultural level, the Democratic party has become undemocratic.

Feeling this anti-democratic contempt, many middle-class Americans (including a disproportionate number of ethnic Catholics) resentfully left the Democratic party, despite their sympathy with much of the party's economic agenda. These new, reluctant Republicans, who have little affinity with the oligarchic libertarianism of "Reaganism," simply could not abide the Democrats' essentially anti-religious moral permissiveness or relativism. Cuomo promises to bring back to his party these middle-class moral or "social" conservatives by opposing, consistently, all forms, both oligarchic and intellectual, of the irresponsible excesses of moral permissiveness that pervade this "consumer society."[8]

This opposition is perhaps most strikingly clear in Cuomo's exemplary personal life. He lives, as a Catholic, with moral integrity. He goes to church and confession, hopes, above all, for his soul's salvation, is faithful to his wife, devoted to his large family, has always worked hard, was a model student and teacher (diligent, brilliant, and concerned), lives modestly and is of modest means, and has not forgotten and is not ashamed of his working-class, ethnic origins.[9] He was educated at St. John's (and very well), not at Harvard or even at

Notre Dame. The comparisons with the essentially secular, wealthy, Ivy league, and often personally irresponsible Kennedys are obvious. Cuomo, for all sorts of reasons, might be called some day the first genuinely Catholic American president.

CUOMO ON THE CONSTITUTION

Cuomo's most impressive contribution to American political discourse, expressed in his Notre Dame address, is his contention that the First Amendment protects the right of Americans to persuade their fellow citizens that certain of their "religious values" have more than a "narrowly sectarian" significance because they are expressions of desires or values that Americans, generally, hold to be good. According to Cuomo, "Almost all Americans accept some religious values as part of public life. We are a religious people. . . ."[10]

In what his biographer calls his "most inspiring speech,"[11] delivered at the Cathedral of St. John the Divine, Cuomo was more specific concerning the relationship between religion and America's fundamental political principles. "Our Constitution," he said, "isn't simply an invitation to selfishness, for it also embodied a central truth of the Judeo-Christian tradition, a sense of the common good." Hence, "if we have been given freedom, it is to encourage us to pursue that common good."[12] This sense that human beings have been given the freedom to apprehend the same truth about the human good, and hence are free to pursue and share that good in common, is the central tenet of the tradition of "Catholic realism" to which Cuomo explicitly refers in his Notre Dame address.

The Constitution, Cuomo properly went on in the spirit of this tradition, affirms the "Gospel" distinction between liberty and license, and hence the thought "that liberty creates responsibility." The foundation of America "as a people, as government" is at least partially biblical in inspiration. Cuomo also suggests that the liberalism particular to the Democratic party is similarly rooted, in its affirmation that government has the responsibility of caring for "our brothers and sisters," to whom we owe more than, say, we do to those whom we perceive as merely our fellow human beings or even our fellow citizens.[13] If all Americans and human beings are brothers and sisters, it is because they all have the same Father.

For Cuomo, reasoning about the common good begins with the common experience of the existence of a personal or "loving" and "compassionate" God.[14] But this creationism is a great distance from "fundamentalism." The view of the common good in the tradition of Catholic "realism" is emphatically rationalistic and public; human beings can really share the same perception of the good. Cuomo's religious thought is not the unreflective "peasant mysticism" of the Italian immigrant, which was, the sociologists say, apolitical and even amoral in its familial partisanship.[15] His mind led him from the tradition given him by his parents to a tradition of thought, which he chose for his own.

Cuomo's political application of theology, and his discovery that follows John Courtney Murray's,[16] that Catholic realism expresses many of the presuppositions of constitutional discourse in America, are meant to show a way of overcoming the politics of competing interest groups, and of grounding a nonarbitrary or genuinely constitutional political community, and hence providing reasonable support for "communal strength and obligation to the whole."[17] Political discourse can be moral without being moralistic and religiously based without being sectarian if reason can judge moral arguments when they are introduced into politics according to the standard of the common good.

ABORTION POLITICS AND CATHOLIC POLITICIANS

The abortion controversy would seem to lead Cuomo to reexamine his assertion that being a good Catholic can make one a better Democrat. The bishops say that Catholics are antiabortion, and this opposition should be reflected on the positions Catholics take on public policy. Yet for Cuomo to take such a position, the evidence suggests, would make him ineffective as a Democratic leader. The "pro-choice" conversions of Jesse Jackson and Richard Gephardt seemed to have occurred out of expediency. It seems to be impossible to be in any respect antiabortion and become a serious contender for the party's presidential nomination. For a Catholic, this is surely a lamentable fact, and there is much irony in it. The Democratic party seems today to be more "monolithic" on abortion policy than the Catholic Church. But this fact, however lamentable, is one with which Cuomo and the bishops must deal.

Cardinal Bernadin, the "mainstream" spokesman of the American Church, has proposed, repeatedly, that Catholics evaluate candidates according to their position on a number of "pro-life" issues, most of which call for extensions of the welfare state. This partisanship on behalf of a "consistent ethic of life" gives no special precedence to abortion. Cuomo, it turns out, has the correct position on about every issue but abortion. As Timothy Byrnes observes, this "broadening of the bishops' policy agenda, and the deemphasis on abortion it unavoidably implies, meshed more readily with the Democratic moral agenda than with the Republican one."[18] The bishops' mainstream political prudence, some Catholics complain, is a covert endorsement of Cuomo, with the result that the political and moral significance of the bishops' opposition to his abortion position is trivialized. Could it really be true that one's stand on abortion is no more important than one's stand on the minimum wage?[19]

Such prudential calculations are not altogether out of place, but they do not give Cuomo the credit he deserves. He does not view his abortion stand as expedient. He has an argument, and it differs from the bishops'. It is best to assume that his argument developed out of Cuomo's reflection concerning how best to apply antiabortion moral principles to the political circumstances he encounters.

CUOMO'S ANTIABORTION MORALITY

Cuomo is antiabortion, and he explains why in his Notre Dame address. He says that he accepts "the Church's teaching authority on abortion," and he and his wife "felt" that it was "in full agreement with what our hearts and consciences told us."[20] They did not submit blindly to exterior authority; they followed the heartfelt call of conscience.

Cuomo goes on, as he must given the intellectual nature of his religion, to say that his mind made the same affirmation. The fact that "the full potential of human life is indisputably there [in the fetus]" was enough for his "mind" to "demand respect, caution, indeed. . . reverence." For him, the evidence is clear, "even if five of nine justices on the Supreme Court and my neighbors disagree."[21] At this point, it is the reasonableness of the Church's teaching that distinguishes it, for Cuomo, from what the opinion of any particular majority might be.

Cuomo's view at least approximates that of the bishops. He accepts their teaching authority, and he has affirmed their teaching with his heart and mind. His disagreement with them, he says, is merely concerning what prudence or reason dictates, not concerning the principles that guide this practical reasoning.

Cuomo applies quite nicely in principle some of the understanding of prudence within "the American-Catholic tradition of political realism." He asserts that there is no consensus in America for antiabortion legislation, and its absence "can't help but determine our ability—our realistic political ability—to translate our Catholic morality into civil law." He also says "that what is idealistically desirable isn't always feasible, that there can be different political approaches to abortion besides an unyielding adherence and absolute prohibition."[22] On both these dictates of prudence, it turns out, the bishops disagree not at all with Cuomo.

CARDINAL O'CONNOR'S ANTIABORTION PRUDENCE

Cardinal O'Connor, doubtlessly Cuomo's most severe ecclesiastical critic, believes the acceptance of the bishops' antiabortion argument requires two things from an office holder. First, he or she should "issue a statement opposing abortion on demand." Second, he or she should demonstrate " a commitment to work for a modification of the permissive interpretations of the subject by the U.S. Supreme Court."[23] O'Connor leaves open what might be done to "modify" the Court's interpretations. One way, the most obvious and perhaps ultimately the most effective way, is public persuasion. The public official who opposes abortion should use his or her rhetorical talents to convince his or her fellow citizens why it is reasonable and constitutional to hold that human beings have a responsibility to protect fetal life. It would not be necessary for him to work for any particular legislation until the persuasion has had some effect, until there was an antiabortion consensus in place.

O'Connor's position is supported by the leading scholarly expositor today of the tradition of "American Catholic realism," Richard Regan. According to Regan, "rational argument," with "no appeal to religious authority or creed," shows that "the human fetus," because of its humanity, "represents a public interest worthy of legal protection."

But he goes on to contend, prudently, that "restrictive public morals legislation," even when such legislation is perfectly reasonable, "depends upon a broad popular consensus behind it." There is no such consensus today in America " to sustain and support a legal prohibition of abortion." Consequently, "current attempts . . . to overturn *Roe v. Wade* seem doomed to fail and unwise from the viewpoint of consensus if the attempts were to succeed."[24]

Regan's conclusion, however, is not that realistic opponents of abortion should do nothing. As a precondition for prudent legal action, they "need first to revive a broad national consensus against abortion." They must engage in a "campaign" of political education. It "is not likely that . . . [it] will succeed in the near future, but that is no excuse for failing to make a resolute effort."[25] The effort itself is the decisive evidence of one's antiabortion resolution or commitment, that one really believes that the fetal life deserves protection.

CUOMO ON PRUDENCE

Cuomo acknowledges that there is nothing unconstitutional in the bishops' arguing, with respect to abortion, that "the whole community, regardless of its religious belief, should agree on the importance of protecting life—including life in the womb."[26] But Cuomo refuses to use his constitutional right to make this argument himself, because he believes, contrary to O'Connor and Regan, that the argument itself is imprudent. This belief is not rooted in the unreasonable thought that the issues surrounding abortion are intrinsically merely personal or private ones. "Even a radically secular world," Cuomo explains, "must struggle with the question when life begins, under what circumstances it can be ended, when it must be protected . . . [and] what protection to extend to the helpless and the dying, to the aged and the unborn, to life in all phases."[27] The question of whether the fetus deserves protection, and hence the question of its human status are by nature public questions, which demand public answers. The bishops make a reasonable or prudent distinction in acting publicly and resolutely on abortion, but not on divorce or birth control.

But, for Cuomo, the question of whether or not to introduce a "religious" argument into public debate "depends on a consensus view of right and wrong." He says that "values derived from religious belief will not—and should not—be accepted as part of the public morality unless they are shared by the political community, at large, by consensus."[28] He seems to mean in context that one ought not to make a religiously based political argument unless it is already accepted by consensus.

This position does not square with, say, Cuomo's unpopular public position against the death penalty. It could not justify his praise of the bishops' intrusions into the debate over public policy through their letters on nuclear weapons and the economy, both of which are meant, as Cuomo himself says, to contribute to the creation of new consensus on controversial public questions. It also could not justify the other examples he gives in the address of salutary introductions of religious values into politics: the Civil Rights movement and "the alliance of the left and clergy against hunger, the arms race, and exploitation."[29] Such movements, of course, at least begin unpopularly and oppose the reigning consensus. The idea that "religious values," especially ones with "realistic" foundations, cannot be used to improve public policy is, most fundamentally, at odds with Cuomo's theory of constitutional interpretation and the impression he creates that his "progressive" or change-oriented political opinions have theological roots.

CUOMO ON *ROE V. WADE*

Cuomo simply does not say whether *Roe v. Wade* was decided correctly. He refers to it as a "given."[30] In view of its existence, he says, the hands of public officials are tied. He has even articulated a constitutional theory which opposes almost all criticism by elected officials of judicial interpretations of the Constitution. In its perspective, not only President Reagan, but also good Democrats such as Andrew Jackson and Franklin Roosevelt, were wrong to act politically, or even speak politically, against the Court.[31]

Cuomo himself makes no such effort. He says that "the Supreme Court has established a woman's constitutional right to abortion." Even more tellingly, he speaks of "the constitutional right *given* by *Roe v. Wade*."[32] The inference is the Constitution means what the Court says it does, and hence its interpretations are beyond criticism. The Court, consequently, can *give* rights to Americans. This doctrine of "judicial finality" is of relatively recent origin, was invented by the Court, and is really quite controversial.[33] It was, obviously, not the approach Lincoln took with *Dred Scott v. Sanford.* Lincoln spoke and acted on the principle that the decision itself must be implemented, but public officials who understood the Constitution correctly must speak and use the power given to them by the Constitution to work against the Court's erroneous interpretation of the Constitution. The president's oath binds him to oppose, especially in principle, constitutional misinterpretations.[34]

The doctrine of "judicial finality," taken to the extreme Cuomo appears to take it, is nothing but legal positivism. (Chief Justice Taney was the first positivistic or merely historical interpreter of the Constitution on the Supreme Court.[35]) It is, as a result, contrary to the key principle of "realism" that the common good can really be known by rational creatures, and hence there is a standpoint from which all political decisions, including judicial decisions, can be criticized. It is the standpoint Cuomo says he himself used to formulate his own opinion concerning the "indisputable" responsibility human beings have to protect fetal life, a standpoint that was different from that of the judicial majority. The Constitution, he has said, must be viewed as embodying such a standpoint. The Constitution could not simply be what the Court says it is.

Cuomo's contention, nonetheless, is that the courts (including, when necessary, the state courts of New York[36]) have given him no choice on abortion. They have given the Constitution a radically pro-choice interpretation which he is not at liberty to oppose, either in word or deed. The bishops, consequently, are wrong to demand such criticism, because he, as a public official, cannot provide it. Anything he might say must presuppose the givenness of *Roe v. Wade*. This conclusion is at the foundation of his otherwise incomprehensible statement that "there is a perfect consistency between everything I believe privately and everything I am free to do publicly."[37]

Cuomo's acceptance of the givenness of the Court's giving of rights does not produce what he says prudence ought to produce, "a measured attempt to balance moral truth against political realities." It does not produce a position between "unyielding adherence" and "absolute prohibition."[38] It produces "unyielding adherence," an unreflective conservatism. It seems at this point to be unconstitutional, given *Roe v. Wade*, for *Cuomo* to create an antiabortion consensus. Apparently, Cuomo's position is different from the bishops', because public officials, unlike bishops, must accept, through their oath of office, the absolute authoritativeness of judicial interpretations of the Constitution.

Prudence, according to O'Connor and Regan, cannot justify Cuomo's silence, because silence implies agreement with the Court's thought that there is no reason for government to restrict abortion on demand, and hence all such restriction is an arbitrary violation of liberty.

Cuomo, it seems, regards this restriction on his judgment as "moral fundamentalism," but his practical conclusions seem more one-sided than those of the bishops. The bishops seem less fundamentalist or positivist because they have a greater faith in the authority of reason.

Cuomo's decision not to evaluate *Roe v. Wade* can be viewed as brilliant political strategy. It allows Catholics to believe that he must agree with the bishops on *Roe* in principle, although prudence prevents him from doing anything about that fact. It allows liberal Democrats to assume that he views the Court's opinion as basically sound. After all, if there is an argument that can appeal to all Americans for protecting fetal life on the basis of its humanity or potential humanity, then *Roe* cannot be sound. Consequently, liberals conclude that Cuomo does not accept such an argument, and that Cuomo's disagreement with most of them on the morality of abortion is merely personal. It has no political significance whatsoever, and it does not even suggest a criticism of their moral choices.[39] Is this an example of what McElvaine means when he says that the views of Cuomo and other liberals "coincide," although Cuomo makes much of reaching these views in a different, specifically religious way?

But it is almost surely unfair to reduce to political strategy Cuomo's decision to accept uncritically *Roe v. Wade*. The more persuasive explanation is his uncertainty concerning the status of his antiabortion morality. He sometimes seems not to be certain that it is "realistic" to affirm the humanity or potential humanity of the fetus. He says several times in his Notre Dame address that he holds his antiabortion principles "as a Catholic," and he calls them "our [Catholic] religious values."[40] The inference at these points may be that they *could* not become persuasive in a pluralistic society in which Catholics are in a minority.

Cuomo's account of the "realism" of antiabortion principles is inconsistent. He, in truth, sometimes agrees and sometimes disagrees with the bishops. When he disagrees with them, "realism" seems to come to mean caution rather than a common apprehension of the human good, and "prudence" comes to mean not effective action on behalf of moral principle affirmed by the "mind" of a rational creature, but simply uncritical conservatism or acceptance of the *status quo* because there is no real reason to oppose it (the prudence of a Burkean conservative).

Cuomo's uncertainty, he himself suggests, also stems from the fact that those with whom he agrees on most political issues do not accept his personal stand on abortion. His attempt to persuade them of its correctness for all human beings and its political relevance would inevitably offend them. It would be perceived by them to be morally degrading, and hence it would arouse their animosity. Cuomo, prudently, does not seem to want to disturb the harmony among liberal Democrats that seems indispensable for political success. Consequently, he does not want to appear to degrade anyone with a sincere attachment to the "progressive" vision of social justice. He suggests that antiabortion politics is suspect because it is the only thing that separates the bishops, politically, from their fellow liberals.[41]

In suggesting that an absence of consensus is the sign of a theoretical uncertainty that somehow justifies *Roe v. Wade*, Cuomo seems to be in agreement with part of the Court's opinion. The Court said that there is no "consensus" on when life begins. Consequently, it will not "speculate" concerning the question's answer "at this point in the development's of man's knowledge."[42] The absence of consensus, it appears, is taken as evidence that human beings do not know enough to answer that key question, and perhaps never will. The absence of consensus means none of the competing opinions is true, or more true than the others.

But the question is one that needs a public answer, and the Court could not help but give one, implicitly.[43] Its real thought was that the true answer must be one restrictive enough not to offend or impose upon anyone's sense of privacy or liberty, one that is not controversial in its limitation upon liberty. Hence the Court contends that no legislation can be constitutional that is based on the thought that human life exists before birth. The uncontroversial thought is that the postnatal offspring of human beings are to be accorded the protection government grants to human beings. (The Court was blissfully unaware of how controversial, especially among experts, even this thought is.[44])

ANTIABORTION MORALITY AS CATHOLIC APPEARANCE

Cuomo's silence on or even implicit affirmation of *Roe v. Wade* creates the impression, whether he intends it to or not, that antiabortion morality is an "appearance" to those with Catholic faith rather than a reality for human beings. For Catholics, then, abortion is wrong, but not for non-Catholics. Can one conclude, as a result of this line of thought, that the Catholic conviction should not limit the liberty of those who do not share the conviction? But it cannot be affirmed by Catholics, even if (as is clearly not true, after all) no non-Catholics shared their antiabortion conviction. If the fetus deserves protection, that fact does not disappear because the person acting against the fetus is doing so with no subjective perception of wrongdoing. The Catholic, with his or her conviction, would still have the responsibility, insofar as he or she is able, to provide such protection.

If there is no "realistic" argument against abortion that is compatible with the American Constitution, then Catholics cannot be good Americans without abandoning a fundamental conviction about the protection of life. It would be, in principle, impossible to be a good American and a good Catholic, and even more impossible to be a good liberal Democrat and a good Catholic. This line of thought, of course, is radically opposed to the one Cuomo promotes, and hence he seems actually to *need* a "realistic" and hence politically relevant argument against abortion to defend his religiously based principle of constitutional interpretation.

CUOMO'S OPPOSITION TO THE "NECESSITY" OF ABORTION

Cuomo does, to some extent, present himself as a proponent of public policy that discourages abortion. He does not oppose those who say that a woman should be able to choose abortion. He opposes abortion as a "necessity." Through redistributive social welfare programs providing food, clothing, jobs, education, Medicare, and child care for poor women, he would "reduce the incidence of abortion without coercing women."[45] He would have government do what is required to keep any woman from "being driven to abortion by a sense of helplessness and despair about the future of her child." Those who oppose abortion without supporting such policies, he says, do not "prove" their "regard for life in the womb."[46] They are hypocrites. By support of such policies, Mary Segers contends, Cuomo proves that he "does not embrace either a religious or political quietism on the subject" of abortion.[47]

Cuomo is, of course, partially right. It would be hypocritical, not to mention unrealistic, to restrict abortion legally without supporting, as much as possible, childbirth, child rearing, and adoption services for those in unfortunate circumstances. The bishops recognize this; they, to be pro-life consistently, agree with Cuomo's agenda of social welfare policies. Even allegedly Republican O'Connor joins his fellow bishops' firm support of liberal social welfare policies.[48]

But Cuomo is also misleading. His policies coincide with those of "secular" liberals, because they understand them as pro-choice or pro-personal liberty, and not at all antiabortion. Their view is that there is nothing human beings as human beings can know about abortion that makes it intrinsically wrong, that there is nothing "really" wrong with it. Abortion should occur not out of necessity, but out of choice. From this perspective, one does not point to a perfectly just society where abortion would no longer be a necessity and hence would no longer occur. Such a society would be an absolutely free-choice, unconstrained by any necessity, be it economic, social, or legal.

Whatever the effect of any social reform we can imagine, there will always be plenty of reasons for women to choose abortion if abortion itself is not viewed as intrinsically evil. Pregnancy and its natural results will always impose burdens of responsibilities. They will always involve pain and limitations on one's freedom. The question of abortion is less a matter of the necessity felt as a result of poverty than the necessity felt as a matter of duty, a duty which, if felt and thought about, extends beyond the fetus in one's own body to all fetuses. One's duty to protect life, for a reasonable being, extends beyond the lives of one's own children. The merely "personal" opposition to abortion produces an argument in agreement with the familial selfishness of the "peasant" religion Cuomo explicitly rejected in the name of reason.

THE "PRO-CHOICE" ARGUMENT

The "pro-choice" argument is best understood as one of the excesses of the "consumer society" Cuomo abhors. Its foundations are moral skepticism about intrinsically public questions of life and death and personal selfishness. It uses, in defending "reproductive freedom," arguments Reagan Republicans use in defending the excesses of unrestricted economic freedom.

Pro-choice thought is unbridled Lockean contractualism. It purges from the Constitution all of the "creationist" presuppositions that Cuomo says limit such selfishness.[49] A woman must consent before a child may be born from her body, and she may withhold her consent for any reason she chooses, including merely personal convenience. The mere existence of the fetus, despite its distinctive humanity (and the science of genetics has shown that the fetus, from its beginning, is distinctively human[50]), give it no rights, nothing that deserves protection, because a woman must consent before anyone or anything may use her body.

The thought that the fetus deserves, by its nature, protection, and that human beings, by their nature, love and feel duty-bound to protect their own, that they, as Cuomo is fond of saying often, feel compassion, especially, for the least or the most vulnerable among their own, is dismissed as controversial, because acknowledgement of its truth would allow the fetus to use the woman without her consent. It is only the absolute priority of rights to all human duties, a view which, contrary to Cuomo's more noble or inspiring interpretation, reduces the Constitution to a selfish compact that can justify the conclusion that all legal restrictions on abortion are unconstitutional.

If Cuomo agrees with the bishops on the moral evil of abortion, then he is simply wrong on the level of prudence. In accord with his general approach to his constitutional duties, and hence on behalf of his moral and political integrity, he should speak against the Court's decision in *Roe v. Wade* and attempt to persuade his fellow citizens that the law should at least restrict abortion. If he were to do so, his claim to oppose the permissive excesses of both oligarchs and intellectuals (or "liberal activists") would be more credible, as he would join the bishops in attempting to base such opposition on being consistently pro-life. He would show that he can truly distinguish his political position from that of other liberals, that he does have a greater respect for the sense of moral and political responsibility, the "common sense" which forms the American political community.

NOTES

1. Mario Cuomo, Keynote Address, *Vital Speeches of the Day*, 50 (August 15, 1984), p. 648.

2. Richard John Neuhaus, "Nihilism without the Abyss," *The Journal of Law and Religion*, 5 (1987), p. 55.

3. Bishop Malone, as quoted in "Sorry Mario," *Crisis*, 4 (May 1986), p. 3.

4. Mario Cuomo, "Religious Belief and Public Morality" [Address delivered at Notre Dame], *The New York Review of Books* (October 25, 1984), p. 34.

5. Robert S. McElvaine, *Mario Cuomo: A Biography* (New York: Scribner's, 1988), pp. 88–89.

6. Cuomo, Speech at Sunday Service, St. John the Divine (November 27, 1983) in *The Diaries of Mario M. Cuomo* (New York: Random House, 1984), p. 464.

7. McElvaine, p. 89.

8. See the reference to the "consumer society" near the beginning of Cuomo, "Religious Belief," p. 32.

9. This summary is based upon impressions gathered from the reading of McElvaine's biography and Cuomo's *Diaries*.

10. Cuomo, "Religious Belief," p. 32.

11. McElvaine, pp. 395–396.

12. Cuomo, Speech at St. John the Divine, p. 466.

13. Ibid., pp. 466–467.

14. Ibid., p. 466.

15. See Maria Laurino, "Mario, Italian Style," *The Village Voice*, 33 (May 3, 1988), pp. 22–29, with her references to the work of Edward Banfield, Nathan Glazer, and Daniel Patrick Moynihan.

16. See Kenneth Wald, *Religion and Politics in the United States* (New York: St. Martin's Press, 1987), p. 37, with my "Natural Law and the American Regime," *Communio* 9 (Winter 1982), pp. 366–388.

17. Cuomo, Speech at St. John the Divine, p. 467.

18. Timothy Byrnes, "Politics '88: What Role for the Bishops?" *Crisis*, 6 (March 1988), p. 36.

19. See Michael Novak, "Giving Consistency a Bad Name," *Crisis*, 6 (April 1988), pp. 4–5.

20. Cuomo, "Religious Belief," p. 33.

21. Ibid., p. 34.

22. Ibid.

23. John J. O'Connor, "Human Lives, Human Rights," *The Human Life Review*, 11 (Winter/Spring 1985), pp. 50–51.

24. Richard J. Regan, *The Moral Dimensions of Politics* (New York: Oxford University Press, 1986), pp. 101–103.

25. Ibid., p. 103.

26. Cuomo, "Religious Belief," p. 32.

27. Ibid., p. 33.

28. Ibid., p. 32.

29. Ibid. See also Cuomo's article on the bishops' economic letter, tellingly titled "Toward a Consensus," *America*, 152 (January 12, 1985), pp. 9–11.

30. Cuomo, "Religious Belief," p. 35.

31. See R. W. Apple, "The Question of Mario Cuomo," *The New York Times Magazine* (September 14, 1986), p. 50.

32. Cuomo, "Religious Belief," p. 34. Emphasis added.

33. See John Argesto, *The Supreme Court and Constitutional Democracy* (Ithaca: Cornell University Press, 1984), pp. 102–107.

34. Ibid., pp. 89–95.

35. See Kenneth Holland, "Roger Taney," *American Political Thought: The Philosophic Dimension of American Statesmanship* (Itasca, Ill.: F. C. Peacock Publishers, 1983), p. 170.

36. See p. 34, where Cuomo says, in effect, that the courts of New York have been more consistent in deducing the implications of *Roe v. Wade* than the United States Supreme Court. The former has struck down, but the latter has upheld the legislative denial of public funding for abortion.

37. Cuomo, *Diaries*, p. 17.

38. Ibid., p. 34.

39. See Nat Hentoff, *John Cardinal O'Connor* (New York: Macmillan, 1988), p. 149.

40. Cuomo, "Religious Belief," pp. 32–33.

41. See Cuomo, ibid., p. 34.

42. *Roe v. Wade* 410 U.S. 113.

43. For a persuasive criticism of the Court's contention that it is avoiding this question, see William Mathie, "Reason, Revelation, and Liberal Justice: Reflections on George Grant's Analysis of *Roe v. Wade*," *Canadian Journal of Political Science*, 19 (September 1986), pp. 456–459.

44. Some contemporary thinkers, deducing the consequences of the "pro-choice" argument, have no problem finding postnatal cases in which human beings are to be denied personhood and hence legal protection. See the sources cited by Mathie on p. 460.

45. Mary C. Segers, "Religious Conviction and Political Choice," *New Catholic World* (July/August 1988), p. 160.

46. Cuomo, "Religious Belief," p. 35.

47. Segers, p. 160.

48. See Hentoff, *passim*.

49. See George Grant, *Technology and Justice* (Notre Dame, Ind.: University of Notre Dame Press, 1896), pp. 117–130 and Neuhaus, "Nihilism," pp. 56–57.

50. Consider Grant, p. 120: "The fetus is a living member of our species. It is a fact, accepted by all scientists, that the individual has his or her unique genetic code from the moment of conception. He or she is therefore not simply part of the mother's body."

PART III

THE POLITICS OF SEXUALITY AND REPRODUCTION

The essays in this section focus on issues of sexuality and reproduction, one of the major areas of modern life in which Catholic teaching is openly countercultural. These essays describe the concerns of American Catholics about the morality and legality of contraception and abortion, the ethical implications of new reproductive technologies, and the tensions between church teachings on sexuality and institutional recognition of the civil rights of homosexuals. Patrick Allitt describes how Catholic conservative intellectuals associated with *National Review* magazine fought the permissiveness associated with the sexual revolution and cultural liberalism of the 1960s and 1970s. In voicing Catholic moral perspectives on abortion and homosexuality, these Cold War conservatives argued that the defense of American capitalism and the security of the West were closely connected with the preservation of monogamy and the nuclear family. They thus anticipated many arguments of fundamentalists, conservative evangelicals, and Reagan conservatives in the 1980s.

Through the first half of the twentieth century, American family law reflected Catholic teaching on sexuality regarding the impermissibility of contraception and abortion. However, the U.S. Supreme Court in *Griswold v. Connecticut* (1965) invalidated anticontraception statutes, and in *Roe v. Wade* (1973) discovered a constitutional right to abortion. Mary C. Segers compares the U.S. Catholic bishops' accommodation to legalized birth control in the 1960s with their militant opposition to legalized abortion in the 1970s and 1980s. Jo Renee Formicola offers a case study of the efforts of one Catholic institution—Georgetown University—to comply with antidiscrimination and civil rights laws without appearing to endorse sexual behavior the church regards as immoral. Thomas A. Shannon discusses Catholics teaching on the new reproductive technologies and finds an unlikely congruence between the opposition by some U.S. bishops to surrogate motherhood and the critique of surrogacy made by many prominent feminists.

CHAPTER X

CATHOLIC CONSERVATIVE INTELLECTUALS AND THE POLITICS OF SEXUALITY: 1950–1980

Patrick Allitt

William F. Buckley, Jr., founded *National Review* magazine in 1955. He designed it as a forum for American conservative intellectuals seeking political influence on the right to match the liberal influence of *The New Republic* or *The Nation*. The central concerns of *National Review* were resistance to communism abroad, and resistance to liberalism at home. Buckley, a Catholic layman, argued from the Catholic natural law tradition against what he saw as the characteristic relativism of liberal thought. Although *National Review* was not a Catholic journal in the sense of seeking Church approval for its editorial posture, many of its contributors were Catholic laymen, and Catholic issues usually won a sympathetic hearing in its pages. Moreover, a succession of *National Review* editors and contributors *converted* to Catholicism: Willmoore Kendall, Russell Kirk, Frank Meyer, Brent

Bozell, and Jeffrey Hart. Even those who were not Catholics, such as the journal's first religion editor, Will Herberg, made declarations of their admiration for Catholicism, saying that they saw in the Church the strongest bastion of anti-communist principle in the West.[1]

In the 1960's this group of conservatives and cold warriors confronted the sexual revolution and the legal and political disputes which came in its wake. Some of these disputes, particularly those surrounding abortion and homosexuality, affronted Catholic and conservative principles so directly that by the mid–1970s the clinic and the bedroom had become as important as the Berlin Wall and the floor of Congress in the conservatives' fight against their adversaries. These Catholic conservatives argued, in opposing the sexual revolution, that the defense of American capitalism and national security were connected with the preservation of monogamy and the family.

THE SEXUAL REVOLUTION AND THE CATHOLIC CONSERVATIVE RESPONSE

The term "sexual revolution" developed popular currency in the early 1960s. It designated a series of changes in Americans' sexual behavior and sexual morality. The Kinsey Institute phrased its reports on male and female sexuality (1948/1953) in value-neutral language, and presented them as scientific studies of human behavior. They reported high levels of premarital and extramarital sexual intercourse among both men and women, and documented the frequency with which, at differing times of their lives, individuals of both sexes were homosexually active. During the 1950s and 1960s, a popular Freudianism encouraged the view that sexual repression was potentially a source of mental illness; sex therapy boomed. Kinsey, Masters and Johnson, and their cohorts studied the affective and expressive aspects of sex more than its reproductive function. *Playboy* magazine, founded in 1953, challenged American sexual conventions in the name of its ideal modern liberated man. Journalists noted a weakening in the tradition of premarital celibacy among women. Many women, by 1960, regarded premarital sexual experience as no impediment to their dignity or marriageability.[2]

The development of dependable female contraceptives in the late 1950s (the anovulent pill and the intra-uterine device) facilitated this attitude in favor of a sexuality separable from both procreation and marriage. It is unlikely that these technological innovations actually *caused* the "sexual revolution": deeper cultural forces were at work with which these technologies coincided. While avoiding any technological determinism, it is at least worth echoing one journalist's remark that "without birth control, the very idea of a married woman's entitlement to full sexual pleasure, not to mention that of a young woman's freedom to pursue sex outside of marriage, would be an idle and rather bitter joke." Many American Catholics disliked these changes in sexual attitudes and activities, which conflicted with the principles of Catholic moral theology.[3]

Pope Pius XI wrote the encyclical letter, *Casti Connubii*, in 1930. It described contraception as "an offense against the law of God and of nature" and those who employed it as covered with "the guilt of a grave sin." Abstinence from sexual intercourse was the only method of contraception the Church would countenance; each sexual act had to be open to the transmission of new life. In the 1920s, studies of the female menstrual cycle had established the existence of fertile and infertile periods each month, on the basis of which various systems of "natural family planning" were developed. The logic of the Catholic position would have been to deny the legitimacy of these methods, if they were used to forestall conception. But Pope Pius XII, in an allocution to Italian midwives in 1951, signalled his approval of the "rhythm method." This concession was a foot in the door for Catholic advocates of contraception; if human ingenuity could be used to prevent conception with the aid of thermometers, charts and mucus tests, why not with the pill? Herein lay the origin of bitter intra-Catholic disputes in the 1960s, 1970s and 1980s.[4]

American law and Catholic teaching on sex coincided through the early part of the twentieth century. Some states prohibited the sale and use of contraceptives, every state had antiabortion laws, homosexual intercourse was a criminal offense, and the family enjoyed special privileges at law. In the 1960s and 1970s, however, legislation and Supreme Court findings brought to a close the era in which Catholic moral teaching coincided with American law relating to sex. The Supreme Court, in *Griswold v. Connecticut* (1965), invalidated anti-contraception statutes, and in *Roe v. Wade* (1973) discovered a constitutional right to abortion. The Gay Liberation movement of the 1970s rolled back many of the sanctions imposed on homosexuals, while courts and legislators increasingly accorded rights to individuals in themselves rather than as family members. Justice Brennan, invoking the notion of a constitutional right to privacy in *Eisenstadt v. Baird* (1972), wrote: "If the right of privacy means anything, it is the right of the *individual*, married or single, to be free from unwarranted governmental intrusion into matters so fundamentally affecting a person as the decision whether to bear or beget a child." Catholic conservatives were dismayed by this emphasis on the individual *per se* rather than his or her family status, especially with regard to such issues as teenage girls' access to contraceptives.[5]

Catholic opposition to these trends developed gradually during the 1960s. As laity, William Buckley and many of his collaborators favored the use of artificial contraceptives within marriage, and expected Pope Paul VI's pontifical commission to rule in their favor. They shared with liberal Catholics the view that a celibate clergy might not be the best judge of their difficulties in raising large families. Buckley told an interviewer in 1969, "I tend to the conclusion that it is not an obvious violation of the marital ideal to permit contraception . . . I would consent, subject to prior consent by the Church, in any collective endeavor to suggest means by which the size of a family can be regulated by couples who desire to do so." A majority of the American Catholic laity, liberal and conservative alike, had similar hopes by the mid–1960s. Michael Novak, a Catholic advocate of contraception, was careful to emphasize that their use would *strengthen* the marriage bond, first by enabling Catholic couples to give birth only to so many children as they could afford to nurture and educate, and second by affording them an anxiety-free expression of their love. When Pope Paul VI overruled the majority report of his pontifical commission, and upheld the ban against artificial contraception in 1968, *National Review* shared the view of many Catholic publications when it editorialized that his encyclical, *Humanae Vitae*, would not win acclaim or assent from the world's Catholic people.[6]

One of the intellectual preoccupations of the mid-1960s was the "population explosion." Paul Ehrlich argued in *The Population Bomb* that the world's population was catastrophically inflated, and that only drastic measures could restore ecological stability. Ehrlich's strictures applied as much to America as to China and India. He and many other participants in the population debate took it for granted that both contraception and abortion would be necessary tools for population restriction. They argued not about whether to use these devices but about the degree to which governments could use them coercively. These experts argued that population pressure against resources was so grave that contraception and abortion were the ethically benign alternatives to mass starvation. They treated the large Catholic family, by contrast, as an example of heedless folly.[7]

In 1965, the editors of *National Review* ran a special edition on the population explosion, in which they too took current predictions of calamity seriously and discussed measures to control it, including contraception and abortion. In view of subsequent developments, its emphases are surprising. It included an article by the President of the Planned Parenthood Federation (PPF), Alan Guttmacher. In the 1970s, Guttmacher became an arch-villain of the antiabortion movement when he reversed the traditional antiabortion policy of the PPF. In his book on the development of prenatal life, written in 1952, Guttmacher wrote that as soon as conception took place, the life of a new baby had begun. In his re-issue of the book in 1973, when PPF had adopted a pro-abortion position, he deleted this section. Antiabortion conservatives accused him of acting in bad faith, trying to veil the fact that he was knowingly advocating the killing of children. It would have been unthinkable to welcome Guttmacher to *National Review* after 1973 but in 1965 he was introduced respectfully as an expert on population.

A few months later, a *National Review* column by Buckley argued that Catholics should not oppose the current movement to liberalize abortion laws. The gravamen of the declarations of the Second Vatican Council (1962–1965), he said, was to let the holders of different religious convictions make up their own minds on such questions. Besides, population pressures were such that abortion might indeed be a necessary option for the contemporary world.

> Surely the principal meaning of the religious liberty pronouncements of Vatican II is that other men must be left free to practice the dictates of their own consciences, and if other religions and other individuals do not believe that under certain circumstances abortion is wrong, it would appear to contradict the burden of the Vatican's position to put pressure on the law to maintain the supremacy of one's own position . . . Some Catholics may understand themselves to be pleading as defenders of the rights of unborn children of whatever faith, and the stand is honorable, but not viable: and the means by which the case is pleaded must be suasive rather than coercive.

In light of his later advocacy of the antiabortion position, Buckley's 1965 position is surprising, but not inexplicable. He was one of the first Catholic intellectuals in America to break out of the "Catholic ghetto" which had enclosed his co-religionists since the nineteenth century. Buckley's primary concern was to create a viable political conservatism in America, not to fight for the particulars of Catholic moral theology. At that time, besides, proposed abortion law reforms were incremental; in 1965 few voices were claiming abortion as a *right*.[8]

In the later 1960s, the new feminism first gained public notice. Some American feminists made the claim that women should have unqualified sovereignty over their bodies, and they began to interpret laws restricting abortion as examples of male oppression. Those who saw the issue in this light campaigned for a woman's right to choose abortion without the involvement of the doctor, the state, or even the father of a prospective child. To the extent that conservatives and feminists alike criticized sexual promiscuity and pornography, they had common objectives, but Catholic conservatives would never accept the rhetoric of women's autonomy or the feminist endorsement of abortion.[9]

As feminists and "populationists" lobbied for abortion law reform in the late 1960s and early 1970s, Catholics became increasingly alarmed, and lines for and against abortion began to harden. Many lay people had hoped for Church approval of contraceptives, but they drew the line at abortion. Effective contraception prevented the creation of new lives, they said, but abortion was the killing of new lives. In 1970 *National Review* changed its mind about the population explosion. The journal now saw it, at least with regard to the United States, as an intellectual fad, unjustified empirically and deployed cynically by the champions of abortion law reform, whose real interests lay in gaining a woman's right to discretionary abortions.[10]

The first stirrings of the abortion reform movement led to tensions not only between American conservatives and their liberal opponents, it also precipitated a split within the ranks of Catholic conservatives. L. Brent Bozell, Buckley's old Yale debating partner, who had converted to Catholicism in the early 1950's and was now a stout defender of the Church, criticized Buckley's early laissez-faire attitude towards abortion reform. With a group of Catholic loyalists who had also worked for *National Review*, Frederick Wilhelmsen, Michael Lawrence, Charles Rice and others, Bozell founded a new journal, *Triumph*, in 1966, which celebrated Catholic orthodoxy in all matters. Rice warned Buckley's group that they had erred in supporting contraception reform. Such reforms, said Rice, were based on the fallacy that the generation of new life is under human rather than divine control. Accordingly, a woman who used contraceptives, finding herself pregnant "by accident," would be disposed to seek an abortion because she had not intended to become pregnant in the first place. *Triumph* contributors did not believe that sex and procreation were separable. The editors of *Triumph* and a group of their supporters, decked out in the regalia of Spanish Carlists and calling themselves "The Sons of Thunder," were arrested in 1970 for damaging property and scuffling with police while demonstrating at a Washington, D.C., abortion clinic. *National Review* denigrated the *Triumph* "action" as likely to do more harm than good, whatever the merits of the antiabortion position.[11]

The Supreme Court decision in *Roe v. Wade* was the catalyzing event for all parties in the abortion controversy. This decision overturned abortion laws in all fifty states, and gave pregnant women the right to choose abortion in their first trimester on grounds of privacy (with limited restrictions thereafter). *National Review* criticized the decision as bad law, bad social policy, and an abuse of the constitution. A month later James McFadden established the Ad Hoc Committee in Defense of Life to lobby congressmen for legislative redress. McFadden then gathered a large group of donors and activists, launched the Human Life Foundation, and began publication of the *Human Life Review* in 1975. McFadden was a Catholic layman, a political conservative, and an anti-communist. He had worked as associate editor of *National Review* since 1956, and the offices of his new journal were in the same New York building as *National Review* itself. Then and subsequently, the two journals had many contributors in common. Like *National Review*, the *Human Life Review* was not an explicitly Catholic publication, but the influence of Catholicism on it was profound. James McFadden shared Charles Rice's view that contraception and abortion should be seen as parts of a continuum:

> When you use contraception, you willingly deny the gift of children from God. That sounds theological but I'm making a psychological case . . . you have devalued the gift . . . Once you have said that to yourself, then find you are pregnant, it is the classic case of feeling that it's not your fault. When you have the abortion, you didn't *want* to have that either. You are not willing it in the sense of *wanting* to sin . . . Contraception is the John the Baptist to the Antichrist of abortion.[12]

Mindful of the American separation of church and state, however, which a succession of Supreme Court decisions in the 1960s had widened, Catholic antiabortion intellectuals emphasized that they protested against *Roe v. Wade* not solely on religious grounds but *as citizens*. A nation which permits the killing of children at their most vulnerable moment, they argued, will not long preserve the reverence for life upon which civil society depends. Protestants, Jews, and secularists, they added, had every reason to share their concern both on empirical grounds and on the basis of a commitment to human rights.[13]

Catholic conservatives opposed abortion because they believed that human life starts at the moment of conception. Human life from the moment of conception is a scientific fact, not a religious belief, they said—a fact rendered increasingly clear by recent advances in embryology. They struck hard against the view that the question of when life begins is metaphysical rather than scientific, or that pregnant women should be allowed to choose whether or not to give birth to a baby. As John Noonan put it for the antiabortion position, the moment of conception is the most certain place for establishing an objective discontinuity between mere biological tissue and a distinct human life. From that moment forward a distinct human being is fully genetically encoded and needs no further genetic enhancement to grow to adulthood.[14]

John Noonan, legal scholar and antiabortion activist, offered a potent historical analogy by describing *Roe v. Wade* as his generation's *Dred Scott* case. In *Dred Scott v. Sanford* (1857), the Supreme Court took upon itself the right to decide who was and who was not fully human. Like the slaves victimized by *Dred Scott*, said Noonan, the unborn were now being denied their fundamental human rights by the twisted interpretation of a constitutional principle. Moreover, if taxpayers' money funded Medicaid abortions for poor women, an analogy with the 1850 fugitive slave law would also apply. Just as anti-slavery Northerners were obliged to connive at the re-enslavement of fugitives against their principles, so now anti-abortion taxpayers would have to subsidize what they considered to be the killing of children.[15]

The *Human Life Review* was preoccupied with the abortion controversy at first, but its interests broadened over the next decade to include other issues of bioethics: euthanasia, surrogacy, in vitro fertilization, as well as family policy, pornography, homosexuality and AIDS. It acted as the cynosure of the antiabortion political struggle, carrying legal analyses of the Supreme Court's abortion cases, drafts and discussions of Constitutional Amendments, and reports of progress or reversals in Washington. Speeches and papers by Congressman Henry Hyde of Illinois, Surgeon General Everett Koop, Judge Robert Bork and other public figures, were published alongside the arguments of conservative Catholic jurists, John Noonan, Robert Destro and Basile Uddo.

THE NATURE OF SEX

Catholic conservatives and their adversaries meant different things when they used the word "sex." For Catholic conservatives, the family rather than the individual was the basic unit of society. The particular circumstances in which an act of sexual intercourse took place, therefore, had a profound bearing upon its nature, depending on whether it strengthened or violated the familial bond. Intercourse between a husband and wife must be conceived in a way quite differently from intercourse between any other two persons. The animal function might be the same but the natural law context was quite different. Catholic conservatives accorded sexual intercourse a sacramental significance as the most binding component of marriage. Michael Novak described this sacrament in a characteristic passage:

> the human body is a dwelling place of God, and the joining of a man's and a woman's body in matrimony is a privileged form of union with God. The relationship is not merely that of a mechanical linking, putting genitals here or there. It is a metaphor for (and an enactment of) God's union with mankind. Marital intercourse thus re-enacts the basic act of creation. It celebrates the future.

Sex for pleasure outside of marriage violated this sacramental union and perverted a divine gift. It violated the natural law orientation of sex towards procreation and violated the natural law ordinance of marriage.[16]

Homosexuality, in the eyes of Catholic conservatives, represented an even more serious deviation from the natural law. Joseph Sobran, a polemicist for the *Human Life Review,* noted: "The use of the word 'sex' to refer to an activity rather than to a gender is, I believe, fairly novel. It is even used to refer to genital activities between members of the same gender. This implies the conception of such activities as ends in themselves, with procreation a mere possible by-product." In other words, homosexual acts might not warrant the name of sex at all. The relational aspect of intercourse, rather than the action itself, determined its meaning: it was primarily a spiritual rather than a bodily event. Catholic conservatives differed as to whether criminal sanctions should be retained on homosexual acts between consenting adults, but they agreed that such acts should be made socially odious. Sobran, arguing against the granting of rights to homosexuals, noted: "The full legalization of homosexuality will have results that are hard to foresee while our ears are being dinned with slogans about 'dignity.' It would, for instance, rule out considering homosexuality as even a *possible* disqualification for adoptive parenthood."[17]

Catholic conservatives sustained a theory of the origin of homosexuality which, by the 1970s, was losing favor among American doctors; namely, that it was a psychological disorder, a form of infantile regression. Homosexuality, insofar as it was an involuntary condition, should be regarded with sympathy, they admitted. But at the same time, individuals should be counseled to resist the temptation to act upon their homosexual inclinations:

> It would be a victory of humanity to undo the damage of the gay rights movement by persuading its members, without humiliating them, that they need not pretend that their vice is a virtue in order to belong to the moral community. To put it another way, homosexuals should be encouraged to realize that homosexuality is unworthy of them.

Catholic conservatives also pointed to a paradox in the development of the rhetoric of the gay movement. If the condition of homosexuality was innate, why did advocates of gay liberation describe it as a "lifestyle" or a "choice" rather than as a destiny?[18]

CATHOLIC CONSERVATIVE WOMEN

Catholic women writers as well as men played an active role in the conservative antiabortion movement. Clare Boothe Luce was the first person to write a major article on abortion for *National Review*, in 1971. For Luce, another of the many Catholic converts in the conservative movement, resistance to abortion was the genuine feminist position, because it fulfilled the woman's natural law function of child bearing. Her thoughts on the issue, like Buckley's, did not solidify until after *Roe v. Wade*, and at the beginning of the 1970s she could still sympathize with women electing abortion in hard cases. Luce criticized abortion books by John Noonan and Daniel Callahan when they neglected women's experience. "Like so many of the books which learned men have written about "women's problems," this is really a book about the problem men are having with other men who refuse to see the "woman's problem" as they do . . . not a single woman lawyer or moralist is quoted on a subject which is a uniquely female experience."[19]

Luce did not expand on this feminist discernment in the years following *Roe v. Wade.* Making a united stand against abortion was, for her, more important than criticizing gender bias within the debate. She withdrew her support for the Equal Rights Amendment (ERA) when its leading advocates argued in favor of abortion, even though she had actively supported the Amendment for fifty years. "If the ERA fails to pass, as I now fear it will," she wrote in 1978, "a large part of the blame must fall on those misguided feminists who have tried to make the extraneous issue of unrestricted and federally-funded abortions the centerpiece of the Equal Rights Struggle." The "Natural Law (and the Divine Law) is the rock" on which the American Constitution was founded, said Luce, and an ERA in violation of that law was doomed.

> Nature made man to be the inseminator, woman to be the childbearer . . . It is natural—and normal—for the woman who conceives to carry her child in her womb to term, to give birth to her, and her mate's baby . . . It is not the nature of women to abort their progeny . . . Induced abortions are against the nature of woman.[20]

Ellen Wilson, Juliana Peron, and Janet Smith, three other women who contributed to The *Human Life Review*, shared Luce's views, that *by nature*, childbearing was a woman's highest calling, and that the moral instinct to protect the unborn child was innate. Feminism, they said, did women a disservice by denigrating the dignity of a woman's role as wife and mother. Janet Smith argued, in 1978, that childbirth had never been safer, the demand for children to adopt had never been greater, and that only an ideological aversion to motherhood could have motivated the feminist advocates of abortion:

> Behind women's demands for unlimited access to abortion lies a profound displeasure with the way in which a woman's body works and hence a rejection of the value of being a woman. Whereas one might hope that the women's movement would be based on the assertion that it is great to be a woman, and that women would endeavor to promote the powers and qualities which are theirs, the popularity of abortion indicates quite the opposite. Abortion is a denigration of a woman, a denial of one of the defining features of being a woman.[21]

There is no necessary consonance between a conservative political posture and opposition to abortion. A majority of all American Catholics followed Church teaching by taking the antiabortion position; Peter Steinfels, editor of the liberal Catholic journal, *Commonweal*, was a case in point. Catholic antiabortion conservatives believed, nevertheless, that adherence to the natural law prompted conservative convictions on other issues, and that those who violated the natural law by appealing for abortion or gay rights were prone to radicalism in other respects. Ellen Wilson made the connection explicitly:

> Homosexuals cannot propagate by means of homosexual liaisons; since homosexual unions are barren, in the literal sense, they are antithetical to family life. Thus militant homosexuals are spared the strong, sentimental attachment toward the family which poses a hurdle of greater or lesser proportions to many social revolutionaries. In other words, homosexuals who campaign for universal acknowledgment of their normality are likely to be social revolutionaries in all areas, since their definition of normality dethrones the family from its sovereign position as the foundation of society.[22]

CONCLUSION

Catholic conservatives hoped for a sexual counter-revolution when President Reagan was elected in 1980. They anticipated a pattern of "pro-family" legislation, an antiabortion constitutional amendment, and a stronger traditionalist representation on the federal bench. Evangelical Protestant groups during the 1970s had entered electoral politics in a more co-ordinated way than hitherto; in defending religion and the family, Catholics and Evangelicals shared a pattern of interests and objectives. In any event, the Reagan presidency disappointed both groups. The American conservative movement championed not only traditional values, but also free-market capitalism, and the "Reagan Revolution" was, in practice, largely an economic phenomenon. Workable family policies would have necessitated new bureaucracies—one of the targets of the Reagan electoral campaign—and seemed likely to prove costly and unworkable.[23]

Catholic conservative intellectuals made an energetic case against the sexual license of their age, against homosexuality and against abortion, but were unable to translate their ideas into policy. The tensions within the conservative movement account for some of their disappointments, tensions within the Catholic Church account for others. The case against homosexuality and abortion rested on arguments from the natural law, but Buckley, Novak, Noonan and other Catholic conservatives argued *against* the traditional natural law teaching as it applied to contraception. In so doing they showed the natural law to be a protean conception rather than an unmoving rock of assurance; the natural law had to be *decided*, not simply discovered. They did not show earlier generations' habitual deference to Church guidance. American Catholic unity was shattered in the 1960s over the questions of Vatican II reforms, the vernacular, contraception, and discipline. The Church, indeed, suffered an authority crisis; radical Catholic groups mounted many more dramatic challenges to the tradition than these conservatives. Where once the American Catholic Church had been able to hold a negative veto over such matters as access to contraceptives and film censorship, it now lost its ability to do so.[24]

The Church, which might have been a strong point of resistance to the sexual revolution in matters of law, was too internally divided by the mid-1960s to mount a concerted opposition. Even in its more unified resistance to abortion after 1973 the Church had little impact on legal and political developments. Catholic conservatives and their Evangelical allies could not reverse the sexual revolution during the Reagan administration, but there is every prospect that the issues raised by this revolution will continue to generate political controversy. The ultimacy of sex, raising questions of the origin of human life, the structure of a healthy society, and the spiritual superiority of America over its adversaries, are comparable to the ultimate issues raised, in the nineteenth century, by the question of slavery.

NOTES

1. George Nash, *The Conservative Intellectual Movement in America: Since 1945* (New York: Basic Books, 1976). Patrick Allitt, *Catholic Lay*

Intellectuals in the American Conservative Movement: 1950-80 (Berkeley, CA: Doctoral Dissertation, 1986).

2. Alfred C. Kinsey et al., *Sexual Behavior in the Human Male* (Philadelphia: W. B. Saunders, 1948); Alfred C. Kinsey et al., *Sexual Behavior in the Human Female* (Philadelphia: W. B. Saunders, 1953); William H. Masters and Virginia Johnson, *Human Sexual Response* (Boston: Little Brown, 1966). On *Playboy* see Barbara Ehrenreich, *The Hearts of Men: American Dreams and the Flight From Commitment* (Garden City, New York: Anchor Doubleday, 1983).

3. On the pill see Loretta McLaughlin, *The Pill, John Rock and the Church: The Biography of a Revolution* (Boston: Little Brown, 1982). Quotation is from Midge Decter, *The New Chastity and Other Arguments Against Women's Liberation* (New York: Coward, McCann and Geohegan, 1972), p. 145.

4. Robert Kaiser, *The Politics of Sex and Religion: A Case History in the Development of Doctrine* (Kansas City, MO: Leaven Press, 1985), Introduction.

5. On abortion, John T. Noonan, Jr., *A Private Choice: Abortion in America* (New York: Free Press, 1979). On Gay Liberation, John D'Emilio, *Sexual Politics, Sexual Communities: The Making of a Homosexual Minority in the United States, 1940-70* (Chicago: University of Chicago Press, 1983). The *Eisenstadt* finding is cited in Rosalind P., Petchesky, *Abortion and Woman's Choice: The State, Sexuality and Reproductive Freedom* (Boston: Northeastern University Press, 1984), p. 290.

6. On Catholic hopes for a new teaching on contraception see Michael Novak, *The Experience of Marriage* (New York: Macmillan, 1964); John Noonan *Contraception: A History of its Treatment by the Catholic Theologians and Canonists* (Cambridge, Ma: Belknap Press of Harvard University, 1965). John Noonan was a member of the pontifical commission. For *NR* on *Humanae Vitae*, see "The Encyclical," *NR*, August 13, 1968, p. 786. Buckley quotation is from Robert Campbell ed., *Spectrum of Catholic Attitudes* (Milwaukee: Bruce Publishing, 1969), p. 101.

7. Paul Ehrlich, *The Population Bomb* (New York: Ballantine, 1968). See also Daniel Callahan, ed., *The American Population Debate* (Garden City, New York: Doubleday, 1971).

8. Special report "The Population Explosion," *NR*, July 27,1965. For Catholic conservative attacks on Guttmacher in the 1970s, see John Noonan, *A Private Choice*, p. 37; Germain Grisez, *Abortion: The Myths, The Realities and the Arguments* (New York: Corpus, 1970). William F. Buckley, Jr., "The Catholic Church and Abortion," *NR* April 5, 1966, p.308.

9. Sheila Rothman, *Woman's Proper Place: A History of Changing Ideals and Practices, 1870 to the Present* (New York: Basic, 1978), Chapter 7, "Liberation Politics"; Kristin Luker, *Abortion and the Politics of Motherhood* (Berkeley: University of California Press, 1984), Chapter 5, "Women and the Right to Abortion."

10. For *National Review* refutation of population explosion theory, see Colin Clark, "World Power and Population," *NR*, May 20, 1969, p. 481; editorial "The Population Firecracker," *NR*, Oct 7, 1969, p. 999: ("More nonsense is currently being talked on the subject of population than on any other subject that comes to mind.") For Buckley's changed position by 1970, see "Catholics and Abortion," *NR*, Dec 15, 1970, p. 1366.

11. Brent Bozell's letter, *NR*, May 3, 1966, p. 390. Charles Rice, "Government and the Copulation Explosion," *Triumph*, March 1969, p. 16. See also Charles Rice, *The Vanishing Right to Live: An Appeal for a Renewed Reverence for Life* (Garden City, New York: Doubleday, 1969). For the "Sons of Thunder" demonstration, *Triumph*, June, 1970, pp. 7,11. For *National Review* strictures, "Abortion," *NR*, June 30, 1970, p. 658.

12. "The Continuing Battle Over Abortion," *NR Bulletin*, Feb 9, 1973, p. B12. Personal interview with J. P. McFadden, Oct 12, 1987, New York City.

13. Joseph Sobran, "Abortion, Rhetoric and Cultural War," *Human Life Review* (hereafter *HLR*) Vol. 1, No. 1 (Winter 1975), Joseph Sobran, "Abortion and the Right to Speak," *HLR*, Vol. 1, No. 3 (Summer 1975).

14. John Noonan, "An Almost Absolute Value in History," Chapter 1 of John Noonan, ed., *The Morality of Abortion* (Cambridge, MA: Harvard University Press, 1970). Joseph Sobran, "Roe and Doe: Six Years After," *HLR*, Vol. 5, No. 1 (Winter 1979), p. 10.

15. John Noonan, *A Private Choice*, pp. 80–83.

16. Michael Novak, "Men Without Women," *Human Life Review* Vol 5, No. 1 (Winter 1979), p. 64. Novak was a Catholic radical in the 1960s but became sympathetic with conservatism in politics and religion during the 1970s. See his *Confession of a Catholic* (San Francisco: Harper and Row, 1983).

17. Joseph Sobran, "In Loco Parentis," *Human Life Review*, Vol. 5, No. 4 (Fall, 1979), p. 14. For conservative debate on decriminalization of homosexuality, see *NR* July 19, 1974. When the New York legislature debated a "gay rights bill" in 1974, *National Review* editorialized against it as an attack on the moral integrity of the Western tradition. It noted that the language of the New York bill, "reflecting the avowed goals of various 'gay liberation' organizations, would make homosexuality merely another life-style in the eyes of the law, and would both break down social resistance to it and stigmatize such resistance as 'bigotry.'" Editorial, "Gay Rights," *NR*, June 7, 1974, p. 635. See also Ernest Van Den Haag, "Reflections on Gay Rights," *NR*, July 19, 1974, pp. 802–803.

18. Joseph Sobran, "Bogus Sex: Reflections on Homosexual Claims," *HLR* Vol. 3, No. 4 (Fall 1977), p. 105. On the ambiguities of the movement's rhetoric see Michael Novak, "Men without Women," *HLR*, Vol 5, No.1 (Winter 1979), pp. 61–67. On the changing medical attitude towards homosexuality, see John D'Emilio, *Sexual Politics, Sexual Communities*.

19. Clare Boothe Luce, "Two Books on Abortion and the Questions They Raise," *NR*, January 12, 1971, p. 27.

20. Clare Boothe Luce, "A Letter to the *Womens' Lobby*," *HLR* Vol. 4, No. 2 (Spring 1978), p. 7.

21. Ellen Wilson wrote thirteen articles for *HLR* between 1976 and 1985. See in particular "Mother Didn't Know," *HLR*, Vol. 4, No. 4 (Fall 1978). See also Juliana Geran Pilon, "Semantic Problems of Fetal Research," *HLR* Vol. 2, No. 2 (Spring 1976); and "Cost Benefit Ethics and Fetal Research," *HLR*, Vol. 3, No. 1 (Winter 1977). Janet Smith, "Abortion as a Feminist Concern," *HLR*, Vol. 4, No. 3 (Summer 1978), p. 64.

22. Personal Interview with Peter Steinfels, New York, Jan 6, 1986. Ellen Wilson, "Young and Gay in Academe," *Human Life Review*, Vol. 3, No. 4 (Fall 1977), p. 95.

23. On the internal tensions of the conservative movement, between traditionalists and free-marketeers, see George Nash, *Conservative Intellectual Movement* Chapter 6, "Fission and Fusion: The Quest for Philosophical Order."

24. On the fragmentation of American Catholicism during the 1960s, see Jay P. Dolan, *The American Catholic Experience* (Garden City, New York: Doubleday, 1985).

CHAPTER XI

THE BISHOPS, BIRTH CONTROL, AND ABORTION POLICY: 1950–1985

Mary C. Segers

An examination of the American Catholic bishops' public policy initiatives on reproductive issues in the period 1950 to 1985 reveals two rather remarkable facts. The first is the accommodation of the American bishops to the legalization of birth control in the 1960s. The second is the militant oppositions of the bishops in the 1970s and 1980s to the legalization of abortion. The juxtaposition of these two facts is at the heart of this essay, which compares the political activity of the bishops on these two issues. The comparison prompts this question: Why, given their acquiescence in policy changes on artificial contraception in the 1960s, have the bishops opposed policy changes on abortion in the 1970s and 1980s?

There are really two points of comparison here. One is the Catholic hierarchy's strict insistence, during the years 1910 to 1960, that public policy reflect the church's moral teaching on the impermissibility of artificial contraception; this was followed by a softening of the bishops' policy position and their acquiescence in the legalization of birth control during the 1960s. The second point of comparison is the bishops' insistence in the 1970s and 1980s that public law reflect the church's moral teaching on the impermissibility of direct abortion. Whether this will be followed by a softening of the church's policy position is difficult to tell. At the moment, the bishops show few signs of relenting in their campaign to translate their moral teaching on abortion into public law. Perhaps our charting the course they took with respect to birth control legislation will provide insight into the future of Catholic lobbying on abortion.

Several considerations lead me to compare the bishops' political activity on birth control and abortion. First, I am interested in how the American hierarchy adapted to different political circumstances in a changing culture and altered its views about birth control policy. Second, I believe the current debate about abortion policy is, in some important respects, a replay of the controversy over family planning policy some twenty-five years ago. Many of the same issues in the present debate about abortion policy—Catholic political and legal thought on the proper relation between law and morals, the limits of law as a method of social control, and on religious freedom and church-state relations in a pluralist society—were raised in the controversy over birth control policy in the 1950s and 1960s. Moreover, the church's moral theology provides a basis for comparing the bishops' accommodation to legalized birth control with their opposition to legalized abortion. Since Catholic moral theology considers both artificial contraception and abortion to be serious violations of natural law and of the procreative purpose of human sexuality, one is led inevitably to ask why the American bishops reacted differently to the legalization and public funding of birth control and abortion. What rationale has the American hierarchy offered to explain its refusal to seek to translate into public law its teaching on birth control, and its willingness to do exactly the opposite on abortion?

In seeking to answer these questions, I have divided this essay into three parts. The first section compares the bishops' political activity on contraception and abortion policy. The second part suggests some reasons why the American church, after long, fierce opposition to the birth control movement, acquiesced in public policies designed to make birth control accessible to all segments of American society. In the third section, I suggest several factors that might differentiate the bishops' opposition to legalized abortion from their accommodation to legalized contraception. Finally, I offer some concluding remarks about the continuing activity of the American Catholic bishops on family planning and abortion policy.

I should emphasize that I approach this topic as a political scientist, as a scholar interested in the broad relation between morality and legality. That is, I am not so much interested in a particular church position on the morality of an action or practice as I am in that church's stance in the political arena, its willingness to work to translate its moral position into public policy. In seeking to understand why the American bishops retreated on birth control in the 1960s but not on abortion in the 1970s and 1980s, it is essential to keep in mind the distinction between the church's moral teaching on the impermissibility of artificial contraception and abortion and the American bishops' views of sound public policy on these issues. The church has traditionally recognized that, while law and morality are related, they are not coterminous. There are limits to the law as a method of social control. Lawmakers must consider whether measures they enact will be acceptable and evoke compliance, and whether they will achieve their intended effect or result in a situation far worse than the original problem the law was supposed to remedy. These questions of sound lawmaking assume greater significance in a pluralist, religiously diverse society such as the United States, which is committed to religious freedom and church-state separation. In such a society, the church's conception of the pedagogical function of the law—that the law is a moral teacher—is difficult to sustain on controverted issues where there is little consensus.

While law and morals are separate, they are nevertheless closely related, and, as we shall see in the cases of birth control and abortion, the persuasiveness—or lack thereof—of the church's moral teaching on these issues had something to do with how actively and effectively the American bishops pursued the task of translating their moral views into public law.

THE BISHOPS' EFFORT TO INFLUENCE PUBLIC POLICY ON BIRTH CONTROL AND ABORTION

From the 1920s through the 1950s, the Roman Catholic Church in the United States vigorously opposed legislative modification or repeal of birth control statutes—largely at the local and state level. These efforts were most effective in states and cities with large Catholic populations: New York, Massachusetts, Illinois, Connecticut, and Pennsylvania.[1]

Municipal hospital physicians in New York and Chicago, for example, were prohibited from prescribing contraceptive devices for any patient, regardless of the religious beliefs of doctor or patient; nor could the doctor tell the woman where she could go for assistance.[2] The situation was similar in small cities and towns. "In [these] communities . . . private birth control clinics sometimes were closed by the police. Catholic charitable organizations pressured community funds and welfare councils to exclude Planned Parenthood. Catholic hospitals dismissed from their staffs Protestant doctors who dared to become affiliated with Planned Parenthood associations."[3]

Despite Catholic opposition to birth control, changing social mores in the United States indicated an increasing acceptance of artificial contraception. By 1959 Planned Parenthood Centers operated freely in 28 states; also by 1959, most of the Protestant churches in America had either approved artificial contraception as a proper method of family planning or decreed that this was a matter to be decided according to individual conscience.[4] By the early 1960s, innovations in contraceptive technology (development of the oral contraceptive and of the intrauterine devices) were considered to have made birth control cheaper, more effective, and relatively safer and easier. Concerns about world population[5] and about welfare dependency in the United States created a climate favorable to government distribution of contraceptives in both foreign aid programs and domestic poverty programs. These efforts culminated with the passage, in 1970, of the Family Planning Services and Population Research Act, which was to make contraceptive services available to all who wanted but could not afford them. From 1957, when birth control services were offered in the tax-supported public health programs of only seven states, until the 1970 Family Planning Act which in effect nationalized family planning services for the poor, an enormous change in attitudes had occurred in American society. In little more than a decade, government had changed roles—from being a force against the dissemination of birth control services to becoming an active participant in their distribution.[6]

In the face of these changes, the opposition of the Catholic bishops to legalized birth control slowly crumbled, then collapsed. At first, the pattern of church resistance was erratic. In New York, over strong opposition from the Catholic Archdiocese, the City of New York lifted the ban on distribution of contraceptives in municipal hospitals.[7] In Illinois, the Archdiocese of Chicago yielded, after initial criticism, to state welfare policy changes that permitted the provision of birth control services to all welfare mothers over the age of fifteen.[8] In Pennsylvania, the hierarchy led by Catholic John Krol of Philadelphia mounted a vigorous campaign against governmental distribution of contraceptives; and the bishops' strong opposition forced concessions from family planners.[9] In Massachusetts, however, the church, while powerful, seemed to recognize the inevitable and acceded to legal reform. Cardinal Richard Cushing of Boston displayed a sophisticated approach to questions of religious freedom and church-state relations; commenting on the Massachusetts birth control law, he stated: "It is important to note that Catholics do not need the support of civil law to be faithful to their religious convictions, and they do not seek to impose by law their moral views on other members of society."[10]

In between the extremes of opposition in Pennsylvania and cooperation in Massachusetts, church resistance to the legalization and government funding of birth control was largely desultory and halfhearted, consisting of the usual statements of church teaching accompanied by warnings about coercing the poor, violating privacy rights, and sliding down a slippery slope to promiscuity, sterilization, and abortion.[11] The hierarchy seems to have recognized that, in some instances (e.g., Illinois), they were fighting a losing battle, while in other cases, opposition to legal reform of outmoded birth control statutes would have been counterproductive. In any case, beyond issuing formal statements, the church hierarchy did little on a national level to oppose changes in birth control policy in the 1960s. The bishops were silent when the U.S. Supreme Court, in its 1965 *Griswold* decision, invalidated an 1879 Connecticut statute banning the use of contraceptives.[12] Even John Courtney Murray, the most respected American Catholic theologian on church-state issues, could find little to defend in the Connecticut birth control law.[13]

By contrast, the national effort of the bishops on the abortion issue in the 1970s and 1980s has been intensive and extensive. Unlike their quiet response to *Griswold*, the bishops reacted immediately and strongly to *Roe v. Wade*, the 1973 Supreme Court decision legalizing abortion. Their 1975 Pastoral Plan for Pro-Life Activities, restated in 1985, contains one of the most detailed, explicit proposals for political action ever to emanate from the offices of the American Catholic hierarchy. Convinced that they face, in abortion, an ethical issue that is not a matter of religious belief but a question of moral reasoning about which all Americans can come to some agreement, the bishops have pressed for change in law and public policy reflective of their convictions.

The bishops' aggressive posture on abortion policy is reflected in their numerous appearances before Congressional committees to testify on behalf of antiabortion constitutional amendments and in their efforts to influence major presidential candidates in the 1976, 1980, and 1984 election campaigns.[14] Moreover, they have supported numerous efforts to attach antiabortion amendments to Congressional legislation on civil rights, women's rights, and budgetary financing of government programs. They have filed numerous *amicus curiae* briefs in state and federal court cases on abortion. In 1984, a regional conference of Catholic bishops declared the abortion issue to be the most important issue of the presidential election, and several prominent archbishops condemned the Democratic vice-presidential candidate, who was Catholic, for her position on abortion policy.[15]

The political activism of the National Conference of Catholic Bishops (NCCB) on abortion is also reflected at the local level in parish-sponsored participation in the "March for Life," an annual march on Washington every January 22nd, the anniversary of the Court's decision in *Roe v. Wade*. In addition, the bishops have asked parishes to observe "Respect Life" Sunday every October, during which priests are encouraged to explicate the church's teaching against abortion and contributions are solicited to fund pro-life activities.

Nothing approaching this level of political mobilization, organization, and activity at the national and parish level was undertaken by the bishops on birth control policy in the 1960s. The question this raises for students of politics and law is: Why has the American church ultimately refused to work to translate into public law its teaching on birth control while seeking to do exactly the opposite on abortion? Why have the bishops drawn the line, so to speak, on abortion policy? To answer this question, we must first consider some factors that facilitated the bishops' accommodation to changing birth control policy in the 1960s.

WHY THE BISHOPS ACQUIESCED IN THE LEGALIZATION OF BIRTH CONTROL

In retrospect, it seems there are many factors that account for the church's willingness to accede to changes in birth control policy in the 1960s. These may be grouped into the following general categories: (1) jurisprudential considerations of good law and sound public policy; (2) the internal debate within the Catholic Church over the morality of artificial contraception; (3) the historical situation of American Catholics in the 1960s; and (4) the increasing success in the late 1960s of the abortion reform movement.

First, jurisprudential considerations. It became increasingly clear in the 1950s and 1960s that state statutes restricting birth control were unwise law and unsound public policy. State laws in Massachusetts and Connecticut were not only inefficacious; they were openly flouted in practice and became the objects of ridicule and contempt. An earlier consensus against birth control in American society had largely evaporated by 1960; and this, of course, meant that the enforcement of restrictive statutes had become increasingly problematic. For the Catholic Church, this meant that an aggressive Catholic defense of such outmoded statutes was becoming increasingly counterproductive. A British Catholic politician, Norman St. John-Stevas, pointed this out in 1961: "Catholics, in campaigning for the maintenance of such laws, gain little for public morality. They do, however, increase the fear of Catholicism in the minds of non-Catholics, and increase the likelihood that when Protestants visualize the Church, the image will not be that of a religious body, but of a political power structure. This is a high price to pay for the maintenance of ineffectual statutes."[16]

Second, the Catholic bishops' ability to put forth a convincing case for restrictive birth control laws was hampered in the 1960s by the internal debate within the church and among theologians about the morality of artificial contraception. Catholic moral theology on this issue had been undergoing a searching reexamination since the late 1950s. The Church had accepted the validity of family planning, but had stipulated that birth control methods must be "natural," not "artificial." Natural family planning, the rhythm method, restraint, and periodic abstinence were held to be morally acceptable methods of fertility control, but the Church's moral theology ruled out artificial contraception on grounds that this frustrated the procreative purpose of sexual intercourse. Continued questioning by respectable theologians of this ban on artificial contraception created uncertainty and heightened expectation that the Church's teaching might change. The Pope's ultimate reiteration of the traditional teaching in his 1968 encyclical, *Humanae Vitae*, shocked the Catholic world, and the ensuing deluge of protest and criticism made it even more difficult for the church to insist upon a restrictive public policy.

For their part, public policymakers felt little if any internal compulsion to conform policy enactments to the Roman Catholic view. The case of Joseph A. Califano, Jr., former Secretary of Health, Education and Welfare, well illustrates the effect of internal controversy upon policymakers. From 1965 to 1969, Califano, a Roman Catholic, served as a domestic policy advisor to President Lyndon B. Johnson, who vigorously advocated birth control, especially in population policies for developing nations. Although the Catholic bishops publicly disagreed with Johnson's policies, Califano noted that birth control was a subject of intense debate among theologians, and that he himself inclined toward the liberal view of artificial contraception. He therefore felt free to support government funding of family planning programs.[17] The absence in Califano of moral qualms about such policies should be contrasted with the acute conflict he felt between his private moral views on abortion and his public duties, as HEW secretary during the Carter Administration, to administer Medicaid funding of poor women's abortions. In his memoirs, Califano devotes an entire chapter to a discussion of the major dilemma the abortion issue posed for him as a Catholic in public office—a conflict he clearly did not feel over birth control.[18]

A third factor that may have influenced the Church to accede to legal changes in birth control statutes was the historical context of the 1960s for American Catholics. Catholics seemed to have reached political maturity in the United States in the 1960s—not only because of the election of President Kennedy but also because of the Second Vatican Council's stress on ecumenism and the pioneering work of the Jesuit theologian, John Courtney Murray, which culminated in the Vatican II *Declaration of Religious Liberty*. There had been a growing conviction within the American Catholic Church that it should not impose its moral beliefs on others through public policy embodied in law; among other things, such an approach seemed antithetical to ecumenism. The new maturity of American Catholics meant escape from a fortress or siege mentality into dialogue with persons of other denominations as well as with agnostics and atheists. It meant a growing acceptance and recognition of the American commitment to religious freedom and separation of church and state in a pluralist society. Largely because of the work of Murray, political, civil, and social tolerance came to be seen as a moral duty for Catholics.[19]

Given the irenic tone of American Catholicism in the 1960s, a triumphalist, church–militant approach to public law on birth control seemed reactionary—that is, a reaction back to the pre–Vatican II, anti–birth control crusades of the 1930s and 1940s. In the context of Vatican II, with its stress on ecumenism, it seemed incongruous for the American Catholic bishops to insist that public policy reflect what was, after all, a distinctly minoritarian view on the morality of artificial contraception.

Fourth, and finally, a review of events and trends in the 1960s indicates unmistakably how the abortion issue overtook birth control as a major preoccupation of Catholic bishops and theologians. A movement for reform of the nation's restrictive abortion laws gathered momentum throughout the sixties, bringing about changes in public opinion and in state statutes. In view of impending changes in state laws, Catholic theologians and lawyers began to discuss at length the question of abortion law and policy. From 1967 on, a lively debate regarding the legalization of abortion filled pages of such publications as *America*, *The Catholic World*, *Commonweal*, *Theological Studies*, and *The Proceedings of the Catholic Theological Society of America*. And the American bishops themselves, in numerous statements from 1968 on, expressed deep concern over what they perceived to be imminent changes in state abortion laws.[20]

Thus, in retrospect, it seems that from 1967 on, concern over public policy on birth control was overtaken by concern about abortion policy. The American church was too embroiled in internal debate about the morality of artificial contraception to press for public laws reflective of the traditional teaching. Moreover, considerations of jurisprudence and sound public policy suggested that it was counterproductive for the church to stake its power and influence on what had become, by 1967, a losing battle. Instead, American bishops as well as scholars and theologians found their attention diverted to what must have seemed a more important public debate, the attempt to shape changing abortion policy.

A COMPARISON OF THE BISHOPS ON BIRTH CONTROL AND ABORTION POLICY

If we ask why the American church acceded to legal changes on birth control but not to the legalization of abortion, several answers come immediately to mind. First, a strong pro-life movement among lay Catholics keeps pressure on the American bishops not to accede to permissive laws regarding abortion. Any analogous movement among the laity on birth control in the 1960s was noticeably lacking.

Second, the bishops have adjusted to a different political context in the 1980s. Both family planning policies and the American Catholic hierarchy may be said to have undergone a "nationalization" process over the last twenty-five years. With the poverty and healthcare programs of the 1960s and 1970s, the federal government has become a major provider of family planning services. Moreover, the Supreme Court's decision of *Roe v. Wade* in effect federalized the abortion issue and required state lawmakers to be cognizant of federal law in all future deliberations. As for the bishops, changes in the organizational structure of the American hierarchy in the wake of Vatican II resulted in the emergence, in 1966, of a strong, centralized, well-financed national episcopal conference.[21] The NCCB and its staff arm, the United States Catholic Conference (USCC), enable the American bishops to speak with one voice (at least most of the time) and to address national issues such as war and peace, economic justice, and federal abortion policy. Whereas the bishops' fight against reform of birth control laws in the 1960s was conducted on a state-by-state basis, their struggle against permissive abortion laws in the 1970s and 1980s has been conducted at both the national and state levels. This phenomenon of nationalization helps to explain why the bishops reacted silently to *Griswold*, which, after all, concerned a single state statute, while protesting vigorously against *Roe v. Wade*, which invalidated 46 of 50 state laws.

A third difference between the 1960s and the 1980s is the emergence of the contemporary women's movement. Second-wave feminism generated a conception of reproductive freedom as essential to the emancipation of women and emphasized a new set of arguments concerning the political-legal right of women to control their procreative ability. Whereas the church saw the abortion question as primarily a moral issue, many women conceived the abortion debate to be, at least at the level of public policy, a controversy about decisionmaking. They asked: *Who* shall decide when, if ever, a fetus is to be aborted—doctors, lawyers, government bureaucrats, clergymen, individual women? *Who* is making these decisions—in *whose* interests? Granted that such decisions are hard choices, *who* can be trusted to make them?[22] By phrasing the question in this way, feminists succeeded in democratizing the abortion issue, in translating it from a concern of elites (doctors, lawyers, clergy, demographers, social workers) to an issue of concern to millions of ordinary women. They also defined the issue differently from these traditional elites, construing it as an issue of procreative choice and fertility control. Like the old Catholic moral theology, feminists saw abortion, contraception, and sterilization as related matters on the continuum of sexual ethics. At the same time, they offered a strikingly different perspective, which declared that women had an intrinsic right to reproductive self-determination. Their novel definition of abortion as primarily an issue of women's autonomy presented an unexpected challenge to the Catholic view and, I suggest, influenced the bishops to present their public policy arguments in a different manner.

This leads me to the fourth and perhaps the most important factor differentiating the church's approach to birth control and abortion policy—namely, the merits of the church's moral teaching on these issues. As should be evident from the reception accorded *Humanae Vitae* in 1968, the substantive argument against artificial contraception is strained and ultimately not compelling, whereas the case for prohibiting abortion on moral and legal grounds has more than a little plausibility. Catholics like Califano were convinced that, while the church condemns contraception and abortion as violations of natural law and the procreative purpose of human sexuality, the two issues are qualitatively rather than quantitatively different. Artificial contraception was understood to be the prevention of the creation of new life, whereas abortion was understood to be the taking of new life, once begun; and this the church must oppose—morally and even legally. The plausibility of this argument undoubtedly accounts for the support by lay Catholics of the bishops' opposition to changing abortion policy.

However, it should be noted that, over the last twenty-five years, there has been a subtle shift in the way the bishops have presented the church's policy position. This shift of emphasis was done partly in response to the continuum arguments of family planners and feminists that abortion is simply another method of birth control. The change is this: Whereas in the 1960s Catholic teaching stressed continuity between contraception and abortion, in the 1980s these two issues are viewed as "apples and oranges," and abortion is seen as a far more serious violation of natural law than artificial contraception. For strategic purposes, the church's rhetoric shifted—from defining abortion as a sexual sin to conceiving it as an issue of human rights. For purposes of public policy, contraception is seen as a matter of sexual morality, whereas abortion is seen as violating the ethic against unjustifiable killing. This has allowed the church to employ the language of human rights with respect to the abortion issue and to speak of a "consistent life ethic" which applies to a variety of issues across the political spectrum.[23]

This kind of strategic redefinition of the abortion issue was necessary, I think, for two reasons. By 1970, it was apparent that Catholic arguments about the immorality of artificial contraception could not command assent and could no longer be upheld by force of law, and this meant that the church's opposition to abortion had to be dissociated from its moral teaching on birth control if it was to have any realistic chance of success in the legal arena. Secondly, feminist conceptions of reproductive self-determination tended to lump together abortion, sterilization, and contraception; against this the church insisted that abortion was more serious than artificial contraception and should not be viewed as "another form of birth control."

To summarize, the following factors distinguish the American church's approach to public policy on birth control and abortion. On birth control the church's position was distinctly minoritarian and therefore more readily perceived as sectarian, whereas the church has offered a nonsectarian rationale for its opposition to abortion, which, though not commanding majoritarian consensus, nevertheless finds support among many non-Catholics (Mormons, Orthodox Jews, Fundamentalist and Conservative Evangelical Christians). On birth control, a disaffected laity offered little support for clerical efforts to keep restrictive laws on the books, nor was there any feminist movement in the early 1960s to make disturbing new claims; by comparison, a strong pro-life lay movement and a powerful women's movement have democratized and polarized discussion of proper public policy on abortion. Finally, the historical context of American Catholicism is important: in the 1960s an American church, anxious to prove its commitment to tolerance in a pluralist democracy, and distracted by Vatican II and the possibility of a change in its own teaching, was willing to acquiesce in the liberalization of birth control laws and policies. By contrast, a reorganized, stronger hierarchy was leading an American church in the 1980s, which clearly felt it must resist the legalization and social acceptance of a practice the church regarded as intrinsically immoral.

On the basis of this essay, we may offer some tentative conclusions about the future activity of the American Catholic bishops on family planning and abortion policy. The opposition of the NCCB to liberalized abortion policies will probably continue as before. However, the activity of the bishops on family planning policy is likely to be discontinuous rather than continuous with the trends shown in this essay. That is, we should not be surprised if there are renewed efforts by the bishops to shape public policy on contraception.

It seems unlikely that the bishops will tone down their resistance to legalized abortion. They are bound by the inner logic of their moral teaching to continue campaigning for the reinstatement of restrictive abortion laws. To them, abortion is a *public* issue precisely because it affects a third party, a human being or potential human being, who cannot be consulted but whose interests deserve protection. This is not the case with birth control, which affects chiefly the couple involved and can therefore be defined as a *private* issue—about which government need not legislate. Given the Catholic understanding of abortion, the bishops cannot retreat on the public policy front. Perhaps the most they can do is work toward a consistent life ethic on a variety of issues; this allows them to preserve integrity while avoiding a narrow, single-issue focus.

With respect to contraception, the situation is different. Recent controversies about birth control suggest that contraception is not all that private an issue, and that the American bishops have not abandoned completely their hope of influencing family planning policy. In the 1980s, the archbishops of New York, Boston, and Chicago have strongly opposed dispensation of contraceptives in public schools. The AIDS crisis has provoked heated controversy among the bishops themselves over allusions to condoms in preventive education and in TV advertising. Pro–lifers regularly remind the bishops that some contraceptives (e.g., the I.U.D., some forms of the pill, and the newer RU-486) are abortifacients. It may be that the bishops' strategy in political discourse of separating abortion from artificial contraception cannot be sustained—since the two issues continue to be seen as aspects of a single ethic having to do with the regulation of sexuality and with reproductive self-determination.

One of the ironies of the Catholic politics of reproduction in the late 1980s is that feminists like Rosemary Ruether agree with conservative pro–lifers such as James McFadden in seeing continuity between contraception, sterilization, abortion, and homosexuality.[24] These Catholics, from both ends of the political spectrum, see these issues as inextricably linked in the deeper Catholic view that human sexuality cannot be divorced from the possibility of procreation. Here, perhaps, is the real "seamless garment"—not a consistent life ethic, but a Catholic sexual ethic that seeks to subordinate sexuality to the service of family and society. While feminists like Ruether emphasize the sanctity of marriage and the family, they detect in the church's traditional view of sexuality a refusal to recognize and acknowledge women's moral autonomy. They suspect that the real effort here is to use the ideology of natural law, which holds that the purpose of sexuality is procreation, to keep women subordinate and subject to biological forces beyond their control.

NOTES

1. C. Thomas Dienes, *Law, Politics, and Birth Control* (Urbana, Ill.: University of Illinois Press, 1972), p. 93.

2. Thomas Littlewood, *The Politics of Population Control* (Notre Dame, Ind.: University of Notre Dame Press, 1977), pp. 2–3.

3. Ibid., p. 14. See also Norman St. John-Stevas, *Life, Death and the Law* (Bloomington, Ind.: Indiana University Press, 1961), chapter 2; also Daniel Callahan, *The Mind of the Catholic Layman* (New York: Scribner's, 1963), p. 92.

4. See Norman St. John-Stevas, *Life, Death and the Law*, pp. 50–115, for a concise legal history and analysis of birth control and public policy in the United States from the passage of initial legislation in 1873 until 1960.

5. See the debate in successive issues of *Science* in the mid– to late 1960s as an example of the controversy over "the population explosion." See also Littlewood, chapter 1.

6. See the discussion in Gilbert Steiner, *The Futility of Family Policy* (Washington, D.C.: The Brookings Institute, 1981), p. 78.

7. St. John-Stevas, *Life, Death and the Law*, p. 100. It should be noted that not all Catholics supported the New York Archdiocese in its opposition to this proposed policy change; see James Finn, "Controversy in New York," *Commonweal*, September 12, 1958, p. 583, where Finn questioned the wisdom of the Church's position.

8. Dienes, *Law, Politics, and Birth Control*, pp. 274–277; also Littlewood, *The Politics of Population Control*, p. 42.

9. Dienes, pp. 277–278.

10. Quoted in U.S. Congress, Senate, Subcommittee on Foreign Aid Expenditures of the Committee on Government Operations, *Hearings on S. 1676, Population Crisis*, 89th Cong., 1st Sess., 1965, pt. 1, p. 17, as cited in Dienes, pp. 149–150.

11. See the 1966 statement of the NCCB, the strongest of the three major episcopal statements made during the 1960s. "Statement on the Government and Birth Control," November 14, 1966, in Hugh Nolan, ed., *Pastoral Letters of the U.S. Catholic Bishops*, Vol. III (Washington, D.C.: USCC, 1983), pp. 69–73.

12. *Griswold v. Connecticut*, 381 *U.S.* 479 (1965).

13. John Courtney Murray, *We Hold These Truths: Catholic Reflections on the American Proposition* (New York: Sheed & Ward, 1960), chapter 7.

14. For a discussion of the bishops' interventions in the 1976 presidential campaign, see Timothy A. Byrnes, "The Bishops and Electoral Politics: A Case Study," chapter 6.

15. See M. Segers, "Ferraro, The Bishops, and the 1984 Election," in C. W. Atkinson, C. H. Buchanan, and M. R. Miles, eds., *Shaping New Vision: Gender and Values in American Culture* (Ann Arbor: UMI Research Press, 1987), pp. 143–167. For the Statement of the New England Regional Council of Bishops, see *The New York Times*, September 5, 1984, p. A20. Twenty-two other bishops questioned the New England episcopacy's single-issue concentration on abortion; see National Catholic Documentary Service, *Statement by 23 Bishops on Nuclear Arms*, released in Washington, D.C., October 22, 1984.

16. Norman St. John-Stevas, *Life, Death and the Law*, p. 96.

17. Joseph A. Califano, Jr., *Governing America: An Insider's Report from the White House and the Cabinet* (New York: Simon & Schuster, 1981), pp. 52–53. See also Gilbert Steiner, *The Futility of Family Policy*, pp. 58–88.

18. Califano, *Governing America*, pp. 49–87.

19. John Courtney Murray, *We Hold These Truths*, chapters 1–5.

20. The complete citations for this review of the literature are: Robert F. Drinan, "Strategy on Abortion," *America*, Vol. 116, No. 5 (February 4, 1967), pp. 177–179; *America*, Vol. 117, No. 24 (December 9, 1967), pp. 706–719; Thomas A. Wassmer, "The Crucial Question About Abortion," *The Catholic World*, Vol. 206 (November 1967), pp. 57–61; Norman St. John-Stevas, "Abortion, Catholics, and the Law," *The Catholic World*, Vol. 206

(January 1968), pp. 149–152; Robert F. Drinan, "Catholic Moral Teaching and Abortion Laws in America," *Proceedings of the Twenty-third Annual Convention of the Catholic Theological Society of America*, Vol. 23 (Washington, D.C.: June 17–20, 1968), pp. 118–131; *Theological Studies*, Vol. 31, No. 1 (March 1970), entire issue. For the American bishops' statements of concern about changes in abortion laws from 1967 on, see Vol. III of Hugh Nolan, ed., *Pastoral Letters of the United States Catholic Bishops* (Washington, D.C.: USCC, 1983).

21. Mary T. Hanna, "Catholic Bishops as Political Leaders," unpublished paper presented at the Annual Meeting of the American Political Science Association, Chicago, September 3–6, 1987; subsequently published in Charles W. Dunn, ed., *Religion in American Politics* (Washington, D.C.: Congressional Quarterly Press, 1989), pp. 75–86.

22. The issue of who could be trusted to make abortion decisions was very important to contemporary feminists; they feared the arbitrariness of hospital joint-review committees, judges, and physicians. Historically, they had reason to be concerned. Luker shows the tremendous arbitrariness that characterized medical regulation of abortion. Physicians' control of abortion was highly variable, with the inevitable bias toward upper-class women. Moreover, physicians' discretion was essentially uncontrolled, unregulated, and unsupervised within the medical community. See Kristin Luker, *Abortion and the Politics of Motherhood* (Berkeley: University of California Press, 1985), chapter 3.

23. The major proponent of a "consistent ethic of life" is Joseph Cardinal Bernardin, Archbishop of Chicago. See his statements in *Origins* 13:29 (December 29, 1983), pp. 491–494; *Origins* 13:43 (April 5, 1984), pp. 705–709; and *Origins* 14:8 (July 12, 1984), pp. 120–122.

24. Speaking of Catholic concern over abortion in the 1980s, Rosemary Ruether writes: "While appearing to shift the focus to defense of 'life,' and hence to principles analogous to those defended in the bishops' peace pastoral, in reality the anti-abortion crusade was largely a continuation of the inability of the hierarchy to accept birth control. The Pope was as vehemently opposed to birth control as to abortion. The issue of reproductive rights was linked together with the inability to accept the rights of women as autonomous persons." Rosemary Radford Ruether, *Contemporary Roman Catholicism: Crises and Challenges* (Kansas City, Mo.: Sheed & Ward, 1987), p. xvi. Another continuum perspective is that of James McFadden, editor of *The Human Life Review*, who argues that "Although it is much the lesser sin, contraception

acts as the entering wedge for abortion, because sex undertaken with contraceptives is designed to avoid procreation. A pregnancy resulting from contraceptive failure, therefore, would be regarded as unwanted, and the temptation to abort significantly increased." From an interview of McFadden by Patrick Allitt, reported in "Catholic Lay Conservatives and the Politics of Reproduction," presented at American Catholic Historical Association Meeting, December 29, 1987, Washington, D.C., published above in this volume. In addition to Ruether and McFadden, a third position is represented by John Noonan, law professor and federal circuit court judge, who disputed church teaching and public policy views on contraception in the 1960s, but has advocated vigorously the church's position on both the morality and legality of abortion in the 1970s and 1980s. See his books, *Contraception* (Cambridge: Harvard University Press, 1965) and *A Private Choice: Abortion in America in the Seventies* (New York: The Free Press, 1979).

CHAPTER XII

THE GAYS, GEORGETOWN AND THE GOVERNMENT

Jo Renee Formicola

In 1978, Georgetown University faced an educational dilemma, having been placed in a position to choose between its religious principles and its political responsibilities. At that time, an organization of gay students petitioned the University for official recognition, thus challenging the Catholic school's traditional religious opposition to homosexuality. As a result, a series of minor clashes between gay students and college administrators escalated into a major lawsuit involving the homosexuals, the government of the District of Columbia, and officials of Georgetown University. During the ensuing nine–year battle, as the issues became more polarized and the stakes more valuable, the focus of the case turned increasingly toward the broader question of "principles." Was this really a case of personal vs. institutional rights? Of tolerance vs. endorsement? Or was it a matter of society vs. theology? Of democracy vs. autocracy? Of church vs. state? Of the First Amendment vs. the Fourteenth Amendment?

The Federal Court of Appeals eventually settled the matter quite simply, holding for the homosexual students and requiring that Georgetown University recognize them officially. However, the "principles" were never clearly resolved or placed in proper perspective. This chapter will explore the complexity of the problem and analyze the equity of the solution. And it will argue that a reorientation of the relationship between church and state has occurred as a result of the Georgetown/gay rights case.

THE CHURCH AND HOMOSEXUALITY

As a result of Vatican II, 1962–1965, the Catholic Church has been in theological flux. Its *magisterium*, that is, its teaching, has been reinterpreted often since then to accommodate to the exigencies of time, place, society, and politics. Certainly, hierarchical statements on ecumenism, human rights, religious freedom, disarmament, the economy, and the liturgy attest to this fact.

One of the last bastions of theological orthodoxy, however, is the Church's traditional teaching on homosexuality. Based on Biblical passages[1] and the natural law, Catholic moral opposition to homosexuality is specifically directed against overt genital acts. The Church maintains that such actions are intrinsically disordered, and that they lack "essential finality,"[2] that is, that they prevent sex from being life-giving and life-uniting. At the same time, however, the Church does not officially stand in judgment or condemn homosexual individuals, their preferences, or condition. Rather, bishops are expected to provide pastoral care. Clergy are encouraged to serve the sacraments to *all* their parishioners. And homosexuals, themselves, are encouraged to lead chaste lives while playing an active role in the life of the community.[3]

There are also those within the Church who challenge this hierarchical view of homosexuality. Groups such as Dignity, the Catholic Theological Society of America, and other members of the clergy and laity argue for a more humane treatment and understanding of Catholic homosexuals. Their reasoning is based on the belief in the intrinsic worth of each individual and the need for a pragmatic, pastoral response to homosexuality. Therefore, they argue for gay acceptance, rather than discrimination, for the restoration of self-esteem, for an understanding of sexual orientation, and for the evaluation of individual sexual relationships rather than a condemnation of all homosexual choices.[4]

Georgetown University, as a Catholic institution of higher learning, has openly admitted homosexuals as part of its admissions policy. It had never rejected gay students for their personal sexual preferences, but had instead set up a campus ministry program to help homosexual students with their special pastoral needs.

Lines were drawn, however, when the University was petitioned in 1978 by a gay rights student group, the Gay People of Georgetown University (GPGU), for official recognition. According to administrators, that status would have required University endorsement of GPGU's activities. It would also have allowed GPGU to apply for University funding, a privilege granted only to student organizations that fostered the educational mission of the school and performed a service for the University. In the case of GPGU, the University withheld official recognition, arguing that it would be "an inappropriate endorsement for a Catholic University," since one of the purposes of the GPGU was "to foster theories of sexual ethics consonant with one's personal beliefs."[5] In both 1979 and 1980, GPGU was denied official University recognition, but was granted, instead, student government endorsement. This limited standing allowed it to advertise in student publications, to use university facilities, to receive counseling from a comptroller, and to apply for lecture monies. But GPGU was not allowed to have an official mailbox, to use University mailing services, to use computer labels, or to apply for organizational funds. The lack of official recognition for GPGU did not result in the denial of extensive financial grants or space for its twenty-three members, but the organization claimed that it suffered a greater, intangible loss; that of credibility, respect, and equality. And so, in 1979, GPGU sued Georgetown University for violating the District of Columbia's Human Rights Act, specifically that section that held sexual discrimination to be illegal.

THE LEGAL BATTLE

The original case against Georgetown University was brought by GPGU's attorney, Ronald Bogard. Heading a diverse legal team of young and inexperienced people, Bogard took on Georgetown

University and the prestigious law firm of Williams and Connelly. The David and Goliath scenario only added to the drama of the case.

Bogard filed a motion for a summary judgment in a pretrial hearing before Judge Leonard Braeman of the Superior Court of the District of Columbia. His argument was based on the fact that Georgetown University was in violation of the District of Columbia's Human Rights Act. That law made it illegal to restrict, abridge, or limit access to facilities and services in the District of Columbia on the basis of sex.

Georgetown countered with different arguments. It claimed that the enforcement of the District of Columbia's Human Rights Act against the University was an infringement of the free exercise clause of the First Amendment of the Constitution. Attorneys for the University argued that as a Catholic institution, Georgetown was compelled to adhere to its religious principles. If a conflict were to exist between church law and state law, Georgetown argued that the Constitution should yield to the guarantee of religious freedom. Judge Braeman, however, held that the action of Georgetown University violated the standard of the Human Rights Act of the District of Columbia unless the University action would be protected by the First Amendment guarantees of religious freedom.

At this point, Judge Sylvia Bacon of the District of Columbia Superior Court, who had also been petitioned by GPGU for a civil decision, enlarged the decision of Judge Braeman. In October 1983, she held for the University even though the District of Columbia had intervened as a plaintiff to enforce the Human Rights Act. Her decision had four major findings. First, she held that Georgetown University was a religious institution even though it carried out secular activities, thus negating the argument of GPGU that Georgetown had over the years lost its religious identity. Second, she claimed that the denial of homosexual recognition was based on religious beliefs and that as a religious institution Georgetown could make such a decision. Third, she contended that the court could not interpret the application of religious beliefs, for to do so would be a violation of the principle of separation of church and state. And fourth, she held that the exercise of religious freedom must take precedence over the law of the District of Columbia in the absence of a compelling federal policy, evidenced by legislation, to eliminate homosexual discrimination nationally.[6]

The arguments of both the plaintiffs and the defendants, as well as the rulings of the justices, all had a certain amount of validity. In hindsight, it is easy to see that the case did not require a decision between right and wrong, but rather that a priority be set between two rights: the rights of individuals versus those of institutions and the rights of the state versus those of the church.

Shortly after Judge Bacon's decision, GPGU decided to take its case to the Court of Appeals of the District of Columbia and seek a reversal. Making the same arguments as it had in the past, GPGU hoped, nevertheless, that a larger panel would agree with the points that it had made previously. Interestingly, a three–judge panel did reverse the Superior Court decision, two to one, but vacated its decision the same day. Laura Foggan, one of the attorneys for the GPGU, called the decision "difficult" and fraught with "dissension."[7] She believed that the court had decided to rehear the case in order to reshape its opinion. The judges, Julia Cooper Mack, John Ferren, and John Terry, who had heard the case, called for an *en banc* decision and the issuance of separate opinions by their fellow judges. Two years later, after the decisions were in, all the holdings had one point in common: that the District of Columbia did have a compelling interest to eliminate discrimination even though national legislation did not yet exist to coincide with the concerns. As a result, the Court required that Georgetown University give formal recognition and tangible benefits to gay rights groups on campus. It also allowed the University to place disclaimers on all posters, ads, and public printings of GPGU.

At this point the University had the option of taking the case to the Supreme Court. Bogard, who had been replaced by Richard Gross at this point, and the GPGU were anxious to settle the case once and for all. Laura Foggan revealed that the strategy had been set, that Gross *et al.* had intended to argue the case on the constitutional issue of the Fourteenth Amendment, that is, state's rights. They would claim that the state statute was constitutional, and that it superseded the First Amendment guarantees of freedom of religion and free exercise.

Several conditions had given weight to GPGU's case during the intervening nine year period. First, a series of legal precedents had developed, which strengthened its position and revealed a consistent line of support for the precedence of "compelling state interest" among the Justices of the Supreme Court. And second, the University had been denied its right to raise monies through bonds, because it was technically in violation of the District of Columbia Human Rights Act.

Case law had been building in support of GPGU's claims since 1983. At that time, as a result of the Supreme Court's ruling in *U.S. v. Bob Jones University*,[8] the University had been denied its tax–exempt status because of its official, religious policy prohibiting interracial dating and marriage among its students. Holding such a policy to be unconstitutional, the Court reasoned that the state may justify the limitation of religious liberty to accomplish overriding governmental interests.

In 1984, the Supreme Court handed down two decisions that continued this line of reasoning. In *Roberts v. The United States Jaycees*,[9] it ruled that Junior Chambers of Commerce must admit women into membership, again basing its decision on the compelling state interest to eradicate discrimination. And, in *Grove City v. Bell*,[10] it ruled that federal funds may be cut from any particular program if illegal sexual discrimination exists within that program. Subsequently, the Congress, in an attempt to broaden the scope of support for affirmative action guarantees, enacted the Civil Rights Restoration Act in 1988. That law enforced the right of the government to withhold federal funds from all university units if discrimination existed in any single agency.

Support for the argument to carry out "compelling state interests" continued in 1987 in the case of the *Board of Directors of Rotary International v. The Rotary Corporation of Duarte, California*.[11] In its decision, the Court held that the Rotary must accept women as members, even though it held that size, purpose, selectivity, and exclusion must be criteria with regard to the right of expressive association. In *McLeod v. Providence Christian School*,[12] the "compelling state interests" argument again gained strength. The Michigan Appellate Court held that a teacher who was discharged from her position at a church–affiliated school because she had a preschool child could not be denied employment, even though the school had a religious belief in the need for mothers to tend to their own children at that age. It held that eradicating unemployment was a more compelling state interest and that to retain mothers of preschool children did not place a burden on the free exercise of religion.

Finally, in 1988, the Supreme Court decided in *New York State Club Association v. The City of New York*,[13] that women could not be summarily excluded from private clubs; that indeed, New York State had a compelling state interest to eradicate discrimination in order to advance business, professional, and employment opportunities. The list of such precedents continued to strengthen GPGU's legal position and its claim that the elimination of sexual discrimination with regard to homosexuals was also a growing compelling state interest.

At the same time, Georgetown University was also being squeezed by the Bond Counsel for the District of Columbia. In the District, the right to bond is granted to certain private institutions by the local government. However, a bond counsel must certify that the institution seeking to sell bonds is in compliance with all local laws. In the case of Georgetown University, which had sought to sell an estimated eighty-five to two hundred million dollars' worth of bonds for University restoration and building during the nine year period of its litigation with the gay rights students, such certification was denied. In short, the University could not carry out its planned maintenance and expansion, although University officials claimed that construction had not been compromised.[14]

On March 17, 1988, the Board of Trustees of Georgetown University met to discuss whether or not to accept the decision of the Court of Appeals and whether or not to bring the case to the Supreme Court. In light of the growing legal precedents that would most likely be used to protect the rights of the homosexual students over the religious principles of the University, Georgetown University chose not to test its position in the Supreme Court. One overriding factor emerged as the most significant consideration in that decision: the fact that the decision of the District of Columbia Court of Appeals was binding only on Catholic institutions within the District of Columbia, while a decision of the Supreme Court, if unfavorable, would enjoin all Catholic universities in America. The trustees reasoned that by taking the brunt of the decision of the District of Columbia Court of Appeals, Georgetown could win a pyrrhic victory and conceivably protect the moral interests of other Catholic institutions beyond the borders of the District of Columbia. With that as its major concern, Georgetown University decided not to appeal its case to the Supreme Court. Father Healy, President of the University, claimed that the loss of bonding authority was not critical to the decision of the Board of Directors.[15]

POST MORTEMS

As the dust began to clear, both the GPGU and Georgetown University claimed victory. Although at first glance, that might have been the result of the wisdom of the consent order that settled the case, religious institutions in general, and Georgetown University in particular, appeared to be the significant losers.

An understanding of the nature of the conflict in this case serves as a point of analysis about the current relationship between church and state in America and the equity of the solution in this specific matter. Broadly speaking, a first step has been taken by the government to limit the right of free exercise by a religious institution. However, such an incursion is justified and clearly the result of the current, conscious voluntary entanglement between the United States government and the American Catholic Church.

Originally, the wall of separation to which Jefferson alluded in his "Letter to the Danbury Ministers" stood like a fortress during most of the nineteenth and twentieth centuries. The Supreme Court, particularly, took a classic hands-off attitude with regard to church–state issues. In 1872, in the case of *Watson v. Jones*, the Supreme Court had been asked to settle a property dispute between feuding factions of the Presbyterian Church. At that time the Court held that the law does not distinguish between orthodoxy and heresy, sects or factions.[16] Therefore, it justified its holding that the Court should not become involved in intra-Church matters and, even more importantly, that it should not play a part in the application of specific religious principles to secular situations.

Moving from a total hands-off stance to a more neutral posture in 1947, the Court in *Everson v. Board of Education* delineated the parameters of the Church/State relationship to reflect the practices of the time. Among other things, the Court ruled that neither the federal nor state governments may legally participate in the affairs of any religious organizations and vice versa.[17] In short, religious activity by the government and political activity by churches were disallowed. However, these Supreme Court decisions and the attitude of both the government and religious institutions began to change in the latter half of the twentieth century.

During the 1970s, the Supreme Court heard a series of cases, and handed down a number of opinions that reflected a new, "cooperative" attitude between church and state in America, particularly in the area of education. This change reflected the increasing, positive political involvement of religious denominations in the civil rights movement and the anti–Vietnam cause. Their experiences continued to catapult religious organizations into the political process for diverse social justice issues, as well, during the decade. The National Conference of Catholic Bishops and its administrative arm, the United States Catholic Conference, along with the National Council of Churches, the Moral Majority and other fundamentalist groups worked politically for a myriad of issues such as school prayer, right–to–life legislation, SALT, and human rights. Their active participation was encouraged by a "born–again" Christian president, Jimmy Carter, in 1976 and supported by the conservative Ronald Reagan in 1980 and 1984.

In the case of *Lemon v. Kurtzman*[18] in 1971, the Court established a threefold test with regard to federal aid to private/parochial schools. The standards required that federal statutes with regard to education must have a secular purpose, that their effects neither promote nor prohibit religion, and that excessive entanglements with religion be avoided. As separatist as that decision sounded, on the same day, based on that precedent, the Court allowed the federal government to expend tax monies for the construction of buildings on four Catholic college campuses.[19] It held that such an action did not constitute an excessive entanglement between church and state. In swift succession, the Court allowed state revenues to be used for the building costs of both public and parochial colleges,[20] allowed states to provide monies to nonpublic schools for books, standardized testing and scoring, diagnostic services, and therapeutic needs,[21] as well as permitted parochial and private schools to be reimbursed for giving and reporting tests required by state law.[22] Finally, in 1976, sectarian colleges were even allowed to receive annual noncategorical grants provided they would not be used for denominational purposes.[23]

In short, the federal government was allowing more and more aid to be channeled into religious educational institutions, and the church schools were accepting it gladly. Yet it was naive of these religious institutions to believe that they could totally maintain their "religious" nature without having to become, at some point, secularized or dual-educational corporations. Indeed, Georgetown University itself, in *Speer v. Colbert* (1906), had argued that it was not a minister, preacher, teacher, a religious sect, or denomination,[24] in order to accept a $10,000 bequest made to the College. It stressed, instead, its secular, educational mission, and over the years has concentrated on getting federal funds for building projects based on this claim.

Presently, Georgetown University, like many other major educational institutions, has an active government relations office. Its two professional lobbyists, Reverend T. Bryan Collins and Reverend William George, have successfully pursued a strategy known as "earmarking." They identify specific pieces of legislation before Congress that could provide funds for projects that the University might be able to use. Then they lobby Congress directly for the monies, thus circumventing programmatic scrutiny by lesser agencies. In the past, this has netted the University funds for experimental buses and the modernization of its power plant.

Georgetown has many friends in Congress, some of whom are alumni, many of whom are Catholic. The proximity of the University to Capitol Hill assures the fact that lobbying will be intense, systematic, and usually successful. In short, Georgetown University is inextricably involved in the political process, playing at lobbying like any other interest group.

Georgetown University is not alone in these efforts. Religious lobbying has become almost commonplace today in a world of highly sophisticated, specialized political pressure groups. The United States Catholic Conference, the administrative arm of the National Conference of Catholic Bishops, has a staff of five full–time, paid lobbyists. Other groups such as the Union of Hebrew Congregations, the Freedom Council, the Lutheran Council, the National Association of Evangelicals, the Christian Voice, the National Council of Churches, and until recently, the Moral Majority, have established political action committees and/or government relations agencies to impact on U.S. foreign and domestic policy. The National Conservative Political Action Committee (NCPAC), the National Right to Life Committee, and the Washington Office on Latin America are specific examples. NCPAC, founded by Terry Dolan, was established to target certain liberal political candidates for defeat, and was extremely successful in the Congressional elections of 1980. The National Right to Life Committee has worked to influence social legislation and judicial decisions with regard to abortion, holding mass rallies on the anniversary of *Roe v. Wade* in Washington each year. The Washington Office on Latin America has worked to impact on U.S. foreign policy with regard to human rights during the decade of the 1980s by focusing pressure on American activities in El Salvador and Nicaragua. The religious lobby has become increasingly successful due to the large scale mobilization of its members, its extensive financial resources, its innovative strategies, and its excellent communication network.[25]

Clearly, the wall of separation envisioned by Jefferson has been falling down during the last twenty years. Religious institutions are intimately involved in the political process, and concomitantly, the U.S. government is financially entangled, at the very least, with parochial schools and universities in America. Therefore, it should come as no surprise to a Georgetown University, a Bob Jones University, a Grove City College, or any other religious institution that such political intermingling would require, at some point, that the sectarian bodies would have to abide by the rules that accompany the granting of such funds. In short, religious institutions cannot have it both ways. They cannot conveniently choose to be Catholic, fundamentalist, or orthodox. At this point, they must either be willing to sacrifice federal monies totally when their religious principles are compromised, or they must be willing to accommodate their immutable beliefs to national laws or compelling state interests. Therefore, the decision of the District of Columbia Court of Appeals and the consent decree issued by that judicial body must be recognized as both an equitable and just conclusion to the matter of *GPGU v. Georgetown University*.

THE FUTURE

As that great sage Yogi Berra once said, "It ain't over till it's over." In the summer of 1988, Georgetown University picked itself up, brushed itself off, and decided to continue to pursue the issue of funding homosexual students on its campuses. It did not intend to reassess or reinterpret its religious beliefs. It did not intend to use judicial means to be heard. Instead, it chose to fight through its strong Congressional contacts. Having lost a significant amount of bonding ability because the Bond Counsel would not certify that Georgetown was in compliance with the District of Columbia's Human Rights Act, Georgetown University chose to hit the District of Columbia in its own pocketbook.

The District of Columbia, although technically an autonomous entity, is dependent on the Congress for its operating budget. In July, officials of Georgetown University were able to hold up final passage of a five hundred and thirty-two million dollar measure. Senator William Armstrong (R-Col.) argued before the Senate Appropriations Committee for an amendment that would exempt religious institutions such as Georgetown University and Catholic University from the District of Columbia Human Rights Act prohibiting discrimination on the basis of sexual preference.

The amendment was approved by the Congress in September, and the District of Columbia was given until December 31 to change the law or risk a cut–off of its funds. In November, Georgetown University Treasurer, George R. Houston, Jr., appeared before the Finance and Revenue Committee of the District of Columbia Council, promising that Georgetown would abide by the agreement it had reached with the GPGU even if the institution were to be exempt from its responsibility to adhere to the District of Columbia Human Rights Act.

At this point, Georgetown had outmaneuvered its opponents. The University had played hardball and won. Philosophically, it had circumvented what it had perceived to be an initial governmental incursion into its religious and institutional autonomy. But pragmatically, and just as importantly, it had also preserved its right to be certified by the Bond Counsel. The need to comply with the District of Columbia Human Rights Act no longer applied to Georgetown, and the University had also maintained its financial freedom.

While Georgetown University had enough clout to win this squirmish, the battle was not over. In December, Judge Royce Lambert of the U.S. District Court of the District of Columbia, ruled, in response to a suit brought by the District of Columbia, that the Armstrong Amendment was unconstitutional. Again, the balance of power shifted between church and state, as "compelling state interests" were invoked to override religious freedom.

The fight continues. An appeal has now been filed by the United States government against the District of Columbia on a freedom–of–speech technicality. The District will be required to reply, and oral arguments are set for April 1989 before the District of Columbia Court of Appeals.

The larger question, however, looms like a specter. Will private colleges, not as wealthy as Georgetown, not as politically well connected and backed by the Catholic Church, be able to protect their religious and financial interests in the future? How pervasive will the argument for "compelling state interest" become in relation to traditions and policies? How will smaller, independent colleges be able to pursue their diverse visions of the educational mission without being forced to capitulate to what might be called "the bludgeon of funding"?

What is clear, however, is that religious institutions such as Georgetown University are in the political process to stay. They know how the game is played, and they are good at it. The time has come for the public sector, however, to become acutely aware of the religious factor in the political process and decide how much denominational involvement is welcome, prudent, or tolerable. Very soon the Supreme Court will be called on to hear a challenge to the tax–exempt status of the Catholic Church. Claiming that such an exemption is unjustified because the Church is politically involved, critics of religious denominations hope to redefine the current rules by which religious institutions operate within the political arena.

Clearly, there is a place for religion in politics. As the voice of the voiceless, the homeless, the disenfranchised, the social justice mission of religion can serve as the conscience of government and act as the conscience of the state. Such a noble, ethical goal is necessary, lest government degenerate to a "political monism" as John Courtney Murray, the Jesuit church-state scholar, cautioned.

Over thirty years ago, Murray argued that the American Constitutional concept of separation of church and state preserved the dual aspects of man's socio-political and spiritual nature by guaranteeing the freedom of religion.[26] Now, however, the delicate balance between the two must be restabilized so that religious denominations do not simply become supportive agencies for their own narrow, institutional, or dogmatic concerns. There is still validity in Murray's belief that the only certain way to assure that the "wall of separation" will continue to stand tall, is to place the responsibility squarely on individuals. Acting simultaneously as members of religious institutions and citizens of the state, individuals must mediate the roles of church and government in the American pluralistic social system. Hierarchy, clergy, and politicians alone, cannot be left to define the relationship between church and state. Instead, the dynamic tension between the two institutions must be constantly reassessed, redefined, and reformulated by an informed and concerned American public.

NOTES

1. The most widely referenced Biblical passages are: Genesis 19:1–11, the story of the men of Sodom; Leviticus 18:22, "You shall not lie with a male as with a woman; such a thing is an abomination"; Leviticus 20:13, "If a man lies with a male as with a woman, both of them shall be put to death for their abominable deed; they have forfeited their lives"; 1 Corinthians 6:9". . . no sexual perverts . . . will inherit God's kingdom"; 1 Timothy 9–10, "[the Law] is aimed, not at good men, but the lawless and unruly . . . murders, fornicators, sexual perverts. . . ."; and 1 Romans 18–32, ". . . all who do such things (homosexuality) deserve death."

2. Sacred Congregation of the Faith, *Declaration on Certain Questions Concerning Sexual Ethics*, Rome, 19 December 1975.

3. Sacred Congregation of the Faith, ". . . *And the Truth Will Make You Free*," Rome, 1 October 1986.

4. See for example Ronald Lawler, Joseph Boyle, Jr., and William May, *Catholic Sexual Ethics*, Huntington, Indiana: Our Sunday Visitor, Inc., 1985.

5. Letter of Father Healy to Georgetown University Alumni, 28 March 1988, pp. 1–2.

6. *Gay Rights Coalition of Georgetown University Law Center v. Georgetown University*. Superior Court for the District of Columbia. Civil Action No. 5863-80.

7. Interview with Laura Foggan, 27 May 1988.

8. *U.S. v. Bob Jones University* 461 U.S. 574. Decided May 24, 1983.

9. *Roberts v. United Jaycees*, 104 S. Ct. 3244 (1984). Decided July 3, 1984.

10. *Grove City v. Bell*, 104 S. Ct. 1211 (1987). Decided February 28, 1987.

11. *Board of Directors of Rotary International v. The Rotary Corporation of Duarte, California*, 107 S. Ct. 1940 (1987). Decided May 4, 1987.

12. *McLeod v. Providence Christian School, 408 NW 2nd 146, Michigan Appellate Court 1987*. Decided May 19, 1987.

13. *New York State Club Association v. The City of New York*, 56 LW 4653. Decided June 20, 1988.

14. Eric George, "Approaching a Resolution," *Georgetown's Blue and Gray*, Vol. 1, No. 3, p. 24. See statement of University Treasurer George Houston.

15. Healy, *op.cit.*, p. 9.

16. *Watson v. Jones*, 13 Wash. 679. Decided 1872.

17. *Everson v. Board of Education*, 330 U.S. 1. Decided 1947.

18. *Lemon v. Kurtzman*, 403 U.S. 602. Decided 1971.

19. *Tilton v. Richardson*, 403 U.S. 672. Decided 1971.

20. *Hunt v. McNair*, 413 U.S. 734. Decided 1973.

21. *Wolman v. Walter*, 433 U.S. 229. Decided 1977.

22. *Committee for Public Education and Religious Liberty v. Regan*, 444 U.S. 646. Decided 1980.

23. *Roemer v. Board of Public Works of Maryland*, 426 U.S. 736. Decided 1976.

24. *Speer v. Colbert*, 200 U.S. 130. Decided 1906.

25. See Robert C. Liebman and Robert Wuthnow, *The New Christian Right* (New York: Aldine Publishing Company, 1983) for more details.

26. John Courtney Murray, "Leo XIII: Separation of Church and State," *Theological Studies*, XIV (June 1983), p. 186.

BIBLIOGRAPHY

Interviews

Foggan, Laura. Attorney, The Gay People of Georgetown University (GPGU). 27 May 1988.

Sincere, Richard. President, Georgetown University Gay Alumni. 27 May 1988.

Books, Documents, Newspapers, Articles

American Bishops' Pastoral. "To Live in Christ." 1976.

Biemiller, Lawrence. "Georgetown University Homosexuals Cite Constitution, Morality, in Quest for Recognition." *Chronicle of Higher Education*, Vol. 29, January 30, 1985.

———. "Homosexual Groups at Georgetown University Get Court Backing." *Chronicle of Higher Education*, Vol. 30, August 7, 1985.

Brandus, Joseph. "Georgetown: A Portent of Future Church-State Relations." *The Wanderer*, March 17, 1988.

Caplan, G. S. "Fourteenth Amendment—The Supreme Court Limits the Right to Privacy." *Journal of Criminal Law and Criminology*, Vol. 77, Fall 1986.

"Chief Justice Delays Effects of a Decision in Gay Rights Case." *The New York Times*, 25 December, 1987.

Coleman, Gerald S.J. "The Vatican Statement on Homosexuality." *Theological Studies*, Vol. 48, December 1987.

Curran, Charles. "Sexual Ethics: A Critique." *Issues in Sexual and Medical Ethics*. Notre Dame: University of Notre Dame Press, 1976.

Gay Rights Coalition v. Georgetown. 536 Atlantic 2nd Dist., November 1987. Civil Action No. 5873–80.

George, Eric. "Approaching a Resolution." *Georgetown's Blue and Gray*, Vol. 1, Spring 1988.

Gold, Phillip. "Gay Rights and the Public." *The Washington Times*, 25 February 1986.

Hager, Philip. "Bias Suit Pits Gays Against Jesuit University's Beliefs." *Los Angeles Times*, 19 November 1984.

Hanigan, James P. *What are They Saying about Sexual Morality?* New York: Paulist Press, 1982.

Healy, Timothy. "To the Members of Georgetown's Faculty and Alumni." Unpublished letter of 26 March 1988. Distributed to faculty and alumni of Georgetown University.

Lawler, Ronald, Joseph Boyle, Jr., and William E. May. *Catholic Sexual Ethics.* Huntington, Indiana: Our Sunday Visitor Press, 1985.

Liebman, Robert C., and Robert Wuthnow. *The New Christian Right.* New York: Aldine Publishing Company, 1983.

McBrien, Richard. *Caesar's Coin: Religion and Politics in America.* New York: Macmillan, 1987.

McNeil, John. *The Church and Homosexuality.* Kansas City: Sheed, Andrews and McMeel, 1976.

Mc Shea, Kathy. "Should the University Have Won?" *The Hoya*, 28 October 1983.

Murray, John Courtney. "Leo XIII: Separation of Church and State." *Theological Studies* XIV (June 1953).

Sacred Congregation for the Doctrine of the Faith. "Declaration on Certain Questions Concerning Sexual Ethics," *L'Osservatore Romano* (Rome), 22 January 1976.

Strasser, Fred. "Panel Backs Gays Students." *National Law Journal*, Vol. 7, 12 August 1985.

———. "A Clash over Gay Rights: Catholic College Balks at Recognition." *National Law Journal.*, Vol. 7, 5 November 1984.

"University Wins Friends on Hill." *Congressional Quarterly*, Vols. 89–92.

Vatican Statement on Homosexuality, 1987. "And the Truth Will Make You Free." San Francisco: Ignatius Press, 1 October 1986.

Will, George. "The Human Rights Bludgeon." *The Washington Post*, 30 October 1983.

Williams, Bruce. "Homosexuality: The New Vatican Statement." *Theological Studies*, Vol. 48, June 1987.

CHAPTER XIII

BISHOPS, FEMINISTS, AND SURROGATE MOTHERHOOD

Thomas A. Shannon

When one sees the words "bishops," "feminists," and "surrogate motherhood" in the same sentence, one can be sure of only one thing: that they occurred in the same sentence! Yet in this case, there is, to some extent, a curious but complementary blending of concerns and principles that link bishops and some feminists.

The purpose of this article is to present a critique of surrogate motherhood from the perspective of the Vatican, some Catholic bishops of the United States, and several feminists. Of particular significance is the way in which several of the concerns of these groups complement each other in an unlikely way. This is not, however, to argue that the methodology of the bishops and feminists are similar; frequently that is far from true. Yet each group, beginning from different starting points, identifies concerns that are similar and comes to similar conclusions.[1]

THE ROMAN CATHOLIC HIERARCHICAL CRITIQUE OF SURROGACY

The following section presents, in summary form, a general overview of Roman Catholic teaching on artificial reproduction from three major sources: The Vatican Instruction on artificial reproduction, a presentation by Cardinal Bernardin, and a statement of the New Jersey Bishops' Conference.

The Instruction on Respect for Human Life in Its Origin and on the Dignity of Procreation

The *Instruction*,[2] issued by the Congregation of the Doctrine of Faith on 22 February 1987, contains nothing new from a methodological perspective with respect to traditional Roman Catholic teaching on sexuality. What the *Instruction* does is to focus that teaching on applications of new or alternative methods of artificial reproduction. In general, the *Instruction* defines the basic ethical teachings on sexuality and reproduction within the context of the broader teaching on marriage and then evaluates methods of artificial reproduction in light of these perspectives.

Five principles are identified by the *Instruction* as being key to the moral analysis of reproduction. First is the subservience of science to the integral good of the human being. This is because science is a method and as such cannot identify appropriate ends. These come from the good of the person. Additionally, such goods of the person serve as a check on scientific proposals.[3] Second is the traditional doctrine of respect for human persons based on their having an immortal soul, moral responsibility, and the destiny of beatific communion. Such dignity is the ultimate check of any exploitation of the person.[4] The traditional standard of avoidance of harms is the third principle in the *Instruction*. Thus persons, right from the moment of conception, may not be subject to disproportionate risks. Any exposure to risk must be justified by the promotion of personal well–being.[5] Fourth is the positive right of a child to be conceived, carried in the womb, and to be brought up within marriage. Such a right secures the identity of the child and ensures its proper development. Also affirmed is the invalidity of a right to a child. Marriage entitles couples only to acts "per se ordered to creation" but does not establish an entitlement to a child as a consequence of being married.[6] Finally, the traditional principle, or good of marriage, is the fidelity of the spouses, which has three aspects: (1) a reciprocal respect for the right to become parents only through each other; (2) the procreation of the child in conformity with the dignity of the person; and (3) a reflection of the unitive and procreative aspect of the conjugal act.[7]

The discussion of surrogate motherhood takes place within this general context and under the specific rubric of heterologous artificial fertilization. Since such a conception is initiated typically from semen from without the marriage, such a means of conception violates many of the principles discussed above. In particular, such a means violates the reciprocity of the marriage, the fidelity of the spouses, and the unity of the marriage. Such a conception also violates the structure of the conjugal act, which is both procreative and unitive. Additionally,

> The child has the right to be conceived, carried in the womb, brought into the world and brought up within marriage: It is through the secure and recognized relationship to his own parents that the child can discover his [*sic*] own identity and achieve his [*sic*] own proper human development.
>
> The parents find in their child a confirmation and completion of their reciprocal selfgiving: The child is the living image of their love, the permanent sign of their conjugal union, the living and indissoluble concrete expression of their paternity and maternity.[8]

This forms the proximate moral background for the negative moral evaluation of surrogate motherhood.

> Surrogate motherhood represents an objective failure to meet the obligations of maternal love, of conjugal fidelity and of responsible motherhood; it offends the dignity and the right of the child to be conceived, carried in the womb, brought into the world and brought up by his [*sic*] own parents; it sets up, to the detriment of families, a division between the physical, psychological and moral elements which constitute those families.[9]

Thus, according to the *Instruction*, surrogacy separates that which is inseparable, harms the child, and attacks the institution of marriage so as to weaken its place and role in society.

SCIENCE AND THE CREATION OF LIFE

In this address[10] to the Center for Clinical Medical Ethics at the University of Chicago, Cardinal Joseph Bernardin continued his practice of speaking to critical issues to a variety of audiences, not all of whom are receptive to his message—and frequently for opposite reasons.

This address focuses on the previously discussed *Instruction* and does so by situating it within two broad principles of traditional Catholic morality: natural law and human responsibility. Bernardin understands natural law as "an inner order or meaning to all that exists which was placed there by the Creator."[11] As such, it is accessible to people of good will who reflect with care on the meaning of life. Bernardin wisely recognizes the historical nature of human understanding and, therefore, affirms that "what appears to be a proper understanding or application of an ethical principle in one age may be found to be wanting or even incorrect in another. It is also possible to confuse the *application* of a principle for the *principle itself*."[12]

The other principle, human responsibility, is characterized by the charge to be fertile and to subdue the earth. In addition to this charge to be a "co–creator with God," there is a similar capacity and responsibility for creativity and insight.[13]

Bernardin joins these principles to draw two conclusions: (1) we are not God and, therefore, we are ultimately accountable to God for what we do; and (2) "all that the human mind or the scientific method is capable of doing is not necessarily worth doing. In fact, it might be something that should not be done."[14]

Thus, the general context that Bernardin sets affirms the goodness of human knowledge and creativity, with the proviso that these need to be evaluated "in the light of perduring and normative human values."[15]

Moving to the *Instruction* itself, Bernardin highlights three major principles. The first is the inviolable dignity of human life, which has broad agreement in principle but disagreement about its breadth and application. The second is the "essential and necessary relationship between human sexuality, marriage and parenthood."[16] Ultimately this means that "Human intimacy yearns for the interpersonal commitment and fidelity of heterosexual marriage and is celebrated in marital intercourse. Marital intimacy, in turn, has a natural propensity, a desire, to be generative of life for the couple and also of new life. In this perspective, then, there is an essential unity between marital sexual intimacy and the generation of new life."[17]

Bernardin concludes that such unity is violated by surrogacy, AID, IVF with gametes other than those of the couple, cloning, and parthenogenesis.

The third principle refers to the nature of marital intercourse: "The making of love is always to be open to life when a couple celebrates marital intercourse, and the making of life is always to be the result of the making of love in the context of marital intercourse. There is an essential unity that cannot be broken."[18]

Bernardin notes that the *Instruction* concludes that AIH and IVF are prohibited. Then Bernardin raises three questions with respect to the reproductive technologies. Is there a qualitative difference between the creation of life and other human activities and if so, does that put any constraints on what may be technically possible? And what consequences are there for the human family if we replace "the ecstatic union of two bodies becoming one-in-love as the source of life with the technology of artificial insemination or in vitro fertilization?"[19] Finally, would unforeseen consequences result from removing the mystery and unpredictability of interpersonal marital communion and making it subject to scientific planning?

Bernardin suggests that the answers to these questions should at least make us approach artificial reproduction cautiously. Overall, however, his judgment is negative about the use of such technologies, because they overstep boundaries imposed by the Creator. Yet, in the context of his acknowledgement of the suffering caused by infertility, Bernardin recognizes that "in the end, after prayerful and conscientious reflection on this teaching, they must make their own decision."[20]

IN THE CASE OF BABY M

Baby M was the first major surrogacy case[21] to have a full judicial review. Essentially, Mary Beth Whitehead agreed to be a surrogate for William and Elizabeth Stern but, after the birth, decided to keep the baby. Although originally viewed as a custody case (in which the Sterns were awarded custody), the New Jersey Supreme Court saw the case as one involving maternal rights and while the Sterns retained custody, Whitehead's maternal rights were restored, as well as visiting privileges.

This document is a friend of the court (*amicus curiae*) brief to the New Jersey Supreme Court from the New Jersey Catholic Conference. In it the six bishops of New Jersey argue against surrogacy primarily from a public policy perspective. Thus the argument is essentially directed to the public rather than being exclusively an ecclesial document.

The first point made is that the issue of surrogacy is a legislative decision to which the courts should defer. This position is then followed with several arguments against surrogacy as public policy and arguing strongly that the legislature is entitled to make further declarations on surrogacy.[22] The more critical issues, for the purposes of this paper, are raised in the second section, in which the bishops argue that there is no constitutional right to use a surrogate mother. While recognizing the right of individuals to decide whether or not to bear a child, the brief argues that such a right does not include a right to use a third party to actualize this right. They approvingly cite another decision, which suggests that surrogacy is not protected by the right of privacy from reasonable governmental regulation.[23] Next the brief argues that since a fundamental right is not involved, the state need satisfy only a rationally related test to prohibit or regulate surrogacy. "Substantive due process is not violated if a state statute reasonably relates to a legitimate legislative purpose and is not arbitrary or discriminatory."[24] Additionally, legislation against baby selling will protect the public welfare.

The document concludes by identifying a number of legal and moral reasons for prohibiting surrogacy. Legally, surrogacy involves the sale of a child, which violates his or her dignity; the surrogate exploits both herself by making conception and birth part of a commercial transaction and the child by selling him or her; and the rights of the child are violated through surrogacy arrangements. Additionally, "surrogacy exploits women as part of a 'human machine'."[25] Finally, the practice of surrogacy may put pressure on poor women to participate in the practice to help support themselves and their families. The moral reasons against surrogacy include: the violation of the biological and spiritual unity of the husband and wife and the dignity of the child; it is a threat to the stability of the family and can harm the family, if any, of the surrogate; and the child may become a pawn between individuals who are biologically related to the child but have no relation to each other.[26]

To no one's surprise, the New Jersey Catholic Conference strongly supports the voiding of surrogacy contracts.

CONCLUSIONS

The essential reasons for the moral wrongness of surrogacy from the Catholic perspective are three. First, surrogacy violates the dignity of the child by making him or her a means to the ends—however noble—of the couple. Second, surrogacy is the intentional separation and, therefore, the violation of the inseparable union between the procreative and unitive dimensions of heterosexual married sexual intercourse. And third, there are limits to what humans can do and these are set by the natural law. All other arguments are variations of these themes, whether they be addressed to the members of the Church or to the public. While recognizing that a child is a tremendous good and that there is significant suffering on the part of couples who are not able to have the children they desire, nonetheless the Church argues that there are limits to what humans can do in achieving their goals and that in the case of surrogacy, these limits would be violated.

FEMINIST PERSPECTIVES

We now turn to a consideration of feminist perspectives concerning surrogacy. One major problem here is to determine who, if anyone, speaks for feminists. There is no official feminist ideology to which one can turn as, for example, there is for the Catholic Church. Additionally, not all feminists, as we will see, agree on the issue of surrogacy. What I will focus on in this section is providing a sampling of pro and con feminist perspectives about surrogacy and identify their critical arguments.

ARGUMENTS AGAINST SURROGACY

A. Mary Gordon

A Catholic, a feminist, and an author, Mary Gordon presents as well as anyone the ambiguities of surrogacy: "I keep changing my mind."[27] There are three things Gordon does not understand about surrogacy: getting pregnant "*for the purpose* of giving the child up";[28]

altruism or heroism that leads women to share their fecundity; and bearing the child for money.

Mary Gordon makes the interesting point that she has difficulty understanding surrendering a child at birth whether this be to permit adoption rather than abortion or in surrogacy. Does one not understand, she asks, "what it is to have carried a baby all those months, to feel it grow inside you, move, take on life?"[29] For Gordon, the issue is the difficulty of nurturing the baby during pregnancy to give it away. The issue of heroism is problematic because the mother rejects an obvious and immediate bond in favor of an abstract bond or principle. Gordon asks: "Why choose the altruism that serves a stranger at the price of never again laying eyes on the child of one's own womb?"[30] Finally, with others, Mary Gordon recognizes that surrogacy isn't very profitable and that any economic gain will be probably be only short–lived.

Such, Gordon says, is what she seems to be sure of, especially the inability to understand bearing a child to give it up. However, she recognizes the dangers of her position: overprotectiveness and callousness. Thus she resists all–out efforts to ban surrogacy—though she is unclear about the legality of accepting payments for this. Additionally, Gordon does not want to take a hard line on the contractual nature of surrogacy. While recognizing and rejecting the sexist perspective that argues that women are too emotional at and after birth to keep their word, she also recognizes the reality that many of us don't keep our word and that this should be part of the understanding of the interpretation of the surrogate contract.

Thus Mary Gordon picks up on several key points in the general surrogacy debate but also recognizes that there are several consequences following from her concerns that need to be carefully addressed lest women continue to be harmed socially and personally. Especially poignant is her concluding comment that "I have always felt it a safe proposition that whatever position the Vatican takes on the sexuality of women, I'm in a good place on the other side."[31] Mary Gordon recognizes the possible harms in surrogacy, but is alert to the numerous problems women face in reproduction.

B. Gena Corea

In her ground-breaking book *The Mother Machine*,[32] Gena Corea early on identified many thematic problems with artificial reproduction and surrogate motherhood.

Corea begins with problems concerning the utilizers of the services. Some of these are men who want children without romantic involvement with a woman, busy or involved women who can use surrogates for convenience, and gay and lesbian couples who can utilize the procedure as well. Then, too, there are children available for adoption who are passed over in the search for having a child. Corea makes the point that one issue here is the preference of the individuals for a child of a particular kind.[33] Such orientations can lead to the child's being viewed as yet another investment these individuals make, or another item to be acquired.

A second major issue for Gena Corea is the motivation for seeking surrogates. These are identified first as the pressures associated with infertility and a poor prognosis for pregnancy. But she also identifies the issues of obtaining affection from children and fear of emotional and economic abandonment as significant motivators.[34] Then, too, there is the problem either of surrogacy's reducing the woman to the role of the vessel for the male's semen or of seeing her as the property of the man. Thus the woman's inferior social position is reinforced by the practice.

Corea also sees the artificial reproductive technologies as a form of reproductive prostitution and the centers in which these activities will be carried on as breeding brothels.[35] Again this imagery picks up on the issue of the commercialization of women and their reduction to objects and thus, their continued devaluation.

Also identified are actual and potential health risks that must be faced by the surrogate as she goes through the pregnancy. Additionally, Gena Corea suggests that women participating in surrogacy will begin to understand pregnancy as an abstract concept, as men currently do. Typically for the woman, reproduction is a continuous experience and one in which she participates directly. By using a surrogate mother, a woman will begin to conceptualize childbirth instead of experience it.

In her book, Corea sets a broad framework in which a variety of issues are explored, which this summary has not attempted to capture. Rather, I have highlighted the key issues Corea makes about surrogacy which summarize her case against its practice.

C. Barbara Hilkert Andolsen

Using her background as a Catholic, a feminist, and an ethics teacher, Barbara Andolsen raises several critical issues about the context in which surrogacy is practiced. While raising points similar to the ones already mentioned, Andolsen also illuminates several contextual issues.

The first of these is surrogacy as a challenge to the cultural ideal of motherhood as "a guarantee of continuous, unconditional love even in the middle of the night."[37] While surrogacy certainly would challenge such an ideal by the relinquishing of the baby, Andolsen's point is that we should not mistake an image of maternal love shaped in a particular set of circumstances for evidence of an immutable, instinctive love between mother and baby. Thus, while there is obviously some degree of bonding between mother and child, "their relationship is culturally malleable."[38]

Andolsen also notes that our acceptance of a right to control our reproductive processes has broadened into a "notion of a *right to experience wanted parenthood.*"[39] Such a right raises issues concerning the dignity of the persons of the mother and child as well as putting the mother at risk of being seen in purely instrumental terms.

A third issue that Barbara Andolsen discusses is the issue of choice. With Mary Gordon, she recognized that Mary Beth Whitehead's change of mind and/or heart led to her being perceived as fickle and untrustworthy, thus imputing to her a whole set of stereotypes about women. Andolsen's point is that we need to recognize that choices are not purely rational or disembodied. "It is out of diverse embodied experiences that human beings begin to sort out conflicting moral claims."[40] This means that we need especially to take into account our bodily experiences when weighing moral choices.

Additionally, surrogacy contracts share the liberal assumptions "about autonomous individuals who exercise radically free choice when entering into contracts."[41] Such an assumption ignores the reality that Mary Beth Whitehead was "an economically embattled woman."[42] Thus her choices must be seen within her economic context and evaluated accordingly.

Finally, Andolsen notes that frequently reproductive decisions "are limited by a social situation in which childbearing is unnecessarily difficult to reconcile with educational and career responsibilities."[43] Thus an individual may delay childbearing only to find that she may be too late in making her decision and is unable to conceive. Whether this condition arises because of age, sexually transmitted diseases, or workplace hazards, the reality is that some women may have an option denied to them because of the way in which other paths were open to them.

While echoing familiar themes, Andolsen also opens up the social context by analyzing the concepts of motherhood, rational control, and choice. These perspectives complement much of what Corea argues while focusing our attention specifically on the social context in which decisions by and about surrogates will be made.

D. Sidney Callahan

Another Catholic, feminist academician, Sidney Callahan has devoted much of her career to issues surrounding marriage, the family, and parenting. Here we look specifically at her concerns about surrogacy, which are set in the context of her analysis of reproductive technologies.[44]

The context for Callahan's analysis is the question of what will further the good of the potential child, the family, and the social conditions of childrearing, while simultaneously strengthening moral norms of responsibility in the area of human reproduction.[45] Thus in general, she limits the use of artificial reproductive technologies to cases in which it is possible for a "normal, socially adequate, heterosexual married couple to have a child as they would, or could, if their infertility were not an obstacle."[46] Thus Callahan approves of IVF and AIH because the joint efforts of the couple will result in natural parenting and a child in which they are both equally invested.

Surrogacy or any other third–party form of reproduction, however, is another issue. For Sidney Callahan, such methods are not ethically acceptable methods of parenting. First, such methods of reproduction are disruptive to the nuclear family as it has evolved, together with the psycho-social advantages it brings, as well as rendering asunder the "bond created by genetic kinship."[47] While not offering naive arguments about the normative role of biology, nonetheless she makes us take our embodiness seriously and recognize its significance. This is particularly true when we acknowledge the problems that various forms of asymmetry have caused in blended or reconstituted families. Second, while recognizing that no child is conceived with his or her consent, Callahan argues that children of surrogates are unconsenting participants in a social experiment that may cause harm to the child. While no one as yet knows whether or not surrogacy will actually be harmful, Callahan argues that the risk of this possibility is too costly to engage in the practice. Then we have the problem of the child's identity: Whose child am I? When numerous permutations of motherhood and fatherhood are biological and social possibilities, such a question is hardly meaningless.

Finally, individuals who are reproductive donors do not assume personal responsibility for their actions. While it is the case that such donors actually do not want to be responsible and that society has made it possible for them legally not to be responsible, Callahan argues that this isolates sexual and reproductive acts from long–term responsibility and that "this moral abdication will exacerbate existing cultural problems"[48] by making us more fragmented, rootless, and alienated.

Such issues are critical and show another face of the problems raised by surrogacy. Callahan, by relating surrogacy to larger issues of sexual and social responsibility, pushes the analysis another step forward.

E. Andrea Dworkin

Coming from a radical feminist perspective, Andrea Dworkin, in *Right-wing Women*[49] and other works, directly attacks artificial reproduction and surrogacy.

Dworkin sees the reproductive technologies as leading to reproductive prostitution. What is sold is the reproductive capacity rather than the sexual one, but there will be "no stigma of whoring because there is no penile intrusion."[50] The legitimacy of both transactions will, Dworkin argues, be conducted on the same basis: the freedom of the woman to act as she wants. If a woman wants to sell her body in some commercial transaction, "what right has the state to deny her this proper exercise of femininity in the marketplace?"[51] Dworkin provides two answers to this. First, the state has brought about the conditions in which the "sale of some sexual or reproductive capacity is necessary to the survival of women."[52] Second, the concept of freedom invoked is quite narrow: "The only time that equality is considered a value in this society is in a situation like this where some extremely degrading transaction is being rationalized. And the only time that freedom is considered important to women as such is when we're talking about the freedom to prostitute one's self in one way or another."[53]

Thus for Dworkin, the key to understanding the ethical significance of the reproductive technologies is their social context, in which it is assumed that issues related to sexuality and reproduction are individual choices unaffected by the patriarchal and capitalist society in which women live. Dworkin also points to another critical aspect of the reproductive debate. She points out that, paradoxically, the Right to Life people, who are the major organized opposition to the reproductive technologies, are also the agents "in engineering legislation that would give the uterus and the fertilized egg to the state to protect and control."[54] Giving to the state the right to define life, such as through proposed Constitutional amendments to define life as beginning at conception or referenda to determine the beginning of human life, means taking that power from religion and making it part of the police power of the state.

"For the sake of religion, they are taking from religion its moral authority to demand obedience from the faithful and turning that authority over to a soulless state apparatus incapable of moral discernment. They are taking from God what no atheist would dare and giving to Caesar what he has never dared claim for himself."[55]

This is an exceptionally critical point not mentioned by any other commentators I have read. Giving the state power to define life implicitly confers the right to make other decisions about life. The two major outcomes that Andrea Dworkin sees from this are that this state power will be used "(1) to redefine when life begins and what life is so that the male becomes its sole creator and (2) to determine and enforce which women reproduce, when, and how."[56]

For Dworkin, then, the key issue is the social status of women and how the power of the state will be used to further disenfranchise them. This will ultimately, in her judgment, give the state the power to determine who will reproduce and under what conditions.

ARGUMENTS FOR SURROGACY

Not all feminists are against the reproductive technologies and surrogacy in particular. In this section I will present a sample of the arguments used to support their position.

A. *Lisa H. Newton*

The Director of the Program in Applied Ethics at Fairfield University, Lisa Newton has written a strong defense of surrogacy. This defense is set in the context of a critique of the Vatican document and argues against other commentators who oppose surrogacy. Here I will highlight her constructive argument.

First, Newton rejects the position that surrogacy involves baby selling. Rather the process is described as providing a service, the services being impregnation, pregnancy, and delivering the child to the biological father. As she notes: "Nothing is 'sold.' The microscopic genetic material of the egg is 'donated,' after the custom of blood or organ donation, and the baby already 'belongs to' the father who takes it home—there is no need for him to 'buy' it."[58]

Second, Lisa Newton understands the surrogacy practice to be free of exploitation, and this for two reasons. (1) While there may be disparity in income between the women involved as surrogates and the other couple, such disparity does not "mean poverty, let alone poverty and desperation."[59] Newton observes that most of the surrogates come forward because they enjoy being pregnant, not because they are desperate. (2) Newton also rejects the argument that they are being coerced by the offering of a fee. She notes that historically, exploitation refers to being underpaid with respect to the market value of one's work. Now, the argument goes, one can be coerced by being overpaid. Newton's comment is that "if overpayment is coercive, then it's the kind of coercion I freely choose to endure, and that, by definition, makes it non-coercive."[60]

Next, Newton argues that in surrogacy the welfare of the child is protected, or at least as well protected as one can guarantee in this world. The key point is that there are no guarantees in life for anyone and if the parents desire the child and are in a position to provide a good upbringing and education, that is an appropriate context for childrearing—irrespective of the origin of the child.

Finally, several benefits accrue to the parties involved: the couple has a child, the surrogate has her fee and the satisfaction of having helped someone, and the child has life and access to the opportunities that life in a good home brings.

Thus the key element in her analysis should be freedom: freedom for consenting adults to conduct their business in their own way; freedom from overmedicalizing the process; and freedom for the couples and the surrogates to come to terms on their own with the assistance of brokers.[61] For Newton, no harm is done, no one is exploited, and everyone benefits.

B. Lori Andrews

As an author and a project director in medical law at the American Bar Foundation, Lori Andrews has spent much time and energy pursuing the questions surrounding artificial reproduction. Through her writing and work on various committees, Andrews has helped inform many people about these new technologies and shown them how to work their way through various problems and systems.[62]

While many of her publications are more descriptive in that they either describe the technologies[63] or present overviews of legal or legislative developments,[64] Andrews is a strong advocate of the legalization of the reproductive technologies and surrogacy.

In Congressional testimony, Lori Andrews identified many of her concerns. One is her conviction that children are unlikely to be harmed by the method of their conception. "A child born after surrogacy or donor insemination should fare at least as well as an adopted child, particularly since the child will be reared by a biological parent and his or her spouse. . . ."[65] Additionally, surrogacy should not be seen as baby selling. Andrews argues that the reason baby selling is prohibited is that children need security and would not have to worry about being sold. She argues that after the payment is made to the surrogate, "the child is never in a state of insecurity."[66] This is because the child is in the care of the biological father and his wife. Thus this child or "*any other existing child* "[67] will not have to worry about being sold.

The way into surrogacy suggested by Andrews is to use the statutes governing informed consent. That is, society already allows competent adults to engage in some forms of risky behavior, even though others might question it or disapprove of it. However, especially in medicine, once the adult has given voluntary, informed consent, typically one may proceed. Thus the key ethical issue for Andrews is making sure that all parties are properly informed and that they consent to the procedures. Additionally, there should be protective layers around these technologies to ensure that parties who may be harmed receive appropriate protection. Thus in a comment complementary to the concerns of Dworkin, Andrews argues,

> There should be vigilant efforts to assure that women have equal access to the labor market and there are sufficient social services so that poor women with children do not feel that they must create and sell another child just to provide for their existing children. If these injustices were alleviated, then all the women acting as surrogates would be doing so out of a true choice.[68]

Then, too, the physical integrity of the participants should be protected. Some surrogate contracts have been extremely intrusive by a detailed and perhaps excessive regulation of surrogates' activities. "It is inappropriate for the government to set standards on women's behavior during pregnancy. Such standards should not be part of a statute covering surrogates."[69]

Finally, the preconception agreement of who the legal parents are should be maintained. This will ensure that a surrogate will consider the situation before she is pregnant, the welfare of the child will be better protected, and postbirth litigation will be avoided.[70] Such a policy will also help screen candidates for surrogacy so that those who are unsure will not come forward. For Andrews the key moral issue is consent as traditionally practiced in contemporary medicine as well as creating an appropriate social climate which guarantees that the choices women make are in fact free. Given this and the appropriate protection of the vulnerable, a couple should not hesitate to enter into the surrogacy process to obtain their desired child.[71]

CONCLUSION

In the critiques of surrogacy by the hierarchy and some feminists, one can note a number of overlapping concerns: human dignity, the welfare of the mother, the interests of the child, the integrity of the family, and a rejection of baby selling. These issues stand out clearly and are argued forcefully. Clearly, though, other feminist authors raise other concerns about these issues and press a different agenda.

The major difference, not surprisingly, is the traditional hierarchical reliance on a narrow version of the natural law to insist upon the absolute inseparability of the unitive and procreative dimensions of sexual intercourse. This position, the same used to prohibit all forms of artificial contraception, is now used to reject any and all forms of artificial conception. Since the arguments about that position continue to be well rehearsed, I will not deal with them here other than to note that one can arrive at a similar—though not as totally prescriptive—position as the hierarchy without adopting that position.

Another major difference is ethical acceptability—typically within traditional heterosexual marriage—for the use of technologies such as IVF, AIH, or GIFT. For the feminists cited here, the means need to be evaluated with respect to their safety and efficacy in terms of the goal of childbearing, not the physical integrity of a single act of intercourse.

A critical difference between the majority of the feminists cited and the hierarchy is the feminist insistence upon a class and gender analysis of artificial reproduction. This is most strongly presented by Andrea Dworkin but is certainly echoed by the other authors cited. Two critical issues are raised: the social situation of women, which leads them to engage in these activities, and the implications of surrendering the power to define life into the hands of the state. This is a particularly powerful element of the argument over reproductive technologies and the hierarchical argument is considerably weakened by its absence.

One concluding observation concerns the tone—either implicit or explicit—in some of the argumentation. And that tone suggests either a lack of confidence in the hierarchy or its arguments or the assumption of patriarchy as the critical issue. This is expressed most clearly by Mary Gordon when she says that her instinctive position on sexuality is the opposite of what the Church says. That many people think the Church's position on sexuality is either wrong or not worth considering is certainly not news. The tragedy of this is that such a predisposition leads one to ignore or not take seriously the positive elements of the hierarchical argument about artificial reproduction.

Thus the wisdom and concern expressed in that position is lost, even though one can see from this essay that there are many points of complementarity in the argument, if not actual identity. Thus I conclude on a somewhat pessimistic note. Although there is a commonality of conclusions reached by many feminists and the hierarchy, there is a substantive chasm between them based on history, experience, and methodology. One can only hope that similar concerns and indeed similar positions can serve to help bridge this chasm.

NOTES

1. For more thorough analysis of these issues, see Thomas A. Shannon and Lisa Cahill, *Religion and Artificial Reproduction* (New York: Crossroad, 1988) and Thomas A. Shannon, *Surrogate Motherhood: The Ethical Use of Human Beings* (New York: Crossroad, 1988).

2. *Origins*, 16, pp. 697–711. The text can also be found in Shannon and Cahill, *Religion and Artificial Reproduction*, pp. 140–177.

3. *Instruction*, II, p. 7.

4. Ibid., Introduction, p. 1.

5. Ibid., pp. 1, 2.

6. Ibid., II, pp. 1, 8.

7. Ibid., II, pp. 1, 4, 5.

8. Ibid., II, p. 1.

9. Ibid., II, p. 3.

10. *Origins*, 17. pp. 21–26.

11. Ibid., p. 23a.

12. Ibid., p. 23b. Emphasis in the original.

13. Ibid., p. 23b.

14. Ibid., p. 24a.

15. Ibid., p. 24a.

16. Ibid., p. 24b.

17. Ibid., p. 24b.

18. Ibid., p. 25a.

19. Ibid., p. 25b.

20. Ibid., p. 25a.

21. *Origins*, 17, pp. 158–164.

22. Ibid., pp. 159–160b.

23. Ibid., p. 161b.

24. Ibid., p. 161b.

25. Ibid., p. 162b.

26. Ibid., pp. 161c–164.

27. "Baby M: New Questions About Biology and Destiny," *MS Magazine* (June 1987), p. 25.

28. Ibid.

29. Ibid.

30. Ibid.

31. Ibid., p. 27.

32. New York: Harper and Row, 1985.

33. Ibid., p. 218.

34. Ibid., p. 220.

35. Ibid., pp. 272ff.

36. Ibid., p. 287.

37. Barbara Hilkert Andolsen, "Why a Surrogate Mother Should Have the Right to Change Her Mind: A Feminist Analysis of Changes in Motherhood Today," in *On the Problem of Surrogate Parenthood: Analyzing the Baby M Case*, ed. Herbert Richardson (New York: The Edwin Mellen Press, 1987), pp. 41–55.

38. Ibid.

39. Ibid. Emphasis in the original.

40. Ibid. Emphasis in the original.

41. Ibid.

42. Ibid.

43. Ibid.

44. Sidney Callahan, "Lovemaking and Babymaking: Ethics and the New Reproductive Technologies," *Commonweal*, 114 (24 April 1987), pp. 233–239.

45. Ibid., p. 235.

46. Ibid.

47. Ibid., p. 236.

48. Ibid., p. 238.

49. New York: Coward-McCann, Inc., 1983.

50. Ibid., p. 182.

51. Ibid.

52. Ibid.

53. Andrea Dworkin, quoted in Corea, *The Mother Machine*, p. 227.

54. Dworkin, *Right-wing Women*, p. 192.

55. Ibid., p. 193.

56. Ibid.

57. Lisa H. Newton, "Surrogate Motherhood and the Limits of Rational Ethics." Forthcoming, *Logos*, Vol. 9.

58. Ibid.

59. Ibid.

60. Ibid.

61. Ibid.

62. See for example her *New Conceptions: A Consumer's Guide to the Newest Infertility Treatments* (New York: Ballantine, 1985). This is literally a how–to–do–it book which in addition to describing the various technologies, shows individuals what steps to take, what problems to watch for, and how to protect one's interests. The book has a storehouse of valuable information.

63. See for example, "Yours, Mine, and Theirs," *Psychology Today* (December 1984), p. 20ff.

64. See "The Aftermath of Baby M: Proposed State Laws on Surrogate Motherhood," The Hastings Center *Report* 17 (October/November 1987), pp. 31–40.

65. Testimony on Reproductive Technologies. Select Committee on Children, Youth and Families. 21 May 1987.

66. Ibid.

67. Ibid. Emphasis in the original.

68. Ibid.

69. Ibid.

70. Ibid.

71. *New Conceptions*, p. 179ff, provides a step by step procedure for locating and contracting with a surrogate and what legal issues to be aware of.

PART IV

CHURCH POLITY AND INTERNAL GOVERNANCE

This section focuses on matters of church polity, ecclesiology, and internal governance. Leonard Doohan discusses the implications of Vatican II theology for the role of the laity in both church and society. He sees in the Council's renewed ecclesiology a conscious acknowledgement that lay life is foundational for all levels of church living, and he explores what this might mean for political participation. One of the most controversial topics of the 1980s has been the U.S. Church's position on the movement for justice and equality of the sexes. Karen Sue Smith provides an overview of the current status of women within the Catholic Church. Finally, from the vantage point of their personal experience, Maureen E. Fiedler and Charles Curran, participants in two of the more notable cases of church discipline in the 1980s, discuss the politics of faithful dissent within the church. Maureen E. Fiedler's analysis is in the form of a presentation to the 1987 Women-Church Conference in Cincinnati, Ohio; Charles Curran was interviewed by Anne Lally Milhaven.

CHAPTER XIV

DISSENT WITHIN THE U.S. CHURCH: AN INTERVIEW WITH CHARLES CURRAN

Anne Lally Milhaven

Editorial Note: Charles E. Curran is a highly respected moral theologian who holds a licentiate and two doctorates in theology from the Pontifical Gregorian University and the Academia Alfonsiana in Rome. A priest in the diocese of Rochester, New York, Curran taught at St. Bernard's Seminary there from 1961 to 1965. In 1965, he joined the faculty of the graduate school of theology at Catholic University of America in Washington, D.C. In his scholarly work during the mid-1960's, Father Curran worked within the neoscholastic tradition of Catholic moral theology but also appealed to the practical experience of Christians and to a less biological, more personal understanding of natural law. Like many other Catholic theologians in the Vatican II era, he took exception to official church teaching on artificial contraception. Inevitably, his writing, teaching, and lecturing occasioned criticism from within the American Catholic community.

In 1967, when Catholic University's Board of Trustees rejected its faculty's unanimous recommendation that Curran be promoted to the rank of associate professor, the faculty and students called a protest strike, shut down the university, and forced the Board to reverse itself and promote Curran. In 1968, when Pope Paul VI issued an encyclical reaffirming church condemnation of artificial contraception, Curran was one of the ten theologians who wrote a statement publicly dissenting from the encyclical (this "Washington Statement" was eventually signed by 600 U.S. Catholic theologians). Again the University's Trustees called for an inquiry to determine if those Catholic University theologians who signed the statement had violated their contractual responsibilities as university professors. After a year-long inquiry, a faculty hearing committee vindicated the declarations and actions of the professors.

In 1979, ten years after these controversies, the Vatican Congregation for the Doctrine of the Faith (CDF) began a formal investigation of Father Curran's theological positions. The areas in question were his writings on contraception, direct sterilization, abortion, euthanasia, homosexuality, premarital intercourse, and the indissolubility of sacramental marriage. The underlying issue was the legitimacy of theological dissent from noninfallible teaching. The CDF's investigation took seven years. At its conclusion, in 1986, Joseph Cardinal Ratzinger, head of the Congregation, informed Father Curran that he was "no longer considered suitable or eligible to exercise the function of a Professor of Catholic Theology." In stripping Father Curran of his license to teach Catholic theology in an ecclesiastically approved program, the Vatican requested that Catholic University take similarly strong action against the theologian. In 1987, James Cardinal Hickey, Chancellor of Catholic University's Board of Trustees, cancelled Curran's theology classes and suspended him as a theology professor.

Charles Curran has brought suit in federal court charging Catholic University with breach of contract and with violating the academic freedom to which he was entitled as a tenured professor. At stake in this suit is Father Curran's career as a Catholic theologian, his future at Catholic University, and the autonomy of the University vis-à-vis American civil law and Roman canon law. Also at stake are larger issues of academic freedom in American Catholic colleges and universities and responsible dissent by theologians within the church.

Since leaving Catholic University, Father Curran has served as visiting professor at Cornell University and at the University of Southern California. He was interviewed by Anne Lally Milhaven in Ithaca, New York, on April 22, 1988.

PART I: WHERE CHARLES CURRAN COMES FROM

Q: *Although 1967 and the student strike on your behalf at Catholic University seem ages ago, still ecclesialdom has a long memory. How much of your present plight stems from resentment of your great victory and promotion back then?*

I have often phrased the question to myself in terms of why I was the one picked out. Certainly part of that has been the visibility that I have had: I taught at Catholic University; I have been president of the Catholic Theological Society and the Society of Christian Ethics; and I have published quite a bit in my area. I think also the student strike on my behalf at Catholic University in 1967, and the fact that I was promoted at that time, as well as my reaction to the 1968 encyclical "Humanae Vitae" all figured in. I acted as a spokesperson for more than 600 Catholic scholars who signed a statement saying that one could dissent from this particular teaching and still be a loyal Roman Catholic. As a result then of all this visibility, I think that I was probably a logical choice to single out.

In this connection, I read a book about two years ago called *The Politics of Heresy*. The author is named Kurtz, who has a degree in divinity (a Master's) from the University of Chicago, but is also a sociologist. His book was a study of the reaction of the official church to the Modernist crisis. The author established that the church ordinarily does not publicly go against those who are the radical or the more further removed from the church, but rather against the one who might be called the deviant insider, who tends to be closer to the church and not just looked upon as a greater threat to the institution of the church. This helped me to understand why even though my positions were not as radical as many others, I may have been the one who was singled out.

COMPASSION FOR PEOPLE

Q: *You are not in a position of dissent just to have "the powers" after you. Would you describe the forces that give you a feeling of compassion for the human being, making you take the road you're taking?*

You expressed in your letter to me the term "compassion" and that got me thinking prior to this interview. I think compassion is an accurate reality. It's always hard to analyze oneself and I was glad that you gave me the chance to be more self-critical. I think that compassionate is accurate. Maybe it's even broader than that: a respect for persons even when you disagree with them.

I never intended early on to be an academic. I purposely decided to go into the diocesan priesthood because I wanted to deal with people. I greatly appreciate the academy; I have learned a tremendous amount, and I think I've contributed my share to it. It was a joy being in the academy. But when you get right down to it, I think honestly, I have always seen my function in the academy and my intellectual pursuits as in the service of the church. And in the service of people. That is how I put the two together, even if there are two different publics. Some people come to be much more oriented toward the academy, but just by who I am, what I am, I tend to be much more oriented toward the church. And that also deals with the fact of the subjects in which I am interested: people's lives, people's actions, rather than more esoteric abstract subjects like Christology.

An important part of my theological method has been to give great significance to the *experience* of people. There is an old theological tract that talks about the sources of theology, and what these sources are: Scripture and tradition. I always wanted to include the experience of Christian people. Not that you absolutize that experience, not that you accept it uncritically, but one can and should learn quite a bit through it. There is a theological foundation for that because we claim that the primary teacher in the church is the Holy Spirit and the Spirit does speak in and through the lives and the witnesses of all the people in the church.

I can remember the first issue where I really questioned church teaching was contraception. I remember very clearly that in my dealing with a lot of married couples my own age, they experienced problems and difficulties. My change was certainly initiated by their experiences. Here you had people who were struggling, people who were striving, people who were trying to be honest and open and yet had great difficulty with the church's position on birth control.

Their experiences were instrumental in my change. I then took those experiences, (not uncritically) and I reflected on them. I had done some work on the whole history of human reproduction, and I realized then how much our teaching might be based on inadequate biology. That forced the kinds of questions that I have been raising. I then looked more deeply at the philosophical foundations of Catholic teaching on artificial contraception, and I saw the weaknesses there. I changed in the light of all those things, but it all began with the experience of people.

In the first book I wrote, *Christian Morality Today* (1966), I mentioned how significant in my own change was hearing other people describe their struggles. I just wondered . . . they had to be right, and then I finally convinced myself. Once a colleague of mine, describing me to somebody else, said: "Charlie is the best pastoral theologian in the country." I did not agree. But then I realized what he meant, and I think he was getting at the same dimension.

This feel for the human being . . .

Yes, that's a good way to describe it. Certainly that's the case with regard to the problems of gays, the problems of divorced and remarried Catholics. Behind it was a genuine concern, interest, and respect for other people. I was greatly taken by my mentor, Bernard Häring, all the time saying that God has called each person by name, respecting the individuality of the person. I too always try to follow Häring's influence and do right by the students by making sure I know everybody by name. Not treating people as numbers. In fact, here at Cornell that was quite clear at the end of the first semester. Six different students asked me if I would write a recommendation for them. Thinking they would be better off getting somebody else, I suggested that I'm not a member of the faculty. I've only been here for three months. They said: "Oh, no, you know us better than anybody else. We want you to do it." I've come across that problem in the big university where you have two hundred and three hundred in a class and there isn't that friendly contact with the students.

Q: *The church is full of theologians who write against the use of birth control and quite a few are really harsh on abortion. These are issues women think a great deal about. What are the roots of your sensitivity?*

It's hard to say exactly where they came from. They've always been there; respect for people and willingness not only to listen, but to truly empathize with them and their problems. Whether that's nature, nurture, or grace, I'm not sure where it comes from.

I recall one couple in particular who touched me very deeply. I have stayed and suffered with them over the years. They had a tragedy:

one of their children was killed just after college, and the husband died of cancer about three years ago.

In fact, this morning in answering my mail, I addressed five letters. One is to a former student of mine who is in prison at Pawtuxet Institute in Maryland. Another is a former student who is a minister in the gay church in California, and he helps people who have had all sorts of problems and difficulties. I don't do very much for him, but at least, I occasionally keep a correspondence with him. My emphasis on people's experience probably comes from a more pastoral rather than a more purely intellectual approach to theology.

FOCUS ON SEXUALITY

Q: *Why is there such a focus in the Catholic Church on all these issues of sexuality?*

No doubt that that's where the focus is. The question is why. And it seems to me that there are multiple answers to this one. There is no doubt that the church has had much more invested in sexuality than it has had in other areas. Its teaching in the sexual area has been very well known, taught constantly, in every time, and every place. I was reminded of this here at Cornell teaching a course on Catholic Social Thought. So many of the students had never heard anything about the subject before. So I said: "I bet you all know what Catholic sexual teaching is about?" It is like that famous remark Al Smith made in the 1928 presidential election. Running as a Catholic, people were asking him if he went along with papal teachings. Somebody asked him about a papal encyclical, and Al Smith's famous answer was: "What the hell's an encyclical?" He didn't know anything about the area of Catholic social teaching. It just was not well known, and that is part of a much bigger picture.

In terms of the reality of the church, it tends to be much more in the private sphere than in the public sphere. Some people might say that when the church lost its presence in the public sphere, it intensified its presence in the private sphere, and that the family was going to be the area where the church ruled. As a result, many clear specific teachings had to be known, so they were pounded in time after time. Combine that with the reality (in my judgment) that the Roman Catholic Church was never more authoritarian or overcentralized than it was in the twentieth century. Fundamentally, it had a defensive attitude toward Protestantism, a defensive attitude toward the Enlightenment, toward modernity, toward most of these nineteenth century developments. Scientific developments such as Darwinism were looked upon as bad, and his notion of creation was refuted. You had this terribly defensive posture on the part of the church, and together with the growing technologies of transportation and communication, it all enhanced the church's centralization and authoritarianism.

Why would that be so?

To make it almost flip: I think probably one of the greatest forces in bringing about this overcentralization and authoritarianism was the telephone. Rome was in much closer contact with the rest of the world. Many Roman Catholics in the United States are startled if they ever read that the first Roman Catholics in the United States in the 1780s, in Maryland, were using English in the liturgy. It was generally accepted. The first Catholic Bishop in the United States was elected by the priests. These instances are indicative of the kind of greater autonomy given to the local churches. It was a matter of necessity when there was so little possibility of communication between places. It was the way the Catholics existed most of the time, and it was theologically justified. This was the way it should be. Only in the twentieth century, for example, did Rome start to name bishops. Before that time, bishops were usually not elected or named by Rome, but they would always be accepted in communion by Rome. Just that very thing has given a tremendous power to Rome and it's also led many people to believe that in a sense the bishop is sort of the delegate of the pope. Sort of like the pope sends the lieutenant out to run this territory over here and somebody else to run the next territory.

But that was never the best view of the church. What happened was when the church became overly authoritarian, everything was absorbed into the papacy. To its credit, what the Second Vatican Council tried to do was to move away from it a bit by talking much more about the role of the bishop in the church, even somewhat about the role of the People of God. Certainly by saying also that the pope should never be seen apart from the College of Bishops, but as a part of the College of Bishops. Each bishop, moreover, by being a bishop, is the primary minister of the word and work of Jesus in his own diocese and does it on his own. The bishop is not a delegate of the pope. The bishop is bishop in his own right, so to speak, and is also part of this College of Bishops that then has solicitude for the total church.

In practice, the Second Vatican Council was a good illustration of that conciliar process of the College of Bishops coming together to deal with issues in the church, and fundamentally recognizing that the church just can't be seen as all power in the papacy alone. Beginning at that time, and I don't think it has gone far enough, but it's interesting that Rome is trying to cut back even now on the role of bishops' conferences on a national/regional basis. It is obviously necessary to have more autonomy in the local churches. Rome however is finding great difficulty with that at the present time. I think Rome rightly fears that if you have greater diversity and differences you might cause tensions.

Recently an example of this tension surfaced. It was brought to light much more in the social area today when the United States Catholic Bishops were writing a pastoral letter on peace and war. Many other bishops' conferences did the same thing. Rome was worried that there might be differences among them. Now there are clear differences among them with regard to specific teachings. For example, the American Bishops, to their great credit, say the first use of nuclear weapons is always wrong, even the smallest, tiniest battlefield tactical nuclear weapon would always be wrong. The French Bishops and the West German Bishops don't hold that. The whole French strategy of defense is the first use of nuclear weapons. It is always amazing to me that every French person, be they the farthest left of the Communist to the farthest right of the Imperialist in France always agree on the "Force de France."

They're very close to Russia.

Fair enough, but, so you had differences though in theory. The United States bishops put a great stress on what they call the principal of discrimination or noncombatant immunity as being an absolute moral norm. The West German bishops don't seem to accept that norm.

Q: *Why does the Vatican view those differences on such a* **secular** *issue as problematic?*

They would say that if you use the word *secular* there, you could also use the word *secular* regarding sexuality. What they are going to say is that these are issues where faith should have something to say. I agree. But I think we're going to have to learn to live with a much greater pluralism and diversity than existed in the past. This is also a recognition of what I have always thought to be one of the most significant changes in the Catholic theology of Vatican II. That change was the recognition of historical consciousness, a recognition that so much of what we do is historically and culturally conditioned. Therefore people living in different historical and cultural circumstances are going to approach things differently from people in other historical-cultural circumstances. And that's all the more reason then why we need much more autonomy. Autonomy may not be the best word, but much more possibility for initiative and direct involvement in the local, regional, and the national churches. Obviously that goes against the notion of centralization, and it's also a little bit scary for anybody who is worried about people going off on their own. I think that's precisely why Rome is finding great difficulty with the existence of the Episcopal conferences and the power of the Episcopal conferences as such.

ROME'S WORRIES

Q: If the bishops of this country get strong enough, do you feel Rome might worry about a national church?

I think Rome could very well worry about it. Frankly, I worry about it too. I don't think that's a solution at all. It is very important for me and for all of us to belong to the church which is universal. The great problem with Americans—Americans are not the only ones, but we have seen enough of the problems of American heritage—is if you put the engine of God behind your own arrogance, there are no limits to what you might do. We have talked about American civil religion, and it seems to me very important and necessary to have a universal church, which by its very nature then, is always a way of criticizing my perspective. Even though I come out of the Catholic perspective, a very fascinating argument I heard and accepted regarding the need for universal church arose specifically with regard to the Vietnam War. I remember asking two different Protestant theologians whom I respected and who were early opponents to the Vietnam War, how they came to their position. Both stated they had always started out saying that the United States was right. But it was precisely in the contacts with their church believers in other parts of the world, who belonged to the Christian church, and who said to them: "Can't you see the narrowness of your approach? Can't you see what you Americans are doing. Look at it from a different and a broader perspective."

Fundamentally then, I frankly would be opposed to an American church, because it is so important for us to recognize our solidarity on a much broader universal level and the richness that brings us, and also the consequent responsibilities it brings to us. Ultimately the way I would see the whole thing worked out is very much in keeping with that notion which Catholic theology has used with regard to the understanding of the role of the state and the federal government in political society. It is the *principle of subsidiarity*.

The principle of subsidiarity (it comes from *subsidium* meaning help) states that you allow the local group to do everything that individuals and voluntary groups can do. Everything that can be done on the local level. The higher or the more universal level only takes over those things that the lesser levels cannot do. I think that is an important principle and way of structuring that could be very helpful for the church itself. I see it in total harmony with Catholic ecclesiology over the years. It should be the proper understanding of the church, so we would take a lot of those things off the universal level and bring them back down more to the local, regional, or national levels.

THEOLOGIANS IN THE NIGHT

Q: And how would that affect our prior discussion of issues like birth control?

I think it could in many ways. I think that the primary issue with regard to those sexual issues is definitely the authority of the church. The teaching authority of the church basically is going to have to face the fact: is it willing to admit that the church teaching is wrong? This is really the strongest point in issues of sexuality, and to take me back to your point of my attitude toward people. When I first went to Catholic University, there was a nationally known priest teaching moral theology in the '60s who was about to retire. He was a very decent man. But this was 1965 and he knew that I was arguing for change in the church's teaching on artificial contraception for spouses. He was opposed to it, strongly opposed. And we got together one night and talked. After a long time, he finally said to me; "Charlie, you know, we can talk reasons all night long. In the last analysis, the real problem for me is the problem of my own self-identity. No one has written more than I to defend the Catholic teaching that artificial contraception is wrong. No one has stood up at more lecterns in this country to defend Catholic teaching. Now do you mean to tell me that I have spent most of my life, most of my priesthood, most of my theology, instead of helping people—that I've been hurting people? Do you mean that I told people the wrong thing and it caused them problems? Would God allow that to happen to me?"

Q: What was your answer to that?

I can't honestly remember exactly what I said at that time. I can remember reflecting on it very, very much over the years.

Q: Maybe the answer was not to answer him, but what do you think now?

I think it's very much behind the whole reason why Pope Paul VI could not change the church's teaching on artificial contraception with the encyclical "Humanae Vitae" in 1968. Fundamentally, it was a question of authority. Could he say that the church had been wrong? And if we believed that the Holy Spirit guides the church, would the Holy Spirit allow the church to cause this harm, to cause this trouble for people? And in the end, I, at least, would take the other side. I always attempt to deal with the best arguments of my adversaries. I mean there's no sense trying to take the easiest one. You've got to deal with the strongest side, and I can understand that approach, that feeling behind it.

It seems to me that in the end, all I can say is that I think we as a church bear some responsibility precisely because we inflated the value and authority of church teaching in those areas. Even the textbooks of Catholic theology added (if only in the small print), but they admitted that noninfallible church teachings might be wrong. And I'm afraid that we were not true to ourselves and our own tradition, and therefore we're just going to have to pay the price. We were guilty of that creeping infallibilism which went from everything the pope said, to everything the bishop said, to everything the pastor said, to everything the first-grade sister said.

We really forgot to distinguish that there are some teachings that are core and central to faith, and others that are more remote. That is why I said during the controversies of the last couple of years and why I thought it was so important to make them a teaching moment. I had taken exception even during the papal visit, when people were talking about American church practices as "smorgasbord Catholicism," "cafeteria Catholicism," or "pick-and-choose Catholicism." In fact, on the McNeil–Lehrer Report, somebody talked like that and I said I totally disagreed with such categorization, precisely, because I don't think it's adequate. I said that I don't find many Catholics questioning the existence of God, the divinity of Jesus, the death and resurrection of Jesus, the forgiveness of sin, even the petrine role in the church. To call all of that "smorgasbord Catholicism" is wrong. What it's saying, it seems to me, is we admit that there are certain things that are core and central to Catholic faith. But there are other things that are more remote, and it's precisely on those areas where we can have greater diversity than we've had before. And we must recognize that on those things that are more remote, there can be the possibility of dissent. My own dissent on these issues really comes out of the best of the Catholic tradition. Mainly because the Catholic tradition—to its credit, in my judgment—holds that its teaching on these moral issues is primarily based on human reason. It is not primarily based on scripture, or on faith, or on Jesus, but it's primarily based on human reason. So the question then naturally arises, what if it's no longer reasonable? But at least the best of the Catholic tradition gives me the platform from which to make the criticism in the dissent.

Q: And may I say further that maybe one of the roots of your compassion for human beings is the sense that yes indeed that theologian with whom you were speaking into the night did hurt people. And that you didn't want to be part of it. . . . Is that possible?

Yes, that could very well be. I was always looking at it more as his hurt at the time, and that he could even express it to me in his way. That he felt free enough, and that I could existentially understand his problem . . . Again, it's part of the fact that no one likes to see anybody hurt. Even though we could disagree very strenuously, I could still sympathize with his hurting.

A CHURCH IN REVERSE

Q: But it's fortunate for you that you were born and educated at a time that helped foster your own feelings of compassion? Yet now, the church is trying to force you around to another position. What are your feelings?

It ultimately gets back to the problem I mentioned earlier, the overly authoritarian understanding of the church. And a couple of thoughts about that. I found myself, more than I would have expected, going back to the teaching of Thomas of Aquinas. That was just to recognize what the tradition had held. For example, take Aquinas' position on the concept of authority. He raised that fascinating little question: is something commanded because it is good or is it good because it is commanded? And Aquinas, to his great credit, writes that something is commanded because it is good. In other words, authority is in the service of the true and the good. Authority doesn't make something good; authority must always see itself in terms of the service of the true and good. If you understand in that way, all the more need for the possibility of dissent within Catholic self-understanding. In terms of the general picture, Aquinas' understanding of morality did not follow the legal model: morality seen primarily in terms of the law. Aquinas followed the understanding of what's called the teleological model, where morality was ultimately based on the question of ends and means to ends. An old Dominican once put that to me in a very good way. He said: suppose that most Catholics, especially young ones, had the opportunity to take away one of the commandments, we all know which one they'd take away.

His point was trying to defend the sixth commandment. But it is so opposed to Thomistic morality which never saw the law as coming from outside, telling you to do something you didn't want to do. The basis of Thomistic morality was ultimately human happiness. In fact, Aquinas says the ultimate end for human beings is happiness; something is good if it brings you toward that happiness and it is bad if it prevents it. Morality, therefore, is just really what it means to be truly human. Morality is not something authoritatively imposed from the outside. You always have to be careful; like in Vatican II, you can find a quote to support any position you want. This was not just an isolated quote out of Aquinas.

On the question of morality, Aquinas says in the beginning of his *Second Part of the Summa*, where he treats of morality and the human person: "We've treated of God in the first part, now we'll treat the human being who is an image of God, precisely insofar as one is endowed with intellect, free will, and the power of self-determination." Aquinas says we are images of God insofar as we use our intellect, our free will, and our self-determination. We participate and image not by obeying law, but by using our intellect, free will, and power of self-determination. It was a different way of looking at the moral life itself. It seems to me that so much of this has just been involved in overly authoritarian understanding of things. Aquinas in those two instances I mentioned is a good illustration of one who did not have that kind of authoritarian approach to morality.

Nevertheless, when the authoritarian churchmen speak, they say Thomas is a big factor behind their claims.

In a certain sense, this is the great irony. It's the great proof of the overly authoritarian nature of the church, the fear of plurality and diversity, and it illustrates in a practical way much of what we talked about. Only in the nineteenth century did Catholic authority, namely the pope, make Thomas the patron of Catholic theology and philosophy, stating that Catholic philosophy and theology had to be taught according to the principles, the method, and the approach of Thomas Aquinas. Now if church authority had said that in the twelfth century about Augustine, there never would have been an Aquinas. Church authority used Aquinas in the nineteenth and twentieth centuries to do exactly the opposite of what Aquinas did in the earlier centuries. What Aquinas did then, and why Aquinas is so significant, is that he did precisely what Catholic theology always has to do: understand the word and work of Jesus in light of the ongoing historical, cultural, and intellectual circumstances in which you live. And the tremendous irony was that the church authority used Aquinas for exactly the opposite purpose in the nineteenth and twentieth centuries. As a result, rather than encouraging the kind of dialogue Aquinas himself did, they used Aquinas to prevent dialogue in the modern world.

Q: What are your thoughts on that? Does it sadden you?

It is the temptation of power. It is also the fear that you sort of cannot trust people or you do not trust people, and maybe it's the fact that people don't have that much—in the good sense of the term—self-confidence of their own. They have to rely on those kinds of things. Vatican II obviously recognized the need for dialogue in the modern world. Dialogue had been anathema until that time.

METHODS AND MODELS CONTRASTED

Q: You have studied how the Church moved forward in the last one hundred years in its teaching on social issues. Yet, in issues of sexual morality, it relies on inaccurate biology, excludes people's experience, and bridles at dissent.

Without any doubt whatsoever, if you examine the official Catholic church teaching on sexual issues and the official Catholic church teaching on social issues, there's a great discrepancy in the methodology involved.

I talk about three different aspects of this: The *first* shift that occurred in Catholic social teaching was from classicism to a *historical consciousness*. Classicism talked about the eternal, the immutable, the unchanging tendencies, using deductive methodology. Historical consciousness gave more importance to the particular, the individual, the contingent, the changing, the historical. Now it would be typical of classicism then to talk about that which is eternal, immutable, and unchangeable. The official Catholic documents on sexuality still do that, for example, the Declaration on Sexual Ethics (1975), or even the more recent official church documents of the Congregation of the Doctrine of the Faith with regard to homosexual persons or with regard to human reproduction, these speak about God's Law for human sexuality as being eternal, immutable, and unchangeable.

It is the way God imprinted it in human nature and it always has to be that way, and it always will be that way. Whereas, when they deal with social questions, they are much more willing to talk about historical diversity and change. In fact, it went so far that, in his 1971 apostolic letter, "Octagesimo Adveniens," Pope Paul VI makes a startling statement saying, "It's neither our role nor our ambition to point out what should be done in individual countries. Rather, it's up to the individual communities themselves, reflecting on the Gospel and the social teaching of the church, to come up with what they think should be done in their area." Such great diversity, such historical consciousness, therefore does not say there is one plan for the whole world and it must always and everywhere be the same. I think these differences are just astounding.

The *second* area of difference is that in Catholic social teaching in the last one hundred years there was a great development toward emphasis on *personalism*. Quite frankly, I don't think John Paul II is as accepting of historical consciousness as Paul VI. But to his credit, I think he is as accepting of personalism in social areas and gives great emphasis to the person. The important thing is the human person. In his encyclical on labor, "Laborem Exercens," he says the most important thing is not what is done but who does it. It's the priority of the person over what the person does. Now that could be quite radical in our understanding of what it says about work. It says that the most important thing is the person who does the work, *not* what is done, and what that should say about wages, people's participation, and what's involved in their own sustenance.

That's a big shift from "Rerum Novarum"?

That's correct. "Rerum Novarum," looking at an older model of the nineteenth century, saw everything structured from the top down. In fact, the words that Leo XIII used when talking about the ordinary citizen was the "ignorant multitude," people sort of like sheep had to be told what could be done. Whereas later on, Paul VI says that the two great aspirations of a human person today are the aspirations to equality and to participation.

Also, the U.S. bishops in their pastoral letter on the economy talked about the need for participation: people have the right to participate and to determine their future. It's not something all planned out that somebody else gives them. As a result then, you have this great church development. In sexual church teaching lately you, have the word personalism used, but the major problem with Catholic sexual teaching is what I have called its physicalism. This is especially illustrated in the case of contraception, which states the physical, biological act can never be interfered with. Now I would say, if you take the person seriously, then for the good of the person, or for the good of the personal relationship, you can and should interfere with the biological act. In other words, a natural act is not sacrosanct, but the person can interfere in it for the good of the person. So if you apply that same kind of personalism to sexual ethics, I think you'd come to different conclusions.

Q: Was the church moving toward this approach when the papal commission studied birth control in 1968?

It obviously was but the authority problem got in the way. Ultimately the church has to change. Sometimes I say—depending on what your definition of church is—the church has already changed. I like to point out that it has changed on the social level and I think now it has to change on the sexual. Talking about how methodology differs, seems to me, is inconsistent.

The *third* model is what I call *relationality-responsibility*. The Christian perspective sees the individual person in multiple relationships with God, neighbor, world, and self. It sees a person trying to respond responsibly within those relationships. Now it seems to me not only in social ethics, but in many other ways, there has been a change in Catholic self-understanding toward a relationality-responsibility model. Take the notion of sin; the older definition of sin was an act against the law of God. That is totally a legal model. Now, today, we tend to see sin as breaking or diminishing our relationship with God. We talk about a fundamental option. It's a different model. To the credit of development in regard to understanding of the sacrament of penance, the old name for the sacrament was confession. You confessed your sins according to the number and species. The sins were acts against the law. The new name—reconciliation—is definitely a relationity-responsibility concept. One becomes reconciled with God, neighbor, world, and self. Another example is the pastoral letter of the United States Catholic Bishops on peace entitled, "The Challenge of Peace: God's Promise and Our Response." If you asked the framers of that document what model they were using, they couldn't tell you. That's not necessary, because it's ethicists who study systematically second-order discourse and who go to the deeper question of what models are people using. Yet even the title tells us they're using a relationality–responsibility model.

WHERE SEXUALITY DIFFERS

But on sexuality . . .

Now, however, if you look at recent church teachings on sexuality, they're still using the legal model. And a very good illustration of that is when you use a legal model, you really have only two choices: something is either permitted or forbidden. It's good or it's bad. Whereas if you use a relationality-responsibility model, you're going to come up with a number of gray areas, which, to their credit, the bishops did in their discussions of the nuclear question. They talked a lot about gray areas. I just wish they might do the same thing with some of the questions about contemporary developments in genetics and human reproduction. But if you read their documents, everything is either forbidden or permitted. And there's no room for the gray areas. And I just wish sometime they'd say: "This is a problem and we're just not sure of it at the present time." They are able to say so in the social areas, but we are unwilling to say it in the area of human reproduction.

PART II: WHERE CHARLES CURRAN IS GOING

Q: Will you share with readers the influences you feel your parents had in your formation? Where does your grace under fire come from?

I think I was influenced by both of my parents, but in different ways. My father died in 1979 at the age of eighty and my mother died in 1985 at the age of eighty-five. Of four children in the family, I was third. My oldest brother—five years older than I—just died in September. Generally speaking, we siblings got along very well together. Perhaps the fact that there were four years or a little more separating the three boys made it a little easier since we were never really encroaching on one another's turf. My sister is midway between my older brother and myself, and to this day, we are still quite close and talk on the phone on a regular basis.

My mother was a very strong and active person. She was a housewife who became involved in many different activities connected with school and church. Looking back on her life, I think a very important thing happened near the end. In the middle sixties I was talking with a priest friend of mine in Rochester who had been appointed as the Vicar of the inner city. He needed someone to answer the phone and do voluntary secretarial work in the office. I suggested it would be a good thing for my mother. He approached her, she was very interested, and beginning in the middle sixties until her death, she volunteered one or two days a week at this office. The office went through a number of bureaucratic changes, but it definitely dealt with questions of justice in the city. I look back on it because I think this was very important in keeping my own mother young. She was associating with people much younger than herself, but they always appreciated her. As a result, at a time in life when many older people find themselves growing more and more alone, and their friends dying, she found her own world expanding. She came into contact across generational lines with many young people. I really think it was a marvelous thing for her. Obviously, she was the type of person who was a very loving and caring person, so that people appreciated her presence. I think in many ways I have received from her her vitality, her strong constitution, and her interest in people.

My father tended to be a little bit more on the quiet side, but he was by no means dominated by my mother. My father's contribution to my own personality has been, I think, a "hermeneutic of suspicion." I can only call it that now, but I think it was there from the very beginning. By this I mean there was a realistic assessment of where things were, what could be done, and what were the concrete possibilities. He was also somewhat interested in politics, usually from a behind-the-scene viewpoint of writing speeches and advising others. In fact, at a time in the fifties, he really was the number two person in the Democratic Party in Rochester, New York, although his work was entirely behind-the-scenes. From that approach, as I say, I learned quite a bit about a type of political realism, but not a realism that totally did away with working for change and development. From him also, the whole family learned the importance of public speaking. He insisted that we all get involved in public speaking, and I think that had a very formative effect on all of us. I think these were the major influences of my parents on my personality. There were no great problems of any type at home, but just the usual growing–up questions. In later life, both of my parents were very supportive of me and were always willing to allow me to do my own thing. I remember once in Washington, I took them out to dinner with Dan and Marge Maguire. Marge said to them something about how would you react if Charlie decided to leave the priesthood. Their basic answer was that it was my decision to make and they would go along with whatever I would decide on such matters.

PATRIARCHAL CHURCH AND WOMEN

Q: In Part One we reflected on the church's move to modernity when dealing with social issues. Yet is it stalled in stage one—the legal model—when it comes to sexual issues? Do you feel that the hierarchical reluctance to change in issues of sexuality is even more basic? Does it relate to how these men feel about women in general?

Well I think there's no doubt that it's included, however, I think that the primary hangup or problem is the question of authority. I really think that's the problem. It is the primary one with regard to change there. But I think it's influenced by a number of other things, especially the whole attitude of the church toward women, the lack of roles for women in the church, and the fact that this teaching has always been proposed by males. One of the funniest things in the old textbooks had to deal with masturbation, where all they talked about was the problem of male semen. They had great difficulty dealing with female masturbation because they were dealing with male categories. The discussion had been male-dominated, male-centered, and that certainly has been a glaring weakness of the whole tradition. There were no theologians who were women; women's experience didn't count for anything, and obviously there was a great lack of sensitivity throughout history.

The basic fundamental church teaching is that women are inferior persons with something missing. Theologians and seminarians, particularly in the Catholic church, have imbibed this sexism in their bloodstreams through the centuries.

Sure. But it has to be seen both for good and for ill. The fact is the church was not the only one doing so, everybody was involved. Now that doesn't excuse the church in any way, but what it also says is that the church now must also learn from what is taking place in the world with regard to the role of women. There is no doubt that the church has a tremendous amount to learn in this area. I say this publicly all the time, because I really see part of the teaching moment that I've been given by all of this, is to bring forward the whole question of role of the women in the church. Just last night I gave a talk at a women's college. I wanted to talk on feminist theology, but the president objected.

I don't know why. Maybe they are dealing with whether or not they should continue as a single-sex college. But I've had my consciousness raised to this question in many ways by my own women students over the years. I saw their struggle with these questions. I especially saw the struggles they went through, and almost invariably the crises they would go through once they had some theological background. Then they contrasted what they knew theoretically and theologically with what they experienced practically in the life of the church. I have seen a good number of women students who decided they would leave the Catholic church. I have helped others in joy and in tears look for ministries in other churches. These were women you know who are religious and would have made magnificent ministers and priests of the word and work of Jesus who feel they are called but who just can't serve in Roman Catholicism. They leave to do it elsewhere. Just to be part of the agony they go through, the problems they cause their parents, and in one case the problem caused with a spouse, makes you understand and feel the pain and deep sense of struggle that they have gone through. Many women have courageously stayed to try to get the church to change, and I certainly applaud them. I want to do everything I can to support them. And that's why I say I have tried to see a special responsibility, any time I am public, I get this point across. People picked it up, for example, at the first press conference in the present dissent, when I referred to God as feminine.

I did that purposely, as a way of making this a teaching moment, to raise consciousness to the whole issue. I think it is so important and so central. The Catholic tradition always said that you take the best of your human concepts and use those to explain God better. This weekend, I preach at all the masses at a suburban Catholic church in Ithaca, and the Gospel is the image of the Good Shepherd. It gives me a marvelous way of dealing with images. Nobody has ever seen God; we use images of God, then we are images. We take the best of what we have and say that's God. Whatever is true and good in the human has to be in God somehow or other. But every image is going to be imperfect, because God is mystery and God is perfect. And secondly the danger of exclusion, people can exclude things from God that should be included. The image of the Good Shepherd—a powerful image used through the centuries in sculpture and painting—says God is caring, protecting, willing to give his life. What that says to us then is we can live with some degree of risk, knowing that God will provide, will take care of us in hard time. We will get lost sometimes, but God will come looking for us. I think it's a marvelous image, but it is also an imperfect image. I'm not so sure we know how it has been abused.

The people of the church have been seen as dumb sheep who had to be led around. I'm not so sure that we are dumb sheep, nor should we be called dumb sheep. So even the best of our images of God is imperfect. Some images we don't want to use any more. In an older society, the warrior king was the best thing that you could say about a human being. Then we used it in naming God. I don't think that's a very good image of God today. The image of God as father is certainly a marvelous image. I think we also need the image of God as mother. There's no reason why God shouldn't be mother just as much as God is father. The danger is precisely when you take just one aspect, you exclude something else. It is something that we have done with regard to God. We, as theologians, and we, as church, have a big problem; I phrase it that God is masculine and God is more than masculine, and God is feminine and God is more than feminine. Somehow or other now we try to get people to realize what it says about us if God is only masculine and there's no place for the feminine. We can definitely learn and try to expand our own consciousness. It fits with the best of Catholic theologies that this God is ultimately mystery; any of our images of God are going to be imperfect. We can only strive to recognize the imperfection and that the worst thing is to have exclusive images of God.

DIVISIVENESS IN THE CHURCH

Without a doubt, the question of the role of the women in the Catholic church is going to be the most divisive issue that the church is facing in the next ten years. And I'm afraid it's going to cause a lot of pain, a lot of hurt on the part of women in the church.

People's consciousness grows every day and the consciousness of more people will grow. I'm very pleased with the first draft of the pastoral letter the bishops wrote on women. It could not have been written ten years ago, so to their credit, those bishops' consciousness has been raised.

Why I'm afraid it's going to be a divisive issue is the fact that it concerns so many people. Other issues in the church are very important; the sexual issues we've been talking about, divorced Catholics, celibacy in the priesthood, or a place for gays in the church. But here you get an issue that involves fifty-two percent of humankind; you've just got the critical mass. You can sort of pretend that some of these other issues aren't there, or they're not as purposive or they're not as all–pervasive as this issue. By its very nature, the women's role is so big that it's going to cause more disturbances than other issues which by their very nature don't have that critical mass. In the end the only way to solve the problem is to change the role given to women in the church, and as a sign of that, women in priesthood and ministry. But these are not the only issues; in fact, I believe very strongly with many women who say that we have to change the whole concept of priesthood. I think that's very, very true. And again, I hope this would also be part of that change, but nonetheless, the sign of the whole thing is the fact that the Roman Catholic Church will not allow women to be priests. To change this, you need structural change. On all the other issues we talked about you don't need structural change. (Ultimately you need it, and I want to bring it about, but you can at least solve these problems in the meantime, without structural change.) In other words, you can solve these other problems in your own conscience. Many Catholic couples have come to the decision in their conscience that artificial conception is right and they practice it. I know gays who are committed to a relationship who are trying to be faithful and they think that their relationship is good and continue to frequent the sacraments, fully celebrating the life of the church. I know divorced Catholics who do the same thing. And so those questions in a sense can be solved in people's conscience.

Many of these persons find church communities acceptable to them, and in a certain sense there is no problem. But the role–of–women question cannot be solved that way. It can only be solved through structural change. It's been so hard to bring about any structural change on these other issues, it's going to be that much harder, I think, to bring about change in the women's issue. And it might very well be that people are fearful of allowing the change on some of these other problems we covered because they know if you change there, you're opening the door to changes on the role of women in the church. It seems to me that it's going to be a very, very difficult struggle for the next few years. I can see growing frustration on the part of a lot of Catholic women.

I see my role as starting to bring about that change. In fact earlier today the diocese of Rochester contacted me. The person calling runs a program for priests who were ordained and are in an internship program for their first five years. They get together once a year with the priest supervisors. There are about twenty of them, and they asked me to give a talk, wondering what I wanted to address. I told him I wanted to talk about feminist theology, because it is so important for me to raise the consciousness of people on this issue. Just to acquaint them somehow or other with the pain and the hurt that so many Catholic women feel. It has to be known. Ultimately we have to raise the consciousness of so many people in the church.

Q: You mentioned the next ten years. Do you see such change in this century?

I say to some people it's bad enough being a theologian in the church. I'm not going to try to be a prophet. Unfortunately, I don't see much room for change in the immediate future. Only one thing has given me a little hope in a perverse sense; Xavier Rynne, who wrote those books on the Vatican Council, coined the phrase "Rynne's Law." Rynne's Law is when the Vatican reinforces something, pounds the table, and speaks incessantly on it, that's a sign that they realize the arguments in favor aren't too good and they might begin to start to change. Now I think that might be a little wishful thinking, but at least Rynne's Law might apply in the women's issue today. We have to push the issue and raise people's consciousness. Again, outside of Rome things are happening. In the parish churches here in Ithaca, a lay woman, a pastoral associate, is on the altar with her alb on every Sunday. She makes announcements, distributes communion, is very much a part of things. Five years ago you would not have seen that.

In the long term, I'm hopeful. In the short term, I am more than guarded. I'm just fearful of tension and the hurt and the pain that's going to come because I don't see change coming easily. In the long run, I'm hopeful because again the best of the Catholic tradition can argue in favor of change here. It's interesting to me too that some of the best of the feminist theologians are coming from the Catholic tradition.

And that does say something about the best of the Catholic tradition. Take, for example, the question of the scripture in general. Not just about priesthood, or the role of women, I mean the scriptural question in general, because there's no doubt that the scripture says it's good news to poor people, but I'm not so sure it's good news to women. In a total scale, then, how do you deal with that? Well some people are dealing with it out of the Protestant perspective—the stress of the scripture alone at one time—they have to deal with it out of the scriptures. Their approach is to try to find what has often been called the "canon within the canon" and other terms. You try to find those scriptural quotes which are more central than others and which determine others, and then feminist theology could very well move into Galatians 3:28 where there is neither male nor female, slave nor freeman, Jew nor Greek. Say you use this text to interpret others that don't seem to be so good regarding the role of women. But the Catholic approach has always said that you never use the scripture alone. There is scripture and there is tradition. You can bring something to the scriptures, so therefore Catholic feminist theologians say, well yes, you bring a feminist perspective to the scriptures. And in a certain sense, the Catholic tradition is more open to doing so. The Catholic tradition, therefore, can be freer to bring perspectives to bear on the scriptures and dialogue with the scripture. Ironically, even though the Catholic church has been so slow with regard to recognizing the role of women, the Catholic method is more open to it. That is why I am somewhat hopeful that in the long run, we might be able to recognize that our own method gives us approaches to these things that allow openness.

THE CATHOLIC PRESS AND WOMEN

Q: Were you surprised at the support the liberal press gave you in your struggle and dissent?

No. I was gratified by it. Even at Catholic University, however this thing is going to turn out, there is no doubt that the bishops and the Board of Trustees had been forced to change their mind because of that support. I was quite sure that the theological support was always there. Obviously it is the closest community I had, that is where I worked. Some people I know, and I read their writings; they read my writings and we discussed them in meetings. But I was also very pleased at the strength, and the publicness of that support. There were a number of people who had to put some things on the line too. A group of Catholic moral theologians got together at Notre Dame last year just to discuss the state of the discipline. I was amazed at how hurt a number of them were. I was surprised by the number of hurts they had experienced because of the church: either by the local bishop, or the local religious superior, or something they had written or had spoken.

I got great support from the theological community, my own colleagues. There were a few who disagreed with me, but overwhelmingly at Catholic University, both in the theology department and outside the theology department, there was very strong support. This is not a scientific sampling at all, but I received oodles of letters from supporters. At one time there were two thousand when this whole thing first broke, especially in March and again in August of 1986. But what surprised me most was the support from older Roman Catholics: a group I might have suspected would find my position most difficult. Amazingly, after a while it was almost like it was a form letter these older people were writing. The same refrain came up all the time: "I'm seventy-two years old and I was in Catholic education all my life. I had the Irish Brothers in high school and the Jesuits in college and my wife had the Sisters of St. Joseph and we were very happy with our faith. We were pleased with everything, we've always been good Catholics and never had any problems. But we have seen the problems that our children and our grandchildren are having and we just want you to know we're so glad there's somebody in the church that understands." That's the one thing that surprised me most in the area of support.

Q: Overwhelmingly, the number of women dissenters exceeds those of men in the church. Are you surprised at how little support the Catholic press has given women?

I think people like Elisabeth Schüssler Fiorenza, and Rosemary Ruether had a tremendous amount of support. For example, *U.S. Catholic*, made them both "Catholic of the Year," as I recall. When Sister Theresa came and spoke up to the pope in Washington, she got a tremendous amount of support. I think, very frankly, what you might be referring to is *The New York Times* ad, and I think that was a mixed bag. To be perfectly honest with you I was asked and did not sign it. I thought the thing was poorly drawn up, and did not make the necessary distinctions, and secondly I was opposed to it, because I'm pragmatic. I thought it would hurt Catholic politicians rather than help them. No Catholic politician could come out and question the church's moral teaching on abortion. If the signers wanted to have their document only with regard to public policy, then they would have been helpful to Catholic politicians, but to tell me the ad is going to help Catholic politicians, no. In the end, it turned out to be exactly that way. That case is very complex; I did not sign it. I, however, have written to five or six religious communities strongly urging that no action be taken against the people who did sign it. I don't think anybody should have been thrown out of the community because of it.

Q: Take Mary Ann Sorrentino, who runs or did run Planned Parenthood. She didn't sign the ad, and did many come to her defense?

I know her story. The same canon lawyer who has spent hours with me has also spent all sorts of hours with Mary Ann. Again, that's why it seems to me that you've got to talk about different constituencies. People are working with constituencies—I mean there's no doubt that the group supporting me most strongly is the theological group. My constituency are theologians, including feminist theologians. It is a question of need and, to be honest, one of which I am very conscious. Over the years, I have been a strong believer in the theories of Saul Alinsky. I have written on Saul Alinsky because I believe that organization—community organization—is very important. You must have organized support. In fact, the last time I saw Saul was just after the strike on my behalf at Catholic University in 1967. He said to me: "Charlie, a damn good organization you have got down there. If you were by yourself, you would have been a total loss. But you have a strong organization of students backing you up. Now keep that up; don't lose that damn organization."

So you see, theoretically and practically, I have always said that in order to do things, you have to have organization and you have to make sure you organize avenues of support. With women there have been attempts to do that, and there has been an awful lot of support by women for one another. I think it's an important time and that's why I want to see my role as saying that we who are males in the church now have to show our support for the role of women. We have to raise consciousness to the role of women; make people see the hurt and the pain women are going through; and get men in church ministry to be more conscious of it.

You are bound to have tensions and that's why you must frame the issue. In my dealing with dissent I wanted to make it very clear that the primary issue was not the sexual matters we discussed. They are important; they are very significant, but you get people divided on those kinds of things. I discovered how I could get the theological community to support me, in a context of organization. I had two choices: to seek the broadest support, or to limit it. The more support one wants, the more important it is to frame the issues as least divisive as possible. That's why I got the theologians to agree just on the question of dissent. Back in 1967 some people said: "Let's use Charlie's strike at Catholic University as a forum for the anti-Vietnam movement." All of us got together—we were all opposed to the Vietnam War—but we said "no." We're going to alienate some of our support, so just keep it on this one issue alone.

How do you apply that to the women's issue? I'm not sure. It seems to me that the minimum is to recognize that there can be diverse approaches. Some will take a more radical approach, some will take a more moderate approach. The two should not have sharp divisions. A good illustration might be those two meetings held last fall: a more radical group in the Women–Church meeting in Cincinnati; the more moderate group meeting in Washington.

There's got to be an interest that clearly provokes both kinds of women, and I would hate to see any kind of internecine warfare going on in the process. Women on both sides are big enough to say: "We need both groups; we'll stay together."

Q: How would you respond to feminist scholars who wonder about male theologians—some under Rome's gun themselves—now taking up the Catholic Woman's cause?

I have heard this complaint from a few people, but comparatively few people. I see my role at the present time as calling attention to the issue of the role of women in the church. In this entire process, I have said from the beginning that I wanted to make it a teaching moment. I have very publicly said that I think the question of the role of women in the church will be the primary internal issue which the Roman Catholic Church is going to have to face in the United States in the next years. For that reason, and as a part of that teaching moment, I have tried to point up this issue and its importance. In the process, I also feel it is important for me to give support in whatever way I can and call attention to the work that many Catholic women scholars are doing on the feminist question. I have never experienced any negative feeling from these women for what I am trying to do. I know there are some more radical feminists who would not want to see any male collaboration in what they are attempting to do. I really do not even call myself a collaborator, but one who is very sympathetic to these concerns and wants them to have a greater promulgation within society at large and within the church. In other words, I do not think that one has to be a woman in order to be a feminist. As I mentioned earlier in our conversations, I have learned a great deal from my women students, and from the sufferings of other women in the Catholic church at the present time. I, therefore, feel that I am in a good position to call attention to these facts and to try to increase within the Catholic church in general understanding on these issues.

Q: Where do you see your future?

Oh, my future; what I do best is I'm a theologian, and I can see that having a role in the church. I asked a reporter recently: Where were you people three years ago and where are you going to be three years from now? They, I told them, were interested in me now because of my dissent, and in a certain sense I use it for my teaching moment. I realize that, and I want to be honest about that. But in the end, it still seems to me that what I do best is I'm a theologian and I want to continue doing theology. For lack of a better word, because of all the support I have, I have some responsibility to work to change the church, and that I will do. But I will never give up my primary way of doing it which is, working in and through the people.

CHAPTER XV

DISSENT WITHIN THE U.S. CHURCH: THE CASE OF THE VATICAN "24"

Maureen Fiedler, S.L.

Editorial Note: In response to several archbishops' attacks on 1984 Democratic vice-presidential candidate Geraldine Ferraro for her position on abortion policy, an ad hoc Committee for Concerned Catholics entered a full-page advertisement in *The New York Times* on October 7, 1984. The statement described a diversity of opinion on abortion within the church and the theological community, decried clerical attacks on political candidates over the issue, and called for dialogue on the issue. This public statement drew an immediate reaction from the Vatican and triggered a series of repressive actions by church-related agencies against the ad's signers, particularly those signers who were members of religious communities. Twenty-four women religious resisted the Vatican's demand that they publicly retract the statement or face dismissal from their congregations. From 1984 through 1988, the Vatican Congregation for Religious and Secular Institute (CRIS) reached individual settlements with most of the sisters. (Two women, Sisters of Notre Dame Barbara Ferraro and Patricia Hussey, refused to compromise with Vatican authorities, were not dismissed by their community, but decided to resign from their community in July 1988.) Maureen E. Fiedler was one of the religious sisters who signed the ad. Her analysis here was originally presented at the 1987 Women–Church Convergence in Cincinnati.

Good afternoon, Women–Church! Buenas tardes, Mujer-Iglesia! Today we explore a theme that cuts to the heart of our struggle as women: the exercise of power. Women of the gospel are called to challenge, and ultimately transform, the power structures of patriarchy into systems of equality and mutuality. The question I address today is a very specific and practical aspect of that theme: *How* do we challenge and transform systems of power? How do we claim our power as women and work *effectively* for justice in church and state? I address this topic not only theoretically, but from the depths of my own experience as a woman, indeed, from the pain of my own encounters with the power structures of the Roman Catholic Church. What follows is an analysis of the power dynamics of one of the most significant events in recent Women-Church herstory: the controversy over *The New York Times* ad of 1984. This is not a rehash of the past, but a reflection on that event to see what we can learn about struggling with patriarchal institutions. This was not the first instance of ecclesial repression in recent times, and it won't be the last. Claiming our power as women demands that we critically examine our experiences, especially the crises, and learn for the next time. Although this analysis is drawn from experience in the Roman Catholic Church, the principles are broad enough to apply to any ecclesial structure or to justice struggles with military establishments, corporations, or nation-states. This analysis is strictly my own; it does not necessarily represent the views of other signers or community leaders. I hope all these women will share their reflections in time. I begin with a few basic assumptions:

Power is not a dirty word. Understood in gospel terms, "claiming power" is not a quest to control others; it is a demand by powerless people for a rightful share in decisions which affect their lives. When the powerless (the poor, women in the Church, racial minorities, etc.) act to achieve this, they work for liberation and justice.

Political power in the modern world is vested primarily in systems and structures, not personalities. Long-term work for justice calls us to understand power *systems*, not just the personalities who run them. It is much easier to change presidents or even popes than to change the systems that put them in power. We may, for example, elect a Democratic President in 1988 but make no fundamental change in U.S. domination of Latin America. Pope John XXIII represented a change in papal personalities, but he left behind no real structural change in the centralized authoritarian power of the Vatican. Changing systems is slow, difficult, risky, and hardly ever "ladylike."

The most common problem women have with political power is not copying male models—although that happens. The most common problem is women's reticence to use levers of power at all. Even today, almost twenty–five years into the most recent surge of feminism, too few women run for public office or act as political consultants. Qualified women are reluctant to mount presidential campaigns. In the church, women have rocked the boat enough to be classified as a major "problem," but here too, women are too often reluctant to use real levers of power, e.g., the media or economic organizing.

It is easier for women of faith to deal with injustice from the state than injustice from the church. Church injustice runs against the deep expectations of our faith and touches our inmost being in a way that state repression does not. Although any power struggle is physically and emotionally draining, church struggles are often more traumatic, more isolating, and less supported by our friends.

THE NEW YORK TIMES AD AND THE POWER REALITIES OF THE CHURCH

First: a brief review of the facts. In 1984, I was one of ninety–seven Catholics who signed the "Catholic Statement on Pluralism and Abortion," which appeared as a full-page ad in *The New York Times* just before the presidential election of that year. It described the legitimate diversity of views on this subject in the Church and called for a serious and respectful dialogue on the issue of abortion. By standards of contemporary protest, it was mild in the extreme. Columnist Ellen Goodman said it was like the American colonists asking King George III if they could please discuss the matter of tea!

It would have passed into oblivion had not the Congregation for Religious and Secular Institutes (CRIS) in Rome given it worldwide publicity. That Congregation singled out signers who were members of religious communities, wrote letters to their leadership, and demanded that the signers either retract or face dismissal.

Politically speaking, the signers exercised a human and Christian right to speak their consciences in a responsible public way. People may agree or disagree with the *content* of what was said; that is *not* the political point here. Adult, responsible Catholics have the right, even the duty, to speak out for what they believe is the good of the Church.

Rome's response to the ad exhibited all the characteristics of a centralized authoritarian structure threatened by a public exposure that it was losing control—not only of the "masses"—but of its "professional" workers, i.e., priests, nuns, brothers, theologians. First, it turned a substantive cry for dialogue into an issue of power and obedience. Second, it made an "example" of the canonically vulnerable signers as a deterrent to others who might have similar ideas. Third, the plan was launched in secrecy, without consulting even the U.S. bishops, let alone community leaders. Fourth, messages were sent from the top down the hierarchical ladder, expecting that community leaders would do the dirty work, i.e., secure the retractions, or if that proved impossible: dismiss the recalcitrants. Implicit in this demand of community leaders was an unspoken threat that failure to comply risked one's status in the hierarchy, and maybe even the official status of one's community.

This was a raw and arrogant exercise of patriarchal power of the worst kind: a "case study" in how *not* to run a church.

After sixteen months of intense struggle, all but three of the nun signers "settled" their cases with Rome or had them settled by community leaders. Rome did *not* get the public retractions it demanded, but officials did get some type of compromise statements either from signers or leaders reporting signers' views. Two women, Barbara Ferraro and Patricia Hussey of the Sisters of Notre Dame, have put up heroic resistance: refusing to give CRIS anything remotely resembling an ameliorating statement, and refusing to be silenced on the subject of reproductive rights. We need to support those women wholeheartedly.

The third signer with an unsettled case is Rose Dominic Trapasso, a Maryknoll Sister from Lima, Peru. Maryknoll's leadership received a letter from the Congregation for Evangelization more than a year after everyone else. (Maryknoll does not come under CRIS in the Roman bureaucracy.) That letter contained no threat of dismissal, but the case remains open.

I muddled through months of this painful struggle myself and ultimately made a compromise settlement with Rome, which I now deeply regret. And so I have asked myself for many months: What happened? What didn't we all hold out? Why did so many of us feel demoralized by these events? Why did most of us act more like victims than assertive feminists? Analyzing this is not easy for me because I share responsibility for what was done, but I offer you my reflections in the hope that we are not doomed to repeat mistakes.

PRINCIPLES OF ACTION FOR WOMEN CLAIMING POWER

This analysis looks at the events of that struggle, extrapolates principles of action for women claiming power, and then reflects on what we did well and what we did poorly in the light of those principles.

Principle #1: Claiming power demands a rigorous analysis of the power dynamics of a situation and action based on that analysis. We *did* analyze the situation: theologically, canonically, communally, and to some extent politically. And we *did* resist, many of us for sixteen long months. The first letters from our leaders to CRIS almost uniformly rejected dismissal as totally inappropriate to the situation.

But we spent far more energy analyzing words and concepts in letters from Rome than analyzing the political motivation behind these words. CRIS was *not* interested in words, or ultimately even orthodoxy on the issue of abortion. CRIS was interested in control, obedience, and submission: anything that sounded like a genuflection to their unshared power. Had we *really* understood that and acted accordingly, we would have realized that *any* statement satisfactory to CRIS implicitly sanctioned their unjust exercise of power and ratified their judgment that signing the ad was wrong and needed reparation. We would not have spent months groping for words that would preserve our integrity and yet "satisfy" Rome. We might have guessed that CRIS would do what it ultimately did: totally misrepresent those carefully crafted statements to the public so CRIS could reclaim the power it lost when the ad was published.

Principle #2: Women claiming power cannot allow oppressors to become the sole public definers of the issues in a struggle. We need to define the issues publicly on our terms, denounce injustice and announce actions for liberation. Some signers did this individually, but it was never done publicly as a group. Had community leaders and signers put together a common *public* stance early in the struggle and denounced the Vatican's injustice, the entire dynamic of the controversy would have changed. The media would not have focused exclusively on the "abortion nuns," but on the Vatican's denial of free speech, religious liberty, and rights of conscience. There might have been articles on Vatican interference with the U.S. political process inasmuch as the ad appeared in the midst of a heated presidential campaign in which the Catholic hierarchy was making abortion a central issue. The *Vatican* and its actions needed to become the issue, not us.

Our lack of denunciation, however, set a *tone of compliance* from the beginning that implicitly accepted—at least in public—CRIS's definition of the controversy. Without a public case for our side, it was difficult to generate public sympathy, organize solidarity actions or even maintain resistance over the long run.

Principle #3: It is no longer true that women are to be seen and not heard. Women claiming power need to be public and use the media. Again, many of us did this individually, but there was no *group* media strategy, and there was strong internal pressure from some community leaders *not* to do media. In retrospect, it is clear that this was based on an early and unarticulated decision by some community leaders that CRIS would have to be "satisfied" in the end and media would make their satisfaction more difficult. In other words, pressure not to do media came from a structural submission to the power of patriarchy and ultimately fear of what they might do.

It is instructive to compare this with the active use of media by Charles Curran. He defended his writings in many public forums, defined his issue as the "right to dissent," and won a great deal of public support. Although the fact that he was a male cleric and prominent theologian were surely important factors in his garnering support, his effective use of the media was indispensable in his struggle.

Refraining from public answers to public injustices is not wisdom; most often it is active fear generated by an internalized patriarchy by which we silence ourselves.

Principle #4: When threatened with repressive action, women claiming power need to remain unified and in constant communication so that anger is not turned inward

and "divide and conquer" strategies won't work. We signed the ad as individuals, not as a group. But for the sake of effective strategy in the struggle, we needed to become a group. Our first moves in this direction were excellent. While the men under fire dealt individually with their leaders, we women called meetings, shared feelings, and developed common strategies. Early meetings included lay and nun signers.

But try as we might, this initial unity lasted about six weeks. We did not remain a cohesive group for the long haul. We did not establish structures that might have helped us, like a central office or a legal defense fund. Eventually, community loyalty and community processes overrode signers' solidarity and settlements followed, one by one.

Forging unity isn't easy when there is no group to begin with, but we need to find ways to do that if we ever hope to claim power as Women-Church.

Principle #5: Women claiming power need to treat each other as sisters in struggle, that is—with the ethic of a discipleship of equals. That means full sharing of information and full participation in decision-making by those whose lives are affected by the decisions. Many of us *did* follow these ethics *within* our own community groups; that was certainly true in meetings within the Loretto Community. But we fell sadly short of this ideal in the larger signers/leaders group as a whole. Both community leaders and signers felt battered by patriarchy and many reverted to old hierarchical modes of action. It's hard to say some of these things, but they need to be named if they are not to be repeated. Community leaders held meetings, consulted with canon lawyers and theologians, and made decisions—all without the presence of the very women whose community lives were on the line: the nun signers of the ad. There was a reversion to pre-Vatican II models which segregate by status and role.

Pressures for community loyalty cut across the solidarity the signers needed as a group. Over time, there was even pressure from some community leaders on their respective signers *not* to share information with other signers! In most cases, this pressure was disregarded, but it often blocked the necessary information flow for days or weeks.

These models carried over into relations with lay signers. The nun signers met with lay signers on several occasions, but we never incorporated them fully into strategy sessions. And with one exception, community leaders flatly refused to meet with them at all. Even though several lay signers were disinvited from Catholic institutions or suffered at their jobs because of the ad, we nun signers never organized for true "common cause" with them.

Perhaps worst of all, some leaders actually "settled" cases for their sisters in ways that the sisters did not know, or in ways that misrepresented the signers' real beliefs. There are some nun signers who do not know to this day what was written to CRIS about their beliefs! Some of this represented a subtle, silent—but nonetheless real—choosing of sides. (This was certainly *not* true of Loretto.)

We need to understand the fears that underlay these actions, but we must resolve that this will *never* be repeated in future struggles. We must work to transform not only *external* patriarchy, but that version which lies *within* us.

Principle #6: When in struggle, women claiming power need to foster solidarity in every way possible. We did some of this. We urged people to send Christmas protest messages to the Vatican when the issue first broke into the media. Community leaders declared a Day of Prayer and Fasting that implied that the Vatican needed help as much as we did. (CRIS made clear later that this prayer and fasting was not appreciated!)

But we refrained from *strong* solidarity actions for many months. When a joint nun–signer and lay-signer group proposed the most powerful action of all, the "Declaration of Solidarity" or the so-called "second ad" in *The New York Times*, LCWR leaders led a campaign to stifle it. More negative emotion was vented on that ad than any reasoned disagreement over strategies could have stirred. Leaders of women's and men's communities made strong pleas—issued orders in some cases—that members not sign that ad. And the *National Catholic Reporter*—theoretically progressive in its viewpoint—indulged itself in the worst of yellow journalism in its editorial condemning the second ad. Catholic theologians who later scrambled to be on the Curran and Hunthausen bandwagons were nowhere to be found.

In future struggles, women need to organize, nurture and promote solidarity—not discourage it.

Principle #7: Women claiming power need to use words, symbols, and images carefully, especially those with power implications. For the most part, we *were* careful with words and definitions among ourselves. But one glaring misuse stands out: we talked a great deal about "dialogue" with the Vatican. Dialogue is a conversation between two roughly equal parties, either one of which is open to modifying his or her views as a result of that conversation. Dialogue is exceedingly difficult, if not impossible, when one party is threatening the other. The Vatican does not "dialogue" with internal progressive "dissidents." Roman officials sit and talk, yes—but consider talks concluded only when the other party makes substantial concessions to their point of view. Whatever that is, it's not "dialogue." If we use such words inaccurately, we wind up fooling ourselves and getting snookered.

Principle #8: Women claiming power don't act through intermediaries; they speak and act for themselves. All through the struggle, we signers allowed community leaders to communicate our views to Rome in writing. Until the end when a frustrated Vatican sent officials to talk personally to the "holdouts," we dealt with CRIS through the intermediary of our leadership. Only one signer attempted direct letter-writing to Rome and was rebuffed.

We never discussed this strategy as a signers' group; we accepted this implicit hierarchical structure as a "given." But adults speak for themselves. Men such as Curran and Hunthausen argued their own cases. In the future, we women must insist on doing the same thing. Perhaps our communication will include our own counterproposals to the Vatican, something we did not do in this case.

Principle #9: Women claiming power recognize that crises are excellent opportunities to promote the issue of justice which led to the crisis. The struggle over *The New York Times* ad did help the cause of reproductive rights for women by showing the world that dissent on this issue is wide and deep in the church. It led many communities to have serious discussions of abortion for the first time. But we did not do what those in secular trials for antinuclear actions or granting sanctuary to refugees usually do very well: promote the substantive issues involved in the public arena. We might have contributed a great deal more to public discussions of reproductive issues because many of our views do not fit the rigid, polarized public debate—but are nuanced and qualified, growing from a theological perspective.

Principle #10: If a struggle reveals a structural impediment to the effective challenging of patriarchy, women claiming power need to work to remove that impediment. If there was one structural reality that loomed large throughout the struggle, it was the fact that our communities all had canonical status, i.e., official ties with the ecclesiastical patriarchy. Many members of our communities value that status, and feared that this struggle might lead to losing it. It was principally those members who created internal pressures on the signers to settle with CRIS.

Scenarios went like this: What if the signers don't settle, and the leaders refuse to dismiss them? Would CRIS depose the leaders? Would the community then lose canonical status? What would happen to the retired sisters, the community property, and the assets built for so long with women's labor? Rome's power operated from within us very effectively.

In short, we discovered that canonical status makes it extremely difficult, if not impossible, for us to challenge patriarchy effectively.

It is canonical status that keeps the case of Barbara Ferraro and Patricia Hussey alive in the Sisters of Notre Dame. I do not believe that their community leaders would ever consider—as they are now—dismissing members for speaking their consciences if Rome weren't watching every move and if the community did not worry about its status with Rome.

This struggle suggests that the time has come to challenge that structure and move away from it. I am not suggesting that we leave the church or the tradition of women's ministering communities. I *am* suggesting that we find a *new and independent space*—and I'm not sure where that is—from which we can be the prophetic challengers we are called to be.

CONCLUSION

This is not an exhaustive list of principles or an all–inclusive analysis. But it's a beginning.

Our hope for the future lies in our ability to be self-critical, to examine our experiences, however painful, and learn from them. It lies in our courage and resolution to claim our rightful share in the decision-making of the Church. It lies in our ability to heal, to understand, and to love as we muddle through struggles. And it lies in Women-Church as we work to shed the layers of internal, as well as external, patriarchy. We may not handle the next crisis perfectly, but we will surely be wiser, less hierarchical, and more unified. We will take longer and firmer steps in the direction of mutuality and equality. We will, as true revolutionaries in our church, take two steps forward for every one back. We will move the church closer to being that sharing and caring community which is the legacy that Jesus left us

CHAPTER XVI

CATHOLIC WOMEN: TWO DECADES OF CHANGE

Karen Sue Smith

Whatever the shape of tomorrow's Catholic church, women will be among the primary shapers. This claim is not intended to diminish women's invaluable contribution to the church in times past, especially when so many of those contributions are only now being uncovered by scholars. Rather, it is to confirm and continue that history, and, further, to suggest that Catholic women are beneficiaries of a global shift in consciousness: the human dignity, inherent rights, and full potential of women are beginning to be recognized by women themselves and by men, by tribes and whole societies.[1]

This change is as sweeping in its ramifications as was the realization by the world's peoples that slavery is immoral. And while this shift in understanding is occurring at differing speeds among differing societies, creating enormous tensions and raising new problems in its wake, it is of such magnitude that established structures are already showing visible signs of its impact. Those structures include family, business, government, and church.

Of course, cultural change is never neat or easy, as the history of the suffragists in this country and earlier women's movements in Europe attest. It is ironic that in previous periods, some Catholic women—particularly those in religious life—attained not merely education and a kind of independence beyond that of their peers, but positions of immense influence. St. Catherine of Siena, St. Teresa of Avila, and the Mexican poet Sor Juana Inés de la Cruz readily spring to mind.[2] Recently, however, women in the Catholic church *seem* to have fallen behind their peers in opportunity. Perhaps this is because an authoritarian church is more resistant to pressure than is either business or government; there is no civil law to bring "affirmative action" to the parish, no women's vote to keep or remove the hierarchy of the church, and very little buying power, since women do want to support the church, in general: the aging sisters, the work with the poor, education, etc.

Nevertheless, it is the thesis of this essay that women have in actuality moved ahead within the institutional Catholic church, even though they have not been admitted to the ordained priesthood. They have progressed by combining (1) the democratic belief in equality of opportunity; (2) the scriptural injunctions against dividing the body of Christ on the basis of gender, race, and class; and (3) the New Testament concepts of worship leaders as possessing certain gifts of the Spirit recognized by the worshipping community itself. And they have appealed to both public opinion and the U.S. hierarchy with organized acts of protest, sustained intellectual achievement, and by participating in established centers of decisionmaking wherever possible. In other words, one can read the signs of the times and argue that as far as women's roles in the Catholic church today are concerned, the cup of progress is half full rather than half empty. It would be difficult to argue, however, that the cup is brimming over.

One cannot say that unlimited progress toward equality of opportunity is inevitable. Gains in public opinion on the issue of women's ordination, for example, have slowed to a crawl. Even so, given the momentum of women's leadership gains in society at large, the recent backlash of traditionalism among some Catholic women's groups has little chance of stopping the tide of progress or changing its direction for Catholic women in general. That is, unless a wave of traditionalism were to sweep over society itself.

How will Catholic women shape the opportunities afforded them over the next several decades? This is the question of the hour. To address it, the church as a whole must recognize the new opportunities and responsibilities women are already assuming and realize the extent of attitudinal changes that have occurred during the last two decades—over the issue of women's ordination to the priesthood and the growing leadership role of women at all levels in the church. Attitudes have changed among the press, among bishops, among feminists, and among the laity. What follows is a brief sketch of these developments, along with the questions and issues that continue to occupy the church.

NEW OPPORTUNITIES AND ACHIEVEMENTS

Catholic women—regardless of their personal views on these developments—may all partake of the new opportunities for service and responsibility that have swept into the church during the last two decades on this tide of change. Many Catholic women are moving into expanded roles for laity as pastors, scholars, organizers, advocates, and leaders of worship. A few are re-envisioning the church and its ministry, examining its hierarchical structure, and calling it into question. The possibility of a new dynamism within Christianity in this outpouring of women's intellectual and spiritual contributions is at hand.

Catholic women in the United States today are chancellors of dioceses, canon lawyers, hospital and prison chaplains, members of marriage tribunals, administrators of parishes, pastoral counselors, superintendents of Catholic schools, heads of departments and presidents in Catholic universities, faculty and spiritual directors in seminaries. Women plan liturgies, and at Sunday Mass are cantors, lectors, eucharistic ministers, and ushers (ministers of hospitality). Catholic women—lay and religious—may and do preside at public liturgies of the Word, the Divine Office, and may preach on these occasions. Women are active on diocesan and state commissions. They have also created and are leading various social ministries—political lobbying on arms control, education, health care, welfare benefits, family issues—as well as offering direct social services to those in need. Catholic women are active in the arts and in media, writing columns and articles, producing films, editing newspapers and magazines that deal with religion.

While this list is necessarily incomplete, it does indicate the breadth of new roles now open to all women vis-à-vis the church.

Formerly, such occupations as president of a hospital or university were open only to members of the religious orders who founded or sponsored them; most orders provided direct care for the sick or poor or were involved in teaching.

These new roles, for the most part, require highly educated women. Catholic women are among those whose advances in education and participation in the paid work force comprise two of the most sweeping cultural changes of the last century in American history. In the field of theology alone, Catholic women have been receiving seminary degrees in unprecedented numbers. Catholics (overwhelmingly lay women and men) have comprised the largest single denominational group at Harvard Divinity School for the last ten years or so (and are well represented at other Ivy League seminaries). This is a far cry from the experiences of women during the fifties and sixties, who, like feminist theologian Mary Daly, could not fully pursue theology in U.S. Catholic seminaries because of gender restrictions.[3]

Catholic women scholars—most notably, theologian Rosemary Ruether and New Testament exegete Elisabeth Schüssler Fiorenza—have been at the helm of the Christian feminist movement, building an ecumenical coalition of scholars and producing an impressive body of new research on Scripture, theology, language theory, ethics, feminist methodology and analysis, church history, and spirituality.[4] Several of their books have entered the culture's literary mainstream and have been reviewed by the national press.

In addition to academic achievements and honors, a few outstanding Catholic women working in religion have been elected to lead professional societies: In 1987, the Society of Biblical Literature elected Elisabeth Schüssler Fiorenza as its first woman president; Monika Hellwig was elected president of the Catholic Theological Society of America in 1986; women have also presided over the National Council of Catholic Charities, the Religious Education Association of the U.S. and Canada, and the Canon Law Society of America.

Catholic women have also been recognized at the popular level. *U.S. Catholic*, a monthly magazine published by the Claretians, has established an annual "Catholic of the Year" award for "furthering the cause of women in the church." (Recipients include Sister of Loretto Mary Luke Tobin, Elisabeth Schüssler Fiorenza, and Donna Hanson, the woman who addressed the pope on behalf of the laity during his 1987 U.S. visit.) The Paulist Center in Boston has established the Isaac Hecker Award for Social Justice, which has honored several women, including lobbyists (Carol Coston of NETWORK) and feminist liturgists (Mary Hunt and Diann Neu of WATER).[5] I mention these offices and awards to indicate that Catholic women leaders—including leading feminists—are receiving a significant degree of support from their colleagues and peers.

Catholic women have also established organizations to promote equality within the church, such as the Women's Ordination Conference (WOC), the Leadership Conference of Women Religious (LCWR) committee on women's ecclesial role, Chicago Catholic Women, The Grail Women Task Force, and the National Coalition of American Nuns (NCAN), organizations with differing characters, emphases, and political strategies. Some women are creating base communities to exemplify a more inclusive church, one that is open to discovering how to fully incorporate the experience and insights of women. One such movement, called Women-Church, will be described briefly later.

THE OLD RESTRICTIONS

These cumulative advances make it particularly troubling for many Catholics to admit—to themselves and to others—that women still may not officially be installed as acolytes or lectors—both roles subsumed in the progression toward priestly ordination.[6] And because women are barred from ordination as deacons and priests, they cannot regularly perform such sacramental functions as presiding at Eucharist, baptisms, marriages, funerals, and reconciliation rites.

Why? Attitudes have yet to be changed sufficiently within the hierarchy—worldwide—to allow it. In a highly centralized church, structural change is essentially the only route open to ordination.

Meanwhile, according to polls, the percentage of Catholics favoring women's ordination increased 12 percent, jumping from 29 percent to 41 percent in 1977, two months after the Vatican issued an encyclical against it.[7] Yet between 1977 and 1985, the increase had slowed to only 6 percent. In a 1985 Gallup survey Catholics were evenly divided on the issue of ordination: 47 percent in favor; 47 percent opposed.[8]

Of course, the pace of social change is a somewhat relative perception. It seems particularly slow for those who have steadily fostered increased opportunities for women since the Second Vatican Council or before; it seems rapid for those overwhelmed by the depth and scope of the social change that burst on the cultural scene during the sixties.

In the next four sections, I will discuss in brief: (1) the movement for women's ordination—the context, the arguments, the attitude shifts, and the stalemate; (2) why, despite the tensions and stalemates, so many proponents of women's equal opportunities remain within the Catholic Church; (3) the Christian feminist movement—its phases and challenges; and (4) the draft pastoral letter on women's concerns written by the U.S. Catholic Conference. The draft, which will eventually become a consensus statement by the bishops, gives some indication of how some feminist goals for a more just church are in fact moving the larger church in the U.S.

ORDINATION

A skeletal chronology helps to contextualize the issue of women's ordination: the Second Vatican Council began in 1962; Betty Friedan's *The Feminine Mystique* was published in 1963; Mary Daly's *The Church and the Second Sex*, 1968; Germaine Greer's *The Female Eunuch*, 1971; the ERA was first passed by Congress (though never fully ratified) in 1972. The first Women's Ordination Conference was held in 1976. Sister of Mercy Theresa Kane addressed the pope, asking that women be "included in all ministries of our church," in 1979.[9]

The rapidity of rising expectations of women for an increased role in the church (as well as in secular society) was not impeded by the staunch Vatican resistance it received. In 1976—in spite of the Pontifical Biblical Commission's conclusion that there are no scriptural grounds to deny women ordination—the Vatican under Pope Paul VI issued its "Declaration on the Question of the Admission of Women to the Ministerial Priesthood."[10] *Inter Insigniores*, released in English January 27, 1977, outlines the Vatican's case against women's ordination: in brief, women cannot image Christ; and tradition has consistently barred women from priestly ordination.

The document's explicit prohibition, however, only stoked the debate already raging in this country. A nationwide prayer vigil led by women was held in protest. Don Zirkel of the *Brooklyn Tablet* described it as "the first time in the 2,000-year history of the church that such a large number of women rejected a decision about them by the exclusively-male decision-making process."[11] Sadly, but not surprisingly, some fifty Catholic newspapers surveyed by Zirkel refused even to report the widespread rejection of the declaration by Catholic laity.

Meanwhile, a group of faculty members from the Jesuit School of Theology, Berkeley, published an open letter of protest addressed to Jean Jadot, the Vatican's apostolic delegate.[12] Many in the liberal Catholic press expressed dismay at the Vatican's statement, but even so, the expectation of a reversal or an amendment of the ban was still palpable at that time. Peter Steinfels, who in 1977 was a columnist for *Commonweal*, predicted that "within a decade" women would be ordained.[13] And sympathizers mindful of the age of Paul VI settled in to await the next pope. Needless to say, on this issue they are still waiting.

Ordination, it should be recalled, is pastorally distinct from other issues, such as the prohibition of divorce/remarriage or artificial contraception, which many Catholics have resolved individually—and with the help of clergy—by making acts of conscience, the so-called "internal forum." Ordination cannot be solved by any personal act of conscience. It is an ecclesial issue, one that poses the question: What kind of church are we, and will we become? The ordination of women to the Catholic priesthood depends upon structural changes within the church.

How, then, have advocates of women's ordination accommodated to the papal prohibition? For over a decade, Catholics in favor of women's ordination have had few choices open to them. They can (1) disobey, trying to find some bishops to ordain women despite church law; (2) quietly allow women to preside at masses, where the priest shortage is genuine, or among small communities that choose to "obey a higher law"; (3) celebrate communion services in lieu of masses; or (4) wait.

The first option, once thought possible, now seems most unlikely. Certainly, any bishops ordaining women, and those women ordained, would be readily excommunicated. This option would be short-lived and accomplish little. Virtually no Catholic feminist is clamoring for such a move. Ordination of women to Roman Catholic priesthood ultimately requires an egalitarian pope.

The second option continues to be practiced, and in some places with genuine success, although—because women presiding is a public act contrary to official church teaching—it carries with it the possibility of divisiveness within the larger church, even schism. Some feminist communities have been experimenting with alternative liturgies that do not pretend to be "Roman Catholic masses" per se, but are celebrations of shared symbolic meals with women presiding. These have also met with considerable success (as with WATER's liturgies), though the effectiveness and meaning of alternative uses of symbolism is worthy of discussion.[14]

The third option holds a strong initial attraction, because it allows congregations without priests to continue to worship regularly and to celebrate *Communion* led by the laity (consecrated during an earlier mass and held in reserve). But there are serious theological problems involved here also, which liturgists and theologians have begun to point out.[15]

The fourth option—wait—is most prevalent and practical for most Catholics. Even so, waiting need not imply passivity, nor has it.

Over time the collective arguments for the ordination of women have sharpened. They have never been clearer or more compelling than they are today: (1) God became flesh, i.e., human, not merely male; (2) by the grace given at baptism all Catholics take on the likeness and mission of Christ; (3) the past custom of ordaining only males was the result of cultural limitations—as was the custom of accepting slavery—and should not be given the weight of tradition. To continue such a custom today is to practice the structural sin of sexism; (4) while ordination is the right of no one—man or woman—neither should anyone be excluded solely on account of gender; (5) that although Jesus did not ordain women, neither did he ordain anyone; (6) that the pastoral needs of God's people to receive the Eucharist—in light of an increasing priest shortage—deserve to be met.[16]

While the priest shortage is a pastoral matter of concern for parishes, it cannot be the major justification for women's ordination, lest a married clergy fill the shortage and close the argument. Rather, the overriding considerations remain theological.

Finally, it should be stated that the ordination of women is a growing concern in other countries, particularly but not exclusively in the developed world of Western Europe. (It was an Irish bishop who called for women's ordination at the 1986 synod on the laity.) Although support for it is not now overwhelming, the question of women's ordination will continue to arise as women take their place in societies alongside men.

CATHOLIC FEMINISTS: WHY THEY STAY

Many Catholic feminists ask themselves (and interested observers ask them) why they remain in such an inequitable church. It is an intensely personal question, on the one hand, but it is ecclesiological, on the other.

Some feminists have found that they cannot remain Catholic, some not even Christian, in view of the corruptions of sexism within the church; some find the maleness of Jesus and the maleness attributed to the entire Trinity to be profoundly limited.[17]

Some, in order to pursue a call to ordination (including men who seek both priesthood and marriage) have joined Protestant Christian denominations. Some feminists, who insist they will not leave the Catholic church, have publicly professed that they remain to change it, adding that they won't give the hierarchy the satisfaction of their leave–taking.[18]

Many progressive women and men, who see clearly the ancient discrimination patterns within the church and deplore them, are also deeply rooted in Catholicism. They find their quest for internal justice to be at the core of their faith, not at odds with it. They intend to remain active Catholics, holding the church they love to its own best teachings. Many simply realize in pragmatic terms that no institution is perfect, that every religion has its own set of problems and injustices. Catholicism is the religion they know best. It is their home.

Some Catholics who hope for increased equality within the church have experienced attitudinal and practical changes, especially at the parish level, that feed their hope for more substantial changes. Why should they leave now? For those engaged at the academic level, the new feminist scholarship and theological construction brings its own excitement and rewards.

It is also possible—though difficult to determine or document—that many Catholics have realized the long-term change they hope for will not occur in their own lifetimes, so they have decreased their immediate expectations, postponed their hopes. This frustration-coping mechanism allows them to continue worshiping within a community that both nurtures and stifles them.

For many Catholic feminists, the recognition that the church discriminates unjustly toward women and has a history mired in patriarchy is only one part, albeit a tragic part, of a much broader understanding of church. For them, the Catholic church is more than its structure, and the Catholic faith is infinitely more.

Their understanding of Catholic faith goes deeper than cultural ties, local community friendships, and family roots, though these are surely important. Such faith rests on a solid understanding of the Christian message of justice, equality, love—including sacrifice, forgiveness and mercy, service to the powerless of this world, and reconciliation of the estranged. It is rooted in the example and message of Jesus Christ, including his friendships with and relation to women.

These Catholic feminists are aware that they have learned this very message within an unjust, male-dominated church, a church that needs to learn how to live up to its own vision. The church has both nurtured and exploited women—among others.

Despite the very real problem of exclusive language, for example, in Scripture, prayers, and rites, Catholics enriched by the church's sacramental life and symbol system have found that symbols and sacraments carry levels of meaning not solely dependent upon words. What these symbols and sacraments have provided is a challenge to the church to embody the full theological meaning associated with them. The power and subconscious depth of archetypal human symbols—fire, light, darkness, bread, blood, wine, water—cry out against their own diminution.

The Eucharist, for example, is, among other things, a symbol of unity, an inclusive banquet where class, gender, age, race, and other barriers between people are broken down. Experienced fully, the Eucharist reveals to worshipers the shortcomings of their own celebrating community: Have race and class divisions in the parish been transcended? One need only look up and down the pews. Gender divisions? The practice of admitting only men as presiders at the banquet visibly tarnishes the sign of unity and the act of communal thanksgiving. (Even a child, upon hearing that the Eucharist is a sign of unity, could articulate the many visible ways it is not, in practice.) Yet unity remains possible through Eucharist.

Catholic feminists who remain within the church continue to be nurtured by the strength and beauty of the nonverbal elements of the liturgy. Few are interested in exchanging these ancient symbol systems, rituals, gestures, postures, rites, and aesthetics for anything less substantial. Nor do they want worship that is separate but equal. They want, rather, to reclaim these symbols for all worshipers.

Catholic feminists are committed to trying to make the church's power structure, the parish's pastoral life, and the language of ritual and prayer truly egalitarian, open to women at every level, to women's experience and decisionmaking.. These are enormous goals calling for significant change, not merely the addition of God "the mother" or brothers and "sisters," though the revision of hymns, liturgical books, and Scripture has already begun, albeit at a halting pace.[19]

Many progressive Catholics have also been shaped by the vision of an inclusive community that works for social justice. They are part of a tradition that has spawned orders of religious dedicated to the poorest of society—lepers, prostitutes, drug abusers, the hungry, the ignorant, the sick and dying, and those whose economic, political, and human rights have been trampled or ignored. Social justice is part of the Catholic ethos, as are other values and an ethical system that give meaning to their lives and provide guidance through the difficult decisions required in adulthood.

Perhaps that is why the gap between the papal and episcopal injunctions to achieve justice in the secular sphere and the practices of injustice in the ecclesial sphere is clear and painful for them.

CATHOLIC FEMINISTS: ON THE MOVE

The Catholic feminist movement—which could be called the Christian/Jewish feminist movement, because from the outset there has been cooperation and collaboration among scholars—has undergone several phases of development. First, a critical analytical phase uncovered the pervasiveness of patriarchal structures underlying most major human institutions.[20]

Second, a constructive phase began as women researched their own religious history, added to emergent liberation theologies of inclusion, and formed coalitions and conferences, using democratic and consensual patterns of collective decisionmaking.[21]

Groups such as the Women's Ordination Conference continue to play an educational role, hold protests and counter conferences, and engage in dialogue with bishops. WOC was among the twenty-four national organizations officially invited to testify before the bishops' committee that drafted the letter on women's concerns.[22]

Third, a community-building phase is in process. Communal groups grew out of the drive for women's ordination as questions about the role of priest and church were considered more deeply, and the vision of a renewed church emerged. The movement called Women-Church is a product of this third phase, an attempt to build now a church where women's contributions and charisms are fully engaged at all levels.

Much has already been written about the development of Women-Church.[23] On the one hand, it is a loose coalition of organizations that coordinate regional and national conferences. For example, the Cincinnati Conference (October 9–11, 1987) was sponsored by twenty-five women's groups and defined itself in the program as "rooted in the Catholic tradition and commitment to Women-Church." On the other hand, Women-Church is a composite of local ecumenical women's groups that meet for diverse purposes—discussion, study, worship, action, service—which they themselves determine. The variations of style and substance are numerous, making the movement difficult to categorize or define sharply.

Women-Church is an alternative for women who are unwilling to participate in any *institutional* church; it is also a support group for those who seeking to develop a language, spirituality, and equal place for women at all levels within their own denominations.

As a rather new movement, Women-Church must ask itself a lot of questions in order to shape a mature identity. How will Women-Church evaluate the contributions of its members and determine its direction? How will it learn from internal criticism and conflict? What will its relation to the established churches be over time? Such questions are impossible to answer now, but they must be asked and, of course, addressed.

The diversity of those within the Christian feminist movement today is both a major strength and a challenge to its future. If the phases of the women's movement are to progress, Catholic feminists must develop:

- an inclusive theology while maintaining a credible Christian identity. To retain continuity with the church's past will require building upon the history and symbol systems already available.
- a renewed clergy and ministry based on service and equality, faithful to the demands of justice for diverse groups and peoples outside the church.
- a message of hope—not of cynicism or despair—and a language that communicates this God-given hope to those most in need.
- a spirituality that can nurture those whose expectations for equality in the established churches have outrun the actual pace of reform.
- conversations among themselves and the whole church on controversial sexual issues, including abortion. Women's voices are varied on these matters. Catholic feminists have differing opinions among themselves. Feminists must create a space where people can listen to one another, allowing differences, while staking out common ground. If it is true that one's position on abortion has become the

litmus test for both Catholic orthodoxy and secular feminism, must it be true for Catholic feminists? I think not.[24]

- some means of constructive self-criticism. Catholic feminists must hold themselves up to the same standards by which they judge other movements and institutions, and when necessary, feminists must be able to admit their faults and move on.
- arguments for the feminist cause within the church that can persuade other Catholics. For instance, many conservative Catholics have understandable concerns about the current malaise surrounding marriage and family. Some associate such social problems as teenage pregnancy and sexually transmitted diseases with a secular feminism "that has destroyed traditional values." Catholic feminists must have some means of communicating with persons whose perception of recent American history and the forces that have shaped it differs from their own. Others argue that for women to be concerned about power is inappropriate, given Christ's message that we are to serve one another. A truism such as—women do not need to become priests or anything else to achieve wholeness or sanctity—is a block to understanding Christian feminism. Indeed, Pope John Paul II's own meditation, *On the Dignity and Vocation of Women (Mulieris Dignitatem)*, expresses these latter two views, by emphasizing what he calls the "genius of women" found in the vocations of motherhood and virginity, period.[25] Catholic feminists must have some persuasive way of communicating with persons who hold such views.

Curiously, the greatest challenge to Women-Church is the same as that facing the established churches today: how to establish a substantial identity and maintain unity while allowing for a measure of pluralism among members? Also, by what authority or by what process will disputes and competing ideas be resolved?

Perhaps one of the greatest contributions the feminist movement could offer others within the church is an effective working model of collegiality. The movement already serves as a training ground for women leaders. And the ecumenical dimension of the Christian feminist movement appears to be flowering at a time when formal dialogues between churches are stalled.

THE BISHOPS' DRAFT LETTER

Anyone familiar with the tensions in the Catholic church today over women's roles knows that, just as new roles have been created and filled with willing women, not all Catholics support the direction feminism has taken, and would like to take, the church.

The wide spectrum of women's concerns is clear in the draft document released April 12, 1988, by the U.S. Catholic Conference of bishops, *Partners in the Mystery of Redemption*.[26] In addition to scope, the draft is a particularly good indication of current divisions and convergences among Catholic women. It gives some indication of just how and how much the church in the U.S. is willing to be responsive to women's concerns.

After listening to 75,000 women and participants from 24 organizations and 100 dioceses, the bishops discovered that there is "no typical" Catholic woman. On the conservative side, Women for Faith & Family sent petitions signed by 50,000 women declaring their allegiance to the pope and reaffirming church teachings, which, presumably, include the prohibition of women's ordination. Despite the fact that this number is only a fraction of one percent of U.S. Catholics, it is significant. On the liberal side, and explicitly calling for ordination of women, were NCAN, WOC, the Grail, and the LCWR—all participants in the Women-Church Convergence of 1987.

Most Catholic women, of course, fall in between these poles. Their views are represented in the draft's "most frequently mentioned" concerns, and these often coincide with ideas that feminists have been espousing for decades: for example, the desire to eliminate sexist language appeared in almost every diocesan report (par. 191).

The Committee also found that "Concern for closing the gap between teaching and practice within the life of the church dominated the listening sessions in comparison to concerns related to roles within family and society" (see draft's footnote 8).

While a widespread affirmation of the church's teaching on abortion was reported, so was a frequent request for women's input on matters of reproduction and sexuality in general (see par. 72–76).

The most "alienation" was expressed by college-aged and single women "with leadership ability" (par. 188)—a fact notable since college-aged women are tomorrow's leaders and many will mother the next generation of Catholics.

What the bishops' committee heard moved them. That is palpable throughout the draft. Taken as a whole, *Partners* is a landmark boxed in by unsightly fences. It is a landmark because the bishops emphatically declare sexism a sin and apologize publicly for the church's sins of sexism.

Such a confession could not have been made even a decade ago. Then, the bishops did not yet realize the significance of the women's movement for either Catholic women or the church as a whole. Catholic women had not yet developed the organizations, pastoral experience, or scholarship that has, in part, persuaded the bishops to follow through with the task they set for themselves.[27] Surely the bishops' strong denunciation of sexism serves to legitimate—for the rest of the church—feminists' own efforts and aspirations for a more egalitarian church. The bishops may open up additional church positions for women, although their call to admit women to the permanent diaconate was issued in the form of a "study" to be undertaken "soon." And the call to officially *install* women lectors and acolytes will merely legitimate those women who are already performing these roles (normative practice throughout the U.S.) without the installation.

The draft illustrates other small signs of progress in terms of feminism. Care was taken to use inclusive language throughout, which required editing Scriptures and excerpts from papal documents. This practice should be continued in future pastorals. (Unfortunately, the text of the pope's meditation on women's dignity was not amended in this fashion.) Scripture passages, many of which have been used traditionally to exclude and demean women, were used positively throughout, another example of the bishops' commitment to reclaim an unworthy past.[28]

Several women have commented on the strengths and weaknesses of the draft in the Catholic press.[29] All interested Catholic women may respond in writing to the bishops' committee.

Having stated the document's major strengths, it is fair to point out its limitations. The very idea of thousands of women stating their concerns before a committee representing scores of men finally ready to listen is the most obvious. Of course, that process expresses the present reality: that there are no women bishops to speak from their experience.

Furthermore, precisely because the papacy has centralized control of the hierarchy during the last century, the bishops find themselves unable to move in progressive or independent directions—even if they wanted to. Now that the pope's meditation has been released, the bishops may find themselves even more hamstrung.

For example, the bishops felt unable to discuss the question of women's ordination to the priesthood because of the 1977 Vatican statement denying women that possibility. They were reduced to restating the arguments against women's ordination.

That the bishops are trying to address very disparate groups—the pope, their fellow bishops, women at opposite poles and at all points on a long spectrum—is visible in the letter, causing inner tensions and ambiguities in content. But that fact makes even stronger their clear proclamation of sexism as sin. The bishops might have waffled here, too, but they did not. At least so far.

The letter still must be presented to the whole conference for discussion, amendments, and a final vote, a process which could drag on past 1989. In the episcopal repartee the draft may be strengthened or weakened. Exactly who will measure (and how) the progress on the bishops' recommendations needs to be decided.

CONCLUSION

Current events can be read in a number of different ways. To focus on women in today's Catholic church might, for example, have involved an examination of women whose activities have been curtailed by its official leaders: the excommunication of Rhode Island's Planned Parenthood director, Mary Ann Sorrentino, and the questioning of her daughter about abortion before her own Confirmation; the signers of the *Times* ad who were asked to retract; members of religious communities who were asked to step down from positions of public office because abortion-funding was under their jurisdiction in some way; the recommendations to seminaries that women not be spiritual directors or teachers of theology for seminarians, and other cases of clampdowns. These are important parts of the current story.

To my own thinking, however, the best measure of what is happening in the church today vis–à–vis women, has to be much broader in scale than such isolated, often abortion-related, incidents. That is why I chose to highlight the issue of women's ordination and to show that support among Catholics in general is evenly split on the issue.

Second, the feminist movement within the church indicates how much creativity and energy are going into women's organizations, education, and spiritual life. The important questions now facing the movement will gradually be addressed, and as they are, they will shape the future not only of the women's movement, but to some extent, the whole church.

Third, while the draft pastoral letter on women's concerns reveals diverse views held by women on a number of issues, it also indicates commonalities. The drafting process shows that women's concerns are of high priority to the U.S. hierarchy; as the committee listened to women, it was led to condemn sexism outside and inside the church. It is broad movements and issues such as these—along with the steady contributions of women in theology and related scholarship, and in positions of recognized leadership in religion—that evince how powerful are the changed and changing attitudes of women themselves and toward women as a group.

NOTES

1. See Robin Morgan, ed., *Sisterhood Is Global* (New York: Doubleday, 1984).

2. Michael Wood's review of two new books about the nun from seventeenth-century New Spain appeared in *The New York Review of Books*, October 13, 1988, pp. 39–43.

3. In the early sixties Mary Daly enrolled in the University of Fribourg, Switzerland, because no U.S. Catholic institution would give a doctorate in theology to a woman. See Mary Daly, *The Church and the Second Sex* (Boston: Beacon, 1968), p.8.

4. For a selected bibliography, see Anne E. Carr's *Transforming Grace* (San Francisco: Harper & Row, 1988).

5. NETWORK is a political lobbying group originally organized by Catholic sisters. Operating out of Washington, D.C., NETWORK lobbies Congress on social justice issues and keeps its own members informed of pending legislation through a regular newsletter, legislative and skills training seminars, and associate and internship programs. Each congressional session, particular issues are selected for attention: housing, welfare reform, budget, jobs, arms control, Central American or South African policy, etc. WATER

(Women's Alliance for Theology, Ethics, and Ritual) was founded in 1983 to draw together for discussion and study persons interested in combining all three areas. WATER publishes feminist liturgies and offers workshops.

6. The focus is on the installation itself. Women now serve as lectors, but they are not officially installed, installation being reserved for candidates for ordination. In the case of "extraordinary" Eucharistic ministers, women and men may be officially installed to assist the priest and deacon.

7. See Rosemary Ruether and Eleanor McLaughlin, eds., *Women of Spirit* (New York: Simon and Schuster, 1979), p. 381.

8. George Gallup, Jr., and Jim Castelli, eds., *The American Catholic People* (New York: Doubleday, 1987), p. 56. In 1974, 29 percent agreed and 65 percent disagreed that women should be priests; in 1977, 36 percent agreed and 57 percent disagreed; in 1985, 47 percent agreed and 47 percent disagreed—a steady increase in support of women's ordination. Also, John Deedy, *American Catholicism and Now Where?* (New York: Plenum, 1987), p. 207. In a 1986 Catholic University survey, support for women's ordination had reached 47 percent, compared with 18 percent eleven years earlier; more men than women supported women's ordination in the 1986 study.

9. Kane's brief welcome to the pope included: "Our contemplation leads us to state that the church in its struggle to be faithful to its call for reverence and dignity for all persons must respond by providing the possibility of women as persons being included in all ministries of our church. I urge you, Your Holiness, to be open to and to respond to the voices coming from the women of this country who are desirous of serving in and through the church as fully participating members." For the entire text see: Anne Lally Milhaven, ed., *The Inside Stories: 13 Valiant Women Challenging the Church* (Mystic, Connecticut: Twenty-Third Publications, 1987).

10. The declaration refers to women's ordination as "an ecumenical problem," something the church has never felt it could "validly confer" on women, as long as it is faithful to the "model left by the Lord." "Jesus did not call any women to become part of the twelve"; and "it is impossible to prove that this attitude is inspired only by social and cultural reasons." "Eucharist is not only a fraternal meal, but . . . the memorial which makes present and actual Christ's sacrifice and His offering by the Church." "The whole sacramental economy is . . . based upon natural signs on symbols imprinted upon the human psychology." ". . . priesthood does not form part of the rights of the individual .

. . it cannot become the goal of social advancement . . . for the greatest in the kingdom . . . are not the ministers but the saints."

11. Don Zirkel, "When Dog Bites Man That's Not News (Except in the Church)," *Brooklyn Tablet*, 7 April 1977, p. 14. Zirkel surveyed some fifty Catholic diocesan papers and found only 17 reported the February 27 protest vigil against the pope's declaration. The rest had apparently practiced self-censorship.

12. The Jesuit's letter was widely published; it can be obtained from the Office of Women's Affairs of the General Theological Union, 2378 Virginia St., Berkeley, CA 94709.

13. Peter Steinfels, "A Matter Preordained" *Commonweal*, March 4, 1977, p. 136.

14. See my "Women–Church: Claiming Our Power," *Commonweal*, November 6, 1987, pp. 613–615.

15. Robert W. Hovda, "The Amen Corner," *Worship*, Vol. 62, No. 2, March 1988, pp. 154–159. Hovda cautions against "a widespread practice" of "communion" versus Eucharist because it promotes "a general lack of appreciation of the difference between the two services." Also, Gabe Huck, *Liturgy* 80, October 1987 (Chicago: Liturgy Training Publications), pp. 4–5.

16. See "Ordination for Women and Christian Thought: History, Theology, Ethics," in Carr, *Transforming Grace*, pp. 43–59.

17. In the post-Christian feminist introduction to Mary Daly's, *The Church and the Second Sex* (Boston: Beacon, 1985), p. xii, Daly writes: "It is my observation and conviction that Living Faith propels women out of patriarchal religion, whereas blind faith in dead symbols keeps women lost/trapped inside its gynocidal, spirit-deadening maze."

18. Milhaven, *The Inside Stories*, p. 168. Frances Kissling, director of Catholics for a Free Choice (CFFC), is quoted as saying: "But I'm not going anywhere; I have no reason to leave. I won't give them [the hierarchy] the satisfaction of leaving." And, "I feel an obligation to other women to stick with it. It's not up to me to leave other women alone in the church." This book of interviews is interesting particularly for the variety of feminists' points of view on the question of remaining in the church.

19. The New American Bible's recently revised New Testament is a very slight improvement in terms of inclusive language. See the editorial, "The Good News on 'Man,'" *Commonweal*, April 24, 1987, pp. 228–229.

20. The first two books by Mary Daly, *The Church and the Second Sex* (Boston: Beacon, 1968) and *Beyond God the Father* (Boston: Beacon, 1973); Rosemary Radford Ruether, *Religion and Sexism* (New York: Simon and Schuster, 1974); the anthology by Carol Christ and Judith Plaskow, eds., *Womanspirit Rising* (New York: Harper & Row, 1979); Marina Warner, *Alone of All Her Sex* (New York: Alfred A. Knopf, 1976) illustrate this first phase.

21. Elisabeth Schüssler Fiorenza, *In Memory of Her: A Feminist Theological Reconstruction of Christian Origins* (New York: Crossroad, 1983); Mary Jo Weaver, *New Catholic Women* (San Francisco: Harper & Row, 1985); Jane Schaberg, *The Illegitimacy of Jesus* (San Francisco: Harper & Row, 1987); Carolin Walker Bynum, *Jesus as Mother* (Berkeley: University of California, 1982; and Elaine Pagels *Adam, Eve, and the Serpent* (New York: Random House, 1988) illustrate this second phase.

22. It should be pointed out that Anne E. Carr, originally asked to be part of the drafting committee, was disinvited after she signed *The New York Times* ad (October 7, 1984), with the headline: "A Diversity of Opinions Regarding Abortion Exists Among Committed Catholics," sponsored by Catholics for a Free Choice (CFFC).

23. Rosemary Radford Ruether, *Women-Church: Theology and Practice of Feminist Liturgical Communities* (San Francisco: Harper & Row, 1985).

24. Consider JustLife (713 Monroe St., N.E., Washington, DC 20017). These supporters of "a consistent prolife ethic" are opposed to the nuclear arms buildup, capital punishment, and abortion; and favor policies to safeguard the environment, the poor, children, minorities. Feminists may embrace much, perhaps all, of the JustLife agenda, abortion being debatable.

25. The pope's meditation can be ordered from *Origins*; Mrs. Bessie Briscoe, 1312 Massachusetts Ave., N.W., Washington, DC 20005. It dispatches with the possibility of women's ordination through the logic of *Inter Insigniores*: "In all of Jesus' teaching, as well as in his behavior, one can find nothing which reflects the discrimination against women prevalent in his day" (par. 13). "Consequently, the assumption that he called men to be apostles in order to conform with the widespread mentality of his time does not at all

correspond to Christ's way of acting." ". . . It is the Eucharist above all that expresses the redemptive act of Christ, the bridegroom, toward the church, the bride. This is clear and unambiguous when the sacramental ministry of the Eucharist, in which the priest acts *in persona Christi*, is performed by a man" (par. 26).

26. A copy of *Partners* can be obtained from *Origins*.

27. In 1972 the bishops in the U.S. formed an Ad Hoc Committee on the Role of Women in Society and the Church. In 1983, the bishops decided to write a pastoral letter that would discuss the concerns women themselves had raised.

28. Jesus "emptied himself, taking the form of a slave, coming in human likeness; and found human in appearance . . ." (Phil. 2:7–8). Usually translated "became a man like us." "In the divine image . . . male and female (God) created them" (Gen. 1:27). This has been translated "man in His image" for centuries, and spawned a male-centered theology. The letter gives many such examples of inclusive language.

29. See "Women and the Pastoral" *National Catholic Reporter*, April 29, 1988, pp. 4–6 and "Sin, Sexism, & Grace," *Commonweal*, June 17, 1988, pp. 361–366.

CHAPTER XVII

THE ROLE OF LAITY IN CHURCH AND SOCIETY

Leonard Doohan

CHANGES IN THE CONTEMPORARY CHURCH

The Vatican Council referred to change as a global sign of our times, "Profound and rapid . . . individual and collective . . . a true social and cultural transformation" (*Pastoral Constitution on the Church in the Modern World* (*Church Today*, 4:2). The Pastoral Constitution takes the various changes as a basis for pastoral reflection, and most conciliar decrees, in their first paragraphs, mention the changed conditions of our times. However, change constitutes a sign of the times because its characteristics are different now than at any time in history. Today's change is profound, constant, accelerated, universal, and ambivalent, and the Pastoral Constitution speaks of a resulting new period of history (4:2–3; 11:1). This has produced a new scale of values and different ways of thinking not only about society, but also about the nature of the church and people's roles in both its internal life and in its outreach of service. Moreover, social emphasis on human dignity, progress, community, and freedom has produced similar developments internal to the church. Contemporary change is so profound it leads to tension that is not always strategically good but frequently stressful.

Since the turn of this century, the church has experienced several changes that have profoundly affected its self–understanding. A series of outstanding popes, beginning with Leo XIII, up to the present pope, John Paul II, has called the members of the church to renewal in social involvement (Leo XIII), liturgical life (Pius X), canon law (Benedict XV), lay apostolate (Pius XI), faith development (Pius XII), and ecumenism (John XXIII). In addition to these leaders' efforts, several movements with world impact—such as the biblical, liturgical, lay apostolic, and ecumenical movements—have stimulated the people to think in new ways about the place in life of scripture, worship, ministry, and church unity. A further phenomenon of the twentieth century has been the growth of grass roots spiritual movements of parish, family, and social renewal. Thus, since the turn of the century, the faithful have been urged to rediscover the importance of their baptismal vocation, to accept a call to personal and communitarian conversion, to share spiritual experiences, especially the liturgy, to witness to mutual love, and to revalue the religious significance of daily life and work.

For four years, 1962–1965, the Second Vatican Council met in Rome. Partly the result of the ecclesial trends of the previous half century, and partly John XXIII's response to changed contemporary circumstances in society, this gathering of over three thousand bishops set the future direction of the church both in the teachings of the sixteen conciliar documents and in the new experience of a universal church made up of increasingly independent regional churches.

The Council's major contribution was its ecclesiology, and all other teachings need to be filtered through the new vision of church as a community, in the world, to serve the world. Chapters one, two, four, and five of the Dogmatic Constitution on the Church led to a new way of appreciating the life and dedication of the laity, an upgrading of the image of laity, an appreciation of their roles in ministry, an acceptance of their charisms as part of a collaborative approach to church, an openness to their unique spiritualities, an insistence on their indispensable role in secular circumstances, and a conscious acknowledgement that lay life is foundational for all levels of church living.

The Council's teachings have produced a series of new emphases in ecclesiology: stressing church as community instead of institution, service instead of power, participatory government instead of hierarchies, world involvement instead of withdrawal, coresponsibility instead of obedience, and personal charisms instead of ecclesiastical offices. Without excluding the second part in each case, the pendulum swung to aspects of church life that made lay contributions important.

The Council's desire to upgrade the role of the laity met with notable obstacles before the end of the sixties, partly because of institutional concern at a lack of clarity regarding the specifics of lay contributions to the church, and partly because of disagreements among laity, some of whom wanted greater participation in the internal life of the church, while others wanted an almost exclusive emphasis on the specific contributions of laity to secular development.[1] The decade of the seventies focused on the specifics of the relationship between laity and hierarchy, at times giving rise to encouraging collaboration, and at other times to fear of regression in the roles of laity.[2]

The upgrading of laity in the church is due to the Vatican Council's teaching on the autonomy of earthly realities and to a focusing on lay values in the church. The international and local church's new pastoral priorities are frequently in areas where laity have expertise, such as family life, social justice, politics, and peace. This increased role of laity, due also to a humanizing of church structures, an emphasis on local church, and a dedication to coresponsibility, has led to new styles of discipleship, a focus on the centrality of the family, and an increased interrelationship between religion and politics.

The shift in values, caused in part by social change and in part by the Council, has produced polarization and division in the church. Formerly a unified, monolithic organization, the Catholic church, like other churches, has become structurally diffuse into sub–groups, some of which identify more with similar sub–groups from other denominations than different sub–groups within their own tradition. Thus, we see conservatives from various church traditions uniting to attain their common goals, while liberals do likewise.

The shortlived liberal renewal of the post–Vatican II years has yielded to a rebirth of conservatism. In fact, the Catholic church has at least two parties that now seem as polarized as their political counterparts, if not more so. The former desires more of the changes the Council gave rise to, while the latter wants to change back to the way things were in the recent pre–Council past. This two party system in the church looks increasingly like two parallel churches, evidencing little effort to unity.

Any examination of the role of laity in church and society must take account of social and ecclesial developments since the turn of the century, especially the challenges of Vatican II's new ecclesiological vision, and the lived experiences of laity who continue to struggle to incarnate Christian values in ever changing circumstances.

VATICAN II'S CHALLENGE TO LAITY

The Extraordinary Synod of 1985 insisted that the vision of church as community was the most important teaching of Vatican II.[3] This emphasis led to a refocusing of the guidelines distributed to local churches in preparation for the Synod on Laity in 1987 and substantially influenced the synod debate and final propositions.[4] Rather than view the vocation and mission of laity to be service to the world, the synod viewed the vocation of laity to be the same as all members of the church, namely to be an integral part of the "communio" of the church. All the faithful have a common calling in baptism, a common sacramental source of life, a common community, a common source of charisms in the Holy Spirit, a common ministry in the sharing of the priesthood of all the baptized, and an equal opportunity to give life to the church.[5] The Synod on laity then viewed the mission of laity to be primarily involvement in world transformation. This double focus was a faithful expression of Vatican II (*Decree on the Apostolate of Laity* 3:3; 16:3), whose members restructured the principal document, the Dogmatic Constitution on the Church, to reflect this understanding of laity as integrally church, speaking first of the mystery of the church and the people of God before considering the hierarchical nature of this institution. Full membership and recognition of equal dignity lead to responsibility in developing the church (*Church* 33:2), participating in its saving mission (*Church* 33:2), contributing to its expansion and growth (*Decree on the Church's Missionary Activity* 36:1).

Laity share in Jesus' mission (*Laity* 10:1; see *Church Today* 43:7), and their responsibilities internal to the church's life include liturgical participation (*Constitution on the Sacred Liturgy* 11; *Laity* 10:1), community building (*Laity* 10:2), and coresponsibility (*Laity* 10:3). The last topic, referring to internal church governance, encourages laity to participate in diocesan projects, offer their special competencies, administer church goods, present catechetical instructions, bring back those who have strayed from the church, serve on parish and diocesan committees, and take the priest's place where he cannot go (*Laity* 10; 17; 26). Lay contributions to the internal life of the church are so essential the pastor's work is ineffective without them (*Laity* 10:1), and the church cannot be considered as fully alive without this lay involvement (*Missions* 21).

This coresponsible contribution to internal church life, a sign of communion, complements the laity's principal mission of being church in the ordinary circumstances of life. After all the church's primary mission is to serve and evangelize the world and respond to its hopes and anguish (*Church Today* 1:1; 3:1). The principal mission of laity is to evangelize the world by the quality of their lives (*Church* 31:4; 35:3, 5; *Laity* 6:1), by appropriate words of inspiration, encouragement, and education (*Laity* 6:3), and by transforming their environments to reflect Christ's teaching (*Laity* 7:2). Their faith should activate laity to aid the needy (*Church Today* 21:6), and to foster the Christian growth of family life (*Laity* 11:1; *Church Today* 52). The Council stresses the social responsibilities of laity (*Laity* 13:1), claiming this includes cooperating for justice in economic and social matters (*Mission* 12), defending the dignity of the human person (*Church Today* 26), counterattacking new forms of social and psychic slavery (*Church Today* 29:4), educating at all levels of society (*Church Today* 60:1), being involved with mass communication (*Decree on the Instruments of Social Communication* 14), and working in political issues, both by increasing one's participation in the process (*Church Today* 75), and by running for office (*Laity* 14).

Post–conciliar documents such as those which came out of the synods on justice (1971), family (1980), and laity (1987), together with pastorals from the United States Catholic Bishops' Conference on the laity (1980), peace (1983), and the economy (1986), presume the vocation of laity in the internal life of the church, but focus primarily on the lay contribution in secular spheres of life. This emphasis has been strengthened by theological syntheses[6] and by the expressed concern that emphasis on internal church issues should not weaken the main focus of lay life to be an effective, transforming, presence to the world.[7]

The Council pointed out that the church is essentially "both human and divine . . . present in this world and yet not at home in it" (*Liturgy* 2), and because of its mission and nature "is bound to no particular form of human culture, nor to any political, economic or social system" (*Church Today* 42:5; *Missions* 12:5). However, the church's spiritual mission does imply a moral responsibility in secular matters.

Benefitting from the experiences of the centuries (see *Church Today* 43:11), the church can dialogue with human institutions (*Church Today* 29:4) and can indirectly serve these institutions (*Church Today* 42:6).

Always open to the signs of the times (*Church Today* 11:1), and appreciative of human institutions (*Church Today* 42:6), the church discerns "the birth of a new humanism" in which a person is defined by responsibility to others and to history (*Church Today* 55), and the church concludes that because of the increased complexity of modern life government intervention on behalf of the dynamically conceived common good in social and economic affairs is more often required than it used to be (*Church Today* 74:5; 75:4). In this context of change the church calls all "to work for the rightful betterment of this world" (*Church Today* 21:7), affirms its respect "for the political freedom and responsibility of citizens" (*Church Today* 76:4; 75:1).

The church achieves its indirect moral impact on society through the direct involvement of laity (*Church* 36:5). This work for world development and peace is a collaborative venture with all people of good will. This fervent desire of the Council for collaboration (*Church Today* 77:2; 92:7) directly relates to baptismal responsibility (*Church Today* 60:1; see also 72:1).

Christians cannot remain neutral in political matters, but their faith ought to lead them to respect the freedom of everyone, to develop a sense of international solidarity (*Church Today* 57:6), to foster a "renewed education of attitudes...in the area of public opinion" (*Church Today* 82:7), and to intelligently and effectively pursue the common good (*Church Today* 84:1). The Council urges "all Christians [to] appreciate their special and personal vocation in the political community" (*Church Today* 75:7; 55; see *Missions* 12:4), to be conspicuous in collaborating with others (*Church* 36:5), insisting that this is a resulting challenge of their baptism (*Church Today* 93:1).

The Council teaches that the political community is based on human nature, and as such is divinely ordained (*Church Today* 74:4). Laity who belong to the nation in which they were born must cooperate in its integral advancement (*Missions* 21:2). In fact, the Council continues, there is an intimate connection between individual human progress and the advancement of society (*Church Today* 25:1). Christians should recognize that in political and temporal affairs "various legitimate though conflicting views can be held" (*Church Today* 75:8), and while respecting others' views, Catholics "should make the weight of their opinion felt" (*Laity* 14:1) by voting freely and selecting suitable leaders (*Church Today* 74:4; 75:1). In two different documents the Council singles out for praise those Catholics who dedicate themselves to political service in public office, expressing the hope that they will be "adequately enlightened in faith and Christian doctrine" (*Laity* 14:1; *Church Today* 75:1).

The Council longs for a more humane society, built on justice and animated by love (*Church Today* 26:4), and rejoices in an increased political awareness among people (*Church Today* 73:2). It urges Christian politicians to protect the welfare of the people (*Church Today* 79:5), to dedicate themselves with fairness and political courage (*Church Today* 75:9), and to encourage others to participate in the political process (*Church Today* 73:3). Such political servants should lead "primarily as a moral force" (*Church Today* 74:3), conscientiously discharging duties to serve the political and economic interests of the common good.

The Council's challenge to laity includes a broad range of options for dedicated involvement, including inner church activities as well as service to the world. However, social and political involvement is considered to be particularly significant for laity, an exclusive dimension of their baptism, and the way in which the Christian message can influence society.

DEVELOPMENTS SINCE THE COUNCIL

The Council's commitment to political involvement is seen particularly in chapter 4 of the Pastoral Constitution. Unlike the other conciliar documents, this one is principally inductive, and as our experiences change, so does its validity.[8] Chapter 4's view of church–state relationships, seen by some to be medieval, is already out of date and in places not reflective of modern secular society.[9] However, the Vatican Council's call to laity to be more involved in their church and in society has been reinforced by a series of church documents that have reinterpreted the Council for changed times and manifested a consistent concern for social involvement. Several of the post–conciliar popes have issued major challenges to social involvement, such as John XXIII in his encyclicals "Christianity and Social Progress" (1961) and "Peace on Earth" (1963), or Paul VI in his "Development of Peoples" (1967) or "Call to Action" (1971). In 1971 the Synod on Justice affirmed that action on behalf of justice and participation in the work of the world is a constitutive element in the preaching of the Gospel.[10] In September 1981, John Paul II published his encyclical "On Human Work," in which he proposed a personalist approach to work as a dimension of the gospel of work and a major component of any adequate solution to society's social problems, thereby centering on laity as the effective agents of social change.[11] In November of the same year, the pope's "Apostolic Exhortation on the Family" synthesized Catholic teaching up to the Synod of 1980 and focused again on the laity as the cutting edge of the church's mission to society.[12] In 1988, John Paul published his seventh encyclical, "On Social Concern," in which he claimed that the church's mission of evangelization implies its right to address the moral dimension of development (no. 34), to criticize the structures of sin (no. 38), and to confront the selfishness, fear, indecision, and cowardice that lead to the neglect of the urgent needs of multitudes (no. 47). The pope reaffirmed the church's pastoral duty to apply the word of God to the life of society by offering "principles for reflection," "criteria of judgment," and "directives for action" (no. 8). In October of the same year the pope published his "Apostolic Letter on the Dignity and Vocation of Women," in which he addressed women's "active presence in the Church and in society." He then promised a further document that "will present proposals of a pastoral nature on the place of women in the Church and in society."[13]

The pope's claims that the church's social doctrine guides people's lives ("On Social Concern," no. 41) complements the documents of the United States episcopal conference on laity, peace, and the economy. Although these documents of the pope and U.S. bishops support the church's right to be involved in directing society by a moral understanding and imply the laity's obligation to be involved, they have not produced a uniform strategy. Many have found John Paul II's positions confusing: at times he is challenging regarding the work of social transformation, on occasions he has denounced political involvement by the church and restricted the involvement of priests and bishops, while being himself more politically involved and outspoken than any pope of recent times.[14] The bishops' pastorals fail to establish a strong common Catholic vision, especially when powerful individual bishops pursue their own agenda for the public realm.[15] Moreover, the bishops' recent teachings contrast with earlier positions. Mary T. Hanna states "most Catholic leaders enthusiastically supported American wars and championed the basic tenets of business culture," and Dorothy Dohen referred to "the seeming acquiescence of the American Catholic prelates to the status quo of capitalistic industrialism."[16] Recent pastorals show a new direction and have dealt with issues in which laity are the experts, and the bishops have involved large numbers of laity in the drafting of their letters. This process has generated admiration in some circles of the church and opposition in others who see a politically liberal and theologically untrained national bishops' staff manipulating the focus of the documents.[17] Some laity strongly opposed to the documents established their own committee of political conservatives to write their own pastoral letter.[18]

In addition to the documents, and the clash of opinions that some of them have generated, there have been other influences on lay involvement in society. Representative Geraldine Ferraro, a vice–presidential nominee, was openly attacked by church administrators.[19] Agnes Mansour was driven out of her religious community over the same issue of a Catholic implementing a public policy on abortion. Governor Cuomo, challenged on the same topic, held his ground and presented his response in his Notre Dame address.[20] Priests have been told to leave politics, and we have witnessed international ecclesiastical interference in academic freedom, together with sexist attitudes, financial misconduct, and examples of oppressive ecclesiastical government, that make calls for justice in contemporary civil and political communities more difficult in view of the institutional church's many lapses.

Political conservatives have found a ready ear in the Vatican and have been able to bring pressure on their bishops and on laity. The Vatican's, and John Paul's personal support of the ultraconservative Opus Dei, with its silence, secrecy, and questionable financial involvements, has also influenced the direction of Catholic involvement in society by raising fears of institutional interference in the laity's career of public service.[21]

A further influence on lay involvement in society is the interpretation one gives to the constitutional doctrine of church–state separation. Some Catholic members of Congress understand this to mean there is a wall between one's private affairs of religion and the public domain of politics. This understanding implies a separation of competence; church–spiritual, state–political. Bryan Hehir states a different interpretation: "We accept the separation of Church and State; we do not accept the separation of the Church from society."[22] To do so would imply an odd and irrelevant understanding of the nature of religion. Thus, Cardinal Bernadin, claiming the support of the thought of John Courtney Murray, challenges laity to resist any division of religion and politics,[23] and Bishop Malone applies this to political candidates, denouncing the dichotomy between personal morality and public policy as illogical and untenable.[24] When the state suggests that religion is a private matter for individuals, and some members of the church say that politics is a private matter outside the domain of the church, then we see that this approach to separation is itself political.[25]

American history evidences an anxiety that Catholics would impose a Catholic agenda on the nation. However, many Catholics seem to have gone to the opposite extreme of cutting themselves off from all religious influences in public affairs. This regretful absence of an effective Catholic presence in the social and political arenas led forty–seven prominent Catholics in 1971 to sign the "Chicago Declaration of Christian Concern." "The Declaration was an ambitious undertaking. It sought to redirect the Church's strategic approach to social action and to urban ministry; to refocus attention on the secular role of the laity; to update the peace and justice agenda of the Church."[26] Believing that God teaches people in the ordinary circumstances of their lives, the Declaration not only reinforced the specific lay role in transforming society but also saw lay experience as a source for the church's teachings in secular matters.

A century since Leo XIII wrote "The Workers' Charter," and a quarter century since the Council challenged laity to deepen their awareness of their responsibility, we still struggle to distinguish the specifics of the institutional church's social and political responsibilities and the scope of concrete lay applications of this moral guidance.

While the struggle for clarity of roles continues, we can identify the following areas of consistent institutional service of the church to laity. Amidst the sad experiences of obstacles to justice and peace, the church serves as a sign of hope. The institutional church claims its doctrine guides people's moral understanding and behavior, since no aspect of humanity can be fully understood without consideration of a person's interior dimension. While not committed to any specific form of political system, the church encourages democratic and participatory forms of government, and prophetically challenges all to care for the poor and oppressed. "The Church's social doctrine is not a 'third way' between liberal capitalism and Marxist collectivism, nor even a possible alternative to other solutions less radically opposed to one another: rather, it constitutes a category of its own."[27] This social doctrine can only be implemented effectively by laity through their participation in the broad areas of public life, public opinion, and political processes. Some confident and competent laity suggest that "With creative reapplication . . . Catholic social thought may provide a way out of the 20th century U.S. paradox of poverty amidst plenty."[28]

LAY INVOLVEMENT IN SOCIETY

Prior to the Council, lay Catholic political and social involvement was generally the official involvement of church leadership through laity who worked for the institutional church. However, many previously politically inactive Catholics have been drawn into political issues since Vatican II. Early political involvement was due to the prophetical challenges of a small number of individuals—for example, Dorothy Day and the Catholic Worker Movement (1940s), and Cesar Chavez and the Farm Workers' Movement (1960s). Prior to the sixties, most Catholic lobbying was done by one person, Monsignor John O'Grady, on behalf of one organization, the National Conference of Catholic Charities; generally working for institutional issues rather than social justice. Later, we witnessed the civil rights activism of the 1960s, involvement in anti–Vietnam War projects, and initial signs of a war on poverty. The Catholic Worker Movement continued to develop, as did the Catholic Peace Movement. By the mid–seventies Catholics were the largest religious group in the United States. They became the best educated, financially and socially successful group in the nation. Their upward mobility together with their dedication to the renewal of Vatican II brought many of them into leadership positions in their church and in society. More influential than ever before, "The American Catholic is secure now, feels secure about saying what he thinks."[29]

Since 1958 Catholics have been the largest religious group in Congress, often having over a hundred representatives in the House and more than a dozen in the Senate. The names of Catholic political leaders recall much of recent national history: the Kennedy brothers, Eugene McCarthy, Mike Mansfield, Edmund Muskie, Sargent Shriver, Thomas Eagleton, John Tunney, James Buckley, Robert Drinan, Thomas (Tip) O'Neill, Alexander Haig, Peter Rodino, William Casey.[30] Nowadays, Catholicism is not a monolithic organization with ability to deliver a block of votes. However, the varied concerns of Catholics should be viewed with political interest, since there are currently over thirty Catholic lobbying groups based in Washington, D.C.[31] Catholics have always been strong in the trade union movement, both nationally and locally. In addition to well known individuals, groups have arisen on a regional and local level, focusing on right to life, peace, nuclear opposition, sanctuary, undocumented aliens, and labor.

The increase in the numbers of Catholics in public service should not be equated with an increased unified Catholic presence. Politicians evidence no common Catholic position, no block voting. In fact, those whose career is influenced by their Catholicism are certainly in a minority. For most, their religion is accidental to their politics, and they are more likely to let their politics influence their religion than the other way round.[32] The Chicago Declaration expressed concern at a decreased Catholic lay presence, and the nation's Catholic bishops considered this failure the single greatest problem facing the U.S. Church.[33]

There are all kinds of Catholics in public life; they are as disparate as membership in their churches, and most show little identification with the policies of the institutional church.[34] Moreover, involvement may steadily decrease and further disintegrate without a clear institutional commitment to new goals and strategies.

Many Catholic laity now separate their Catholicism from politics. When the Council foresaw laity playing an increasingly active part in society, the document added that this required a well-informed Christian conscience (*Church Today* 43:5). While the layperson should be the expert of the church's living and active involvement in society, this leadership has not materialized on any broad scale. When some are more active politically in social justice issues, their involvement is quickly labeled liberal rather than Catholic. Some have worked against the arms race, and involvement in Latin America, and have striven for more welfare aid, increased civil rights legislation, approval of the equal rights amendment, and support for illegal aliens. Those who give these groups a liberal label are conservative Catholics who themselves generally reduce Catholic morality to privatized, and frequently exclusively, sexual sin, and show little interest in social issues, except abortion, which is often not approached as a social issue but rather as the target issue to attack the liberalizing tendencies of society. The conservative groups have opposed the equal rights amendment, pornography, rights of homosexuals, and increased government involvement in creating jobs. In addition to their efforts against abortion, they have striven to restore prayer in public schools.

In analyzing current Catholic lay involvement in social and political issues, there are several different ways of understanding and living the relationship. The first is an understanding that the spheres of religion and politics are absolutely separate, and thus, involvement in society is seen as a non-religious activity. John Coleman expresses concern that such "privatization of religion, its relegation to the peripheries of American institutional life, is a genuine American danger."[35] This understanding accounts for the absence of a Catholic focus in government or business. A second understanding sees laity as instrumental to the hierarchy in channeling the church's influence over society. The Opus Dei movement, as well as many right to life groups, would fit into this category. This position has serious drawbacks: the hierarchy, seen as official church, runs the risk of jeopardizing their non–partisan approach; it thwarts the originality of lay responsibility in society; the laity thus involved are frequently seen as agents of the institution; and the hierarchy run the risk of becoming too involved in matters outside their competence.

A third understanding views laity as having an independent transforming presence in society. In this "the laity are the key social action agents of the Church in the world and the critical point of insertion of transforming Christian actions in the arenas of economics, politics, the erotic, aesthetic, and intellectual spheres."[36] These spheres are proper, some writers would insist exclusive, to laity, who are "the church at work in the world," caring for society.[37] The unique experiences of laity enable them to provide a prophetical challenge in the ever–changing circumstances of public life. At the level of involvement interpretations will be multiple, some laity even disagreeing with the hierarchy. Governor Cuomo commented on such a situation, and criticized "This whole notion that we are somehow 'failed Catholics' because we disagree with the bishops' political judgment. It's not good logic, it's not theologically sound, and it's not true."[38]

A fourth understanding of the lay role in society implies a restructuring of the church. The exaggerated clerical dimension of the church leaves the laity as a disenfranchised, passive clientele, whereas the church's primary mission of service to the world requires a firm emphasis on lay competence, initiative, responsibility, and control. One author, searching for an appropriate organizational form, declares: "I am arguing for two changes in our self–understanding of the Church. The first is an institutional change which would provide a serious platform for the laity to address social questions. The second is an assumption that the laity are the key action agents of the community of faith in its mission to transform societal structures."[39] After two thousand years the church still has no mechanism "for tapping the huge reservoir of Catholic lay talent."[40]

The previous understanding often produces the undesirable side–effect of maintaining a clergy–lay split in the church, a division which a collaborative understanding seeks to remedy. The U.S. bishops' recent pastorals established a process that integrated the varied visions of clergy and laity while maintaining appropriate teaching roles to the bishops and competence to laity in concrete situations. Such processes are viewed as liberal and evoke conservative reactions from groups or individuals who consider the bishops should just repeat papal generalities without interpretation or application,[41] and also from those who insist the hierarchy should not interfere in lay control of secular matters.[42] This approach to lay involvement in society will generate more conflict in the diverse interpretations of the most suitable application of church teaching. Nevertheless, while Vatican II has no direct statement on participatory government, collaboration and solidarity in the mission of the church are clearly implied in its teachings,[43] and such collaboration will clearly lead to a more socially active church. Only a collaborative approach respects the magisterial foundations of Catholic political action and the necessity of lay experience in the formulation of the teaching and lay life in the implementing of it. In this understanding the hierarchy legitimately hold a middle ground between the gospel and concrete involvement in the practical lay decisions of each day.

While laity are the ecclesial agents of world transformation their mission is exercised within the context of church. This presumes mutual service on the part of hierarchy and laity—a presumption not easily verified in contemporary Catholicism, focused as it is on ecclesiastical power and control.

The hierarchical church does not have, or claim to have, technical solutions to societal problems, and laity have no authority to "compel the assent of the institutional Church as such, whose worldly vocation is restricted to the guardianship of orienting principles and a nonpartisan . . . leadership role."[44] Nevertheless, theologians like John Coleman speak of "the entire Church" as "magistral," claiming that the hierarchy not only should consult the laity, but indeed that "the specific area of political theology is primarily a lay prerogative."[45] Together they must plan a new pastoral strategy that capitalizes on faith in the church; both the hierarchy's task and charisms, and the laity's energies, dedication, and charisms. It must be a creative ecclesial and social vision that will discern what is appropriate for the contemporary church. The strategy for involvement must take cognizance of Catholics' upward mobility, increased knowledge, commitment to Vatican II's renewal, and at the same time be aware that Catholics are now so numerous that Catholicism is necessarily diffuse and no longer unified in approaches to political activity.[46]

The ecclesial challenge to work for social justice, seen as integral to Christian responsibility, focuses on major issues of public policy and urges Christians to struggle for change. The issues include poverty, war, the homeless, peace, the plight of minorities, reform of prisons, housing, welfare, women's rights, control of the activities of FBI and CIA, and all kinds of discrimination. However, all these are overshadowed by antiabortion protests. Attempts to broaden this latter issue into right to life and respect for life have so far failed to influence the majority of those involved.

Catholic lay involvement in society is the filter separating conservatives and liberals. The gospel and the traditional teaching of the church are never always conservative or always liberal. Rather, at times believers are called to be unyielding in their values and will be judged conservative by their neighbors. However, the same sources call believers to assume positions of social reform that contemporaries could judge to be liberal. When some members of the church always espouse conservative positions, they are generally reading their own psychological conservatism into religion. The same is true of liberals who are always liberal.

CONCLUDING REFLECTIONS

Changes provoked by the Council have led to greater independence among Catholics. This is true of both liberals and conservatives, neither of whom feel obliged to identify with the collective official positions of the church in social and political matters. It is no longer possible to speak of a Catholic political position.[47] Since the watershed issue of abortion, which drew even the reluctant into political involvement, people across the spectrum of opinions are more involved in politics, and the lack of identification with official church positions does not evidence a loss of faith but is a side–effect of the maturing to adult independence to which religion should lead. Contemporary Catholicism shows considerable diversity and remarkable unity in core essentials. When they confront modern life as both Catholics and Americans, many see "a religious space for a religious substance in society,"[48] finding that "the themes of religion, morality and politics are woven through the American experience" as they always have been in the nation's history.[49] Differences in the political arena may help in the emergence of a mature understanding of the church, with greater clarification of the roles of pope, bishops, and laity.

Vatican II spoke of an increased awareness of political responsibility among the faithful, as well as an increased sense of independence, claiming "Such a development is of paramount importance for the spiritual and moral maturity of the human race" (*Church Today* 55). Adult faith requires an awareness of one's responsibility for others within the human family. Such political action is a corrective for the privatization of religion. However, in addition to the need to be politically involved, Catholics must discern their motives for political action. While Catholic political involvement was previously directed to the betterment of the church, it now seems to be focused on the benefits of humankind. The broad issues of social responsibility are not well exemplified in the antiabortion fight, noble though it may be, many of whose dedicated members show little interest in the theological awareness of social involvement. Cardinal Bernadin's efforts to formulate a consistent ethic by pushing "the moral, legal and political debate beyond an 'ad hoc' or 'single issue' focus, setting our moral discussion in a broader context" has not yet succeeded.[50]

Christians prove the quality of their religious commitment in the ordinary circumstances of each day. Dedicated to their own country and its traditions (*Mission* 21:4), their vision is for the integral human development of a worldwide family, and they enthusiastically strive to attain it (*Laity* 8:4; *Church Today* 75:6). This is no easy task, but rather "a monumental struggle against the powers of darkness" (*Church Today* 37:2).

Awareness and conviction that justice is a constitutive component of Christianity are clearer and firmer than before the Council, but the specific strategies of episcopal or lay involvement have not been formulated, and efforts in that direction, seen for example in the U.S. bishops' pastorals, have been thwarted by post–conciliar polarization. It is increasingly evident that the post–conciliar problems of striving to renew the church are most vividly seen in the spheres of social reform and politics, where many Catholics impose their political agendas on religious reform. Different priorities in social and political life at times show pluralism and at times divisive polarization in the community of the church. Polarization in politics often manifests the polarization felt in the church. Social issues chosen as the focus of dedicated concern portray one's social and political position more clearly than a coherent ecclesiological stance. Thus, serious dedication to lay involvement in society could also bring healing to a divided and polarized church and lead to a more integrated renewal of the internal life of the church.

The church has a prophetical mission to imbue societal values with the gospel, and while respecting society's independence, the church challenges it to build on morally acceptable values. I conclude with ten reflections:

1. Respect freedom of conscience. The church is free to challenge and criticize society, but society is free to criticize the church, and members of the church are free to criticize and challenge their own institution.

2. Show personal and structural authenticity. A ministry of prophetical denunciation and challenge is seriously impeded when Christians' families and church structures do not embody what they seek in society.
3. Plan for integral development. Genuine growth in social matters must include the whole person and all people.
4. Offer a hope–filled vision. Social and political involvement should be based on a utopian vision of mutual compassion.
5. Search for a theology of social criticism. It is not the church's principal task to present an integrated social doctrine, but rather to be an institution of social criticism.[51]
6. Be aware that we are always within the structures we criticize. Strategies for social involvement are provisional and need to be directed to ourselves and our contributions to society, before they are directed to anyone else.
7. Be dedicated to a new prophetical ministry of working for structural change. This task will be directed to both civic and ecclesiastical structures.
8. Let the church's social and political involvement be the work of a lay–centered church. This will not be a unified approach, but the church will need to work with a variety of lay groups that only partially identify with official positions and with each other.
9. Preserve a Catholic tradition of pluralism that dialogues and strives for unity. The tradition empowers and enriches but needs to be applied in varied ways.
10. Begin social and political involvement with personal conversion.

Many of the changes in the contemporary church, together with the challenges of Vatican II, stress the roles of laity. While many of these changes primarily affect their work for society, they develop attitudes that are remolding laity's approach to inner church governance. Since the Council, laity have increasingly dedicated themselves to social and political involvement. However, their involvement is not a uniform Catholic strategy but varies with the value systems of those involved. There is an intermingling of religion and politics, and it is not always clear which is influencing the other.

NOTES

1. See chapter 2 in my book, *The Lay–Centered Church* (San Francisco: Harper and Row, 1984).

2. See *The Lay–Centered Church*, pp. 1–4; also my *Laity's Mission in the Local Church* (San Francisco: Harper and Row, 1986), chapter 1.

3. See Extraordinary Synod 1985, "Final Report," II C, 6, *Origins* 15 (1985), p. 440.

4. See Working Paper for the 1987 Synod of Bishops, *Origins* 17 (1987), pp. 1–19.

5. See my "Critical Issues for Laity," *Way Supplement* 60 (1987), pp. 23–32.

6. See Yves Congar, *Lay People in the Church* (Westminister, Md.: Newman Press, 1957); *Laity, Church and World* (Baltimore: Helicon Press, 1960); Edward Schillebeeckx, *The Layman in the Church* (New York: St. Paul Publications, 1963).

7. See "Chicago Declaration of Christian Concern," and the accompanying articles in *Challenge to the Laity*, Russell Barta, ed. (Huntington, Ind.: Our Sunday Visitor, 1980).

8. Church documents are nearly always deductive, arriving at conclusions from unchanging principles rooted in Scripture and constant church teachings. The Pastoral Constitution was based on people's experiences, not stable principles, and as experiences change, so do this document's conclusions. Chapter 4, dealing with the life of the political community, considers modern politics, the goal of politics, political participation, and the church's relationship to politics—all issues that have changed substantially since the Council. The document's methodology remains valid, but its analysis and resulting conclusions are out of date.

9. The 1962 edition of the document which became *Church Today* alluded to politics, but politics was little mentioned in the third session of the Council. In fact, only one bishop, Mendez Arceo of Cuernavaca, planned to speak exclusively on politics, and while we have his address, he never had the

chance to give it in the Council. Politics was not mentioned at all in the later 1965 edition. When chapter 4 was presented in October 1965, there were only four interventions.

10. See Synod of Bishops, *Justice in the World*, No. 6.

11. See "On Human Work," *Origins* 11 (1981), pp. 25–244, especially No. 6.

12. See "Apostolic Exhortation on the Family," *Origins* 11 (1981), pp. 437–468.

13. John Paul II, "On the Dignity and Vocation of Women," No. 1, *Origins* 18 (1988), p. 264. For other speeches of the pope on aspects of lay responsibility in society, see my book, *John Paul II and the Laity* (New York: Human Development Books, 1984), pp. 25–53, 99–125.

14. Rev J. Bryan Hehir says: "Many of you know the texts in which John Paul II, while making very powerful social statements, continually stresses that the Church is not to be political. For many the texts are very confusing; for some they are handily used to argue against the whole social ministry." See his untitled article in *Religion and Public Life: The Role of Religious Bodies in Shaping Public Policy*, Joseph A Bracken, ed. (Cincinnati, Ohio: Xavier University Press, 1986), p. 15.

15. See Langdon Gilkey's comments in an untitled article in *Religion and Public Life*, p. 30.

16. Mary T. Hanna, *Catholics and American Politics* (Cambridge, Mass: Harvard University Press, 1979), p. 38.

17. See for example Brian J. Benestad, *The Pursuit of a Just Social Order: Policy Statements of the U.S. Catholic Bishops, 1966–1980* (Washington, D.C.: Ethics and Public Policy Center, 1982), especially pp. 93–118.

18. See A Lay Letter, *Toward the Future: Catholic Social Thought and the U.S. Economy* (New York: 1984). For a critique of the Lay Commissions action, see William E. Murnion, "Early Reactions to Economic Justice for All: Catholic Social Teaching and the U.S. Economy," *Horizons* 15 (1988), p. 141.

19. Joseph Gremillion and Jim Castelli, *The Emerging Parish: The Notre Dame Study of Catholic Life Since Vatican II* (San Francisco: Harper and Row, 1987), p. 189, concluded that 46% of those interviewed wanted less involvement in elections by church officials, and only 16% wanted more.

20. Governor Cuomo, Address at Notre Dame, "Confessions of a Public Man," *Notre Dame Magazine* (Winter 1984–1985).

21. For a rare inside view of Opus Dei, based on information from former members, see Peter Hertel, "International Christian Democracy (Opus Dei)," *Concilium*, 193 (1987), pp. 95–105.

22. See Hehir, p. 12.

23. In "Religion and Politics," in *Religion in Politics*, Richard McMunn, ed. (Milwaukee, Wis.: Catholic League for Religious and Civil Rights, 1985), p. 60.

24. See Virgil C. Blum, "Moral Values in Democracy," in *Religion in Politics*, p. 4.

25. See John Baptist Metz, *The Emergent Church* (New York: Crossroad, 1986), p. 68.

26. Ed Marciniak, "On the Condition of the Laity," in *Challenge to the Laity*, Russell Barta, ed., p. 30.

27. Pope John Paul II, *On Social Concern* (Boston: Daughters of St. Paul, 1988), No. 41.

28. See William L. Droel and Gregory F. Pierce, *Confident and Competent* (Notre Dame, Ind.: Ave Maria Press, 1987), p. 83.

29. Hanna, p. 22.

30. See Hanna, p. 5.

31. See Paul H. Chalfant, Robert E. Beckley, and C. Eddie Palmer, *Religion in Contemporary Society* (Palo Alto: Mayfield Publishing Co., 1987), pp. 244–266, and especially pp. 247–250; "Religious Lobbies and Pressure Groups." The authors (247) distinguish between transformationist religious pressure groups, that "become involved in politics to sway public policy toward

religiously sanctioned ends," and separationist religious pressure groups that "advocate a pragmatic separation between church and state, and become involved in politics in order to insure this continued separation."

32. For an excellent analysis of Catholics in Congress, see Mary T. Hanna's book, chapter 3.

33. See Arthur Jones, "Bishops: Laity Invisible to the World," *National Catholic Reporter*, 30 March 1979, p. 12.

34. See Gremillion and Castelli, pp. 36–47.

35. John A. Coleman, *An American Strategic Theology* (New York: Paulist Press, 1982), p. 4.

36. Coleman, p. 42.

37. See Droel and Pierce, p. 24; Robert L. Kinast, *Caring for Society: A Theological Interpretation of Lay Ministry* (Chicago: The Thomas More Press, 1985).

38. Quoted in Droel and Pierce, p. 79.

39. Coleman, p. 53.

40. Michael Novak, "What the Laity Can Teach the Church," in *Challenge to the Laity*, Russell Barta, ed., p. 55.

41. See Benestad, pp. 93–118.

42. See the comments of David O'Brien, "Choosing our Future: American Catholicism's Precarious Prospects," in *Rising from History*, Robert J. Daly, ed. (Lanham, Md.: University Press, 1984), p. 20.

43. See *Church Today* 26:1; 68:1; 82:1; 88; 89; 90.

44. Coleman, p. 54.

45. Coleman, p. 4.

46. See Hanna, p. 202.

47. Gremillion and Castelli, p. 189, concluded that religious beliefs determine the voting of 9% of Catholics, influence "to a large degree" the voting of 34%; "only to a small degree" 35%; and not at all for 21%.

48. Cardinal Bernadin, p. 61.

49. Cardinal Bernadin, p. 59.

50. See Cardinal Bernadin, p. 64.

51. See Johann Baptist Metz, "The Church's Social Function in the Light of a 'Political Theology,'" *Concilium* 36 (1968), p. 10.

ABOUT THE CONTRIBUTORS

Patrick Allitt is an assistant professor of history at Emory University in Atlanta where he teaches courses in American religious history and intellectual history. He served as Henry Luce Fellow in Theology at the Harvard Divinity School from 1985 to 1988. His articles have appeared in *American Heritage* and in *U.S. Catholic Historian.* His forthcoming book is *Catholic Lay Intellectuals in the American Conservative Movement: 1950–1980.*

Timothy A. Byrnes is an assistant professor of political science at the City College of the City University of New York. He is the author of several published articles on the political activities of the American Catholic hierarchy. His doctoral dissertation, "Mixing Religion and Politics: The Catholic Bishops in Contemporary America," was completed at Cornell University in 1987.

Leonard Doohan is professor of religious studies at Gonzaga University in Spokane, Washington. He has written many articles and twelve books. Among his books are six on the roles of laity in the churches including *The Lay–Centered Church, The Laity's Mission in the Local Church, The Laity: A Bibliography,* and *John Paul II and the Laity.* With his wife, Helen, an associate professor of theology, he has lectured and given workshops throughout the United States, Canada, and Europe, as well as Australia, New Zealand, and the Far East.

R. Bruce Douglass is associate professor in the Department of Government at Georgetown University in Washington, D.C. He has written extensively on issues pertaining to the relationship between politics and religion, publishing in such journals as *Commonweal, Christianity & Crisis,* and *The Christian Century.* He edited *The Deeper Meaning of Economic Life* (Georgetown University Press, 1986), and is co–director with David Hollenbach, of a new interdisciplinary scholarly project on "Catholicism and Liberalism" which is being jointly undertaken by the Woodstock Theological Center and the Department of Government at Georgetown.

Maureen E. Fiedler, scholar and activist, is a Co–Director of the Quixote Center, a national Catholic–based justice center located in Mt. Rainier, Maryland. She co–founded and co–directed "Catholics Act for ERA" from 1972 to 1982. In 1982, she was one of the seven women who fasted for 37 days for the ERA in Springfield, Illinois. She presently serves on the board of the Women's Ordination Conference. She holds a doctorate in Government from Georgetown University; she has written and lectured widely on women in the church, feminist spirituality and the Equal Rights Amendment. Her current work focuses on the Quest for Peace, a program of humanitarian aid for the people of Nicaragua. She is a Sister of Loretto.

Jo Renee Formicola is assistant professor of political science at Seton Hall University in South Orange, New Jersey. Her articles have appeared in *Journal of Church & State*, and the *American Political Science Review*. She is the author of *The Catholic Church and Human Rights* (Garland Publishing, forthcoming). She is also elected Councilwoman on the Borough Council of Madison, New Jersey, serving the second year of a three–year term.

David Hollenbach, S.J., is professor of moral theology at the Weston School of Theology in Cambridge, Massachusetts. He has written many articles for *Theological Studies* and other journals and is the author of *Claims in Conflict: Retrieving and Renewing the Catholic Human Rights Tradition* (1979) and of *Justice, Peace, and Human Rights: American Catholic Social Ethics in a Pluralistic Context* (1988). He was a principal adviser to the National Conference of Catholic Bishops in the drafting of their pastoral letter, *Economic Justice for All: A Pastoral Letter on Catholic Social Teaching and the U.S. Economy*.

Peter Augustine Lawler is associate professor of political science at Berry College, Mount Berry, Georgia. He has published widely on the relationships among politics, philosophy, and religion in America. He is the editor of *American Political Rhetoric* and the author of *Tocqueville's Defense of Human Liberty*. His current research is on religious dimensions of the American idea of liberty.

Anne Lally Milhaven is the editor of *The Inside Stories: 13 Valiant Women Challenging the Church* (Mystic, Conn.: Twenty–Third Publications, 1987). She holds a graduate degree in theology from Harvard Divinity School. She is also president of Milhaven and Associates, a retirement–preparation center in Providence, Rhode Island.

James Muldoon is professor of history at Rutgers University in Camden, New Jersey. He is the author of *Popes, Lawyers, and Infidels: The Church and the Non–Christian World, 1250–1550*, as well as a number of articles on the place of infidels in medieval canon law.

Thomas J. O'Hara, C.S.C., is assistant professor of political science at Kings College in Wilkes–Barre, Pennsylvania. He is author of "The Multifaceted Catholic Lobby" in Charles Dunn, ed., *Religion in American Politics* (CQ Press, 1989). His chapter here is based on his doctoral dissertation, "Religious Lobby Groups: The Pluralism of the Catholic Community," American University, Washington, D.C.

Mary C. Segers is associate professor of political science at Rutgers University in Newark, New Jersey, where she teaches political theory and women's studies. She served as Henry Luce Fellow in Theology at the Harvard Divinity School from 1987 to 1989. Previously, she was Visiting Lecturer and Research Associate in Women's Studies in Religion at Harvard Divinity School during the 1985–86 academic year. She is co–author, with James C. Foster, of *Elusive Equality: Liberalism, Affirmative Action, and Social Change in America* and has written many articles on abortion politics, equality and public policy, and on the Catholic bishops and public policy.

Thomas A. Shannon is professor of social ethics at Worcester Polytechnic Institute in Worcester, Massachusetts. He is co–author, with Lisa Sowle Cahill, of *Religion and Reproduction* (Crossroad, 1988) and co–editor, with David O'Brien, of *Renewing the Earth: Catholic Documents on Peace, Justice and Liberation*. He has edited *Bioethics* (Paulist Press, 1976).

Karen Sue Smith is associate editor of *Commonweal* and Director of the Iona Center for Pastoral Liturgy, Iona College, New Rochelle, New York. She holds advanced degrees in theology from the University of Notre Dame and the Harvard Divinity School. Her articles, interviews, and reviews have appeared in *Commonweal, Crosscurrents, America, The National Catholic Reporter*, and *U.S. Catholic*.

SELECT BIBLIOGRAPHY

For specialized bibliographical references associated with each chapter, see the notes for each essay. The following are general sources relating to American Catholic History, the Contemporary Catholic Church, and Religion and Politics.

1. FOR PAPAL, CONCILIAR, AND AMERICAN EPISCOPAL STATEMENTS, THE FOLLOWING SOURCES MAY BE CONSULTED:

Abbott, Walter M., ed. *The Documents of Vatican II*. New York: America Press, 1966.

Catholic Bishops of the United States. *Pastoral Letters of the United States Catholic Bishops*. Ed. Hugh J. Nolan. 4 vols. Washington: National Conference of Catholic Bishops/United States Catholic Conference, 1984.

National Conference of Catholic Bishops. *Economic Justice For All: A Pastoral Letter on Catholic Social Teaching and the U.S. Economy.* Washington: NCCB/USCC, 1986.

National Conference of Catholic Bishops. *The Challenge of Peace: God's Promise and Our Response. A Pastoral Letter on War and Peace.* Washington: NCCB/USCC, 1983.

Origins. Weekly documentary service of the NCCB/USCC. Available in seminaries, diocesan chanceries, and many Catholic colleges and universities. Published by United States Catholic Conference, 1312 Massachusetts Avenue, N.W., Washington, D.C.

Papal encyclicals of recent popes (John XXIII, Paul VI, and John Paul II) may be obtained from the USCC also.

2. BOOKS AND ARTICLES

Annarelli, James John. *Academic Freedom and Catholic Higher Education.* New York: Greenwood Press, 1987.

Benson, Peter L., and Dorothy L. Williams. *Religion on Capitol Hill.* New York: Oxford University Press, 1986.

Cahill, Lisa Sowle. *Between the Sexes: Foundations for a Christian Ethics of Sexuality.* Philadelphia: Fortress Press, 1985.

Callahan, Daniel, ed. *The Catholic Case for Contraception.* New York: Macmillan Company, 1969.

Carey, Patrick W., ed. *American Catholic Religious Thought.* New York: Paulist Press, 1987.

Carmody, Denise Lardner. *The Double Cross: Ordination, Abortion, and Catholic Feminism.* New York: Crossroad, 1986.

Carr, Anne E. *Transforming Grace: Christian Tradition and Women's Experience.* San Francisco: Harper and Row, 1988.

Castelli, Jim. *A Plea for Common Sense: Resolving the Clash Between Religion and Politics.* San Francisco: Harper and Row, 1988.

Curran, Charles E. *Faithful Dissent.* Kansas City, Mo.: Sheed and Ward, 1986.

Daly, Mary. *The Church and the Second Sex.* New York: Harper and Row, 1968.

———. *Beyond God the Father.* Boston: Beacon Press, 1973.

———. *GYN/ECOLOGY: The Metaethics of Radical Feminism.* Boston: Beacon Press, 1978.

Deedy, John. *American Catholicism—and Now Where?* New York: Plenum Press, 1987.

Dolan, Jay P. *The American Catholic Experience: A History from Colonial Times to the Present.* Garden City, N.Y.: Doubleday and Company, 1985.

Dulles, Avery. *Models of the Church.* Garden City, N.Y.: Doubleday and Company, 1974.

Dunn, Charles W., ed. *Religion in American Politics.* Washington: CQ Press, 1989.

Ellis, John Tracy. *American Catholicism.* Second edition, revised. Chicago: University of Chicago Press, 1969.

Fowler, Robert Booth. *Religion and Politics in America.* Metuchen, N.J.: Scarecrow Press, 1984.

Gallup, George, and Jim Castelli. *The American Catholic People: Their Beliefs, Practices, and Values.* Garden City, N.Y.: Doubleday and Company, Inc., 1987.

Gramick, Jeannine, and Pat Furey, ed. *The Vatican and Homosexuality.* New York: Crossroad, 1988.

Greeley, Andrew. *The American Catholic: A Social Portrait.* New York: Basic Books, 1977.

Greenawalt, Kent. *Religious Convictions and Political Choice.* New York: Oxford University Press, 1988.

Hanna, Mary T. *Catholics and American Politics.* Cambridge, Mass.: Harvard University Press, 1979.

Hennessey, James. *American Catholics: A History of the Roman Catholic Community in the United States.* New York: Oxford University Press, 1981.

Hertzke, Allen D. *Representing God in Washington: The Role of Religious Lobbies in the American Polity.* Knoxville: University of Tennessee Press, 1988.

Holland, Joe, and Anne Barsanti, eds. *American and Catholic: The New Debate.* South Orange, N.J.: PILLAR Books, 1988.

Hollenbach, David. *Justice, Peace, and Human Rights: American Catholic Social Ethics in a Pluralistic Context.* New York: Crossroad, 1988.

Jung, Patricia Beattie, and Thomas A. Shannon. *Abortion and Catholicism: The American Debate.* New York: Crossroad, 1988.

Kaiser, Robert. *The Politics of Sex and Religion.* Kansas City, Mo.: Sheed and Ward, 1985.

Kantowicz, Edward R., ed. *Modern American Catholicism, 1900–1965: Selected Historical Essays.* New York: Garland Publishing, Inc., 1988.

Keane, Philip S. *Sexual Morality: A Catholic Perspective.* New York: Paulist Press, 1977.

Kennedy, Eugene. *Tomorrow's Catholics, Yesterday's Church: The Two Cultures of American Catholicism.* New York: Harper and Row, 1988.

Kissling, Frances, and Mary E. Hunt. "*The New York Times* Ad: A Case Study in Religious Feminism." *Journal of Feminist Studies in Religion* 3 (1987), pp. 115–127.

Kolbenschlag, Madonna, ed. *Authority, Community and Conflict.* Kansas City, Mo.: Sheed and Ward, 1986.

———, ed. *Between God and Caesar: Priests, Sisters and Political Office in the United States.* New York: Paulist Press, 1977.

Lawler, Ronald, Joseph Boyle, and William E. May. *Catholic Sexual Ethics.* Huntington, Ind.: Our Sunday Visitor, Inc., 1985.

Leege, David C., and Joseph Gremillion. *Notre Dame Study of Catholic Parish Life.* Reports Nos. 1–14. Notre Dame, Ind.: Center for the Study of Contemporary Society, University of Notre Dame, 1984–1989.

McBrien, Richard P. *Caesar's Coin: Religion and Politics in America.* New York: Macmillan, 1987.

Marty, Martin E. *An Invitation to American Catholic History*. Chicago: Thomas More Press, 1986.

May, William W., ed. *Vatican Authority and American Catholic Dissent: The Curran Case and Its Consequences*. New York: Crossroad, 1987.

Murnion, Philip J., ed. *Catholics and Nuclear War*. New York: Crossroads, 1983.

Murray, John Courtney. *We Hold These Truths*. New York: Sheed and Ward, 1960.

Nelson, James B. *Embodiment: An Approach to Sexuality and Christian Theology*. Minneapolis: Augsburg Publishing House, 1978.

Neuhaus, Richard John. *The Catholic Moment: The Paradox of the Church in the Postmodern World*. San Francisco: Harper and Row, 1987.

Regan, Richard J. *The Moral Dimensions of Politics*. New York: Oxford University Press, 1986.

Reichley, A. James. *Religion in American Public Life*. Washington: The Brookings Institute, 1985.

Ruether, Rosemary Radford. *Sexism and God-Talk: Toward a Feminist Theology*. Boston: Beacon Press, 1983.

———. *Contemporary Roman Catholicism: Crises and Challenges*. Kansas City, Mo.: Sheed and Ward, 1987.

Schüssler-Fiorenza, Elisabeth. *Bread Not Stone: The Challenge of Feminist Biblical Interpretation*. Boston: Beacon Press, 1984.

———. *In Memory of Her: A Feminist Theological Reconstruction of Christian Origins*. New York: Crossroad, 1984.

Shannon, Thomas A., and Lisa Sowle Cahill. *Religion and Artificial Reproduction: An Inquiry into the Vatican "Instruction on Respect for Human Life."* New York: Crossroad, 1988.

Wald, Kenneth D. *Religion and Politics.* New York: St. Martin's Press, 1987.

Ware, Ann Patrick, ed. *Midwives of the Future.* Kansas City, Mo.: Sheed and Ward, 1984.

Weaver, Mary Jo. *New Catholic Women.* San Francisco: Harper and Row, 1985.

INDEX

A

B

C

D

E

F

G

H

J

K

L

M

N

O

P

Q

R

S

T

U

V

W